# The Practice of Modernism

The postwar period saw greater change in the appearance, structure and skyline of cities than any comparable period in modern history. During the late 1950s and the 1960s, municipal councils routinely devised and implemented radical schemes to reshape and modernise their towns and cities. This book, following on from the author's widely acclaimed *The Experience of Modernism*, traces the involvement of modern architects in this process.

Making extensive use of primary documentation and in-depth interviews with architects of the time, *The Practice of Modernism* examines the intricate relationship between vision and subsequent practice in the saga of postwar urban transformation. The first part of the book traces the personal, institutional and professional backgrounds of the architects involved in schemes for reconstruction and replanning. It then goes on to deal directly with the progress of urban trans-formation, focusing on the contribution that modern architects and architectural principles made to town centre renewal and social housing. Finally, the book highlights how the exuberance of the 1960s gave way to the profound reappraisal that emerged by the early 1970s.

At a time when popular understanding of mid-twentieth century urban transformation remains clouded by generalisation and blanket condemnation, *The Practice of Modernism* provides an incisive and timely view of the true complexity of the processes and agencies that brought about change. It will interest urban and architectural historians, urban geographers, planners and all concerned with understanding the recent history of the contemporary city.

**John R. Gold** is Professor of Urban Geography and a member of the Institute for Historical and Cultural Research at Oxford Brookes University.

# The Practice of Modernism

Modern architects and urban transformation, 1954–1972

**John R. Gold**

Routledge
Taylor & Francis Group

LONDON AND NEW YORK

First published 2007
by Routledge
2 Park Square, Milton Park, Abingdon, Oxon OX14 4RN

Simultaneously published in the USA and Canada
by Routledge
270 Madison Avenue, New York, NY 10016

*Routledge is an imprint of the Taylor & Francis Group, an informa business*

© 2007 John R. Gold

Typeset in Univers by Florence Production Ltd, Stoodleigh, Devon
Printed and bound in Great Britain by The Cromwell Press, Trowbridge, Wiltshire

*British Library Cataloguing in Publication Data*
A catalogue record for this book is available from the British Library

*Library of Congress Cataloging in Publication Data*
Gold, John Robert.
  The practice of modernism : modern architects and urban transformation,
  1954–1972/John R. Gold.
      p. cm.
   Includes bibliographical references and index.
  1. Modern movement (Architecture)   2. City planning—History—20th century.
  I. Title.
  NA682.M63G65 2007–02–12 711′.4—dc22              2006037164

ISBN10: 0–415–25842–1 (hbk)
ISBN10: 0–415–25843–X (pbk)
ISBN10: 0–203–96218–4 (ebk)

ISBN13: 978–0–415–25842–5 (hbk)
ISBN13: 978–0–415–25843–2 (pbk)
ISBN13: 978–0–203–96218–3 (ebk)

For Stephen Ward

# Contents

# Figures

# Tables

# Illustration credits

# Preface

In 1963, my family was on an outing to central London. As we headed back to where the car was parked off Tottenham Court Road, I looked up at the emerging skeleton of a building under construction at what appeared to be an enormous traffic island at the junction of New Oxford Street and Charing Cross Road. 'What are they building?' I asked. 'I'm not sure', said my Mother, 'but there are a lot of new flats and offices going up. You won't be able to recognise the place soon.' Recalling that now, it sounds like there should have been a wistful tone in her voice – noting the passing of an era as the historic city in which she was brought up was ripped apart. Yet, as far as I can remember, she said it in a perfectly matter-of-fact sort of way. She was neither excited nor alarmed at the prospect. This was just the way of the world at that time. Things were irrevocably changing, or so it seemed, and the city was changing with them. This was progress, change was normal, and cities needed to be brought up-to-date to match the new sensitivities.

Normality, however, has a habit of being a strangely short-term phenomenon in the world of urban development. Within a short space of time, those 'new sensitivities' were themselves under scrutiny and attack. The structure to which I had addressed my chance remark was none other than Centre Point, the office block built at the site of a proposed, but shortly to be abandoned, traffic roundabout. Centre Point, which remained vacant for many years due to anomalies in the financing and rating of property development, was a powerful symbol. Not only was it a good example of what Ted Heath might have considered the 'unacceptable face of capitalism', but also it was a highly visible symbol of the ills of urban renewal. By the end of the decade, there would be other symbols of equal potency. They included Westway, the elevated section of the A40(M) roadway that divided communities in the west of the city; Ronan Point, the partially collapsed tower block in Canning Town that prompted far-reaching inquiries into the condition and safety of system-built public housing; and the Coal Exchange and Euston Station's Doric arch – two important historic structures demolished because they happened to stand in the way of developers' plans. Each became an emblem of resistance for those who opposed the accepted approaches for redesigning the modern city. Each too, in widely differing ways and with varying degrees of fairness, could be associated with the application of architectural modernism.

London's experience was not unique. Many other British cities witnessed the same cycle in which the peak of enthusiasm for things associated with modernism turned sour within a remarkably short period. Similar protests were experienced elsewhere, particularly in the older cities of the USA, as groups concerned about the transformation of the urban environment started to challenge the prevailing orthodoxies and the values that lay behind them. The trend proved infectious. Inner-city neighbourhoods threatened with clearance saw campaigns mounted that, just occasionally, held off the developers. A number of recently redeveloped housing estates, both low- and high-rise, started to show patterns of social disorder that called into doubt aspects of renewal policy. What started as sporadic protests over specific issues consolidated into something larger that challenged the accepted policies of planned urban reconstruction and undermined the authority of architects and planners deemed responsible for them. 'Modernism', however nebulously defined, became characterised as the derided inspiration for the architecture of another, now happily concluded, phase in the life of cities. Indeed, it was well on its way to becoming the dragon that a new generation of critics queued up to slay.

This dramatically changing climate of opinion provides a backdrop to the ideas, processes and events discussed in this book. In essence, this is the second part of a personal inquiry into the *experience* of architects, who subscribed to a school of thought with many different strands but with a broadly shared sense of direction. My earlier book, *The Experience of Modernism*, traced the ways in which a group of radical architects and their colleagues in the planning, engineering and quantity surveying professions – loosely referred to as the Modern Movement – staked their claim to a place in helping to design the future city. Dealing with the years 1928–53, it focused on what I termed the 'urban imagination' – the anticipation of future urban forms and patterns of city life – exhibited by those who were part of that movement. This book explores what happened when, at last, those ideas came to influence practice. It focuses on the years between 1954 and 1972 and examines the experiences of those architects, working in the public sector or for private practices, as they thought about or participated in projects destined to transform cities. A further and final book, in what has now become a trilogy, will examine the enduring legacy of modernism – direct and indirect, positive and negative, substantive and mythologised – for architectural thought and practice after 1972.

As with its predecessor, this book draws on oral history and so, when turning to acknowledgements, my thanks go first and foremost to all those who agreed to be interviewed for this study. Given that this book draws on more than fifty lengthy interviews, I hope that the individuals involved will forgive me for thanking them collectively for the time that they spared to be interviewed, for their generous hospitality, for the way that they put me in touch with others who 'you really must talk to . . . ', for the trusting way in which they loaned me personal records and documents – 'bring them back next time you are passing' was the sole condition usually placed on the loan. Without them, this book could not have been written. Naturally I have attempted to follow their wishes, whenever it was indicated that material was sensitive or at points where they requested that there should be no direct attribution of source. At the same time, all interpretations of their testimony, along with any errors of omission or commission, are entirely my responsibility.

Next, a special word of thanks goes to a group of colleagues who also share an interest in the history of architectural modernism in Great Britain. In an academic environment that encourages secrecy and publication at all costs in case other people come across the same ideas, it is extraordinarily gratifying to report the willingness with which scholars in this field of research share information. Miles Glendinning and Stefan Muthesius, for example, allowed me access to the unpublished interview transcripts that they had undertaken in connection with their own seminal research on public sector social housing. These not only yielded valuable nuggets that appear in this text, but also supplied me with a series of important leads that I could pursue further. Much the same may be said for Alan Powers and Elain Harwood. Although both working in this field themselves, they willingly shared with me the names of contacts that they had found valuable and pointed me to sources that I never knew existed. David Whitham kindly gave me access to files and unpublished materials on Cumbernauld and allowed me to take advantage of the considerable amounts of effort that he had already devoted to collecting data about that remarkable New Town.

Particular thanks go to the librarians and curators of the following institutions: the National Monuments Record of Scotland Library (Royal Commission on the Ancient and Historical Monuments of Scotland); the Percy Johnson-Marshall Collection (PJMC, Special Collections, Edinburgh University Library); the National Archives (formerly the Public Records Office) at Kew (London); the Royal Institute of British Architects (RIBA, London) and the Architecture Archives at its new partner the Victoria and Albert Museum (South Kensington, London); the British Library and the National Sound Archive (at St Pancras, London); the British Library (Newspapers Division) at Colindale, London; the London Metropolitan Archives (Clerkenwell); the Canadian Centre for Architecture (Montreal), and the Special Collections Archive at the Francis Loeb Library, Harvard University (Cambridge, Massachusetts). Robert Elwall and Jonathan Makepeace, curators of the RIBA's Photographs Collection, again lavished time on my behalf to find many of the images that accompany this text.

Writing books, of course, needs time. In this respect, I would like to record my thanks to the Arts and Humanities Research Council for the grant of a matched sabbatical under its Research Leave scheme. This allowed the conclusion of the fieldwork and a period of concentrated time to work on the manuscript. This would not have been possible, however, without the grant of sabbatical leave in the first place. I therefore owe a considerable debt of gratitude to Oxford Brookes University for instituting and maintaining its enlightened sabbatical policy and to my colleagues David Pepper, Martin Haigh, Judy Chance, Adrian Parker, Simon Carr, Brad Blitz and Helen Walkington for their support. Avril Maddrell covered my teaching marvellously well during my period of leave. My former colleague George Revill was a major source of encouragement and a welcome fellow traveller throughout the years that we worked together at Brookes. At the start of my research, the late Valerie Karn gave me the benefit of her encyclopedic knowledge of the development of British housing policy. Next in this list come a number of individuals who contributed in many different ways to this book. They include: Mike Barke, Peter Carter, Jon Coaffee, Mary Daniels, Roy Darke, Sir Andrew Derbyshire, Derek Elsom, Clive Fenton, Graeme Ford, Margaret Gold, Sir Peter Hall, Dennis

Hardy, Mike Hebbert, Julian Honer, Bob Jarvis, Phil Jones, Peter Larkham, Susan McRae, John Sheail, Colin Ward, Jeremy Whitehand and Sir Colin St. John Wilson. As ever the deficiencies that remain are entirely my responsibility. Maggie, Jennifer, Iain and Josie still somehow seem to put up with me. Finally, this book is dedicated to Stephen Ward, with sincere thanks for his support, collaboration and friendship over the last – whisper it softly – 37 years.

West Ealing, London

Chapter 1

# On the threshold

**Gradually it becomes possible to free more kinds of buildings from controls, and make a serious start on many large projects, such as the office blocks in the City of London. I do hope that building-owners will call for modern architecture and decoration. Our generation wants a style of its own and from what I have seen since I came to the Ministry of Works, if our architects are given the chance, they will create such a style, worthy of the past and expressive of the new reign.**

**Sir David Eccles[1]**

With these words, the newly knighted Minister of Works sent a cautiously optimistic New Year's message via the pages of the *Architects' Journal* to those who might identify themselves as modern architects. Somewhat surprisingly, they were in need of encouragement. However much hindsight suggests that architectural modernism was on the threshold of its profound influence on urban reconstruction and renewal in the postwar period, there was little indication that this state of affairs was imminent in January 1954 – the starting point for this study. Few in power promised that eventuality and equally few architectural commentators predicted it. Most readers would have noticed that the writer prefaced his comments with the word 'gradually' and might well have concluded that they had heard it before. After all, this was the same David Eccles, who positively 'took a pleasure in exercising his responsibilities [as Minister of Works] for the demolition' of the Festival of Britain exhibition site on the South Bank;[2] primarily because his government regarded it as a monument to the socialist ideology of the previous Labour administration. At a stroke, this action symbolically punctured any lingering traces of postwar political consensus about planning for London, gratuitously removed most traces of an event that brought colour to the grey postwar city, and returned a formerly blitzed area to something resembling its former status. It was an unconvincing basis for fostering hope for the future.

Other considerations reinforced the gloom. Severe economic difficulties persisted, with national bankruptcy masked only by the availability of American loans. Queues and shortages had dragged on well into the 1950s. Indeed the prospects for Britain's immediate economic future still alarmed policy-makers at the end of 1953, regardless of the juggernaut of patriotic sentiment about the boundless possibilities of the 'new reign', sometimes optimistically called the 'new Elizabethan age'.[3] The burden of public spending caused grave anxiety, with reports of the 'nation straining at the limit' to meet its external strategic and imperial commitments while somehow trying to reconstruct its battered towns and cities.[4] At this time, as Philip Powell noted, 'we were having worse rationing than in the trickiest times of the war'.[5] The newspapers, almost certainly acting on Treasury briefing, prepared public opinion for more bad news. *The Times*' 'Special Correspondent' warned that longer term improvements in living standards might necessitate renewed short-term sacrifice: 'a temporary level of saving and investment entailing a drastic tightening of belts – or an increase in working hours, effort and skill which apparently many people would regard as no less painful'.[6] In the event, this further extension of hard times did not materialise but the underlying spirit of Austerity persisted. Central government continued to decide the priorities about where to channel scarce investment. Other claimants for reconstruction funds were unlikely to receive resources, especially if meeting their needs meant boosting domestic consumption.

This, of course, did not imply that the results of the necessity-driven approach to reconstruction were negligible. The schools programme had sustained a prolonged wave of construction that kept pace with the 'postwar bulge' of youngsters now reaching school age. At its best, this programme had produced some outstanding new school buildings and acted as an important proving ground for modern constructional methods, especially those involving prefabrication, modularity and system building. The Hertfordshire programme and the Smithsons' Mies-inspired competition-winning design for the school at Hunstanton (Norfolk) had contributed some of the iconic buildings of early postwar architecture. Factory construction in priority sectors continued apace. Lewis Mumford commended the 'brisk rebuilding' of factories of a type that 'England forgot to build in the days of her unevenly distributed prosperity',[7] although in reality only a small fraction of the newly constructed industrial capacity was devoted to replacing archaic plant or to establishing new firms and projects.[8] The housing drive too had had its undoubted achievements. The local authority sector had risen to the challenges thrown down by successive ministers; each of them determined to serve the interests of their political party by playing the 'numbers game' – the colloquial term for the contest between the Labour and Conservative administrations to see which could construct more residential units. Clement Attlee's Labour Government had managed 900,000 new home completions in the first five years after the Second World War. This was somewhat short of its target of 1.25 million dwellings, but commendable enough given the prevailing economic and logistic difficulties. The momentum had continued under the Tories. In 1953, completions surpassed the official target of 300,000, with the public sector authorities contributing just over 229,000 of the new dwellings.

Yet what started to rankle, especially as labour and material shortages eased, was that so much of this effort proceeded unquestioningly on established lines. The vast majority of new housing projects, for instance, perpetuated the pattern of the interwar period. As Chapter 8 shows, 77 per cent of around 195,000 new starts in 1953 were for conventional houses and a further 20 per cent were for low-rise flats.[9] The new estates of 'council flats' almost invariably lacked the breadth of vision that preoccupied the urban imaginings of the Modern Movement during the 1930s.[10] Not only had the agencies responsible for their construction skimped on social facilities and landscaping, which apparently awaited the arrival of better times, but also the designs failed to inspire. When becoming City Architect for Birmingham in 1952, for instance, Alwyn Sheppard Fidler recalled his first impressions of the 12-storey blocks appearing in the city's Duddeston and Nechells Redevelopment Area as being 'the lumpiest things you'd ever seen'.[11] Observers looked in some envy at the advances in practice elsewhere; most notably in Scandinavia but also in France where the housing programme initiated in September 1948 had freely turned to rationalisation of building methods and the use of new techniques of industrial construction (see Chapter 8). Notwithstanding the wholly understandable preoccupation with short-term needs, there was little sense that British policy-makers were seriously trying to accommodate the potential of the future – at least, not the potential of the future that modern architects cherished.

To compound matters, whenever there were opportunities to rethink the design of settlements, practice seemed destined to gravitate towards the tried and tested. The first generation of 14 New Towns created between 1947 and 1950 were a case in point. Modern architects were 'very taken with the New Town idea . . . socially they made a lot of sense'.[12] They applauded the control that the New Towns Act 1946 had devolved to the quasi-independent, task force-like development corporations to design and build their respective towns and noted that this included control over their budgets. They relished the fact that constructing the New Towns required an engagement with the principles by which the building blocks of a city combined to make a greater whole. Modern architects, ever partial to large-scale projects, welcomed the prospect of new, comprehensively planned settlements that might display what was possible when adequate resources came together with analysis of (functional) need to provide an all-inclusive answer to a particular social problem. They also endorsed the planners' commitment to neighbourhood units, which meshed seamlessly with modernist thinking about the nature and function of towns in the modern age. All these elements aroused enthusiasm as part of a paradigm of large-scale construction and centralist planning that might inspire development elsewhere.[13]

Subsequent assessments dispelled the initial optimism. The layout, design and aesthetics of the early New Towns turned out to be direct descendants of the Garden Cities; something that was not a foregone conclusion at the outset. Supporters of modernism castigated the New Towns as never rising 'to anything that was architecturally sufficient' and as missing 'the virtue of civic design'.[14] In particular, they found them 'petty, amorphous and suburban',[15] replete with their low-density residential neighbourhoods, cottage-like housing, picturesque curving tree-lined roads and 'sterile' semi-public open spaces.[16] The passage of the Town Development Act 1952 promised even less. The Act created collaborative frameworks that would allow existing country towns to receive 'overspill' expansion from 'overcrowded' conurbations. Although potentially complementary to the New Towns as an arm of dispersal policy, the so-called 'expanded town' schemes took an inordinately long time to establish.[17] The enabling legislation almost guaranteed that they would be more akin to a modified version of old-fashioned municipal suburbanisation – providing a formula for decanting cottage estates to the countryside – rather than realising their promise as new settlements.[18] The Act made no stipulations about provision of employment and created no more than an outline for the resolution of issues concerned with the associated social and community facilities. Equally, there were no specific provisions for the necessary redesign of town centres to cope with the demands of a larger population – a question left to ad hoc arrangements.[19]

Put more generally, those who regarded themselves as progressive felt a growing sense of dismay that the strategic priorities and patterns of development emerging were a betrayal of the postwar vision.[20] The advisory plans commissioned by municipalities during the war or immediately afterwards may have offered, at best, only a restrained modernism in terms of design, but did hint at a commitment to radical reconstruction.[21] For a brief time,

> science, philosophy, art, psychology, sociology and engineering [had] seemed as one. One imagined a new kind of human rather sensitive and certainly artistic who would poetically enjoy all this and be himself very creative. The machine was going to be the method by which these possibilities were available to all. Housing was going to have all sorts of added facilities, nursery schools, workshops, sports facilities, communal halls.[22]

The euphoria of that moment had long passed and scepticism had set in. Local councils' priorities for rehousing and for the quick restoration of commercial activity militated against the longer time-spans necessary for comprehensive redevelopment and positively discouraged new ways of tackling urban problems.[23] In the country at large, the overwhelming desire to re-establish domestic life and familiar routines as quickly as possible after the dislocations of war had revived traditional housing preferences. As if to mock the pro-urban instincts of many planners and architects, it looked more likely that the future society of Britain would dwell in 'the suburbs and the bungalows' rather than in 'the great cities'.[24] Furthermore, expert opinion seemed to have moved decisively against the visions of the future city favoured by the Modern Movement. In his book *Principles and Practice of Town and Country Planning* – easily the most widely read planning textbook of its day – Lewis Keeble targeted the *Ville Radieuse* and its ilk for particular scorn:

> The proposals just outlined for the creation or re-creation of great cities are hardly of more than academic interest in relation to this country; we

have not the slightest need to create a new great city and it is reasonably certain that the redevelopment of our existing ones is bound to be on fairly conservative lines, since the resources available limit us to a very slow and gradual process of rebuilding, whereas change to a radically new form necessarily involves a rapid process in order to avoid complete chaos during the interim period; indeed, it is doubtful whether a large town, unless it has been virtually destroyed, can possibly be redeveloped on lines completely dissimilar from its existing form.[25]

## Sober confidence?

Despite, or arguably because of this cheerless outlook, one might have expected the architectural press to muster a vigorous counterview. It was perfectly plausible that the prevailing gloom could have triggered the same type of utopian impulse as that seen during the 1930s, when the forbidding extent of urban problems encouraged people of goodwill to campaign in favour of the bold, radical and, above all, untried visions with which the Modern Movement was associated. Such sentiments, however, remained out of step with the dominant view among observers of the architectural scene, who seemingly struggled with the burden of expectation over hope. Although editors of mainstream periodicals did their best to exhort their readership to look to the future with 'sober confidence',[26] their contributors stubbornly preferred sobriety to confidence. They might retain a powerful urge to wave the flag for modernism and repeat familiar injunctions about the virtue of the approaches that underpinned the new architecture, but their surveys of the state-of-the-art contained only a slowly increasing inventory of familiar buildings and structures. Their prevailing introspection about the immediate prospects for modern architecture gave no impression of conviction that the hour for change had come.

Recent books by those associated with the interwar Modern Movement, for example, underlined the uncertainties of the moment. Naturally, they continued to affirm the value of modernist principles for the task ahead, at least in broad terms. In a reissued edition of a 1932 text, Sir Howard Robertson stressed the importance of modernism's organised and scientific approach to design at all scales, in particular to 'that wider field of architecture, town planning, wherein the organisation is applied to the grouping and setting of buildings and groups of buildings as parts of a perceived and organic whole'.[27] Arthur Korn's highly selective international survey in *History Builds the Town* followed the same policy of regarding town planning as a 'wider field' of architecture.[28] He reiterated the analytical significance of the fourfold classification of city functions associated with the Congrès Internationaux d'Architecture Moderne (CIAM) in a work that emphasised the value of functional purpose, hierarchical organisation and modern design. Although couched in seemingly dispassionate terms, Korn concluded that a 'planned town, in contrast to the chaotic growth of past periods, will have to be based consciously on work, housing, and amenities linked by transport, expressing the spirit of human collective work.'[29]

At the same time, some of their erstwhile colleagues from the interwar Modern Movement expressed what looked suspiciously like second thoughts in their writings. Frederick Gibberd's *Town Design* absorbed modern architecture into the flow of an argument that cast around widely for historical precedents of good practice, but without allotting modernism any privileged place in shaping the city of the future.[30] Christopher Tunnard injected an even greater sense of detachment into his book *The City of Man*.[31] He argued that the next twenty years would see 'a revolution in architectural taste and form which will be of tremendous significance to city planning . . . which will, in fact go hand in hand with the new urbanism'.[32] At the same time, he queried the form that this revolution would take. While 'its name will be "modern"', Tunnard suggested, its distinguishing features would be 'an emphasis on scale and proportion, on *ensemble*, on ornament, on humanism' and would be altogether different from that promised by the 'international style'.[33]

The major British architectural periodicals – all of which, apart from the weekly publication *The Builder*, were broadly sympathetic to modernism by this stage – exhibited a similar wariness. Their coverage provided implicit criticism of the domestic scene by showing that the fine architecture found abundantly in other countries was singularly absent from Great Britain. The monthly periodical *Architectural Design*, for example, opened 1954 with a survey of 'tropical architecture' designed by British practices,[34] quickly followed by a special issue on French architecture guest-edited by Ernö Goldfinger.[35] The *Architects' Year Book* – known to its editor Trevor Dannatt as the *Architects' Last Year Book* 'because we were always so late in publishing it'[36] – followed suit.[37] Five articles on 'developments ahead' surveyed the progress made internationally, by looking at case studies of projects in the Netherlands, Italy and the USA. Four essays drew attention to the general convergence between modern architecture and planning. Jane Drew's account of working with Le Corbusier at Chandigarh,[38] plus the publication of an urban project by Alison and Peter Smithson,[39] showed that some of modern architecture's most innovative activity lay at the city scale. Yet despite these impressions of an abundance of activity, Dannatt's 'Foreword' warned about 'skin-deep' modernism:

> Much of the modern architecture in this country soon ceases to convince us, for examination often shows the old picture making formula, new forms seeming to be used for picturesque purposes rather than from inner convictions about planning or form. For example, 'pilotis' used not to free space but as pictorial elements with a certain modernity value. Language used parrot-wise, without understanding.[40]

When turning more squarely to the domestic scene, there were similar concerns about the results to date. The December 1953 issue of *Architectural Design*, the first issue in which Theo Crosby joined the editorial team, used the occasion of the Silver Jubilee Building Trades Exhibition at London's Empire Hall to remark upon the 'atmosphere of considerable optimism' shown at the opening ceremony. Nevertheless, the commentary also listed the continuing problems faced by architects and the building industry.[41] The results of 'prefabrication and the factory assembly of building components' had proven 'miserably disappointing so far'.[42] Mechanisation, if applied 'badly without thought or planning', might well 'produce less at greater cost than traditional methods'.[43] As if to reinforce these points through contrast, the next page contained the transcript of a typically rousing address by the redoubtable Mies van der Rohe, originally given in 1950 at the opening of an extension to the Illinois Institute of Technology. Presented in the style of blank verse, it concluded as follows:

> I hope you will understand that architecture
> has nothing to do with the inventions of forms.
> It is not a playground for children, young or old.
> Architecture is the real battleground of the spirit.
> Architecture wrote the history of the epochs
> and gave them their names.
> Architecture depends on its time.
> It is the crystallization of its inner structure,
> the slow unfolding of its form.
> That is the reason why technology and architecture
> are so closely related.
> Our hope is that they grow together,
> that someday the one will be the expression of
> the other.
> Only then will we have an architecture worthy
> of its name:
> Architecture as a true symbol of our time.[44]

The weekly *Architects' Journal* approached the task of taking stock by eschewing the philosophical in favour of the biographical. Its list of 'Men of the Year', albeit with the 'men' including Alison Smithson,[45] gave firm indications of the judges' preferences. They commended the film designer Michael Stringer for his efforts to bring contemporary design before the public.[46] They praised Owen Campbell-Jones for getting a diluted measure of modern office design, in the shape of Bucklersbury House, into the City of London, despite opposition from the Royal Fine Art Commission, the client (who wanted neoclassical embellishments) and the conservatives on the City's Corporation. They gave the Smithsons space to air their thoughts on town planning, office organisation, the country's future, their fellow professionals, modular construction and architectural competitions, with Peter commenting that 'there is every hope that there *will* be some real architecture in England soon'.[47] Lewis Womersley, the Chief Architect of Sheffield, showed where some of that 'real architecture' might be in his anticipations of the forthcoming reconstruction of the city's Park Hill district. Gordon Stephenson, however, sounded a more discordant note by arguing that modern architecture had reached several dead ends because it had 'neglected to recognize truths established through the centuries. It is now generally accepted but is not yet an architecture for people of today.'[48]

The editors of their monthly stable-mate chose to ignore the old joke about 'there never being any architecture in the *Architectural Review*', teasingly repeated by Astragal in a concurrent issue of the *Architects' Journal*,[49] and directed their readers' gaze towards the future by considering a selection of architectural projects under construction. 'To assess the state of an architect's opinions on the first day of January 1954', they declaimed:

> one would need the last sheet from his sketching pad, the marginal illustrations on the menu of the table where he lunched, the diagrams drawn on his blotter while he conferred with a client. Such ephemera could be highly instructive – without them we should never know the architectural opinions of Leonardo da Vinci – but they would be too slight and too private to survive publication. A fairly advanced project, however, is meant to be legible to contractors and surveyors, shows the real and practical problems with which the architect is at grips at a given instant of time, and is still sufficiently fluid to be affected by the changing weather of opinion. A project in this state takes us as near to the opinion of a particular moment as we can hope to get.[50]

The ensuing pages of carefully selected projects covered work in widely differing sectors to illustrate the prevailing opinion of that 'particular moment'. Frederick Gibberd's designs for the buildings at Heathrow showed modernism applied to the latest transport technologies, whereas Basil Spence's designs for Coventry Cathedral showed it sensitively adapted to the most traditional of settings. The recent construction of the Television Centre at the White City (London) for the British Broadcasting Corporation showed modern design meeting new functional needs. Judging from the examples depicted, modernism also emerged as the architecture of choice for new housing developments. There were eight examples of flatted estates, mostly around London. These included projects by Chamberlin, Powell and Bon at Golden Lane in the City of London, at Roehampton by the Architect's Department of the London County Council (LCC), and schemes for blocks of flats on adjoining plots of land in Bethnal Green (London), respectively, by Yorke, Rosenberg and Mardall and by Fry, Drew, Drake and Lasdun.[51] The selection from outside London featured a scheme for terraced housing by Norman and Dawbarn at Harlow, the Millpool Hill estate in Birmingham by Sheppard Fidler, and private sector houses in Guildford by Geoffrey Jellicoe. There were abundant examples of hospitals, schools and administrative buildings for the public services, factories, offices, commercial premises, power stations, collieries and hostels to complete an impressive array.[52]

Yet in spite of the scope and variety of the survey, there was no attempt to suggest that the structures included were anything other than exceptions or to conceal the critical debates that lay close to the surface. In characteristically impatient fashion, J.M. Richards highlighted the dangers of the loss of human scale in contemporary buildings, especially through creation of long unbroken façades.[53] He noted the ease with which casual observers heralded small advances as breakthroughs as, for example, with prefabrication: 'It is a sign of our uneasy conscience that we have treated every prefabricated swallow as though summer has finally arrived'.[54] There was keen awareness too that progress was effectively confined to building schools, factories and housing – the priorities recognised by the official system of controls. Apart from cities like Coventry, which had 'consistently pursued the ideal of a city centre redesigned and rebuilt in accordance with a predetermined plan',[55] little had materialised that unequivocally furthered the wider hopes for rational, functional and comprehensive town planning based on modernist principles. In this regard:

> the positions now being taken up we may look back and see how far we have fulfilled or forgotten the ideals with which we began reconstruction after the war, how much we have deviated from them, how far they have proved unreal, and how much farther we may be expected to diverge from them in the years immediately to come.[56]

In other words, those who had campaigned for a shining new future enriched by modern architecture might have to face the unpalatable truth of that future being seriously compromised on arrival.

Elsewhere, others leavened their commentaries on contemporary architecture with similar expressions of apprehension. Arthur Ling recognised that London's skyline was at a 'critical moment' in its history, threatened by tall buildings constructed without any proper thought given to their wider impact.[57] A.G. Jury tempered an essay on multi-storey housing, as illustrated by proposals for the reconstruction of Glasgow's Hutchesontown-Gorbals district, with warnings about its limitations. These included recognising that adopting tall flats would not solve social, economic and cultural problems, that public areas within estates were not substitutes for 'public parks and playing fields in the true sense of these terms', and that the available constructional systems had varying suitability for particular problems.[58] Lady Allen of Hurtwood strongly criticised the lack of open space and children's playgrounds in modern public housing estates, noting 'an almost careless handling of the open space, revealing a total disregard for the needs of families as a whole and of the children in particular.'[59] John Betjeman took time off from directing sideswipes at Nikolaus Pevsner's influence on architectural criticism – as exemplified by writers 'whose pages are an unreadable Germanic display of foot-and-note disease' – to counsel his audience about the dehumanising tendencies of the new architecture and against accepting the favoured view of the architect as an anonymous technician rather than as an artist.[60]

Taken together, the cumulative weight of these individual statements might seem symptomatic of latent cultural pessimism or even as supplying evidence of a groundswell of disquiet about architectural modernism. If so, any such interpretation might gain added force from the identity of those expressing doubts, since their opinions were valued by readers of architectural literature. Gordon Stephenson, for instance, was a member of Le Corbusier's Parisian studio in the early 1930s and held the Lever Chair of Civic Design at Liverpool University from

1948 to 1954. J.M. Richards was the leading architectural journalist of his day, as well as a prominent member of the Modern Architectural Research (MARS) Group and a seasoned observer of the international Modern Movement at CIAM congresses and elsewhere. Trevor Dannatt was then secretary of the MARS Group. His fellow MARS Group member, the landscape architect Christopher Tunnard, had moved to the USA in 1938 after the publication of his book *Gardens in the Modern Landscape* and had become Professor of City Planning at Yale University.[61] Frederick Gibberd was the Consultant Architect-Planner of Harlow, a past principal of the Architectural Association and the designer of Pullman Court – still revered as one of interwar Britain's most significant modern buildings.[62] Arthur Ling was Chief Planning Officer for the London County Council, then the most prestigious office in the local authority sector. Archibald Jury, a municipal grandee who was formerly Chief Architect for Liverpool City Council, had held the combined post of City Architect and Director of Planning for Glasgow Corporation since 1951. Marjory Allen was a powerful voice on the political left who had previously occupied the posts of vice-president of the Institute of Landscape Architects and chair of the United Nations Children's Fund (UNICEF). Even the poet John Betjeman, now easily cast as an enemy of modernism, remained a voice worthy of a hearing. His early career as assistant editor at the *Architectural Review* in the pioneering years of the early 1930s and his continuing reputation for being 'a wonderful . . . person to have an evening with' made him still a confidant of the older generation of British modern architects.[63]

The whole, however, was less than the sum of the parts. In 1954, these reservations never developed into anything approaching expressions of collective anxiety. Whatever the doubts, nothing had yet happened that remotely diluted either the broad social consensus that favoured change in pursuit of progress or, more specifically, the idea that modernism was an integral part of progressive visions of the future. It offered seemingly logical and unambiguous solutions to previously intractable urban problems and, through being largely untried, enjoyed the immeasurable advantage of being untainted by the ways of the past. Commentators who were sympathetic might highlight problems or disapprove of the manner of implementation of particular projects, but their belief in the basic premises endured. Certainly when briefly examining a selection of the articles discussed above, Arthur Ling firmly denied that they constituted either an overarching body of criticism or foreshadowed the strands of denigration that arose 15–20 years later:

> My comments that you see there [about the impact of tall buildings on the skyline] were not just aimed at the Modern Movement, although they bore part of the blame. They were certainly not consciously linked to the other criticisms expressed here; indeed I'm very surprised to see that this range of criticism existed then. They look like the product of more recent years. Had anyone put them all together, well perhaps history might have been different, but I very much doubt it. These were exciting times; bubbling with ideas. We debated everything, so naturally we debated the fundamentals of the new architecture and how it might

be deployed. And yes, there were criticisms. One reason was that there was a fair amount of mediocrity around; especially from those who hero worshipped Le Corbusier but only ever adopted the stylistic elements of his work. And, as I mentioned to you, I also had reservations about the over-reliance on high flats [in paper planning exercises] as opposed to a more balanced mix of residential types. But you have to see those things in context. There was a job to be done, a New Jerusalem to build, if you like. Criticism was meant constructively, not to undermine.[64]

Moreover, there were then battles still to fight:

> There were always those who hated modern architecture in principle . . . and even at this stage, it had still not won the battle for hearts and minds. But I don't recall anyone, regardless of their views about the new architecture, putting these points together into a single body of criticism . . . and especially not from those who wanted modern architecture to have its chance. When fighting battles, you don't start off by pointing to the weaknesses in your case. Opposition is best left to opponents. That probably limited our ability to spot shortcomings, but it was surely understandable in light of the task facing us.[65]

In other words, the exercise of criticism was not to be confused with lack of commitment to the new architecture; nor did expressions of disappointment mean that the task was hopeless. Most architects who then identified themselves with modernism remained fully convinced that it offered the right choices for tomorrow's society. All that they essentially lacked was any clear understanding that its hour was at hand.

## Transformations

This book, which deals with the practice of architectural modernism in the period between 1954 and 1972, therefore opens against a background in which expectation tinged with equal measures of uncertainty and resignation abounded. Moving the clock forward to late 1972, we find circumstances that were curiously similar in so far as the architectural profession was again in need of encouragement, but for completely different reasons. Public and, to a lesser extent, professional attitudes towards modern architecture and about its continuing potential for reshaping cities had changed dramatically – as may readily be appreciated by flicking through to the closing pages of this book. Although some continued to believe in and practise modernism as if nothing had happened, elsewhere the mood was critical, apologetic or simply confused. Architectural historians felt uncomfortable trying to cope with a plurality that no longer easily fitted into the old frameworks. Architectural history, which had long had 'a good run for [its] money',[66] would struggle to cope with the new understandings of the nature and role of modernism. For historians and practitioners alike, the authority of architectural modernism, so carefully nurtured since the 1930s, was under threat.

More generally, architects in 1972 found themselves firmly on the defensive; increasingly forced to reconsider the validity of what had been taken for granted as the correct way to proceed. Noticeably, now, the media actively participated in the debate. Whereas newspapers and the broadcast media showed hardly any interest in architectural matters in 1954, by 1972 many architects might have fervently hoped for rather less extensive coverage. Modern architecture was without doubt newsworthy. Along with their colleagues in town planning, who had also previously enjoyed general endorsement as midwives of essential urban transformation, architects now found themselves vilified as dictatorial figures who betrayed public trust and imposed unwarranted change on society – largely by exploiting their eagerly cultivated status as experts. The erstwhile creators of environments fit for tomorrow's society were rebranded as manipulative social engineers. Root-and-branch criticism, not always accurately targeted, had fallen on aspects of road planning, neighbourhood design, land use policy, town centre development and, above all, public-sector housing. Without necessarily offering evidence to support their judgements, critics in the press began to associate architects with a formidable list of failings. The latter stood accused of authoritarianism, dogmatism, unaccountability, elitism, patrimony, hegemony, lack of ethical concern and, above all, arrogance. The places that they had designed were labelled as visually monotonous, socially sterile, without respect for history and memory, and, quite often, as *folies de grandeur*. That which society celebrated only yesterday as being beneficial now stood condemned as dysfunctional or even dystopic. Suspicions about high-level corruption and misallocation of resources, just starting to break in 1972, would compound waves of growing concerns about the perceived social, cultural and economic costs of redeveloping cities on lines inspired by modernism. It all contributed a corrosive atmosphere of mistrust, with proponents of modernism on their way towards becoming 'the collective roadkill' among theoreticians.[67] To say the least, it was a most extraordinary reversal of fortunes in so short a period.

Yet if the end points of this study found the architectural profession at low ebb and introspective, the intervening 18 years were emphatically not characterised by that mood. After the frustrated aspirations of the interwar years and the lean years of Austerity, there was a remarkable flowering of hope and opportunity. The social consensus heavily backed the principle of progress through technology and supported the idea that architecture could contribute decisively to solving pervasive urban problems. The traditional built environment could not stand in the way, because its present sorry state represented the embodiment of past failures and short-sightedness; its intractable problems positively demanded radical solutions. The forces of conservatism seemed in permanent retreat. Innovative designs had a better-than-average chance of being built. These feelings, coupled with the availability of ample private and public sector resources, fuelled an intoxicating atmosphere of dynamism, vigour and, above all, optimism. Compared with the work-starved 1940s and early 1950s, these were what Patrick Nuttgens rightly called the 'years of euphoria' for the architectural profession.[68]

In looking at these profound transformations from initial disappointment through exhilarating advance to accusatory reappraisal, it is important to bear three points in mind, all of which echo and consolidate themes introduced in this volume's predecessor *The Experience of Modernism*.[69] The first point concerns narrative. The previous book noted the need to challenge the Grand Narratives that dominated historical scholarship about the Modern Movement.[70] We noted there the significance of stories that linked modernism to heroic struggle and identified the remarkably malleable imagery associated with its propagation. In time, reference to this imagery was one of the key bases on which not only modern architects justified their work, but also local politicians and ministers, the construction industry, civil engineers and others. Nevertheless, the ability of this imagery to accommodate different positions was a two-edged sword. The lessons of practice would eventually reveal weaknesses and expose contradictions, especially with regard to the gap between the planned and actual states of many transformed urban environments. When persistent problems and inescapable deficiencies prompted sustained criticism, the outcome was to direct withering scrutiny onto the validity of the claims made for the architecture in solving society's problems. The full impact of that critique on architectural thought and practice was already apparent by 1972 and helped to promote a new and powerful anti-modernist Grand Narrative of urban development by the end of the 1970s.

The second, and related, point involves a note of caution over periodisation. The history of architectural modernism resists placing exact temporal boundaries on the flow of events. Certainly the swings that occurred in the climate of opinion between 1954 and 1972 did not emerge overnight and both these dates are treated permeably. Understanding trends that emerged in the 1950s, for instance, has meant occasionally revisiting events occurring in earlier times, sometimes considerably earlier. Dealing with public sector projects in progress in the early 1970s means that references are made to events occurring well after 1972. Perhaps most important, analysis of some aspects of late 1960s avant garde thinking are held over until the succeeding volume because they had their major impact on the evolving debates of the 1970s and later.

The third and most complex point involves issues of the architect's accountability. Modern architects essentially played three roles in the processes that led to the transformation of British cities: namely, as visionaries, propagandists and practitioners. Dealing with the period up to 1953, the previous book focused attention on the first two of these roles, tracing the architect's involvement in and unequivocal responsibility for paper plans, exhibition projects and a handful of experimental schemes. The development of practice, however, changed matters completely. Unlike the earlier period, modern architecture and its practitioners were no longer marginal to the process of remaking cities. At least stylistically, modernism provided the visual language of urban reconstruction and renewal, strongly influencing their aesthetics and shaping the key relationship between built forms and the circulation system. Understandably then, when the results of urban transformation proved less than satisfactory, attention turned to attributing blame for errors of judgement.

At one level, that is a perfectly tenable response. The decision-making environment for urban renewal in the 1960s was relatively enclosed. The conceptual problems of differentiating 'structure' – the underlying patterns that determine society – from 'agency' – freedom of action and ability to determine outcomes – are therefore less problematic than in many areas of social and cultural inquiry.[71] Yet, at another level, it is important to recognise that the process of revisualising and transforming British cities rested on a coalition of forces. The different degrees of power and access to resources that these groups possessed fluctuated over time and diverged between sectors and from place to place. In some cities, for example, City Architects had considerable influence over architecture and cognate areas of activity. Other cities lacked a City Architect until the mid-1960s, with prime powers over transforming the urban environment vested instead in the hands of the City Engineer or Borough Surveyor. Private sector architects, often supplying much needed design skills at a time of labour shortage, worked under varying conditions of design freedom. Construction firms and system builders often replaced the contribution of independent architects by their own in-house design professionals, who sometimes lacked architectural training. Local politicians, with their security of tenure dependent on the electoral characteristics of their town, could drive the processes of reconstruction and renewal forward or might demand greater prudence and retrenchment. Central government took a back seat, especially with regard to housing, but could pull strings through the subsidy regime and chose active promotion of industrialised building methods. All these and other actors played a role in the practice of modernism as it unfolded in the 1950s and 1960s, each complementing the others in activity that enjoyed broad social consensus.

## Aims and sources

This book continues *The Experience of Modernism*'s prime focus by examining what occurred when the urban imagination of the Modern Movement – its anticipation of future urban forms and patterns of city life – encountered the reality of practice in the years between 1954 and 1972. 'Practice' in this instance means more than just the work of architectural offices, since it is interpreted in the senses of both output (completed buildings, plans, unbuilt projects) and the underlying debate that led to that output. This book, however, does not seek to offer a comprehensive handbook of all aspects of architectural modernism and its relationship to the redevelopment of British cities during the postwar period – a coverage that would require a text several times larger than this one. The empirical chapters, given the concern with urban transformation, focus on the two spheres of activity that did most to reshape the contemporary city – town centre renewal and rehousing. By contrast, this text deals only in passing with subjects such as the schools programme, new universities, power stations, cathedrals, bridge-building and bus stations which, although important to modern architecture, had relatively less impact on the wider shape of the city.

With regard to sources, this book follows its predecessor in building its experiential approach on interviews and documentation. Wherever possible, I have sought to use in-depth interviews to gather personal testimony. Some of this material was already in hand, stemming from interviews undertaken for my earlier book. This comprised portions of interviews with older architects from the interwar Modern Movement whose careers continued into the postwar period. The greater part, however, came from a new round of interviews conducted in 2004–6. These proceeded on a semi-structured basis, guided by schedules of questions arranged in major segments that covered personal background, training and major career episodes. Other sections covered specific aspects of the individual's experience, in appropriate chronological sequence. The resulting interviews usually lasted 1½–2 hours, although some were considerably longer. After transcription and amendment, the final version became the definitive basis for citation in this text.[72] In several cases, due to the recency of events, respondents asked that particular points either should not receive direct attribution or should omit personal details. I have observed these conditions throughout.

Asking people to recollect the past through the 'prism of memory' is inevitably more reliable when accompanied by supporting documentary evidence.[73] The latter primarily came from recourse to the major journals of the time, which proliferated in this period, and from archives of papers. The growing interest in architectural modernism and the increasing amount of personal, local authority and government papers now reaching libraries and professional organisations provide steadily improving sources for research in this area of inquiry.[74] Unlike the previous volume, I have also been able to draw on sound archive collections, most notably, the holdings of the National Sound Archive (NSA) in London. Through gifts and direct commissions, the NSA offers valuable material on the lives and work of significant twentieth century architects compiled by skilled interviewers. At the time of writing most of this material remains in the form of tapes or CD-ROMs with only brief interview summaries. Full written and on-line transcripts now exist for a small number of respondents, although frequent transcription inaccuracies emphasise the importance of working from the tapes rather than the transcripts or summaries.

## Structure

This book has an overall chronological trajectory, although the chapters can essentially be considered as comprising three thematic parts. The first three chapters set the scene by considering the careers of architects practising modernism and aspects of the professional environments in which they worked. Chapter 2 traces the postwar career paths of members of the interwar Modern Movement, alongside those of their younger counterparts who entered the profession after 1945. Among the topics considered are their training, sources of inspiration, career choices and the continuing internationalism of their outlook. Understandably, this chapter's emphasis on the biographical dimension tends to emphasise individual motivation and intentionality. Chapter 3 then examines the experience of becoming an architect in the 1950s, considering the typical working environment found in the public and private sectors. In doing so, it recognises the complex relations between the public and private sectors, highlighting the power struggle between the two sectors for influence and patronage. Chapter 4 recognises that the profession of modernism existed in a wider professional context that both empowered and limited the architect's contribution to the transformation of British cities. It opens by briefly considering the ways in which the development of professionalism differentiated architecture from building and how that relationship became blurred with the advance of industrialised building methods. It then examines the vital question of interprofessional relations, which, though often cordial, led to real struggles for influence during the years of reconstruction and renewal. This was frequently the case with the engineers over access to, and influence over, town planning in general and road planning in particular. After briefly sketching the historical background, this chapter considers the turf wars that broke out.

The second and longest part of this book contains five chapters that deal directly with urban transformation. Chapter 5 opens by contrasting the vigorous progress made by private-sector-led development during the office and commercial boom of the late 1950s with the slow pace of public-sector-led attempts to reconstruct town centres during the same period. The remainder of the chapter discuss the way that two pressure groups – the Modern Architectural Research (MARS) Group and the Society for the Promotion of Urban Renewal (SPUR) – attempted to contribute to the formulation of public debate. Chapter 6 notes the way in which reconstruction, now rebranded as renewal, finally sprang into life in the late 1950s and the ways in which architects contributed to the process. The first section presents a case study of central Portsmouth, a heavily blitzed city that moved comparatively slowly towards redevelopment. The central theme of public–private partnership noted there is reiterated in the ensuing sections, which outline the contrasting town centre development strategies pursued by the authorities in provincial towns and then in London. Chapter 7 focuses on town centre renewal ventures in the British New Towns, an unfamiliar territory for a book on modernism. In this instance, it examines the development of the megastructural town centre at Cumbernauld in Scotland as well as its counterpart, the unbuilt private New Town scheme for the LCC at Hook in Hampshire.

Chapter 8, the first of two chapters on housing, looks at provision from the point of view of quantity, highlighting the way in which public-sector housing providers, and their allies in the construction industry, attempted to accelerate the production of housing dramatically in the 1950s and 1960s. After drawing attention to the relationship between the central and local state in housing provision, it turns to the local situation by considering the experience of three provincial cities: Birmingham, Glasgow and Liverpool. These case studies highlight the deployment of high-rise flats, an issue distinct from, but overlapping with the spread of industrialised building. The third section reflects on the particular advantages supposedly gained from industrialised building methods and the role of official sanction and commercial pressures in ensuring their propagation. The final section reflects on the myths that sustained the boom in industrialised building and their consequences.

Quantity, however, was only part of the picture. Despite the pressures towards standardisation and economy, housing was still an essential arena for sociologically inspired innovation and attracted the attentions of those that wanted to use design to engage with the prospective way of life for the inhabitants of public housing schemes. Chapter 9 examines attempts by architects to produce 'urban living' by design. After examining the sociological underpinnings of their designs, it explores a series of case studies that follow the development of thinking from the early 1950s through to the 1970s. These concern, in turn, 'cluster blocks', 'streets in the sky', and schemes that sought to show that high-density need not mean inhuman conditions or necessitate the use of high-rise buildings.

This discussion, touching on avant-garde ideas about housing, leads on to the third part of the book, comprising three chapters that recognise the increasing plurality of architectural modernism during the 1960s. Chapter 10 turns attention to the international avant-garde. It opens with the question of succession, before turning to the events that led to the disbandment of MARS and CIAM. The tensions and indecision of CIAM X at Dubrovnik (1956) led on to Otterlo (1959), a gathering that still carried the CIAM name but scarcely represented the same constituency as earlier in the decade. The final part discusses the work of Team X through into the 1970s. The companion Chapter 11 focuses more on the British domestic scene, identifying groups actively developing powerful new images of future cities, albeit with ever-decreasing connection with the world of everyday practice. It identifies and explores preoccupations with two prototypes – linear cities and megastructures – at a time when technological utopianism again fuelled architectural approaches to major social problems. The concluding section takes stock of efforts to map the plurality of modernism in the early 1970s, showing the strains encountered by attempting to retain the idea of a singular 'Modern Movement' as an overarching framework.

Chapter 12 shows that the exhilaration of the 1960s was not destined to last. This chapter discusses the way that the critique mounted in intensity and its implications for the reputation and future of architectural modernism. Its initial sections show how the weight of criticism by professional and academic researchers about problems of the built environment built up over the decade and was given focus by the *Architectural Review*'s 'Housing Issue' of November 1967 and the Ronan Point disaster of 16 May 1968. Nevertheless, even by 1972 there was still no collectively held view among architects as to how to judge the changing situation, let alone how to respond. Some preferred to dismiss the furore as ill-informed scaremongering and to continue with business as usual. Others believed that present problems were just temporary difficulties, stirred up by the media's partiality for sensation and politicians' instincts to identify scapegoats. Others felt that these shocks to the system pointed to a general crisis within architecture. Each position had different implications for the future of both architecture and the architectural profession. The resolution of those positions and the dilemmas that they posed, coupled with the changes in external circumstances, would shape what would become the legacy of modernism.

# Chapter 2

# Practising modernism

**Much of the story of the 1920s generation remains untold, and certainly, at present, unresearched. It is clearly part of a much larger and continuing picture and one that takes in MARS, CIAM, Team X and the Archigram group, as well as more recent High Tech developments (the role of Peter Fogo and Peter Rice for example) and the consistent work of architects like Trevor Dannatt . . . and Leonard Manasseh who were not hugging the limelight of publicity afforded by the Independent Group and *Architectural Design*.**

**Dennis Sharp[1]**

Just as there are many narratives available to explain chains of events in the history of modern architecture, so is it possible to choose a variety of actors to populate those narratives. The names of the elite and the avant-garde – sometimes, but not always, the same – readily suggest themselves. Certainly, their works do comprise an important element in this book, but the story of the practice of modernism justifiably embraces other, less celebrated architects. It includes those who worked in local authorities and private practices up and down Great Britain, whose contribution, as Dennis Sharp suggests, never enjoyed the immediate 'limelight of publicity'. This chapter, therefore, introduces the dramatis personae of this study. Its first section analyses the rapid growth of the architectural profession after the Second World War. The next part reviews the backgrounds of those who worked in local authority architects' offices and in private practice in the years from the mid-1950s through to the early 1960s. The ensuing segment adds insight into the business of becoming an architect. It considers what made modernism attractive and deals with education and training, the common ground of ideas and working approaches, sources of inspiration, and career choices, including the continuing attractions of internationalism. From this diversity of experience, we initially glimpse the plurality that characterised the practice of modernism in the postwar period.

## Recruitment

There are no internationally consistent employment statistics for architects, but the non-standardised figures available for different countries give some impression of the impressive pace of postwar expansion. The USA, for instance, had 19,000 registered architects in 1950, 30,000 in 1960 and 47,000 in 1970, giving architecture a rate of growth that exceeded even that of the legal profession.[2] Western Europe saw equally impressive increases when measured in relative terms. In Italy, for instance, there were approximately 4000 registered architects in 1959 and 6344 in 1969, a rise of 58 per cent over the decade.[3] Architectural employment in France expanded from an estimated 5200 in 1957 to 8400 in 1968 – more than 61 per cent in eleven years.[4] Despite starting off from a somewhat higher base level, architectural employment in Great Britain increased from 15,824 in 1949, to 19,183 in 1959 and 21,947 in 1969, a rise of almost 40 per cent over the two decades.

While allowing for distortions due to extending accreditation to previously non-registered practitioners, these statistics clearly reveal the rapid entry of a new cohort of architects into the profession. Their recruitment reflected both the need for more personnel to take on the extra volume of work arising from reconstruction and the growth of specialism. The architectural profession gained notable success in asserting a sense of ownership over what might be termed 'architectural knowledge' – the intellectual property arising from the interaction of the ability to design, an understanding of the ways in which user requirements affect design, and the capacity to lead the procurement and construction processes.[5] Not everyone, of course, accepted the architects' proprietorial claims. Engineers, in particular, could lay claim to areas of that knowledge, especially in areas peripheral to the architect's core competencies. This, indeed, occurred in the case of industrialised building (see Chapter 4).

Increases in architectural employment also depended on prevailing conceptions of the relationship between the architect and kindred professions, which varied from nation to nation. In Italy, the need for new skills in handling new materials, building technologies and design also benefited engineers given the close association between architecture and engineering in that country, although architects remained the major beneficiaries. In North America, observers associated rising demand for the services of architects primarily with the need for greater knowledge about how to handle the increased scale of building projects and to manage greater complexity in plan, structure and fabric.[6] An Australian commentator reached similar conclusions, somewhat grumpily linking growth in the architectural profession with the changing state of the world. *Inter alia*, this included 'rushing headlong into an era of rampant technology' in which buildings became larger, architectural offices 'increased in size and included specialist consultants on their staffs', and that the 'realization of a building became the work of a team rather than that of an individual'.[7]

With regard to Britain, the emergent nature of employment patterns became clear with the publication in 1962 of a report entitled *The Architect and his Office*.[8] Commissioned by the RIBA and dealing first and foremost with the architects' function as designers of new buildings, it reported on how work was handled in an architect's office and how the efficiency of architects could be raised.[9] Its findings, based on a census of RIBA members carried out in 1957 with subsequent interview studies, were particularly valuable in providing a portrait of the sectoral distribution of the profession. As shown in Table 2.1, when omitting the residual category of 4 per cent of RIBA members who were teachers, retired or working abroad, employment divided into 58 per cent in the private sector and 38 per cent in the public sector.

Dealing first with the private sector, roughly 7 out of 10 of the architects employed by private practices worked for firms with 6 staff or fewer, although there was a discernible trend towards larger offices with more than 50 architects. Whereas there were only 32 firms employing over 50 architectural staff in 1954, by 1960 there were 66 such firms, with almost all the recent entrants to this category comprising newly founded practices.[10] The heterogeneous industrial and commercial sector, which employed 6 per cent of all registered British architects, included those working for large manufacturing firms, retailing organisations, property groups and building contractors. Besides employing architects in-house, they also sometimes hired qualified architects on a freelance basis to work on specific contracts, for example, when needing to produce working drawings in substantial numbers. The commercial and property boom itself impacted on the organisation of the profession. Given the complexity of building regulations, developers would often call on the services of architectural practices which specialised in offering intimate knowledge of how to exploit planning regulations to best advantage. At their most successful, such practices grew rapidly (see Chapter 3).

Switching to the public sector, the report showed that 6 per cent worked for central government (in ministries such as Housing and Local Government,

**Table 2.1** The structure of architectural employment, 1957

| Sector | % | Description |
| --- | --- | --- |
| Private practice | 52 | Primarily small offices employing six or fewer; tendency towards greater scale |
| Local government | 28 | Freestanding Architect's Offices primarily in county councils and county boroughs; smaller authorities tended to employ architects in Surveyor's or Engineer's departments |
| Industrial and commercial | 6 | Particular growth in office sector |
| Central government | 6 | Housing and Local Government, Health, Education, and Building and Public Works |
| National boards | 4 | Hospital boards, National Coal Board, British Railways Board or the public utilities |
| Other | 4 | In other activities, e.g. teaching, abroad or retired |

Source: Based on J.M. Austin-Smith, A. Derbyshire, D. Howard, J.H. Madge and J.M.N. Milne, *The Architect and his Office*, London: Royal Institute of British Architects, 1962.

Health, Education, and Building and Public Works) and 4 per cent for national or regional boards (the regional hospital boards, British Transport Commission, British Electricity Authority, the divisional coal boards and the other statutory authorities). By contrast, 28 per cent worked in local government offices: a sector that had grown dramatically since 1945. Before the Second World War, most local authorities had no separate Architect's Departments, with both trained and unqualified architects working as none-too-significant members of offices run by the Borough Surveyor or City Engineer. To some extent, this pattern persisted in the smaller authorities, which still had little need of a separate Architect's Office. While job titles were not always an accurate guide to division of functions,[11] architects employed at 28 metropolitan boroughs, 318 non-county boroughs, 564 urban district councils and 474 rural district councils continued to work in offices headed by an engineer or surveyor.[12] For larger authorities, however, the situation had changed dramatically by 1957, when all the 62 county councils, with the sole exception of the Soke of Peterborough, had instituted separate Architect's Departments; 47 out of 83 county boroughs had followed suit. In total, offices run by Chief or City Architects employed nearly 3700 architectural staff (of whom 250 were principals and their deputies, 2150 assistant architects, and 1300 architectural assistants).[13]

## First generation

Practising modernism was a different proposition in the mid-1950s than in the late 1930s. Instead of relying on infrequent contracts from enthusiastic supporters for shops, flats or interior design, modernism now represented the mainstream. To design according to modernist principles was a normal course of action or even an expectation rather than a statement. The underlying sense of critical mass was enhanced by the fact that, for the first time, there was a full age range of architects who identified themselves with the Modern Movement. They ranged from a 'first generation' of older practitioners born around the turn of the twentieth century, to a middle-aged group born after the First World War who were now occupying senior positions in the public sector, to a cohort of newly graduated trainees born after 1930 who had commenced their careers in the mid-1950s.

The 'first generation' included those that enjoyed respect for their part in the historic struggle to overthrow the Beaux-Arts establishment.[14] They included the hard core of British modernists who had organised pressure groups, crafted manifestos, staged international congresses, held exhibitions, drawn plans, made models, lobbied the rich and powerful, charmed potential sympathisers, participated in public debates, written letters to *The Times*, created schisms, vilified opponents and, just occasionally during the 1930s, completed buildings. In the period after the Second World War, they had initially found difficulty in obtaining work and sometimes looked for opportunities overseas. Wells Coates, for instance, gradually shifted his activities back to North America, although not formally moving back to Canada until 1957. Maxwell Fry accepted commissions that began with contacts made during service with the Royal Engineers in the Gold Coast (now Ghana). After the war, he and Jane Drew worked on projects for schools and other public sector projects in the Gold Coast, subsequently branching out into Togoland (later the Republic of Togo), Nigeria and the Middle East. Between 1951 and 1954, they also worked, often uneasily,[15] alongside Le Corbusier and his cousin Pierre Jeanneret on the master plan for Chandigarh (Punjab, India).

Many of their contemporaries (Table 2.2) founded firms that struggled during the years of Austerity, despite later ranking among the key 'prestige practices' of postwar Britain. Basil Spence, Ernö Goldfinger and Frederick Gibberd became principals of the private practices that they headed. Elsewhere co-equal partnerships were the vogue. F.R.S. Yorke, Eugene Rosenberg and Cyril Mardall (Sjöström) had formed their eponymous partnership in 1944, later known as YRM. In 1945, Eric Lyons resumed his partnership with Geoffrey P. Townsend (Lyons and Townsend), which was originally formed in 1938. The socialistically-minded Architects' Co-Operative Partnership (later known as the Architects Co-Partnership), founded by eleven students from the Architectural Association (AA) in 1939, was relaunched in 1946 with the eight remaining partners. Philip Powell and J.H. Moya left Gibberd's firm to form their own partnership in 1946 after winning the open competition to rebuild a large area of war-damaged housing in Pimlico (Churchill Gardens).[16] Similarly in 1947, Richard Sheppard formed a partnership with Geoffrey Robson, one of his former students from the AA, to renew a practice that originally dated from 1938.

Others looked to the public sector for employment (see Table 2.2).[17] In the past, this was distinctly not a popular course of action. When the journal *Official Architect* had first appeared in 1937, the pseudonymous 'Staff Architect' ironically commented on the prejudices about architects who worked in the public sectors:

> A confusion of thought appears to becloud the minds of some who maintain that an architect when he assumes an official capacity becomes an administrator of the work of others, and in consequence he must thereby cease to be an architect proper.[18]

Although changing circumstances had rectified some of the problems of low esteem, opinions still varied about entering public service. Hubert Bennett, for example, observed:

> There was no private practice until about 1950; very little indeed. All materials were regulated; you had to have a licence for this and a licence for timber, a licence for bricks. It was no good, practice, so all I could do was official architecture. . . . I didn't want to, but I just had to do it.[19]

Oliver Cox responded to the same situation in a wholly different manner:

> There was not that much choice. There were a few private practices, some of which had survived since before the war, but so many had died. There were very few in private practice and many were keen to offer their services to put up a school or two. . . . However, I think you must

**Table 2.2** Biographical details of selected senior architects practising in the mid-1950s (career details to 1972)

| Name | Born | Training | Relevant offices held (postwar) |
| --- | --- | --- | --- |
| A.W. Cleeve Barr | 1910 | Liverpool University | Housing, LCC Architect's Department (1951–7); Development Architect, Ministry of Education (1957–8); Chief Architect, Ministry of Housing and Local Government (1959–64); Director, National Building Agency (1964 onwards) |
| Eric Bedford | 1909 | Articled, private practice | Chief Architect, Ministry of Public Building and Works (1950–70) |
| Hubert Bennett | 1909 | Manchester University | County Architect, West Yorkshire (1945–56); Architect, London County Council (1956–71) |
| Walter Bor | 1916 | Prague University and Bartlett School, London | LCC Architect's Department (1947–62); Liverpool City Planning Officer (1962–6); private practice (1966 onwards) |
| Kenneth Campbell | 1909 | Regent Street Polytechnic, London | Principal Housing architect, LCC and GLC (1960 onwards) |
| Cecil Elsom | 1912 | Northern Polytechnic, London | Private practice (1933–40 and 1946 onwards) |
| Donald Gibson | 1908 | Manchester University | City Architect and Town Planning Officer, Coventry (1938–55); County Architect, Nottinghamshire (1955–8) |
| Percy Johnson-Marshall | 1915 | Liverpool University | Planning Officer in charge of Reconstruction Areas Group, LCC (1949–59); Edinburgh University (1959 onwards) |
| Stirrat Johnson Marshall | 1912 | Liverpool University | Deputy County Architect, Hertfordshire (1945–48); Chief Architect to the Ministry of Education (1950–6); private practice (1956 onwards) |
| Denys Lasdun | 1914 | Architectural Association | Private practice (1935–40 and 1946 onwards) |
| H.J. Whitfield Lewis | 1911 | Cardiff University | Principal Housing Architect, LCC (1950–9); ChiefArchitect, Middlesex CC (1959–64) |
| Arthur Ling | 1913 | Bartlett School, London | Chief Planning Officer, LCC (1949–55); City Architect, Coventry (1955–64); Professor of Architecture, Nottingham University (1964 onwards) |
| Eric Lyons | 1912 | Regent Street Polytechnic, London | Private practice (1945 onwards) |
| Robert Matthew | 1906 | Edinburgh College of Art | Architect, LCC (1946–53); Professor of Architecture, Edinburgh University (1953–68) |
| Graeme Shankland | 1917 | Architectural Association | LCC (1950–62); private practice (1962 onwards) |
| A.G. Sheppard Fidler | 1909 | Liverpool University | City Architect, Birmingham (1952–64), private practice (1964 onwards) |
| Richard Seifert | 1910 | Bartlett School, London | Private practice (1946 onwards) |
| Lewis Womersley | 1910 | Huddersfield College of Art | Borough Architect, Northampton (1946–53); City Architect, Sheffield (1953–64); private practice (1964 onwards) |

Note: This table complements the information conveyed in Table 4.1 of J.R. Gold, *The Experience of Modernism: modern architects and the future city, 1928–1953*, London: E. & F.N. Spon, 1997, p. 89.

appreciate that at the end of the war there was a tremendous attitude on the part of people coming out of the AA and other places. It was a very exciting time. . . . We had a huge programme of New Towns and new housing. This was where the action was. So instead of having, as we have now, half-baked departments, if there are any departments of architecture at all, every local authority had a highly qualified Chief Architect, some of them very good indeed. At least half a dozen of them were top rank. The idea of service to the community was paramount.[20]

Members of the first generation and some of their younger colleagues had gravitated to the public sector, particularly because some also had planning qualifications. As Chapter 4 indicates, the profound shortage of qualified planners in the late 1940s had quickly propelled those with suitable credentials into senior positions in the local authorities. There were also opportunities in Whitehall. In 1955, for example, Stirrat Johnson Marshall was Chief Architect at the Ministry of Education with former Hertfordshire colleagues such as David Medd and Mary Crowley among the senior architects. J.H. Forshaw was Chief Architect and Housing Consultant to the Ministry of Housing and Local Government. Godfrey Samuel was secretary to the Royal Fine Art Commission. The somewhat underrated Eric Bedford was Chief Architect at the Ministry of Works. Others continued their long-term appointments at the New Town Development Corporations, with Frederick Gibberd as Consultant Architect Planner at Harlow and Lionel Brett (later Lord Esher) as Consultant Architect and Planner for Hatfield. Commitment to the public sector, however, did not have to be permanent. As the 1950s wore on, second thoughts set in. For some this reflected disillusionment with the ethos and bureaucracy of local authorities, but for others it mirrored improving pay and conditions for private practice. Whatever the motivation, as we shall see later, the result was a wave of new formations that included what would become some of Britain's largest and most prestigious practices.

## Becoming an architect

Turning to the 'slightly younger generation',[21] born in the 1920s and early 1930s (Table 2.3), most shared the socioeconomic background of their elders. They were still dominantly from upper middle-class backgrounds and had attended public schools, although a greater proportion of them were British born. Almost all had come through full-time higher education. Training through evening classes still occurred, but the former option of pupillage (articled status) had largely fallen into disuse. They also had career disruption through military service, although the younger ones increasingly had served two years' conscription under National Service.[22] As a result, most were already in their late twenties or early thirties by the time that their careers started to develop. They shared a folk memory of the horrors of the 1930s – the 'reverse of rose tinted spectacles',[23] but their precise politics remained as hazy as those of their older colleagues. It had been a recurrent feature of the first generation that their politics were architecture. Although clearly inclined to left-wing causes, few actively proselytised for the Communist Party or

**Table 2.3** The 1920s generation: biographical details of selected architects (career details to 1972)

| Name | Born | Training | Offices held |
| --- | --- | --- | --- |
| Christoph Bon | 1921 | Eidgenössische Technische Hochschule, Zurich, Switzerland | Private practice (1952 onwards) |
| Peter Carter | 1927 | Northern Polytechnic, London | LCC (1950–7); private practice (1957 onwards) |
| Peter Chamberlin | 1919 | Oxford University; Kingston School of Art, London | Private practice (1952 onwards) |
| Oliver Cox | 1920 | Architectural Association, London | LCC (1950–9); Ministry of Housing and Local Government (1959–64); private practice (1965 onwards) |
| Andrew Derbyshire | 1923 | Cambridge University; Architectural Association, London | West Riding County Architects' Department (1953–5); Sheffield (1955–61); private practice (1961 onwards) |
| Ralph Erskine | 1914 | Regent Street Polytechnic, London; Academy of Fine Arts, Stockholm | Private practice (1946 onwards) |
| James Gowan | 1923 | Kingston School of Art, London | Private practice (1957 onwards) |
| Patrick Hodgkinson | 1930 | Architectural Association, London | Private practice (1954 onwards) |
| Ted Hollamby | 1921 | School of Arts and Crafts, Hammersmith, Bartlett School, University of London | Senior Architect LCC (1949–62); Borough Architect and later Planning Officer, LB Lambeth (1963 onwards) |
| William Howell | 1922 | Cambridge University; Regent Street Polytechnic, London | LCC; private practice (1959 onwards) |
| John Killick | 1924 | Architectural Association, London | LCC; private practice (1959 onwards) |
| J. Hidalgo Moya | 1920 | Royal West of England School of Architecture, Bristol | Private practice (1946 onwards) |
| John Partridge | 1924 | Regent Street Polytechnic, London | LCC Architect's Department (1951–9); private practice (1959 onwards) |
| Geoffry Powell | 1920 | Architectural Association, London | Private practice (1952 onwards) |
| Philip Powell | 1921 | Architectural Association, London | Private practice (1946 onwards) |
| Alison Smithson | 1928 | Durham University | Private practice (1950 onwards) |
| Peter Smithson | 1923 | Durham University | LCC; private practice (1950 onwards) |
| James Stirling | 1926 | Liverpool University; School of Planning and Research for Regional Development, London | Private practice (1957 onwards) |
| John F.C. Turner | 1927 | Architectural Association, London | Private practice (1954–7); overseas (1957 onwards) |
| John Voelcker | 1928 | Architectural Association, London | Private practice (1955–69); University of Glasgow (1969–72) |
| Colin St. John Wilson | 1922 | Cambridge University; Bartlett School, London | LCC (1950–5); Cambridge University and private practice (1956 onwards) |

radical socialist groups – even though they *may* have been members. For example, as John Summerson remarked with regard to Lubetkin, now accepted as one of the most politically conscious architects of his generation: 'it was accepted, without discussion, that he probably held Marxist views, but he was very tactful, very quiet about his Marxism'.[24]

With some notable exceptions,[25] much the same comment applied to their younger colleagues in the mid-1950s. There was a consensus that there were Communist architects in prominent positions in British architecture, sometimes claimed as being organised into 'cells' – that weasel word of Cold War politics. Their main centres of 'infiltration' comprised the Schools and Housing Divisions of the LCC ('Marxists . . . there were meetings at Communist Party headquarters'), groups at the AA ('You were not a student at that time unless you were a member of the Communist Party; everyone belonged') or in the Association of Building Technicians ('concealed Communists, they knew how to control a meeting').[26] Yet, Communist architects tended to see themselves as apart from the rank and file. As Sir Anthony Cox recalled:

> We didn't much like the party discipline, with these awful sorts of study groups reading beastly little pamphlets, almost like Baptists or something. We – I think it was probably Richard's [Llewelyn Davies] influence – our policy was that it was no good just going around preaching the Revolution, because no one would listen to us. What we had to do was to be very good at our job; then people would listen to us.[27]

Moreover, it was hard to see exactly how these political orientations affected the architecture. Colin St. John Wilson, for instance, observed that the

> unarguable existence of a prevalent Communist persuasion in high places of the organisation [the LCC] soon became manifested in an architectural 'house-style' of, paradoxically, the mildest form grounded upon adherence to the works of the Swedish Housing Authority during the War and currently celebrated in the *Architectural Review* as 'The New Empiricism'.[28]

Ironically, the political revolutionaries considered the Corbusian tendency, with its claims to be architecturally revolutionary, as crypto-fascist. For their part, the Corbusians regarded the opposition's architecture as 'unpardonably compromised and ingratiating'.[29]

One undeniable source of difference between the first generation and those who entered practice in the mid-1950s lay in expectations and outlook. The first generation experienced a world of uncertainty, especially for those who wanted to practise modern architecture. By the turn of the 1960s, there were certainties: architects *knew* where they and their profession were going. Those entering practice could rest assured that the battle was over since 'there wasn't anyone much after the war standing up for traditional architecture'.[30] Those in architectural training benefited from the triumph of the 'modernist academy', in that 'modernism continued to be taken up by many schools while formal vestiges of the Beaux-Arts were neglected, edged out in favour of what appeared to be more pressing curricular requirements, or actually abolished.'[31] The sea change in some cases was quick and decisive. Despite its reputation for being interested in the mundane concerns of 'weathering, durability and maintenance costs',[32] rather than flights of design fancy, for example, the Regent Street Polytechnic emerged in the late 1950s as one of London's more progressive schools led by tutors such as Jim Stirling, John Outram, Bill Howell and Michael Webb.

By the same token, outposts of traditionalism remained given the legendarily slow staff turnover at most of the 73 schools that offered architectural courses in 1958. A few, like the Bartlett School, retained the full Beaux-Arts flavour, although allowed final-year students 'to design in a more contemporary idiom'. Bournemouth retained a reputation for conservatism, with a first year devoted to classical studies. One observer noted about Sheffield at that time: 'In the past the course has been such that even the work of the best students contained little but the ingredients of a totally uninspired mediocrity'.[33] When dealing with Plymouth, the epithet merely changed to 'cliché-ridden mediocrity'. Traditionalism also remained embedded in particular aspects of the syllabus. At first-year level, for instance, most schools still taught the history of architecture 'on a series of styles . . . à la Banister Fletcher'[34] – Sir Banister Fletcher's long-established book *A History of Architecture on the Comparative Method*, first published in 1896. So entrenched was use of this book that copies passed down the generations: 'I used my father's copy (1923). If I needed anything more modern I looked at someone else's copy'.[35] It was an approach that contributed to what Reyner Banham described as 'historical expertise of a very high order, but not necessarily harnessed to a constructive view of architecture as a service to the human race'.[36] Drawing classes continued to require students to learn the Orders, replicate Trajan column lettering, and perfect the arts of perspective and washes. Most students then considered such activities to be a waste of time but subsequently reappraised them as promoting valuable skills: 'I despised it all very much at the time and we all rebelled like hell, but actually I was very grateful for the training. Now noone knows how to draw any more.'[37]

Taken as a whole, however, the balance had swung decisively and traditionalism was confined to residual pockets of resistance. Modernism had come to supply the vocabulary of architecture in most schools of architecture and, like any linguistic form, had its ground rules and its taken-for-granted conceptual underpinnings. Students responded to the 'strong, powerful and simple' approach towards architecture associated with the great figures of the interwar era, most notably Mies van der Rohe and Le Corbusier.[38] Those studying in the 1950s in particular frequently found Le Corbusier's work 'captivating . . . dogmatic and seductive [and] intuitively appealing'.[39] The appeal of specific aspects of his work did not always last, but for many the attraction 'was always there'. They might lose the taste for the *unité d'habitation*,[40] but retained appreciation of special buildings like the Villa Savoie and the chapel at Ronchamp. Modernism not only provided what were regarded as the appropriate forms for building, but also was an intrinsic part of how one learned to see things:

> we did not think of it that much as 'modern architecture', we thought of it as the right way to do things. It seemed pointless doing anything else; you built in the simplest way, you used the most rational form of construction, you got your delight out of proportion, rhythm, symmetry and aesthetic in the landscape and that was enough richness. There didn't seem to be any need for anything else. We were trained to have eyes to see those things, but, there again, we certainly didn't give a second thought to anything else.[41]

The aesthetic prescriptions inherent in modernism seemed like commonsense: 'these were times when resources were in short supply; to add ornament seemed wasteful'. Moreover, it helped to differentiate social architecture from 'the speculative builder, because that [lack of ornamentation] does not help sales'. The unreconstructed general public, however, did not always seem to share the same tastes. John Graham noted:

> When I was [a student] in Manchester, I did a design for an exhibition. I did the show house, which was a modern house, and a themed house, which was a period cottage. After the exhibition, I was approached for a commission to build another period cottage. I recoiled in horror; that was not what I felt that I should be doing at all.[42]

This notion of architecture, of course, influenced the conception of the architect. Although the self-effacing idea of the architect as 'anonymous (building) technician' still retained currency, it mainly implied that construction was *morally* important to the architect and that functional analysis was the *sine qua non* for supplying the appropriate forms for contemporary buildings; the key to constructing 'buildings that made the users comfortable and happy'.[43] There had long been a feeling among students at the progressive schools of architecture that 'much of what was built in the name of modern architecture was appearance only'.[44] By contrast, functionalism should imply

> a thesis of tell me what you want to achieve and I will tell you how it can be achieved. Tell me the function that you want and why you want to achieve it in that way. It was form follows function. Sometimes that led to things that the client may not even have thought of.[45]

Such was the attachment to functionalism that some preferred to avoid the term 'modernism' altogether and identify themselves with the mode of analysis. As Oliver Cox pointed out:

> [Graeme] Shankland, [Michael] Ventris and I called ourselves functional-
> ists. We did not like the term 'modernism': modernism was a style. We

did not believe in style. We believed, as Peter Shepheard put it, in doing what came naturally, but it was in fact interpreting a brief in an appropriate way, with modern materials but not creating a style of architecture that would then be a battle, again with styles.[46]

Naturally, there were many possible ways for tutors to communicate the essence of this orientation without the need for heavy-handed proselytising. At Manchester, for example, it was part of the ethos. George Grenfell-Baines recalled that in the mid-1930s the School of Architecture at Manchester had stressed the notion of 'following the programme through, how will it be used'.[47] Its head, Professor Richard Cordingley, would ask students 'to describe an hour in the day of the life of the people who would occupy the building and how it would help them. It was a very good insight into the Modern Movement; things had to be functional.'[48] Experiencing the same department (still under Cordingley) twenty years later, John Graham felt that these views still permeated the syllabus, especially working through 'the Year Masters – the way they criticised your designs; what they approved of and what they didn't'.[49]

Unlike earlier periods, even at progressive schools, students no longer had to worry that handing in a project featuring a modern architectural subject would automatically attract poor marks. Designs that earlier might have been treated as acts of defiance now received sympathetic, even indulgent treatment from examiners. Later on, the spread of 1960s counter-culture further relaxed the canons of criticism. Encouragement to students to rethink the relationships between architecture, technology and economy led to tolerance of anything that seemed suitably 'daring'. This filtered through particularly into student projects. Studies with little formal content but conveying grand ideas might receive as good a mark as others that espoused more traditional virtues. In an environment in which the avant-garde seemed nonchalant about whether their designs were ever built (see Chapter 11), the underlying concept and audacity of vision had become key elements in judging worth – a development that some considered an abdication of critical judgement.

Thinking big frequently seemed at a premium. Instructors actively encouraged students to take on large-scale projects, often on a group basis. This often led to tackling ambitious topics. Long before the term 'megastructure' formally entered the lexicon of modernism (see Chapter 11), student architects were devising proto-megastructural schemes. Among the fifth-year AA projects for 1954 were Stephen Rosenberg's Rhondda City, a linear city scheme for 12,000 people and Ronald Jones' futuristic Life Structure, foreseeing the world of 2054 with Unit-Metropolises able to support 2 million people – a cybernetic-influenced vision that bore a striking resemblance to an early twenty-first century computer server (Figure 2.1).[50] Peter Winchester, whose fifth-year project at the Regent Street Polytechnic in 1958 comprised the rebuilding of the Natural History Museum around an airport-terminal-like central spine, argued that ambitious topics were considered de rigueur for better students. He noted an obsession for the better students to complete projects on double-elephant paper, commensurate with their status.[51] Martyn Smith suggested tutors' assessments of a student's significance could be gathered by the size of paper that they were encouraged to use. This applied even at the determinedly down-to-earth Northern Polytechnic in London:

> I was appalled at the idea that the merit of the drawing tended to lie purely in the size of the drawing rather than was actually written or drawn or depicted on that piece of paper. It has led me to believe that all the tutors have shares in paper companies: it was ridiculous to have a sheet of paper the length of this room and it would have a few lines on it. You were supposed to be impressed by the size of the paper, because you certainly were not going to be impressed by what was drawn on it.[52]

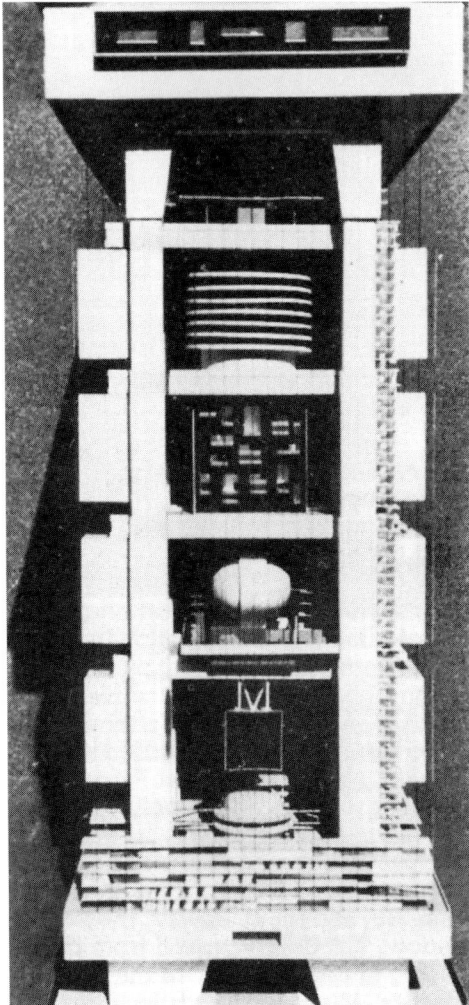

2.1
**End view of model of futuristic 'unit town', from 'Life Structure, Year 2054', Ronald Jones (1954)**

### Visiting the future

The culture of architectural education also inculcated a powerful sense of the importance of seeing what was new in the world of architecture. As Jack Bonnington observed: 'All our holidays were busmen's holidays. There was a new building here or there and we had to go and see it. It was a very single-minded business.'[53] Domestically, the destinations that attracted attention in the 1950s included the central area of Coventry (Figure 2.2), the Hertfordshire schools and the Smithsons' school at Hunstanton, SPAN housing estates by Eric Lyons, flats for the LCC (especially at Roehampton), New Zealand House in London (Robert Matthew, Stirrat Johnson Marshall and Partners) and the new housing estates in Sheffield.

Charles Willis, then a trainee working for the Corporation of the City of Birmingham, recalled a trip that the West Midlands branch of the Town Planning Institute made to Sheffield. His journal entry follows a carefully structured route that took in the problem (slum clearance) and various ways of tackling it through public housing schemes: Radburn principles (Greenhill), high-density mixed development (Gleadless) and deck-access slab blocks (Park Hill: see also Chapter 9). Although Park Hill aroused some ambivalence, the journal also indicates the excitement that he felt on seeing things that manifestly seemed 'on the cutting edge of contemporary development':

2.2
**Lower Precinct,
Coventry
(completed 1958)**

Our six hours in Sheffield was full and interesting. It began with a short introductory talk on the schemes that we were to visit in a Conference

Room of the Council House by Mr Womersley, the City Architect. We were then accompanied in the coach to the Netherthorpe Redevelopment Area near the University where some appalling slums had been cleared on both sides of the steep valley, which will ultimately be open space, and on its western side the first floor of a series of high tower blocks was nearing completion. Nearby other housing schemes included three-storey houses whose ground floors comprised granny flats. . . . In the afternoon we first visited two modern housing estates on the southern fringes of the city. The one at Greenhill embodies many principles of the Radburn layout, with terraces of houses backing on to service cul-de-sacs and facing on to greens. We saw the one superblock within which, apart from the cul-de-sacs, internal circulation is confined to pedestrian ways. The partially complete Gleadless estate is remarkable for the way in which extreme difficulties of relief have been overcome and a high density of 200 persons per acre nevertheless obtained by use of a number of highly unorthodox housing layouts adapted to the relief. These include terraces with one long sloping roof, a double six-storey block with one side stepped down approached by a bridge to an upper floor level, the smaller blocks of about five cubic houses juxtaposed en echelon both in plan and elevation. The whole estate, two thirds complete, is divided into three by densely wooded valleys which are to be retained as part of an open space system. The fine views from the valley sides diminish the need for internal open space and compensate for the high density. The whole area is dominated by three 13-storey blocks on a 700-foot hilltop, which are visible for miles. We next returned to the city centre, downhill all the way, to see the second stage of the Park Hill scheme: slab-like twelve-storey blocks forming a continuous wall along the east side of the Sheaf valley. The design seemed heavy and ugly and they seemed likely to degenerate into tenements if neglected. Every third floor, a rear deck gave access to a flat below and a two-storey house with its lower floor at the same level. Having climbed to the top from an eleven-storey bridge linking two parts of the block, we got a fine view across the industry, bus and the railway stations to the city centre. We could also see workmen whose tasks involved dangerous acrobatics on scaffolding at a considerable height.[54]

Ownership of motorcycles and, increasingly, small cars gave students the possibilities of travelling to see the attractions that lay beyond the shores of the British Isles. In the late 1940s and early 1950s, architects had flocked to continental Europe to see examples of important interwar modern architecture in France, Italy and Germany. Sweden had also joined the itinerary, partly because its neutrality during the war had allowed continued development of modern architecture and also because there was a perceived linkage between Scandinavian architecture and social democracy. By the late 1950s, the itinerary had expanded further. The

masterpieces of the ancient and medieval worlds and the perennial recommendations gleaned from Banister Fletcher remained on the list, but new stops on
the pilgrimage came from reading '*Casabella* and the Danish magazines' and 'the
*Architectural Review* and *Architectural Design* (once Theo Crosby woke it up)'.
'Anything by Corb' always merited a visit. By 1960, this version of the modern
architectural 'Grand Tour' had its list of sites.[55] These included:

- France for Le Corbusier's buildings in Paris, Nantes and Marseilles.
- Scandinavia for Alvar Aalto's sanatorium at Paimio and church at Imatra
  (Finland), Tapiola Garden City (Finland), and Swedish and Danish postwar
  housing.
- Italy for works by Pier Luigi Nervi, BBPR (Banfi, Belgiojoso, Peressutti
  and Rogers), Giuseppi Terragni and Gio Ponti. The Velasca tower in Milan
  (Figure 2.3), Gio Ponti and Pier Luigi Nervi's Pirelli Tower (also in Milan)
  and Terragni's earlier Casa del Popolo in Como ('despite formerly being
  the local fascist headquarters') generated particular interest.
- Switzerland to see modern hospitals and schools, with a particular focus
  of interest at the Doldertal (Zurich) with housing by Marcel Breuer, Emil
  and Alfred Roth, and 'the neglected' Max Haefeli.

2.3
**Velasca tower in Milan (Banfi,
Belgiojoso, Peressutti and
Rogers, 1956–8)**

- The Netherlands for Dudok's Hilversum Town Hall and the recon-
  struction of Rotterdam (especially the Lijnbaan Shopping Centre by van
  der Broek and Bakema).
- West Berlin for the experimental housing displayed in the Hansaviertel-
  Tiergarten district in connection with the 1957 Interbau exhibition (see
  Chapter 8).

For the first time, too, visits to the USA became a practical proposition
with the introduction in the 1950s of affordable transatlantic flights. The growing
fascination with American popular culture added to the curiosity to see what the
USA could offer, with 'expectations of seeing, as it were, what we had strived so
hard to do in England actually built everywhere'.[56] Initially, the fascination stemmed
from the continued presence of the cream of the prewar Modern Movement, who
had been able to carry on their work despite the war in Europe. Projects associated
with Mies and Gropius now rivalled those of Frank Lloyd Wright and the classic
skyscrapers of Chicago and New York as fixed points of interest for the architectural
tourist. For Peter Carter, the lasting attraction with the USA started in the early
1950s, with the Illinois Institute of Technology building 'which we were just
discovering through the *Architectural Forum*'.[57] Similarly, Jack Bonnington recalled
the attraction of going to visit works by Mies, although not always being overly
impressed:

> While I was in the States, I had an opportunity to see some of Mies van
> der Rohe's work. To see it at that time was amazing, but the building has
> to be pristine. The Illinois Institute of Technology, for example, was
> neglected. There is nothing like a steel and glass simple building which
> is rusty and dirty; it does look terrible.[58]

By the 1960s, the centre of attraction moved further west: 'Visits to
America, especially to California, had caused me to believe that there can be a
different way of doing things.'[59] The two cities that drew attention were Las Vegas,
a city in which signs were replacing buildings as the focus of the urban order, and
Los Angeles, with its freeway system facilitating the spread of a decentralised
urban region over hundreds of square miles of southern California (Figure 2.4). Each
would baffle those who believed that good urban form needed the underpinning
of geometric order, but would increasingly intrigue those looking for prototypes to
stimulate new thinking about such issues as the architectural implications of mass
consumerism and the impact of rapidly increasing car ownership (see Chapter 11).

## Associations

As with almost all radical movements, the pioneers of architectural modernism
looked for like-minded individuals with whom they could associate. During the
interwar period, this feeling spurred the creation of many short-lived architectural
or pan-artistic bodies, as well as a handful that had greater durability.[60] Among the
latter, CIAM, MARS and the Architects' and Technicians' Organisation (ATO) took

2.4
**Los Angeles freeways (Los Angeles, CA, April 1979)**

pride of place. CIAM traced its origins to 1928, MARS to 1933, and the ATO to 1935. All continued their activities into the postwar period. MARS and CIAM lasted until 1957 and 1959 respectively (see Chapter 10). The ATO, which had joined with the much larger and older Association of Architects, Surveyors and Technical Assistants (AASTA) in 1938 and had become the Association of Building Technicians (ABT) in 1942, still functioned as a trades union and radical forum, lasting as an independent body until 1969. After a spate of mergers, it finally became part of the Union of Construction, Allied Trades and Technicians in December 1971.[61]

The underlying rationale for these associations had changed by the mid-1950s. Leaving aside professional organisations and trades unions, most modern architects no longer felt the need to cluster together for mutual support in the face of a hostile environment. In that climate, affiliations to associations need not involve much more than paying subscriptions. For example, the MARS Group enjoyed its highest memberships in the years immediately before its disbandment in 1957 despite recognisably running out of steam. Understandably, new issues gave further impetus to the urge to associate, but generally around specific topics. 'Anti-Ugly Action' or the New Architecture Group, established in December 1958 by students at the Royal College of Art and later from three other London architectural schools (the Bartlett, the Regent Street Polytechnic and the Architectural Association), orchestrated a campaign against new buildings they found offensive.[62] The Society for the Promotion of Urban Renewal (SPUR) undertook an extensive programme of activities intended to clarify approaches to urban renewal (see

Chapter 5). None the less, most architects found the world of the speculative and futuristic now constituted a luxury and maybe even an irrelevance. When recalling the demise of the MARS Group, Trevor Dannatt mused that the idea gradually crystallised that there were few prospects of finding successors to replace ageing leaders and that there was also no longer anyway 'a strong enough cause' (see also Chapter 10).[63]

Pan-artistic groupings had also attracted architects' attentions in the 1930s, with the Twentieth Century Group, Unit One and Circle breathing short-lived vitality into creative links between Modern Movements in different branches of the arts. The Independent Group provided a similar forum in the postwar years. Founded in 1952, it brought together architects, painters and sculptors for activities that helped to redefine modernism and explore mass culture.[64] Its swansong was 'This is Tomorrow', an exhibition held at the Whitechapel Art Gallery in August–September 1956. Organised by Theo Crosby in collaboration with Bryan Robertson, the gallery's director, it was conceived as 'the biggest show about design and ways of life since the MARS Group exhibition [of 1938]'.[65] Yet despite two years' preparation it struggled, like its predecessor, to find a larger statement. 'This is Tomorrow' invited painters, architects and sculptors to create their exhibits in mixed collaborative groups – or 'clumps' as Peter Smithson termed them.[66] Individual exhibits attracted considerable attention. The display by Group 2 (Richard Hamilton, John McHale and John Voelcker), laden with selections of consumer packaging, advertising and media artefacts, was seen as an important contribution to Pop Art. Colin St. John Wilson, Peter Carter and Frank Newby (Group 10) created a large piece of architectural sculpture in homage to Le Corbusier's Ronchamp. The Smithsons, Eduardo Paolozzi and Nigel Henderson (Group 6) created their 'Patio and Pavilion' exhibit, based on a Bethnal Green backyard shed, complete with carefully added junk (for example, bicycle wheels on the roof). Although also interpreted as 'proto-Pop Art',[67] or as expressing ideas about the New Brutalism, it could as easily be considered to represent 'the aesthetic of the pigeon-loft and allotment shed'.[68] These projects had a continuing life in the writings of historians, but those participating found more pressing demands on their time than persisting with this type of initiative. As Peter Smithson noted: 'It was a period of very easy collaboration, which then stopped.'[69]

## Choices

Tutors and studio masters exerted considerable influence over their students' forthcoming careers. One reason was that architecture retained the sense of being a 'small world'. It might no longer be possible for the majority of British modern architects to gather in a gallery in London for an exhibition, as had been the case in the 1930s, but the community retained its intimacy at senior level and in the field of architectural training. Formal and informal networks functioned to achieve close connection between the architectural schools and the world of employment. Tutors, themselves often practising architects in either the private sector or public service, remained connected to wider professional networks (see also Chapter 4). In the early postwar period, they provided powerful advocacy in favour of working for the local authorities. Peter Carter, for example, was just one of many who encountered tutors enthusiastic for the work and mission of public service. He recalled that when he was a student at the Northern Polytechnic:

> Michael Powell, my studio master, said to me one day: 'Do you still want to work with Maxwell Fry and Jane Drew?', which I had been doing during the holidays, but now permanently since I had been offered a job. I said: 'Well, yes'. But he said: 'Instead of that, why don't you come and join us at the newly founded Housing Division at the London County Council, where you could design and build your own buildings.' There was a young group of architects starting off there and . . . I spent five productive years there, with an extraordinary group of people.[70]

Sadly perhaps, the evidence suggests that the enthusiasm that stimulated this type of advice had worn thin by the mid-1950s. Public service, which had never won universal endorsement as the ideal source of employment for an architect, found diminishing emotional support. Quite apart from the assorted disillusionments of working for the local authorities, the revival of work in the private sector and the better rewards available there countered the residual aura of working for 'the good of society'. By 1956, Robert Jordan noted that recruitment to the public sector was already 'lagging' and that the 'best postgraduate architects, in the starry-eyed postwar years, turned to such enlightened authorities as Hertfordshire and the LCC, where architecture had a social as well as a technical context'. He continued: 'Now they think of Volta River, Kuwait or Malaya rather than the even darker jungles of Stepney or Lambeth . . . or else in terms of big City offices where the context is neither social nor architectural'.[71]

The relative standing of the public sector deteriorated further during the 1960s. Local authorities found it increasingly difficult to appoint quality staff at the prevailing pay scales and in light of the constraints on design freedom that were considered endemic. The larger public architect's offices, including the LCC, gained a reputation for having lost the edge of their pioneering days and for now being 'impersonal and antipathetic' to young entrants.[72] As one commentator despairingly noted in 1967:

> Private practice offers to all the chance of becoming a principal, and a high proportion of able and ambitious architects either do not enter, or soon opt out of, the public sector because the opportunities of promotion to posts of standing and responsibility and of direct contact with the client committee are often too few. Far from attracting its fair share of good senior staff, the public office has found itself relying too heavily on a late career drift from private practice.[73]

Not surprisingly, then, the traditional advice to consider private practice resurfaced, particularly in relation to the 'prestige practices'. As Jack Bonnington, who studied architecture between 1951 and 1956 at King's College Newcastle, commented: 'In schools of architecture, they concentrated on the idea that you are going to become an architect; one day you will have your own practice and design buildings. And you will design theatres and grand buildings.'[74] That type of work – theatres, cathedrals and universities – was the staple diet of the prestige practices, broadly defined as that 'select band' of practices that 'added to our architectural heritage while using to the full the construction techniques of the mid twentieth century'.[75] For his part, Frank Woods recalled how a recommendation, based on the subject of his final year thesis, had essentially determined the outline of his subsequent career:

> In the fifth year, five of us decided to do a group thesis on a new university, [a subject] which was just beginning to be thought about. We had a philosophy that new universities should not be located in places like York or Canterbury, but should be in places like Harlow or Stevenage. We did a design for a university at Stevenage New Town. We did a group Master Plan, then individual buildings. I happened to do a student residence, a hall. In the process of making it and getting through, I was talking to Sandy Wilson and later Leslie Martin about where to go next. Leslie had said: why didn't I try CPB [Chamberlin, Powell and Bon]? It is quite an interesting crossover. At that time, I walked into CPB with a portfolio of a university building and they had just won the University of Leeds development plan.[76]

Even for those who, unlike Woods, did not choose to remain for a long period, an initial stint in a prestige practice enhanced a curriculum vitae. It gave the chance to participate in the high-profile projects that these practices monopolised and the opportunity to learn through everyday working contacts with distinguished architects. Certainly anyone contemplating joining the private sector was keenly aware of the pecking order. When completing his studies at Brighton, for example, Anthony Blee recalled applying for and being offering starting positions at what effectively constituted a roll call of such practices:

> I applied for and was lucky enough to get jobs at six offices. They were the Architects Co-Partnership, RMJM, Edward D. Mills, YRM, Sheppard Robson and Basil [Spence]. I got out the copy of the *Architectural Review*, which had a strip cartoon on all the architects and I remember sitting on my bed looking at them and thinking which one would I work for.

His eventual decision to work for Spence was that 'he was a hands-on practising architect. . . . I wanted to work for someone who is doing architecture and is not, as is so often the case, the administrative chief of a large office.'[77]

Whichever sector they chose to join, new careers often began with candidate selection methods that would amaze those now used to systematic interview methods and equal opportunities criteria. Public service job recruitment was in the hands of senior officers. They might respond to a word from a trusted colleague or might draw on some recollection from their extra-mural activities, such as seeing some impressive drawings displayed at a student 'crit' or a noteworthy competition entry when acting as a juror. Any of these might be sufficient to prompt an offer. When he was County Architect at West Yorkshire, Hubert Bennett chose to staff his new department 'from schools of architecture, people I knew'.[78] Andrew Derbyshire, one of those that he had then appointed, recalled a similar process occurring when he subsequently joined the Sheffield City Architect's Department in 1955. He noted that Lewis Womersley had hired Jack Lynn and Ivor Smith, the subsequent designers of Park Hill, immediately after seeing their deck-access scheme for Rotherhithe (see Chapter 9). Derbyshire was then

> struggling away at the West Riding trying to devise a prefabricated system for schools, [which] nobody wanted. Ivor got in touch with me and said that there was a job there which was right up my street. That is why I joined Sheffield. Womersley, he just hired people, just like that. If he fancied you, he hired you; there was none of this fuss about advertising or anything. It was a complete oligarchy.[79]

The relationship also worked in reverse. Private and public sector practitioners frequently became the holders of senior academic jobs, strengthening the connection between academy and practice. During the 1950s, two of the Architects to the LCC had left for chairs in architecture: Robert Matthew at Edinburgh (1953–68) and Leslie Martin at Cambridge (1956–72). Others who followed included Colin St. John Wilson (Cambridge, 1956), Percy Johnson-Marshall (Edinburgh, 1959) and Richard Llewelyn Davies and John Weeks, who took up academic posts at University College London in 1960. As Wilson commented: 'I then stepped off the housing and schools belt on to the next available, which was the universities belt, which would then be picking up the next bulge as it came through. It was again a completely different world.'[80] During the 1960s, especially with the expansion of higher education following the 1963 Robbins Report and the establishment of polytechnics,[81] a new round of appointments ensued. Arthur Ling, for instance, became head of the Architecture School at Nottingham in 1964, Michael Blee was appointed as principal lecturer in charge of the interior design course at what would become the Brighton Polytechnic School of Architecture, and John Voelcker moved to the inaugural chair of architecture at the University of Glasgow in 1969.

## Beyond Albion

The prospects of working overseas to gain experience had always attracted young British architects. For the first generation, that meant Western Europe and the prospect of employment, however brief, in the ateliers of the leaders of the Modern Movement. For the next generation, practices in Western Europe and Scandinavia continued to have their appeal although the net now spread somewhat wider. Peter Winchester, for example, left Basil Spence's practice to spend six months working for the Italian structural engineer Pier Luigi Nervi. John Hummerston, who had worked in the Architect's Offices of the Cooperative Society in Sweden as a student, swapped his Scandinavian interests for the rival attractions of Dutch architecture, entering the office of de Weger in Rotterdam, with its portfolio of industrial and naval architecture. This would take him to further work in Ghana before returning to work in Great Britain. Others took advantage of opportunities to work in parts of the developing world, sometimes but not always associated with British colonies. Jim Amos, for example, took the opportunity of a three-year release scheme while working for the Ministry of Housing and Local Government to work in Ethiopia. Others found attractions in building their careers in North America. Peter Carter initially intended to leave the LCC to take up a fellowship at Yale University to study under Louis I. Kahn. When an attractive alternative appeared, he decided to work instead for Eero Saarinen, who had just won the competition for the American Embassy in London. Later, he moved to the Illinois Institute of Technology to study under Mies van der Rohe. Michael Blee left Basil Spence's office to undertake postgraduate research at the Massachusetts Institute of Technology (MIT) and work for The Architects' Collaborative (TAC) under Walter Gropius.

All these architects eventually returned to resume their architectural careers in Britain, but others remained overseas. Pat Crooke's long career overseas began by reviving links with BBPR in Milan. These originally stemmed from contacts made as a student at the Architectural Association. Robert Jordan, when principal of the AA, had established a link with BBPR under which at any one time a senior member of that firm

> would be teaching at the AA and a student from the AA would be working in Milan in their office. I was the first student to go and do that. That would be in the winter of 1949. I got to know [Ernesto] Rogers very well; he was the partner that I worked with while I was there. After I had finished and had spent my 2–3 years out, Robert Jordan invited me to go with him to Italy to BBPR, very much on the spur of the moment. In Milan, we went to BBPR, had lunch there and Rogers asked me if I would come back and work for them in Milan. I said that I would love to do that; by then I was starting to feel the need to do something. This would be early 1955. I took that and spent a year there.

Chance contacts with BBPR's younger staff then led to an appointment at a small university in Bogotá and in squatter housing projects in Peru, where he worked alongside his AA contemporary, John F.C. Turner.[82] Turner himself had graduated in 1954 and arrived in Peru in 1957 after a period of self-employment doing 'the usual jobs as an assistant and various small ones on my own account'.[83] His reason for visiting came from originally meeting Eduardo Neira, a Peruvian architect-planner, at the CIAM VII meeting in Bergamo (1949) where they discovered a shared interest in Patrick Geddes' book *Cities in Evolution*.[84] The eventual invitation to work with Neira in Peru led in turn to projects on self-housing after disaster, to research on the Peruvian barriadas, to a research fellowship at the Harvard-MIT Joint Centre for Urban Studies, a lectureship at MIT, and subsequently to a highly distinguished career of teaching, writing and activism about self-help housing and squatter populations.[85]

Looking back on training that he and Turner had received, Crooke argued that he personally had drawn relatively little on his architectural training in the narrow sense, in that the buildings concerned were 'very rudimentary'. By contrast, the mode of functional analysis and the networks of contacts established, particularly through the AA, were important. Agreeing that the postwar ethos of wanting to build a better world had lain behind much of what he had done, albeit outside of the British context, he added:

> It is like Robert Frost's 'The Road Not Taken'. I can see a series of roads that I never took. . . . Looking back what looks like a series of random decisions turns out not to be random at all. They are the result of real choices. I think that it makes more sense than it might seem.[86]

While this theme resonated equally with the biographies of many other architects, intentionality was only part of the matter; the professional, organisational and broader social contexts that framed the practice of modernism were another. Chapter 3 begins the process of recognising these wider contexts by considering the public and private organisations for which most practising architects worked.

Chapter 3

# Public and private

**As for position, there is no satisfactory model accepted within the profession about how to characterize the various firms by the kind of work they do, the priorities they set, or the market they seek. There are numerous stereotyped distinctions: art or business orientations, money-losing or money-making practice, patron or client centred, star or hack architects, signature or commercial firms, with design or profit motive. The basic drama pits a starving artist against a profit-driven barbarian. Needless to say, few practitioners find these distinctions useful, even though they may structure their own complaints along equally clichéd lines.**

**Dana Cuff[1]**

Central government's decision to make local authorities the vehicles for the schools and housing programmes undoubtedly boosted the image of public service, temporarily giving salaried architects the feeling of being valued partners in the process of rebuilding Britain. The feeling, however, was not destined to last. Many had started to recognise that the state might have entrusted these tasks to the local authorities, but made little attempt to ensure that they were properly equipped to handle that task in organisational terms (see also Chapter 4). Disillusion soon set in. By 1956, Robert Jordan gloomily reflected on the mood of anti-planning sweeping Britain in the wake of the Crichel Down affair,[2] and the revival of prejudice against 'official architecture'. With a tone tinged with sadness and exasperation, he tried to remind the profession that 'Inigo Jones, Wren and Vanbrugh were salaried officials of the State' and that, despite the prejudices of private architects, the LCC represented 'in many ways the most successful architectural office in the world'.[3] The fact that he felt the need to reassert the importance of the public sector was a reminder that ingrained professional value systems were likely to re-emerge as more architectural work became available.

This chapter seeks to provide insight into the working patterns of the two major sectors of architectural employment and their competitive rivalries. It deals first with the experience of working in the public sector, followed by sections on the prestige private practices and the commercial sector. Its final segment examines intraprofessional matters. It notes how architects working in the public sector organised themselves to counter the traditional power base that the titled principals of private firms had enjoyed within the Royal Institute of British Architects. It then touches on private sector concerns about patronage, whereby local authority architects could pass on valuable contracts, with little competitive tendering to those that they favoured.

## Public service

The duties and responsibilities of the local authorities after the Second World War were markedly different from 1939. The government transferred powers that local authorities previously exercised for hospitals and a number of trading services to public boards. In their place came the local authorities' enhanced priorities to undertake school building and, in particular, to provide housing.[4] The government's decision to empower local authorities in this way would dramatically alter patterns of architectural employment, although the way that local authorities responded varied considerably. Some eagerly built up teams of architects to undertake the new work. Others, particularly in the 1950s, did not consider it worthwhile employing architects to undertake tasks like designing dwellings for the working class and continued to use engineers or others to do the necessary work.[5] In the case of Dundee, one observer noted that it was

> one of the very worst places of all, in terms of professional organisation. It always amazed me that here there was a substantial city, without a meaningful department of architecture at all. There was a City Engineer and a City Architect [Robert Dron], with only half a dozen or so staff. Dron's involvement was in making recommendations to committee, in trying to slot away chunks of housing to various agencies.[6]

Size was clearly a factor. Official legislation statutorily confined some work to larger authorities. Only county councils, for example, built schools and smaller authorities seldom undertook research and development work. Architects working in smaller authorities rarely found themselves allocated to specialist divisions in the manner of larger authorities and generally handled a wider spread of tasks – a characteristic that, in many instances, was felt to contribute to job satisfaction.[7] Larger authorities offered greater specialisation. Birmingham, for instance, established a separate Architect's Department in 1952, taking on some but not all architectural functions previously handled by the Public Works Department (see also Chapter 4). By 1960, Sheppard Fidler, the City Architect, and his deputy presided over a department of 264 staff, of whom 82 were qualified practitioners. They were assigned to six sections: housing design, general architectural, schools, research and landscape, quantity surveying, and administration. Liverpool's structure was more complex given that the City Architect, Ronald Bradbury, was also Director of Housing. Two deputies, respectively, headed the Architect's and Housing Departments, with Bradbury having overall charge of these departments and an administrative section. Until 1963 (see Chapter 8), the Architect's Department comprised six sections: two architectural sections (general and redevelopment), alongside quantity surveying, inspectors of works, structural engineering, heating and lighting – with the Housing Department containing four further sections (architectural, surveying, letting and maintenance). Unlike Birmingham, the City Architect also presided over a direct labour force of 470 workers attached to the Architect's Department and 1010 employed by the Housing Department.[8]

Impressive though these figures might seem, they pale into relative insignificance compared with the LCC Architect's Department. In 1956, it had a staff of around 3000, including more than 750 qualified architects, arguably making it the world's largest architectural practice. These, in turn, enjoyed the support of surveyors, engineers, valuers, clerks of works and a vast administrative staff, which meant that the LCC was large enough to handle almost all aspects of the process of designing and constructing buildings for projects that it decided to tackle in-house. Those, therefore, who wanted to specialise in design work could do so without having to bother themselves with such distractions as site supervision. The Director of Housing and the Architect had responsibility for the direct labour force of 600–800 construction workers and 6500 buildings maintenance staff. The Architect's Department had six divisions in 1956, each under the charge of a deputy chief officer: planning, housing, schools, maintenance and improvement, general needs (responsible for fire stations and special buildings) and technical development. The exact numbers employed by the divisions varied over time according to departmental restructuring exercises, with divisions themselves tending to grow or contract depending on the internal politics of the department and institution as well as according to the work in hand.[9] For example, the Housing Division, under H.J. Whitfield Lewis, had grown from a core of 20 architects in 1950 to around 430 in 1956 (including 310 architects, 47 administrative and clerical staff, and 70 clerks of works). By contrast, the General Needs Division, then under Kenneth Campbell, at times had only a handful of architects.[10]

The LCC also stood at the apex of the system in terms of prestige. It was, as John Summerson commented, one of the places that young architects most wanted to work:

> The LCC led the way, particularly once they appointed Leslie Martin as their architect. Martin led the housing team which did the Roehampton flats. You may well ask about what other cities were doing and there is little doubt that they were much slower and much less sophisticated. Immediately after the war, every young man with MARS Group sympathies wanted to be part of Leslie Martin's team.[11]

Part of the initial attraction lay in its distinctive culture. The success in regaining housing from the Valuer's Department in 1949–50 reinforced an ethic that favoured high standards and architectural innovation. This, coupled with available resources, led to the ability to engage in large-scale research activities on building types or experimental methods: 'we had the privilege of being able to put something up just to evaluate it and knock it down again.'[12] John Partridge, for instance, recalled:

> We built a building in Bethnal Green while we were waiting for the planning appeal on Roehampton [the Wellington estate] – 5 and 3-storey buildings. The LCC had resources: it was possible to make a model of the estate, with every tree to the right size . . . and the site was a mile long.[13]

George Bowie, who later became Chief Architect of Crudens Ltd, worked as Group Leader in the Housing Division from February 1953 to February 1955. He marvelled at the approach, fostered particularly by Colin Lucas, of ignoring costings and simply concentrating on finding the best architectural solution:

> Life at the LCC was great fun. We all did as we pleased, there was no discipline or central control. You just ignored the design briefs and got on with designing what you, as an architect, thought was best for people![14]

It also offered, in the early 1950s at least, an environment similar to a 'postgraduate school'.[15] Its group-work ethic and atmosphere of endless earnest discussion were features that served as a powerful attraction for many:

> I put in five years' hard labour there. We worked all hours of the day and night. The only extra pay that we got was 2s 6d for a cup of tea. We were literally leaving the building about midnight, coming out through the tunnel. We were glad to do so.[16]

Time spent at the LCC's Architect's Department added lustre to an individual's curriculum vitae and perhaps to their sense of self-worth: 'Thereafter, wherever you went, because you'd been at the LCC, you thought that you were a bit special. It was easily the liveliest place in the UK, and to get in was quite difficult.'[17]

This ethos, as well as the size of its programmes, saw the LCC draw in staff from beyond Great Britain. Hubert Bennett recalled that there were architects from around 30 countries working at County Hall in the late 1950s, including sizeable contingents from Czechoslovakia, Poland, Sweden, Finland and the USA: 'There was quite a crowd that wanted to come and work with us'.[18] Certainly working at the LCC features prominently in the biographies of many architects in this period and contacts made while working at the LCC assisted career progress. Three LCC architects – Forshaw, Whitfield Lewis and Cleeve Barr – later became Chief Architects at the Ministry of Housing and Local Government. Four others, who held senior positions, became city architects or planners of major cities: Arthur Ling

(Coventry), David Jenkin (Hull), Alan Maudsley (Birmingham) and Walter Bor (Liverpool).[19] Walter Bor's move to Liverpool, for example, followed strong support from contacts made at the LCC. These included: Graeme Shankland, who was already consultant for the city centre but wanted 'the whole city to be planned well'; Robert Matthew, former Chief Architect and one of the assessors on his appointment panel; and Sir William Holford, another assessor with whom he had had close contacts over London planning projects.[20]

However, it is important to place these ideas in context. As a large organisation, it included a wide array of architectural opinion, from traditionalists through to the modernist avant-garde. For example, Frederick Hiorns, an LCC 'architect of the old school',[21] argued for the need for development to proceed in the light of locality and continuity. Seen in that light, he argued, the idea 'that creative work becomes "contemporary" only when torn from any recognisable association with the past is entirely fallacious.'[22] Similar reservations are necessary about the LCC's much vaunted spirit of collegiality. It did not extend, for example, to the London boroughs, which were generally regarded as a 'lower tier' in all respects: 'This was pure snobbishness. We saw ourselves as a special group'.[23] There were those for whom working in even the Housing Division proved less than appealing by the late 1950s:

> I was unimpressed, partly because I think that the Alton estate was largely finished and I was involved in designing children's playgrounds, which was not the most interesting of things to be involved in. My lack of being impressed was due to the fact that no one much ever seemed to do any work. I was amazed: it was not how I believed that life should be in an office. I am sure that work was done but it wasn't done in the vicinity of where I found myself. I had a boss who made model railways; he had a little workshop in his drawer. That was not a very good impression to give those who are working for you. I soon discovered that you had to sign on in the morning before five past nine, which is when they took the book away and you had to sign off in the evening after five to five, which is when they put the book down. It didn't take me long to discover that the book stayed there all night and that if you got in early the next morning, you could sign off for the night before, even though you might have left at three o'clock. I am sure that a lot of other people did exactly the same.[24]

Others positively disliked group-working practices:

> [After the LCC] I went to a practice where there were five or six of us. One man was the boss, but you were given your own job and within reason you could make decisions about it without having to justify everything. In addition, it was your scheme, *personally*. We did hospitals, where you worked as part of a team, but there were other schemes where you did it. You drew it completely.[25]

Finally, and more generally, it is important to retain a sense of proportion. Despite the mystique that the autobiographies of the good and great have attached to working in the LCC Architect's Department in the postwar period, it remained a job, like many others, in the public sector. After the war, working there made good economic sense given the parlous state of private practice in the early 1950s: 'it looked like these were jobs for life, good pension and paid reasonably well'.[26] At the same time, lack of promotion prospects afflicted all levels. At entry or trainee level, one observer commented that what 'they seemed to be doing was to take on young graduates and employed them in a fairly limited capacity for a year or two. As they got dissatisfied, they would move on to jobs elsewhere.'[27] Moreover, as another of his contemporaries noted:

> By 1961–2, all the people that I have mentioned had moved on to other authorities, because they weren't being given any responsibility. The conventional wisdom was that three years . . . was as much as anyone needed to spend there before moving on.[28]

Partly as a result, the Architect's Department experienced considerable labour shortage in the early 1960s, precisely the time when industrialised building methods were canvassed. The most severe scarcity occurred at senior level, with staff leaving as much over internal politics and lack of promotion opportunities as for greater opportunities elsewhere. Oliver Cox, for example, decided to leave for Whitehall when the LCC suddenly scrapped his group's plans for a private New Town at Hook in favour of town development schemes (see also Chapter 7). Walter Bor, who summarised his time at the LCC as 'very exciting but also frustrating', chose to move to another local authority (Liverpool) in part because of dissatisfactions encountered in the planning arena. Besides becoming frustrated with the development control aspect of planning taking precedence over the more imaginative possibilities for urban change, he encountered repeated problems in attempting to formulate policy for high buildings. The relaxation in 1956 of the building height restrictions in place since the passage of the London Buildings Acts in the late nineteenth century added considerable uncertainties.[29] The LCC henceforth judged matters on an individual basis, but with ever-changing advice. At first, prevailing committee argument held that the visual intrusion of such buildings could be prosecuted, 'even though this was never tested in court'. However, the decision in 1961 to build the 28-storey Hilton Hotel on London's Park Lane (Lewis Solomon, Kaye and Partners, 1961–3) set such niceties aside. Unlike the curvaceous Millbank Tower (Ronald Ward and Partners, 1956–63), generally considered to provide 'a good full stop to the upstream prospect from Westminster Bridge',[30] the Hilton, with its oversight of Hyde Park and Buckingham Palace gardens, was undeniably visually intrusive. Its approval rested strongly on a supporting letter from the minister stating that the scheme was important if Britain was to increase tourist earnings, especially from American visitors. Even though smaller than the 35-storey tower originally proposed in 1957, Bor felt 'that opened the floodgates . . . it was very disappointing'.[31]

## Fine distinctions

The history of the private sector during the postwar years remains largely unwritten, apart from monographs on specific practices. Perhaps the key to understanding the way that new entrants and architectural journalists alike regarded the sector is to recognise the fine distinctions applied to firms within it. Most of the many newly established commercial and industrial practices that played a significant role in reshaping British cities received little attention, apart from scorn, from the professional press: 'it was not what the architectural schools said we should be doing'. The prestige practices attracted more attention, although there were even more finely drawn gradations as to worth and stature. Some like the Smithsons, Denys Lasdun, and Powell and Moya had elite credentials and attracted the acclaim of their fellow modernists. Some were recognised to design in ways that 'reflected the new ideas and the core issues that were being discussed',[32] without necessarily aspiring to the avant-garde. Others faced disdain for producing designs in modernistic styles without their buildings expressing the 'correct' ideas. The long-established firm of Easton and Robertson (founded in 1919), for example, was always mistrusted for Howard Robertson being, in Maxwell Fry's words, 'a popularist, who suffered the fate of a popularist in that he was not "pure" or, in the doctrinaire expressions that the Communists used, he was not "correct"'.[33] For those looking back to the 'heroic era', this was tantamount to betrayal.

Some surprising new names, however, now stood accused of this form of deviation. One critic, for example, accused F.R.S. Yorke, Frederick Gibberd and Maxwell Fry himself as purveying 'an *indifferent modernism* attuned to the democratic tastes of the community'.[34] That three key members of the early MARS Group should find themselves in the dock for pandering to public taste revealed distaste towards the eclecticism associated with their firms coupled with a business mentality deemed to reflect commercial compromise. In fairness, these characteristics even troubled members of the practices concerned. Working at Yorke Rosenberg Mardall, the young David Allford found himself 'in awe of the senior partners who knew and had worked with the great men of Modern architecture',[35] but was 'sometimes amazed, even appalled, by the lack of consistency in the work around me'.[36] Yet eclecticism was usually far closer to the norm than contemporary or subsequent critics were willing to admit. Esteemed modern architects, including Le Corbusier of Ronchamp and La Tourette, were designing in ways that would have seemed inconceivable a decade earlier. Those maintaining their own purist versions and consistency of vocabulary were not necessarily more authentic than others accepting greater eclecticism.

The work of Frederick Gibberd's practice provides a good example. Gibberd retained a residual reputation within the Modern Movement for designing Pullman Court (Streatham, London) and was still deemed sufficiently acceptable in 1951 to act as host for CIAM VIII's outing to Harlow. His work – which included his ten-storey block The Lawn at Harlow, the Liverpool Roman Catholic Cathedral, power stations at Hinkley Point, Sizewell and Didcot, civic centres at Doncaster and Hull, and, somewhat astonishingly, the control tower at Heathrow with its brick-built, load-bearing walls – continued to receive coverage from the *Architectural Review* and similar publications.[37] He had certainly moved away from CIAM ideals, believing that the design solution came from the client's brief and abhorred any concept of an international architecture that took no account of regionalism,[38] but his work still emphasised the link between form and function. In the inherently pluralistic world of postwar modernism, it became increasingly hard to agree on the criteria for making judgements about whether or not buildings embraced the right spirit.

## Prestige practices

With private practice again a viable proposition after the 'dreary work-starved years' that followed the Second World War,[39] many architects saw an opportunity to branch out and found their own firms. A number of these new creations quickly joined the ranks of the 'prestige practices'. The group that had worked on the Alton West (Roehampton) estate for the LCC formed a practice in 1959, later joined by Stanley Amis in 1961 to become Howell, Killick, Partridge and Amis (HKPA). When appointed to jobs at University College London in 1960, Richard Llewelyn Davies and John Weeks formed Llewelyn-Davies and Weeks, which expanded in 1965 to become Llewelyn-Davies, Weeks, Robert Forestier-Walker and Walter Bor. Lewis Womersley and Hugh Wilson, two senior figures in the public sector at Sheffield and Cumbernauld respectively, joined forces to head a private planning and architectural practice in 1962. For his part, on leaving the Ministry of Housing and Local Government, Oliver Cox joined Graeme Shankland in 1964 as a full partner in Shankland Cox – a practice that eventually had an extensive multinational portfolio.

Success in competitions, which occurred 'almost every week' in the 1950s,[40] provided a basis on which to found new partnerships. There were potential problems in doing so, not least through clients gaining architects with whom they might have difficulty working, but it did launch a number of important new practices. Peter ('Joe') Chamberlin, Geoffry Powell and Christoph (Christof) Bon, previously tutors in the architectural school at the Kingston School of Art, formed their eponymous partnership on the back of Powell's success in the 1952 competition for the Golden Lane housing estate in the City of London. Competition success similarly attended the creation of Ahrends, Burton and Koralek in 1961 by Richard Burton, Peter Ahrends, Paul Koralek, all students at the Architectural Association between 1951 and 1956. The three founding partners had entered in the 1960 open competition for Trinity College Library, Dublin, where Koralek won first prize. Darbourne and Darke formed in September 1961, based on John Darbourne's success in the Lillington Street Housing Competition for the City of Westminster. Darbourne worked on the scheme as part of his Master's thesis in Landscape Architecture at Harvard. Having won the competition, he immediately contacted Geoffrey Darke, building on contacts developed when the two had previously worked together for Eric Lyons and Partners (see Chapter 9).[41]

As a genre, the prestige practices shared many characteristics. Colin Ward, who worked for the Architects' Co-Partnership, then Bridgwater, Shepheard and Epstein, and finally Chamberlin, Powell and Bonn, observed that they were founded by the generation of architects that 'was nurtured by, and employed by, the Welfare State. They shared its social ideology but also, of course, its paternalistic assumptions'.[42] Their firms had completely different outlooks on design, but usually tried to remain relatively small to avoid the problems of large practices with multiple offices, where the senior partners did less design work, other perhaps than at the conceptual stage. Commissions to build large-scale public projects, in particular, brought the necessity for rapid growth at key times and over long periods. As Frank Woods noted, the partners in Chamberlin, Powell and Bon preferred the firm to remain small, but that contracts led to marked periods of expansion and contraction: 'Leeds [University] was decades, the Barbican was essentially three and a half. The whole ethos of the practice was focused on those, with other jobs coming in and out.'[43] Those not wanting to face that prospect needed to adopt a 'European approach' to production, teaming up with others to handle the necessary tasks. For example, having worked for a large practice (T.P. Bennett) when he first qualified, Eric Lyons preferred to limit his practice to an office of four or five senior staff and student architects as required.[44] Although often doing the more prestigious conceptual design and gifted at persuading local planning committees about the virtues of a scheme, he normally worked with partners – as at World's End, Chelsea (see Chapter 9).

Small size and close working relations had their benefits. Harry Teggin, for example, noted that the working ethos of Brett and Pollen encouraged staff to remain focused on design:

> One of the things that I liked about Esher's firm was that we never had more than twelve people in the office, because if you did you became a businessman instead of being an architect. You got off the drawing board. I made journeys, but for three days a week I was on the drawing board. The other two I was travelling or attending meetings and doing things. I discussed the drawings with Esher or Pollen.[45]

Understandably, working intensively in close proximity with a small group had its drawbacks. For his part, Esher highlighted the significance of long-running disputes and the cumulative weight of petty irritations as being instrumental in the break-up of practices that he had established at different stages of his career. The demise of Brett and Pollen, for example, stemmed from irretrievable differences between senior and junior partners, leading Esher in October 1971 'to give up architecture and take the job as Rector of the Royal College of Art' rather than continue with wearying everyday disputes.[46]

The history of firms founded by co-equal partners tended to reflect the lottery of finding out about one another after formally entering into a business relationship. Many found that they required carefully formulated arrangements if they were to operate effectively in the long run. Although two of the partners in Chamberlin, Powell and Bon lived in the same house, they took considerable care that the third partner (Geoffry Powell) was fully involved in decisions. The abiding rule of the partnership was that the senior partners should supply continuity in design matters:

That was the culture. Inevitably, with practices that stay together over time, there was a very strong throughput of people coming for a year or two and going, but the seniors provided the continuity.[47]

Nevertheless, the various partners gravitated towards the roles in which they felt most comfortable. Chamberlin took the role of the practice's strategist and the Swiss-trained Bon, who 'was technically very strong', often focused on detailing: 'Once the building form was emerging, he actually took it and made it'.[48] Those joining the firm worked on specific projects under the charge of a senior partner. Powell and Moya's firm worked on the basis that Philip Powell would deal with potential clients, with Moya spared the business of having 'to shake hands with people and be nice to [them]'.[49] The founders of HKPA decided at the outset not only that the partnership was an amalgam of equals but also that it should not go on beyond the founding partners, with the initial thinking being that all four would retire on the same day. The early deaths of two of the partners (John Killick and Bill Howell) thwarted that ambition.[50] Sometimes, however, it transpired that partners did not know each other as well as they thought before establishing their business. For example, Robert Matthew and Stirrat Johnson Marshall formed their partnership in 1956 (RMJM), based essentially on knowledge gained through professional contacts. The discovery of different approaches and values led to enduring frictions between the two founding partners and their offices, respectively in Edinburgh and London, which dogged the practice for much of its early existence.

Single-ownership practices, headed by what might be termed 'star architects', generally saw the principal striving to exercise full control over design. Some, such as that run by Ernö Goldfinger, were small enough to see the head of the practice exercise that control on a daily basis, sometimes with legendary ferocity, over design and production.[51] Denys Lasdun consciously created his partnership in a manner that was not a union of equals, since he retained a veto on design matters and on whether or not the practice accepted a building. He also ensured that the practice handled only two jobs at a time, generally specialising in long-term signature projects like the Royal College of Physicians, the National Theatre, the University of East Anglia, and later the European Investment Bank.[52] Frederick Gibberd's practice, with its five-partner London office and two-partner Harlow office,[53] represented a larger firm than that run by Goldfinger, but the dominant figure still exerted command over the design process. As a former partner from the Harlow office recalled:

He always did the basic conceptual design. And being a planner too, he always worked from the larger view of things right down to the details – although he did not necessarily do the detailing himself. That is where others came in. You had to be modest too; he didn't ever promote his partners, although there were partners. They were necessary for seeing projects through although they weren't particularly mentioned. He was hands on [and] was never a front man with others doing the work. Having done the design and presentation, the various partners would then be responsible for the jobs. He worked with them at the beginning and then left them to see the job through.[54]

He also took care to choose 'partners and associates who would not be rivals'.[55] Gibberd's broad policy was to complete the design and presentation to clients, thereby locking the practice into an agreed design. Nevertheless, when confident that colleagues would follow his ideas through, he allowed them freedom to act on issues that he regarded as not central to the practice's reputation. For the City of Bath Technical College (Figure 3.1), for example, one of the working drawings dating from 1965 bore a handwritten note from Gibberd to John Graham stating: 'John will you have a go at this? The City Architect has no artistic sensibility, so exercise yours.'

Basil Spence's practice adopted a different approach to control and scale. Spence preferred to operate within a small group. His Edinburgh office had involved a small group of junior partners and assistants, with Spence and his family living in premises above the office in Moray Place. After leaving for a larger practice based at Queen Anne's Street in central London, Spence decided that he again wanted to work with a smaller section of the office in the business of conceptual design, effectively operating an atelier system within a larger practice. The design section moved to his house at Canonbury Square, where they operated under Spence's direct supervision, leaving the production, contracts and supervision tasks under his junior partner, Andrew Renton, at Queen Anne's Street. A small core of architects remained at Canonbury permanently. Others came from Edinburgh or Queen Anne's Street to work for a short period before returning to their base. This division of labour – 'workshop and . . . the ivory tower'[56] – generated grievances and, in due course, would split the practice.[57] Nevertheless, for young recruits who had

3.1
**City of Bath Technical College (Frederick Gibberd and Partners, photograph 2003)**

caught Spence's eye, selection for Canonbury conferred special status and gave them a stake in the design process. Understandably, this was on Spence's terms. At times when he was particularly busy, as during the time of his presidency of the RIBA in 1958–60, there was less direct daily contact or control but, living on the premises, he could inspect work in progress out-of-hours and leave instructions as to developments or changes. Spence, however, was 'willing to play his hunches',[58] and exercise control in a manner that permitted creativity. Anthony Blee added:

> He could, for example, if he saw something wrong and wanted to correct it [or] had an obstinate assistant or something, he then would do so in a schoolmasterly way. He had a very strong will to bring people to heel when he wanted to, on the one hand, but, on the other hand, if he saw the thing was energised, he would reinforce that creative energy. So it really depended on his reaction, and sometimes he would change his mind with an overnight thought.[59]

## Below the salt

The prestige practices occupied the moral high ground, but represented only a small proportion of employment in the private sector. By contrast, those working in the commercial sector were professionally below the salt – a view generally shared by their colleagues in both the prestige practices and the public sector. With regard to the latter, for example, the 1962 office survey castigated the 'holier than thou attitude of the architect engaged mainly in public work for his fellow working in the commercial field'. This, it was felt, did not help architects working there to persuade clients about the need to invest in good design.[60] These values also permeated the establishment, which tended to assume that those working 'in the development sector were primarily concerned with making money for their developers; they were not supposed to be concerned with architecture'.[61] For their part, educators subscribed to similar ideas. Jack Bonnington argued that schools of architecture strongly conveyed the impression that commercial architecture was somehow unworthy of discussion: it was always the architect as a prima donna figure.

> The schools of architecture had a drought on the subject of commercial architecture. . . . If you work for a developer . . . they were often less interested in the design, [than] in the planning permission and the amount of space. They want a lot of space. The schools never dealt with that. It was always the architect as a prima donna figure.[62]

Quite what constituted a 'commercial practice', however, was open to dispute. After being in practice with Lyons and Israel before the Second World War, Cecil Elsom founded a practice in 1947 as Elsom, Luggage and Robert. Although deemed a commercial practice that started with and continued to take on retailing and office commissions (e.g. Figure 3.2), the firm picked up housing and schools projects for the LCC and won the competition for the town centre at Slough, against opposition that included Ernö Goldfinger. Further town centre schemes followed at Derby, Chesterfield and Tamworth. If Elsom's practice occupied much the same ground as the prestige practices without enjoying the status, that run by his competitor Richard Seifert earned a certain degree of professional condescension for being perhaps *the* major player in office development. Seifert, who Elsom described diplomatically as 'a very successful developer's architect',[63] owed his early success to his skills in interpreting the building regulations, particularly with regard to offices in London (see Chapter 4). Largely as a result, his practice grew from 12 employees in a single office in 1955 to 200 in multiple offices in 1966, with a turnover of £30 million by 1964–5.[64] Yet even Seifert's unequivocally commercial firm often competed against the prestige practices for major contracts. Seifert recalled that for the NatWest Tower in London, for example, the list of competitors interviewed included the firms headed by Spence, Casson and Gibberd.[65]

Architects found that working in this sector had its attractions. For some, it was primarily a matter of getting 'a good grounding . . . I was immediately put on the roundabout of practicality', even though the work involved little design input.[66]

3.2
**C.H. Elsom,
Offices for
Max Rayne,
Duke Street,
London
(1956–8)**

Yet despite Charles Clore's aphorism that he did 'not believe in any great architectural triumphs which end up in bankruptcy',[67] this did not mean that the commercial sector would automatically produce traditional or production line architecture. Developers' architects essentially made their money from maximising the floor area permissible on a particular site within the existing building regulations. If they could meet the space requirements at the right price and on time, even relatively young architects could design their own buildings with no clients to consult or housing committees to placate. The freedom that they enjoyed in design matters varied according to the firm. In Seifert's practice, for instance, the principal continued to control even matters of detail:

> Everything had to go through me. Not a single drawing went out without my vetting it, it was so important to me. Not a single drawing went out without consultation with me. And it meant very hard work, but it was a well controlled office, and I gained the respect of my assistants, of my partners, by doing that. . . . I think that it's the only way that an architect can safely run a practice is to keep it under his own roof and not to spread it. It doesn't work. . . . Because architecture is a very difficult and dangerous profession; you've only got to make a few mistakes and you're in serious trouble.[68]

At the other end of the scale, there were practices where the senior partner's preoccupation with the technicalities of planning regulations and the activity of acquiring new business left staff with considerable aesthetic freedom to build whatever they wished. Rodney Gordon recalled that when designing an entry for the Elephant and Castle Shopping Centre competition for the Owen Luder Partnership in 1959 he found, to his amazement, that the developer had no real concerns what the building looked like provided, first, that it was within its budget and, second, that it would receive planning approval.[69] Gordon developed a series of buildings on this formula while working for the partnership that encapsulate much about the development work in the central city by the commercial sector (see Chapter 5). Perhaps the main drawback arose from the economics of property development. Even when their firms had obtained planning permission, developers' architects did not always get to see their buildings constructed. Developers often took a quick profit by selling on the site with the design and planning permission. Some found this experience profoundly disillusioning. Referring to a design that he produced when working for the office of John de Vere Hunt, for example, Colin St. John Wilson recalled that:

> what I was hired for was my ingenuity, three-dimensionally, to be able to build into an envelope that was prescribed – a continuation of a terrace – the maximum pay-off with the minimum expenditure. In this particular case, this took the form of a maisonette in which one floor was below ground, a house in the middle, and then another maisonette, so that we went from the cornice to the basement with no lift; it was a walk-up. I

got a bit fed up with the fact that the ingenuity [was] all that one was supposed to be delivering.[70]

## Competing interests

This account has so far examined the two main sectors of architectural practice without touching on the changing and sometimes competitive relations between them. Taking a broader view, however, makes it important to recognise that the profession was in the throes of upheaval, as symbolised by the power struggle taking place in the RIBA. In the early 1950s, the RIBA still bore the unmistakable hallmarks of its nineteenth century origins. Founded in 1834 and receiving its Royal Charter in 1837, it developed as a loose federation, with its London office supported by regional branches. Private practice essentially drove the RIBA's agenda, with its council and presidencies dominated by the principals of private firms. This pattern of organisation, with its accompanying social class implications, persisted until the 1950s, when it encountered resistance over two issues. First, the leadership had adopted a cautious line with regard to modernism, especially with respect to education and training, where it tried to steer an even-handed course between the rival claims of modernism and the Beaux-Arts. Second, it had neglected two numerically significant groups: public sector or 'salaried' architects and the junior architects in private practice.

This stimulated various responses once pressure for change appeared. The formation of the Local Government Architects' Society in 1958 and later the Salaried Architects' Group (SAG) effectively recognised that the RIBA had failed to look after the interests of salaried architects and had not faced up to the continuing power of the principal in private practice.[71] Recognising the prevailing distribution of power within the RIBA, a group of public sector architects belonging to the Association of Building Technicians formed common cause with Robert Matthew, Stirrat Johnson Marshall, Donald Gibson and Robert Gardner-Medwin to campaign for 'a fairer representation of public-sector architecture and thus [for] a more [socially] responsible attitude towards building altogether'.[72] The group met before RIBA Council meetings to decide tactics. Group members received invitations to meet for 'the usual lunch discussion' at the offices of RMJM (Robert Matthew, Stirrat Johnson Marshall and Partners),[73] or to supper at the The Bride of Denmark (the faux pub in the basement of the Architectural Press's offices in Queen Anne's Gate). The leadership then relied on sympathetic architects from the public sector ('the Chain Gang') to attend meetings in sufficient numbers to bring about policy change.

Although apolitical in a party political sense, these activities succeeded in bringing about 'an extraordinary about-face in the RIBA', winning a better status for salaried architects and causing the RIBA to pay attention to the working conditions of junior architects. *The Architect and his Office* (see Chapter 2) was part of this initiative. One of its authors noted:

> It (the survey) was to find out how architects are paid – everybody, not just principals; what the financial structure of the offices were like (e.g. how salary costs related to overhead costs and profit when it came to

private architects); what quality of work were they producing (both aesthetic quality and functional performance). It all added up to a series of wide-ranging recommendations about changes in salary structures, changes in office organisation to make people more aware of how they were spending money, changes in the work practices within the office, and a lot about education (the practical training scheme came out of the office survey). Our findings were adopted hook, line and sinker; nobody queried it at all. We seemed to be in tune with the Zeitgeist.[74]

Yet curiously, given that part of the report's rationale was to assert the role now played by the salaried architects in the public sector, the report's findings and 32 major recommendations were most convincing when dealing with the need to improve the economic efficiency of private offices. The tone was also confident when dealing with issues of training and the need to promote standardisation and industrialisation in a manner that 'strengthened rather than weakened' the architect's position.[75] By contrast, the analysis of the position of the salaried architects in the public sector was more hesitant and the resulting recommendations were less specific, arguably sowing 'the seeds of future dissention'.[76] For example, the recommendations about the relative lack of senior posts in the public sector were perhaps more significant for recognising that the problem existed rather than how to solve it:

> The level of salaries and responsibilities of senior architects in the larger offices should be examined in relation to different forms of work organisation to ensure that more satisfactory career prospects are available. This might help to solve present staff shortages and to attract new entrants of high quality into the profession. The relative shortage of senior posts for both principals and assistants in local authority offices when compared with private offices should be one aspect of this study.[77]

## Patronage

The growth of the public sector also had largely unforeseen implications for patterns of patronage. This touched on a relationship that had long played an important role in the history of architecture.[78] Architects, as the designers of special buildings rather than the everyday buildings that were the province of the builder, traditionally looked to wealthy civic authorities or private patrons for their commissions. During the late nineteenth and early twentieth centuries, British municipalities invested their rates revenues in new utilities and fine town halls that reflected well on their power, status and refinement. The choice of local authorities to handle the task of post-1945 urban reconstruction created a wholly new scale and type of official patronage. The state had placed considerable resources, without unduly rigorous accounting procedures, into the hands of the local authorities and, in particular, their planning and housing committees. One observer noted: 'The spirit of the times was one of great optimism and enormous drive to recover from the war; the amount of trust may well have stemmed from that.'[79]

Opportunities and resources followed power. This applied at all levels of the public system. The ministries handed out huge public sector contracts, as with the second generation New Towns or new universities where firms of consultant architects often gained huge contracts without open competition: 'Patronage was the key thing'.[80] Senior figures such as Leslie Martin and Robert Matthew, who combined prestige academic positions with experience of big city architecture, constantly received invitations to take on prestige commissions. When the workload involved was greater than their practices could handle, they routinely handed opportunities on to junior associates, former students or trusted colleagues. This applied to some commissions that latterly became landmarks in postwar British architectural history. Leslie Martin, for example, was believed to have handed on the commission for the University of East Anglia to Denys Lasdun and that for the University of Leicester's Engineering block to James Stirling and James Gowan.[81] In addition, precisely the same cadre of senior architects served as jury members on architectural competitions or as informal advisers whose word carried weight with senior civil servants. They were effectively gatekeepers for the conferment of contracts that, at a stroke, might provide sufficient work to sustain an architectural practice for many years.

Nevertheless, the largest areas for architectural patronage rested with local authorities. The public sector lacked the capacity or expertise to undertake all the work required to rebuild Britain; a deficiency that became acutely apparent in the early 1960s when town centre renewal and the housing drive were in full swing. As a result, the power of senior architects and their colleagues in the Society of Chief Architects of Local Authorities (SCALA) to dispense patronage was legendary, limited more by the internal procedures and working agreements of the local authority than any transparent code of professional conduct or external auditing process. In some instances, this presented opportunities for corruption (see Chapter 12), but even without malpractice, the situation generally allowed them to exercise judgements as to how to allocate work without any requirement to give public reasons for their choice. They could award contracts to private firms to design and build, although the firm undertaking the design would not necessarily gain the contract to build. They could allocate work to direct labour, with 86 per cent of local authorities having a direct labour organisation of some form by 1969.[82] They could seek competitive tendering or arrange design competitions, with the choice of 'open' or 'limited' competitions. Alternatively, they could simply dispense contracts to 'approved' firms. The reputation of a firm was all-important in this respect, leading to invitations to the same group of prestige firms time after time. Harry Teggin remembered the procedure when his firm, Brett and Pollen, were invited to apply to undertake the master plan for central Portsmouth:

> I went with [Lionel] Esher for the interview and, as we were getting off the train at the high level platform by the Guildhall, Leonard Manasseh was getting on to come back. And as we were getting on to come back, Sir Hugh Casson was getting off for an interview an hour later. We had

a bit of a giggle about this, because we realised that we were all being spaced out for our interviews.

By this stage (1968), this was not unusual. If invited for interview, 'you more or less expected that a predictable list of others had also been asked'.[83]

The LCC ran its own list of private practices approved to carry out major contracts. As Hubert Bennett, Chief Architect from 1956 onwards, commented:

> I think that we gave work to Leonard Manasseh, Edward Mills, Powell and Moya, Peter Shepheard, Smithson, Colin Wilson, Walter Bor, Brandon-Jones. We kept it up-to-date. Every year we saw them all personally. Some of them had commissions to keep at least 20 people going in an office and they had only to telephone us and say that they would be running out of work at the end of the month and we would say, 'We have another primary school, would you like it?' . . . We kept them all working. They were part of a team and were doing nice work.[84]

Peter Smithson, one of the beneficiaries, recalled that his firm's direct commission from the LCC for Robin Hood Gardens (in East London) came in 'just a plain letter'; there was no hint of competition or competitive tender.[85] Yet however casual this system might seem, individual architectural practices often depended on these links. Architects invested time and effort in keeping in close touch to find out the client's exact needs and then tailored a bid to suit. Ernö Goldfinger's relationship with the LCC, for example, 'was absolutely fundamental to his career after the war'.[86] He had

> very good contacts . . . they thought of him as someone important. He [also] had very good relations with the planners: it was a very free and easy relationship. It was much easier then, you could talk to people directly. You could walk in with some questions and walk out later with the answers.[87]

Goldfinger's success in the design and developer competition for site B at the Elephant and Castle in 1959 owed much to the team at the LCC effectively wanting him to win and allowing scope for him to improve the financial bid (which was not originally competitive). There was no doubting the significance of gaining the commission: 'That [Alexander Fleming House] was the largest office for development at the time; a huge step up for a pretty small practice.'[88] Equally, there was no guarantee that patronage would persist in the long term. A former architectural assistant who joined the firm in the 1970s noted:

> By the time that I came to work for him [Goldfinger], the body [the LCC] was defunct and Ernö was no longer flavour of the month. No one was building flats, particularly not high ones. That is what killed Ernö's

practice off really. He had ceased to be a good bet for developers in terms of getting planning permission.[89]

Nevertheless, the operations of this system posed problems. Not only did it allow direct channelling of resources to the favoured, but also it relied on perceptions. Basil Spence's practice suffered in the mid-1950s through being associated with cathedral architecture: 'People thought that he was busy doing the Cathedral and thought he was a cathedral architect. However there are not many cathedrals around, so he got very little work.'[90] Chamberlin, Powell and Bon also had 'a name for doing big jobs and it was galling later to discover that people would say that they didn't know that we did smaller buildings because we could have done such and such for them.'[91]

The formation of the Association of Consultant Architects (ACA) in 1973 was a symptom of resistance to these practices. Drawing its membership from smaller independent firms, the ACA consciously countered patronage policies. A pamphlet mapped out their broad position.[92] After noting the historic and contemporary importance of patronage to producing outstanding architecture, the authors noted the problems for the young architects faced with 'the alternative of a position in an anonymous bureaucracy in the public sector or in the often equally large and sterile commercial plan factories'. The attack, however, focused primarily on the public sector, which 'now controls some 80% of the built environment. The sums involved are very large. The temptations of simple, uncontroversial decisions of many kinds are irresistible.' Failure to provide proper open competition for public projects, as was common practice in 'most northern European countries', meant that the architects for official buildings were not necessarily chosen on merit. Most architects employed in local or central government 'are never tested in the marketplace'. Moreover,

> The absorption of the architect into the hierarchical local government career structure has had a divisive effect in the profession, and the quality of architecture has suffered. An easier interchange, a flow of talent between public and private practice, and the universities would benefit everyone.

The resolution of these problems, and particularly the perceived power of SCALA, would come about primarily through the relentless swing of the pendulum when work dried up and local authorities inexorably shed their architects' offices in the 1980s. For the period examined here, perhaps the constraint on the chief architects' power came less from action by architects than relations with other professional groups in the Town Hall – the subject to which we now turn.

# Chapter 4

# Professions

**To the earnest student we would say, put away all that empty talk about the 'profession' and the 'public'. Give up all anxiety to have initials, many or few, after your name; devote yourself with all your power to the study of your art, and strive by every endeavour to keep up enthusiasm. It will take all your time! And if, after a few years of study, you come to the conclusion (or your best friends come to it for you) that your art faculty is very small – if indeed it can be said to exist at all – then with your eyes opened, give up the pursuit of architecture, a pursuit in which you are never likely to excel, and turn to surveying, engineering, or any other vocation to which your best qualities seem to lead.**

**Richard Norman Shaw[1]**

**Architecture is a profession. And that is half the trouble.**

**Stanley Alderson[2]**

Regardless of the significance of the awkward intraprofessional relations discussed in Chapter 3, their overall importance was undoubtedly secondary to the more serious question of interprofessional rivalries. This chapter, which has three sections, deals with the complex and sometimes fraught relationships between architecture and the professions that its members worked alongside in the business of transforming cities in the postwar period. The first section concerns the building team. It traces the way that traditional and accepted divisions of labour were eroded and recast by technological change, with industrialised building methods often serving to detach the architect from direct input into construction of public housing – prima facie, a key arena for developing and judging the practice of modernism. The second section of the chapter deals with the interprofessional tussles between planners and engineers over the question of road planning, providing historical background to rival professional claims for influence over town planning. The third section discusses the turf wars that occurred, most notably between the Architect's and the City Engineer's departments within the local authorities. The discussion draws on the experience of three provincial cities (Newcastle upon Tyne, Birmingham and Sheffield) to analyse the territorial disputes that broke out and the manner of their resolution. The fact that architects seldom won these disputes frequently served to limit the contribution that they made at the wider urban scale.

## The building team

A cursory glance at the names on the spines of bound journals dating from the 1950s and 1960s – *Architecture and Building*, *Architect and Building News*, *Architect and Builder* – reveals the continuing taken-for-granted existence of a professional dichotomy.[3] For most architects, Nikolaus Pevsner's often repeated remark that: 'A bicycle shed is a building; Lincoln Cathedral is a piece of architecture' encapsulated the prime difference between the two.[4] Traditionally, architects designed special buildings as expressions of sublime creativity, a view that architectural schools in the 1950s still cheerfully retained (see Chapter 2). By contrast, builders, with their teams of skilled craftsmen, designed the simpler and repetitive structures of the built environment, from the by-law terrace to the interwar semi-detached house. The advent of modernism, however, had prompted architects to rethink this relationship. Those wanting to see a socially aware architecture making a contribution to building the new Britain favoured a redefinition in which architecture shed its image of an artistic activity in favour of a scientifically based discipline that sought, through functional analysis, to produce a synthesis of the building task that might offer efficiency and economy.[5] Thus reconfigured, architecture might join the various other disciplines contributing to the 'building team' – a phrase with superficially egalitarian connotations – in designing the houses, schools and hospitals that were so urgently needed.

Unwittingly, this was dangerous territory for architects. When conceiving of the 'building team', few architectural commentators doubted that architects would lead the team. After all, the word 'architect' comes from the Greek root *arch* meaning chief and *tekton* meaning 'carpenter' or 'builder'. Textbooks in the field readily asserted that the architect should be accepted as 'the master builder – the leader of the great team which constitutes the Building Industry'.[6] Not everyone, however, accepted that assessment. Changes in the construction process, particularly in provision of housing, had decisively altered the balance of power between architect and builder. Public and private clients, as well as building contractors, allocated work according to needs and skills rather than any moral notions about the 'correct' way to configure the building team. There might well be little argument that the architect's role was essential when dealing with sophisticated buildings such as a national library or a cathedral, with their complex functional and symbolic dimensions. The advantage of architecture-as-art was that the architect's contribution was indispensable, since it involved the indefinable ingredients of artistic creativity. By contrast, architecture-as-applied-science emphasised a rational training and skills that others involved in technologically advanced activities, such as structural engineers, might also possess.

Understandably, architectural theorists attempted to find grounds for preserving the distinction. For example, in an RIBA lecture about the theory of modern architecture (see Chapter 11), John Summerson addressed in passing the question of the difference between the architect and engineer. To Summerson, the architect was at the heart of the building process, whereas engineers are 'concerned strictly with components'. They may 'contribute significant inventions [they] cannot contribute a continuously related system of inventions – i.e. a language'.[7] This was a comforting idea. Leaving aside the problematic aspects of the theory,[8] Summerson effectively suggested that only architects were in command of the language and able to provide a view that turns components into the completed whole.

Unfortunately for them, the large-scale building firms and construction companies did not necessarily agree, as was exemplified by the rise of industrialised building methods. Broadly defined as the adoption of new building site practices and procedures derived from the application of industrial principles of production and organisation, 'industrialised building', in Arthur Ling's opinion,[9] could embrace a spectrum of different methods:

- mechanisation of in-situ processes
- on-site factory or yard producing medium-sized elements for short haul and assembly
- off-site factory or factories for the manufacture of small components for transport to and assembly on the site
- off-site factory producing medium-sized elements for transport and assembly
- off-site factory producing complete room or even dwelling-sized units.

At one end of the spectrum, therefore, industrialised building simply involved speeding up the process of site construction by, say, introduction of pre-designed and reusable frameworks for pouring concrete. For instance, the No-Fines system, developed after the First World War, employed concrete poured into reusable shutters. Within the shell, the on-site construction of dwellings was much the same as for conventional houses.[10] At the other end of the spectrum, the building site became virtually an assembly point for a 'kit of parts' – a group of components and subsystems that could be put together in a large variety of ways to solve a given problem. This option saw substantial sections of buildings or even entire buildings constructed in centralised factories, often at a considerable distance from the point of assembly. Depending on the building system concerned, the component units might be no more than shells, still requiring extensive work on site, or could be modular units complete with wiring, plumbing and insulation and with interior walls ready for plastering.[11]

Collectively, these techniques touched on many themes that modern architects had long seen as touchstones of progress and industrialised building prospered through having the capacity to appeal to many strands of architectural thought. The first generation of modern architects had regarded mechanisation and rationalisation as crucial elements in achieving the new society and saw prefabrication as a way to revolutionise the housing market. For their avant-garde successors, industrialised building was again the way to move architecture forward, having the potential to generate new urban forms and perhaps to revitalise architecture's relationship with society (Chapter 11). Those practitioners with a more unassuming outlook on architecture could also enthuse over the benefits of industrialised building, since they promised to yield a virtuous combination of cost savings through economies of scale, production increases through mechanisation and standardisation, and qualitative improvement through the ability to maintain high production standards. Industrialised building offered the prospects, however optimistic it now sounds, of transforming the building site from its traditional labour-intensive and craft-oriented base towards one that reconfigured construction work as a modern scientific activity. In this regard, the 'multiplication of cells and elements, in accordance with the laws of industrialisation',[12] was not essentially seen 'as a technological issue. It was rational building, particularly in the context of multiple production.'[13] More enthusiastic advocates also argued that industrialised building had a moral dimension; it made 'for civilised work',[14] and addressed the 'moral obligation to meet the demands of progress'.[15] Reflecting on his own work as part of the team at RMJM that designed the buildings and layout of the University of York using a modified version of the CLASP system, for instance, Sir Andrew Derbyshire noted that prefabrication resonated deeply with hopes that modern architecture could contribute a new vernacular:

> I saw architecture as one of the outputs of a social order, like farming, law and everything like that. It sprang from the roots of peoples like vernacular architecture did and my dream, and a lot of people's dream at that time, was to find a new way of achieving a twentieth century vernacular which sprang from the people and was anonymous. . . . [It would be] the twentieth century version of the Cotswold stone vernacular. It was how to reconcile technology with the need for construction that would be flexible enough to reflect the local community that was a true product of the twentieth century.[16]

As such, it might counter the traditional tendency towards treating architecture primarily as an elite art and reconnect building with the needs of society:

> We did not think about architecture as art. There was quite obviously a big aesthetic content in buildings, which was important, but not to any extent the be all and end all. Buildings have to be built within the budget available, within the time available and which make the people occupying them happy, content, and comfortable. That was the top priority. Time, speed, comfort. . . . Prefabrication was seen as a means to build a responsible architecture, both in the sense of responding to the needs of society and making use of the available technology. This is where prefabrication and the social programme came together – a synthesis.[17]

The early experience gave architects hope that their hopes might be realised. The schools building programme, 'always very much under the thumb of ministry and county architects',[18] had seen the use of prefabrication and building systems to create new, light and airy schools by teams that prominently included architects and espoused a strong social commitment. Similarly, the programme of university extensions in the 1950s and new universities in the 1960s saw prestige architectural practices enjoy 'the unusual circumstances of independent autonomy and financial security' to design campuses and campus buildings. These incorporated 'a high degree of brave experimentation and a wide range of different academic and social aspirations'.[19] The more pressing and much larger scale housing programme proved a wholly different matter. As Chapter 8 shows, the failure to generate sufficient production of houses by conventional means had contributed to a government-sponsored shift towards industrialised building. The adoption of system-building, especially where using prefabricated components brought from distance to the building site, fundamentally changed the architect's contribution. The characteristics imparted by standardisation and modularity meant that the decision to adopt a particular system predetermined elements of the design of the building that would appear. In principle, the design task then partly revolved around the arrangement of the units to create the buildings, arranging their layout in relation to one another, and giving thought to landscaping and services. These were tasks that others besides architects could potentially undertake especially when, as with the creation of many public housing estates, they involved considerable elements of standardisation and repetition.

That thought certainly occurred to the engineers. Architects rarely understood, or perhaps chose not to understand, that engineering had its own radical credentials. Official reports by engineers, popular engineering journals and textbooks for trainee engineers long envisaged that multilevel circulation systems and industrialised building would be keys to shaping the urban future.[20] Traditionally, they had their rivalries with architects over issues such as highway design (see p. 74ff), but had had a comfortable modus operandi with architects over building design, whereby they solved particular problems that the architects had referred to them. Their intervention thereby depended on the architects specifying that a particular matter was a problem that required the services of an engineer. The movement towards industrialised building, however, altered the lines of demarcation. When replying to the minister about the terms of reference of the National Building Agency (see Chapter 8), for example, the Institution of Municipal Engineers stressed that its members were 'intimately concerned with provision of housing and municipal buildings of all types' and that the Agency 'should be administered by the highest calibre of professional men, qualified in engineering (civic, municipal and structural) and architecture'.[21] The type of partnership that they envisaged included involvement in design matters. Engineers increasingly saw little reason as to why architects should automatically claim complete control over design and the fees to which this entitled them.[22] A paper presented to a symposium organised by the Institution of Structural Engineers in 1966, for example, provided a robust indication of the changing balance of power:

In the past many structural engineers have tended to be content with a somewhat minor role in the design of the building and the production of its component parts. In order to help in the process of the advance towards industrialized building, it is clear that the structural engineer must play a much larger part in both the design and production aspects as a whole. The days are surely past when a structural engineer was presented with a set of plans with a polite request that he should provide sufficient structure to hold up the building or make a component, without of course allowing any of the structure to be visible or interfere with the already determined size, shape and functions of the building or the component.[23]

Construction firms were willing, at least in practical terms, to accept that logic, even if the design skills of the engineering staff that they could obtain were often not of the highest calibre. At the peak of the industrialised building campaign, they often eliminated the independent architectural professional altogether, using relatively junior staff to tackle production drawings, handle detailing or to advise on layout. Working for the Scottish firm Cruden Homes, for example, George Bowie noted that in the late 1960s, his firm had a staff of 'about 75–100 architects and getting on for 200 engineering staff, plus quantity surveyors'. He continued:

The main professional division within my department was between the architects and the engineers. Designing high blocks was more often far more an engineering problem than an architectural problem: engineering for the foundations, for the roads, for the sewers, for the blocks themselves. For example, there was a sunlight rule that was specific to the Scottish regulations, and it was up to the engineers to sort that out. The architecture, bit by bit, became cosmetics, until a good engineer could say 'Could you not move this . . . ?' Suddenly, you'd find your engineers designing your whole block for you.[24]

This experience was unexceptional. In an environment obsessed by the pursuit of housing completions, local authorities readily accepted arrangements that encouraged a standardised housing product which needed little tangible architectural input. They may also have been perfectly content to adopt a course of action that, among other things, bypassed the architect's standard fee structure.

Perhaps not surprisingly in view of these perceived territorial and economic threats to their core activities, the RIBA did not endorse industrialised building methods until 1967, the time at which the reputation of industrialised building was already becoming tarnished by its association with system-built tower blocks.[25] Prior to that and despite general enthusiasm within the profession for industrialised building, the RIBA's Industrialised Building Study Teams had identified areas of weakness in relation to the application of this technology. In 1965, they reported that the 'basic function of the architect as designer remains', but that the architect should 'become familiar with new spheres of practical knowledge',[26] and that the manufacturer 'has no developed channel of communication with the architect'.[27] These points are notable for what they imply. Certainly, the tacit admission of poor knowledge of industrialised building methods and the lack of appropriate networks of communication placed architects at a disadvantage vis-à-vis others with more readily applicable skills.

Chapter 8 explores the implications of these circumstances with regard to housing, but we may note here that the consequences for architects were an uncomfortable association with trends of which they approved but over which they had limited control. For all their success in riding a wave of postwar expansion, they nevertheless occupied a territory that remained susceptible to incursion from other professionals in the building industry. In the case of industrialised building, that weakness was sufficient for architects to lose their leading role in some localities in public housing and see them unable 'to exert any real influence over the nationwide spread of Modern patterns'.[28] This weakness in interprofessional disputes, however, was not new. It mirrored another, rather older struggle between the architecture and engineering professions over connection with and influence over town planning. This, as the next section shows, would also have a profound impact on the ability of architects to contribute directly to urban transformation.

## A question of planning

The nature of the relationship between modern architecture and planning was always problematic. The urban vision cherished by modern architects emphasised a holistic view that attached equal emphasis to each of the four main urban functions, but also gave expression to the ambitions that architects had long harboured for influence over city planning. Emboldened by modernist rhetoric about the need for a comprehensive view of urban reconstruction and lulled into over-confidence by an astonishing naivety about political realities, architects had pressed to place themselves at the centre of the building team. This inevitably brought them into direct competition with the surveyors and engineers, who already had responsibility in this area and saw no particular reason to cede powers to another profession that wanted to increase its own sphere of influence.

The engineers, as mentioned above, nurtured radical traditions and were fully capable of looking after their own interests. By the 1950s, the engineers and surveyors had recognised the potential threat that architects and others might pose to their position and had mobilised in order to establish closer links between their fragmented branches and to defend areas of common interest.[29] Externally, they sought to consolidate their influence by active participation in the 'road lobby'. The Institution of Highway Engineers, to which the majority of the county surveyors also belonged,[30] formed a joint committee with the British Roads Federation and the Society of Motor Manufacturers and Traders to lobby for the economic benefits of road improvements. This powerful alliance between vested professional and commercial self-interests, augmented by the pivotal recognition that the Conservative governments gave to the road lobby, significantly reinforced the engineers' standing in this field.

These expressions of territorial resistance were a matter of regret for many observers who wanted to encourage an interdisciplinary approach to urban transformation. In April 1962, for example, Colin Buchanan reflected on the current state of relations between the design professions. It was a subject on which he was unusually well qualified to speak. Buchanan held professional qualifications in civil engineering, architecture and town planning and was the author of numerous reports that offer a clear three-dimensional view of the existing and emerging built environment (see Chapter 6). Addressing a symposium attended by a mixed professional audience at the University of Durham, Buchanan circumspectly commented on the prevalence of the constructional approach, whereby the Ministry of Transport and local authority Highway Committees relied on road building programmes to solve urban traffic problems. This approach, he gently suggested, was too narrow and

> what we are really up against is a problem of architecture, and, . . . unless we realise this, we run the risk of doing serious damage to our towns and cities. I hasten to make it clear that I am in no way trying to slight civil engineers, to run down traffic engineers, or to boost architects . . . but I think it absolutely essential to grasp the true nature of the problem and then to distinguish the various contributions that the professions can offer.[31]

The problem for the architects, as Buchanan observed, was 'rooted in history'.[32] To elaborate, engineers also claimed central involvement in town planning as part of their sphere of influence. This had a basis in practice. Long before the establishment of a planning profession, the engineers and surveyors exercised statutory responsibilities for tackling basic road planning and sanitation. These responsibilities necessitated performance of tasks that

> were large in scale and unambiguously seen as falling within the province of engineers, and there were, of course, no other occupational groups in situ to challenge the engineers. Undoubtedly the fact that the engineers were the first 'technical' profession in local government was an important advantage for them over the later professions such as architecture, an advantage that has persisted into more recent times.[33]

When more formal planning activities were required by the inelegantly named Housing, Town Planning Etc. Act 1909, the powers merely assigned town planning to local government.[34] There was no specification about precisely which departments within the town hall would control that function. The architects quickly made a pitch for the new work. The RIBA hosted the first town planning conference held in Great Britain in October 1910, which superficially was an enormous success for the architects. Its final report asserted that 'for the design of the town plan, the architecturally trained mind is as essential as for the design of a single building'.[35] Yet at the same time, there was a distinct undercurrent that recognised that planning was not architecture writ large, with the RIBA's own Town Planning Committee recognising that planning needed interdisciplinary participation if it was to be effective.[36]

Despite some manifestations of alarm,[37] the engineers need not have worried. The 1909 legislation and subsequent Acts saw the surveyors and engineers steadily consolidate their position within the local government sector with respect to land surveys and road schemes: indeed the engineer's ring roads and radial schemes effectively drove the town planning agenda in many cities for the next half-century. Architects continued to press for a stake in town planning, which they still regarded as an outgrowth of architecture and effectively 'covered' by their own profession.[38] Architectural education, for example, continued to offer planning courses. The much-delayed report of the RIBA's Special Committee on Architectural Education, originally commissioned in 1939 but not published until 1946, made the case for including planning within the architect's purview, stressing that: 'Planning, in the sense of the efficient organisation of space, is a fundamental part of the architect and one in which he is specially trained'.[39] However, the reality was that, with certain honourable exceptions, architects lacked a proven record in this area. Although available opportunities were also a factor, architects had tended to 'dabble . . . in a bit of town planning' from time to time rather than develop any systematic approach,[40] with their lack of skills in such areas as 'cost planning, traffic engineering, landscape [and] civic design' proving lasting weaknesses when seeking to make more serious inroads into available work.[41]

The Town and Country Planning Act 1947 ended many uncertainties. The Act's requirement that the county councils and county boroughs prepare development plans within three years of 1 July 1948 specified the need for a more regular and standardised approach rather than the ad hoc methodologies of the past. That approach required skills best provided by a trained and specialist planning profession and effectively blocked the architects' chances of exerting control over planning. Curiously, however, the movement towards the professionalisation of planning worked in the architects' favour in the short term, due to the lack of personnel with suitable skills. In 1946, for example, the Town Planning Institute had only 1700 members, approximately one-fifth of which were not-yet-qualified students. This compared with 1400 planning authorities.[42] The substantial numbers of architects who had acquired planning qualifications in addition to their architectural training, therefore, were in great demand, especially at senior levels where the shortage was most acute. During the period 1946–56, 45 per cent of the associate members of the Town Planning Institute were architects, as against 'direct entry' planners (22 per cent), engineers (14 per cent) and surveyors (9 per cent).[43] Perhaps more significantly, architect-planners filled chief planning officer positions to the extent that almost all of Britain's cities initially had planning departments headed by a trained architect. To some extent, their skills resonated with the apparent needs of reconstruction. They could 'plan in three-dimensions; not just zoning or traffic-oriented',[44] and bring a sense of vision to the task: 'This was a time in which the world was turning to planning, yet there was a vacuum.

[Modern architecture] had people who professed to be planners and were people who had an intensity of view.'[45]

At first glance, this would suggest unprecedented opportunities for architects to influence the course of urban reconstruction but it did not automatically mean, as Crinson and Lubbock asserted, that 'this gave the profession the power to reshape the cities along the lines thought out by Le Corbusier amongst others, before the war'.[46] Nor did it even mean that 'the interpenetration of architecture and planning was thus considerable'.[47] In the first place, the architects' role quickly shrank as more chartered planners appeared on the scene. In 1963, just 143 out of 729 local government chief officers responsible for planning had architectural qualifications (66 being qualified in both planning and architecture, with 77 only in architecture).[48] When looking purely at larger towns and cities, the comparable statistics revealed less than 20 per cent of chief officers as having architectural qualifications.[49] Using figures on a slightly different basis for 1962, only 126 of their 868 planning staff members had architectural qualifications.[50]

Second, and related, the power relationships between the design professions within the public sector usually served to preclude the architects from exercising dominant influence over town planning. Frequently, planning officers continued to work in the City Engineer's or Borough Surveyor's offices, which effectively meant the retention of planning powers by those departments. Indeed, as noted in Chapter 2, this pattern of responsibility was the norm in smaller authorities in the postwar period, with the engineers also retaining control in a number of larger towns and cities until well into the 1960s. Astragal's report on a speech by Henry Brooke, the Minister of Housing and Local Government, to the Institution of Municipal Engineers in April 1960 made precisely this point. While talking about the versatility of engineers, Brookes opined that there was 'a function for the architect and the planning officer separate from those of the surveyor and the engineer'. Astragal remarked that:

> The shouts of protest showed why there are still 38 county boroughs without an architect as a chief officer. (There are many more where the engineer is also the planner.) It only remains for Mr. Brooke to *do* something to help the undervalued architect to find his proper place.[51]

The architects' concerns about their lack of influence over the planning process resurfaced in a report commissioned by the RIBA in December 1962, which opened with the simple question: 'What precisely is the architect's special contribution to [the planning process]?'[52] Its author, Anthony Goss, reviewed the scope of town planning, planning practices by public authorities and the private sector, and the nature of planning education. His assessment argued for the value of a design input at various stages of the planning process, but Goss's four conclusions would scarcely have brought much comfort to his sponsors. Arguing more for the need to recognise town planning as an important multidisciplinary activity in its own right, Goss put the case that architecture, like other professions, should not attempt 'to build up its own empire'.[53] Indeed, his conclusion that the best exercise of the architect's skill was 'at the local level, in town design' was significantly less emphatic than his broadside that 'architects must increasingly be aware of the need for collaboration with other specialists, whose needs must also be catered for' and that

> all the professions traditionally engaged in planning . . . must appreciate how much inter-professional jealousies inhibit the progress of planning, and must be prepared to sink their rivalries in a serious attempt to develop inter-professional training and inter-professional collaboration in mixed teams.[54]

## Turf wars

Given that there was little likelihood of any such outcome, Goss's report was more significant for its critique than its recommendations. It clearly pinpointed a profession whose members regarded themselves as failing to make the contribution that they had hoped and anticipated. This was also borne out by practitioners' experience. Certainly, there were instances, such as the LCC, Coventry and the New Town development corporations, where the organisational structures brought architecture and planning into close contact and achieved a fair measure of integration.[55] Yet these examples were comparatively rare. Even at the LCC, the difference in professional cultures remained. Percy Johnson-Marshall recalled that Arthur Ling's policy as Chief Planner was to bring in 'as many architect-planners as he could to redress the balance of the surveyor-planners. The trouble was that the other type of architects did not want truck with the planners at all – they wanted the clean sheet.'[56] For his part, Arthur Ling found the continuing frictions wearying, citing it as one reason for his own move from the LCC in 1955. He recalled:

> I always wanted to see a strong relationship between architecture and town planning and that was one reason why I eventually left the LCC to go to Coventry, because there as both Architect and Planner I could bring them together.[57]

The separation between planning and architecture led to long-running sagas of division and redivision of functions that acted as a backdrop to urban reconstruction and renewal in the 1950s and 1960s. The government's failure to address the question of the appropriate structure for handling complex and large-scale building programmes, and much less to tackle the problem of outmoded local authority boundaries (see also Chapter 8), meant that arrangements were ad hoc and often arbitrary. Newcastle upon Tyne, for example, had introduced a City Architect's Department under George Kenyon in 1947. Architects had traditionally occupied the dominant role in housing matters, effectively deciding the design and layout of estates,[58] but the Chief Engineer retained the brief of Planning Officer. During the 1950s, this effectively meant little more than development control, given that by 1958 the City Engineer's Department still employed only nine planners.

Several years later, the situation was transformed. In January 1960, Newcastle became the first city to appoint a City Planning Officer in charge of a separate Town Planning Department, with an initial staff of 20 qualified officers.[59] This quickly acquired the reputation of 'probably [having] more power than planning departments in any comparable County Borough'.[60] Its expansion caused some concern in architectural circles. Looking first at the positive side, Astragal praised the decisions both to employ a Chief Planner with responsibility for four times as many planners and to take planning away from the City Engineer, whose department had shown its 'inadequacies' in a recent public inquiry into the massive roundabout planned at the junction of Mosley Street and Pilgrim Street. Yet the writer fretted about where architects fitted into the equation. Favouring arrangements where planning was an integral part of architects' departments, he hoped the changes did not mean 'that architects are to be used for elevational control and not for long-term planning and development'.[61]

His misgivings were justified. The Planning Department's rapidly increasing numbers of employees presaged a similar expansion of functions, including taking over some formerly under the control of the architects. The Planning Department enthusiastically produced plans for all elements of the city's development,[62] with planners and architects progressively working within guidelines produced by Wilfred Burns, the Planning Officer.[63] Architects, for example, found themselves no longer initiating housing schemes, but receiving instructions as to which sites were available and what sort of building was required. Moreover, in 1965 dissatisfaction with the performance of the housing programme led to the splitting of architectural functions between the City Architect's Department and a new Housing Architect's Department, with its own chief officer. These arrangements, motivated by wishing to adopt a task force and multi-disciplinary approach to expedite housing production, lasted until 1974. In organisational terms, they presented an uncomfortable compromise, with the two architectural offices uncomfortably cohabiting within the same drawing office and sharing technical support staff.[64] The City Architect's Department retained greater prestige, although the Housing Architect's Department had a larger budget. The division between the two departments was also far from absolute, in that housing architects often worked on projects other than housing. Although the housing architectural staff found certain advantages in this arrangement, they questioned aspects of the division of functions:

> Eight of the 11 respondents, including those with most responsibility, felt that decisions which should rightfully be made by architects were being made by other groups. Planners were the people most frequently named as encroaching on the architect's sphere of competence. Some antagonism towards them was particularly strongly felt: one man regarded planning as a 'necessary evil'. The architects were resentful of the planners' tendency to dictate what a development should look like, and their reluctance to hand over to the architects after the initial stages of the schemes had been completed.[65]

Thus, even if the changes did provide a central place for architecture, they did not necessarily provide a central place for the architects. It was far removed from the cherished vision of architect-led reconstruction and renewal that encouraged many to join the public sector.

Salaried architects in other cities had similar experiences. The City of Birmingham, which had established a separate Architect's Department only in 1952 (see Chapter 3), saw that event act as the catalyst for long-running battles over the repositioning of responsibilities within the local authority hierarchy. In the event, these were eventually resolved without overt conflict but with lingering tensions. To elaborate, the city had a long tradition of control by municipal grandees and dominant political leaders. In the period after the Second World War, Birmingham's administration was unusual in that it grouped all the functions of urban development and management (engineering, architecture and town planning) in one department (Public Works) under the control of Herbert Manzoni, who had become City Engineer and Surveyor in 1935. Superficially, this might have seemed an ideal arrangement for the architectural profession. After service in the First World War, Manzoni had trained as an architect at Liverpool University, which he then combined with a career in engineering, albeit with a marked leaning towards the latter. Manzoni was a firm believer in large-scale plans and the potential of technology, envisaging a combined onslaught on the city's slums and renewal of the road system. In 1941, for instance, his Public Works Department produced schemes for the comprehensive redevelopment of five large areas of the ring of decay around the city centre.[66] In 1943, it introduced plans for a high-capacity, limited access Inner Ring Road to deal with central area traffic problems (see Chapter 5).

Yet notwithstanding Manzoni's background, the associated results in architectural terms were disappointing. Much of the housing designed by the Public Works Department was poor quality in terms of layout and design, with densities so low that the housing drive threatened to run out of land. City politics, however, demanded the exercise of great tact before suggesting the establishment of an Architect's Department, independent of Manzoni's control, to improve matters. The Public Works Committee's official history, written by one of its former senior engineers, positively exuded diplomacy when referring to this episode:

> In July 1951, the General Purposes Committee reported to City Council that the House Building Committee had asked them to consider whether in the interests of speedier progress with the City's house building programme, it would not be desirable to reduce the heavy responsibilities of the Public Works Department by the creation of another Department of the Corporation to be responsible primarily for house building work, but also concerned with general architecture. The report set out under sixteen heads the various functions of the Public Works Department, and said that it was asking a lot of one man, however good his staff, to control it all, but it was a tribute to Herbert J. Manzoni that it had been so successful. The Council agreed to these proposals for the reorganisation of the architectural work involving the

appointment of a City Architect and the ultimate establishment of a new Architectural Department.[67]

The first head of the Architect's Department, the Liverpool-trained A.G. Sheppard Fidler, arrived from his previous position as Chief Architect at Crawley New Town in May 1952, but the department remained under the aegis of the Public Works Department until 1954. This working arrangement established a power relationship that Sheppard Fidler found difficult to counter, especially given Manzoni's influence with the council. He commented that: 'It was funny to find that I wasn't really wanted at all: the City Council took no damned notice at all'. Although he initially enjoyed support from the Town Clerk, the latter's suicide left Fidler without significant allies within the corporation.[68] Fidler even encountered problems in exerting full control over architectural matters, given that a group of employees with architectural qualifications remained within the Public Works Department.[69] There was little working contact at everyday level between personnel in the Public Works Department and the City Architect's Department, with comparatively small issues having to be deferred to higher levels.[70] Devising architectural policy for the city or even for areas of the city, therefore, became a complex balancing act rather than an exercise in applied vision.

The main focus of Fidler's early years at Birmingham comprised working to raise architectural standards for housing above those of the designs inherited from the Public Works Department. Over time, his department gradually gained greater control over the design of housing, but only within a limited frame of reference. In particular, the architects found it extremely difficult to extend influence over related matters such as road provision.[71] When designing new estates, for example, the Public Works Department mapped out the road lines and only afterwards passed them to the Architect's Department to fill in the housing layouts.[72] Manzoni's unwillingness to cede influence to the architects also applied to central city developments. As Chapters 5 and 6 show, the Architect's Department was not consulted about city centre developments along the line of the Inner Ring Road, where the Public Works Department *deliberately* chose to proceed without a master plan to maximise the possibility of commercial participation.

At one level, this problem involved personalities. Manzoni undoubtedly saw the City Architect as being foisted on him by the council, but also believed in the benefits of keeping all building, planning and engineering under a single control – a model that, in different circumstances, architects would intuitively support. Sheppard Fidler did feel in an inferior position, but was also frustrated at seeing his department's planning capabilities under-utilised. In 1964, he resigned from what he described as 'his prestigious post of City Architect' and moved into private practice. While stating that there were many reasons for his departure,[73] which included failure to convince the council to adopt the French-based Camus system for building flats (see Chapter 8),[74] the long-running failure to gain control of town planning throughout the city was a contributory factor in his decision.[75] Yet differing conceptions of development strategy, underpinned by sensitive interprofessional relations, clearly played their part. The internal dynamics of the organisation established the parameters for the exercise of architectural strategy. Mere establishment of a separate architectural office did not necessarily imply design freedom.

If Birmingham amounted to a situation in which architects struggled without much success to achieve a measure of coordination between architecture and planning, then the redevelopment of central Sheffield saw outright defeat of architectural ambitions. Sheffield had appointed its first City Architect, F.E. Pearce Edwards, in October 1908. The City Architect took charge of a department made up of officers formerly employed in the Surveyor's Department and the Buildings section of the Education Department. During the intervening years, the city's architects had developed a reputation for innovative housing policies, but achieved much less with respect to city centre renewal – as the third incumbent of the position of City Architect, J. Lewis Womersley, found out after arriving from Northampton in February 1953. Womersley established a Central Areas Division to work on a strategy for urban renewal, but quickly found that his lack of powers over town planning constrained his department's ability to bring about change in central Sheffield. Town planning powers came under the control of the City Engineer Henry Foster (later succeeded by his deputy C.R. Warman). Andrew Derbyshire recalled that, when appointed as Assistant City Architect in 1955, part of his job description was to head the Central Areas Division, which

> was invented to try and get central area redevelopment out of the hands of the City Engineer. He was the Planning Officer. Lewis Womersley [the City Architect] desperately wanted to be Planning Officer and he wanted my help. I thought that was quite right, so we struggled away for a long time to try to get it out of that setting. But the City Engineer was a very powerful man and he had a lot of money. The Committee responsible for roads supported him.[76]

For their part, the planners located in the Engineer's Department resisted encroachment on their territory through reallocation of powers to the architects. Their viewpoint, it should again be stressed, was not simply driven by conservatism. They also had their own sweeping plans for the city centre. Driving a series of major roads through the central area, would have allowed the creation of a series of pedestrianised precincts of a type that dated back to the writings of H. Alker Tripp,[77] and found support in the Buchanan Report. The City Engineer's plan saw the central area as being divided into three segments: the Moor, a dual purpose shopping and traffic street; the Centre, containing the major civic buildings; and the Sheaf Valley, a development zone where activities could be separated out by using the gradient or by multilevel solutions.[78] They may well have had, as in Derbyshire's view, a low opinion of the architects, who they regarded as 'completely marginal . . . we were not thought to be serious people at all',[79] but their resistance stemmed, at least partially, from possessing a competing vision about the future Sheffield.

Faced with this impasse, the best that the architects could achieve was to gain powers over development control in the central area. This turned out to be a Pyrrhic victory. Development control involved protracted and largely fruitless negotiations to try to improve the architectural standards of the buildings that developers had put forward as part of reconstructing the city centre. Meanwhile, the engineers

> had given us development control and we weren't making much of that. It relieved them of a lot of worry and anxiety. It was rather a clever move really: it involved us in a lot of useless negotiations and left them free to get on with their roads.[80]

The architects made paper plans that partly overlapped with and partly diverged from those prepared by the engineers. These included schemes such as decking over the Sheaf valley to connect Park Hill with the city centre, for mini-tram systems, for closer access to the northern extension of the M1 motorway, for pedestrianisation combined with multi-storey car parks, and for revitalising the city centre (particularly through rationalising the location of industry within the central area).[81] Although hindsight might question the wisdom of several of these proposals, at the time their failure to progress was blamed on the City Engineer's control over planning and, in particular, over road provision. At Sheffield, as in Birmingham and many other cities, these two significant areas of policy essentially lay outside the architects' sphere of influence until the 1960s – by which time, many key decisions about urban renewal had already been made.

At Sheffield, Womersley and Derbyshire never achieved the aim of linking architecture and planning during their time of office. Both had already left for private practice by the time that Sheffield finally combined the offices of City Architect and City Planning Officer in 1968.[82] As Derbyshire commented:

> My experience of Sheffield was really one of collapsed dreams and disillusionment with local authority behaviour and with the ethos of local authorities of that time, which was why I was attracted to accept Stirrat's [Johnson Marshall] invitation to join RMJM.[83]

His experience would not prove exceptional. Although experiences varied over time and from city to city, in general architects struggled to make an impact against better-placed professional rivals. The course of urban reconstruction and renewal presented numerous instances in which they struggled, and failed, to gain the influence to which they aspired. Indeed, as the ensuing chapters show, it was comparatively rare for them to exert control over the crucial question of the deployment of roads in relation to built forms.

# Chapter 5

# Towards renewal

George Square is regarded as the very centre of the city as this is the location of the City Chambers, Glasgow's main public building. . . . During the Christmas period the square is ablaze with its decorations while, during the hottest part of the summer, office workers flock to the benches in a desperate bid to soak up some sunlight.

David Williams[1]

The climate of Scotland makes it almost impossible for people to gather in the open air.

Lancelot H. Keay[2]

If cities are memory, then in the mid-1950s the city centres served as the lens that brought that memory into focus. For those ports and industrial cities that had suffered most in the Blitz, the townscape remained pockmarked by 'great holes in the ground where buildings used to be'.[3] The new identity of the bomb sites as temporary nature reserves, populated by stray cats and colonised by a carpet of wild flowers, did little to remove their status as open wounds. Rundown street frontages in less fashionable areas, blackened stonework and peeling paint might have been ubiquitous enough not to cause comment, but they served as a daily reminder of continuing dilapidation. Industrial dereliction ate its way almost into the centres of many formerly thriving manufacturing towns. Visitors to Birmingham for the 1950 Annual Meeting of the British Association for the Advancement of Science received a regional survey on arrival that represented the towns of the Black County as haplessly accommodating themselves to the dereliction of the area's 'clinkery' mining and metal-smelting past.[4] Those purchasing the 'About Britain' guides produced for the 1951 Festival of Britain might have heeded W.G. Hoskins' sardonic advice *not* to avoid the six towns of the Potteries ('seven miles of concentrated ugliness and dirt') since their 'ugliness is so demonic that it is fascinating'.[5] Indeed, in the 1960s, the city centre of Stoke-on-Trent still contained an 'unpopulated acreage of . . . derelict land – old clay working, old coal dumps, canal and industrial waste' that 'desperately needs making over anew'.[6]

Besides wanting to restore better days, town councils also faced the question of modernisation. Public transport urgently needed investment. Road congestion had steadily worsened; a problem that became more pressing with the boost that the ending of petrol rationing in 1952 gave to ownership of private vehicles.[7] Attention to provision of open spaces within cities for civic usage, a prominent theme in many of the advisory plans, remained a distant prospect. Beyond that, there was also the problem of air quality, a further visceral indicator of the need for change. One Glaswegian observer recalled a seldom expressed advantage of trams in that, being on fixed rails, they were less affected by thick fogs than motor buses, which were often confined to the garage.[8] Cities then were things that you 'smelt and felt'.[9] The architects working for the LCC at County Hall on the south bank of the Thames, for example, knew that they had a choice on a hot summer's day. They could open a window, in which case they would get airborne grit on their drawings and have to endure the smell of the river, or they could swelter.[10] Latterly, too, London had suffered a traumatic winter hazard in the form of the 'Great Smog' that descended on the city during a five-day spell of anti-cyclonic weather in December 1952.[11] With as many as 4000 additional deaths from bronchitis, pneumonia and other respiratory diseases, the 'Great Smog' was a reminder that pollution could be as dangerous a killer in the mid-twentieth century as cholera had been in the mid-nineteenth century.[12]

These elements, in their varying ways, acted as powerful catalysts of the need for large-scale initiatives for tackling the problems of city centres that went well beyond patching up bomb damage and 'catching up with areas of maintenance and conversion'.[13] For the early part of the postwar period, this activity routinely took place under the multifaceted banner of 'reconstruction'. This implied a socially oriented activity as well as an exercise in physical design. It could also embrace different concepts of change – forensic, cosmetic, beautifying, restorative, revivalist, rational and visionary – in whatever mixture those with the power to transform the city felt it expedient to employ. Yet, with the passage of time, reconstruction became associated with disappointments and interminable wait-ing for something to happen. As in the current era, a rebranding exercise was undertaken to create a cause that would reignite commitment. In the early 1960s, therefore, the term 'renewal' was readily adopted as an alternative, but not entirely identical term. Influenced particularly by North American practice, 'urban renewal' stood for revitalisation of the urban core, rationalisation of physical design, and regeneration of residential districts. Whereas reconstruction grew out of wartime concerns for the coming peace, renewal now implied the spirit of an age of technology, resource availability and progress. The social objectives of redevelopment remained, but rarely with the same moral force as 15–20 years earlier. Although there is no hard and fast divide between the two terms, it is convenient here to use 'reconstruction' to describe activity up to approximately 1960 and 'renewal' for the period beyond that date.

In this chapter, our focus is primarily on reconstruction, but with thoughts firmly on the renewal process that lay ahead. The first section notes the slow progress made in reconstructing the central cities during the 1950s, apart from the seemingly relentless expansion of commercial office blocks. The remainder of the chapter then analyses the diagnoses that modern architects brought to bear on the urban condition. To do so, it studies the work of two pressure groups: the MARS Group, whose 'Turn Again' exhibition at London's Royal Exchange (12–30 July 1955) made a statement about postwar office development, and the Society for the Promotion of Urban Renewal (SPUR), which made a thoroughgoing attempt to influence policy on urban redevelopment.

## Reconstructing the city centre

Lionel Brett (later Lord Esher), who features prominently in the later sections of this chapter, wrote in 1958: 'Except for a few notable examples, by now it is abundantly clear we can produce attractive and often promising plans, models and so on without somehow being able to realise them in concrete form'.[14] The problems were not principally ones of will and imagination. The priorities of the necessity-driven programmes for construction of housing, schools and factories had diverted funds away from large-scale projects such as town centre redevelopment. Admittedly, a few cities took the lead, implementing a Geddesian approach of 'conservative surgery, of cutting out the bad bits',[15] that broadly accorded with the radical approach of the Ministry of Town and Country Planning's handbook *The Reconstruction of Central Areas* (1947).[16] The blitzed centre of Coventry, laid waste by the Luftwaffe raids of November 1940 and April 1941, witnessed the most comprehensive programme. Here special circumstances operated. The government needed the restoration of the city's industrial capacity 'and was not particularly worried about the problems generated in getting it'.[17] Coventry was also notable for the extent that its Chief Architect and Planning Officers – Donald Gibson (1938–54) and Arthur Ling (1955–64) – pushed forward redevelopment on radical lines that offered 'undreamed of scope for many a young architect'.[18] As Percy Johnson-Marshall said of Coventry under Donald Gibson:

> A few of us went up to start the new office, and we went bursting with new ideas . . . [with] Donald Gibson providing us not only with leadership but with a cover against all the complicated difficulties of local government, so that we could quietly get on with the job.[19]

Recent events such as the opening of Broadgate House in 1953 or the Upper Precinct (1955) gave a sense of a city literally arising from the ashes (Figure 5.1). Basil Spence's design for the Cathedral, the centrepiece of the reconstruction, gave the city an international prominence, leading a contemporary observer to declare: 'It's startling, it's controversy, yet it has a defiant grandeur all its own; a commanding symmetry that makes it one of the architectural wonders of the H-bomb age'.[20]

Few other British cities generated such activity at this time. Other cities that had experienced heavy bombing, such as Hull, Swansea and Plymouth, had launched their reconstruction programmes with varying degrees of success, but

5.1
**The Broadgate
Centre, Coventry
(on completion,
1953)**

progress frequently depended on local factors, such as the extent of the involvement of property companies.[21] Early players such as Ravensfield (later Ravenseft) Properties began to expand their retailing interests, with projects in Bristol in 1949 and then Plymouth, Exeter, Hull, Swansea, Sheffield, Sunderland, Yarmouth and Coventry as development opportunities presented themselves in the early 1950s.[22] Their involvement fitted in with a style of reconstruction that implied cosmetic or restorative approaches, tidying up the scars of war and gently modernising city centres to accommodate the shifts in consumer demand, the rise in disposable income and the increasing use of cars. Architectural commentators rarely enthused over the results. A brief commentary in 1959 on the postwar townscape of Swansea depicted in an aerial photograph, for example, lambasted the 'architectural mediocrity which has been added to the planner's inadequacies'. Described as 'another missed opportunity',

> Swansea was one of the blitzed cities of the last war, and therefore, in common with the others, received an added, if bitterly painful incentive, to recreate a city fit to live in. In common with most of the other blitzed cities it has not achieved much, but bearing in mind the potentiality that lay behind the large area of cleared sites, it could scarcely have set itself a lower standard to achieve. A dual carriageway, a roundabout and a lot of infilling, that, in effect, is the new Swansea, an effort as impoverished in imagination as those of Hull and Portsmouth.[23]

The commentator eagerly accepted the opportunity to make comparison with the work of Sir Reginald Blomfield, one of the Modern Movement's *bêtes noires* from the 1930s:

> Connoisseurs of revivalism will appreciate the neo-Tudor shop forming one side of the square . . . and will note that the problem of fitting pitched

roofs on large buildings has been solved no more successfully than it was in Regent Street [London] by Blomfield nearly forty years ago.[24]

Other provincial cities had similar experiences. Glasgow's reconstruction plans after the war revolved less around resolving damage from aerial bombardment, in which respect it had suffered relatively less than many other British ports and industrial cities, than from a swathe of social and physical planning problems. These included crime, poverty, endemic sectarianism and housing conditions that ranked among the worst in Europe. In the early 1950s, for example, the corporation's housing waiting list contained 80,000–90,000 families, with roughly half of the city's households still living in one or two rooms.[25] A fundamental disagreement over rehousing that surfaced in the late 1940s, however, would seriously delay progress both in the field of housing and in wider issues of reconstruction. Briefly, Robert Bruce, the Master of Works and City Engineer for Glasgow Corporation, presented the city's case for not wanting to lose population and for rehousing within the city boundaries. His report, published in 1945, contained sweeping proposals for a 'healthy and beautiful city' that combined a loose modernism in high-rise buildings and neighbourhood development, with a traffic engineer's preference for a high-density inner ring road and multilevel traffic intersections.[26] By contrast, the government had other preferences, as expressed in the Clyde Valley Regional Plan, a strategy document for the modernisation of Clydeside commissioned in 1943 by the Secretary of State for Scotland that favoured a regenerated city surrounded by regional parks and with a lower population achieved by decanting population via overspill.[27] Its strategy for alleviating Glasgow's severe housing problems included proposals for moving 550,000 Glaswegians from central areas either to the periphery or to locations outside the city's boundaries (see also Chapter 7).

This disagreement was eventually resolved by compromise that largely favoured the Scottish Development Office's preference for overspill over Glasgow's wish for population retention, but the struggle had 'far-reaching effects'.[28] In the first place, it delayed the process of building new homes and produced a subsequent overcompensating urgency that dictated a disastrous 'houses only' development policy. That, in turn, stored up problems for the future:

> Politicians and people alike demanded a visible and swift tally of new housing units to relieve inner city misery. Services and amenities could wait, in the prospect of a successful national economy generating sufficient surplus for the provision of town centres, clubs, cinemas, churches and health centres on the pattern of the growing New Towns, once the all-important houses had been built.[29]

Second, the understandable preoccupation with housing delayed progress towards the renewal of central and inner areas of the city.[30] Although there had been formal discussion about creating Comprehensive Development Areas (CDAs) since 1953, the official list of 29 CDAs appeared only in 1957. Work started on the first one –

the profoundly deprived Hutchesontown-Gorbals district – in the same year (see Chapter 8). The other major component of the reconstruction, the Inner Ring Road and its associated links, gained approval only in 1959. For the most part, observers characterised the city in the 1950s as being dowdy and obsolescent. As the American-born poet James Burns Singer wrote:

> Imagine therefore a city with a frontier of smoke, billowing inwards, fluffing outwards, as smoke will in the slightest breeze, and you will have some picture, though vague yet accurate, of the shape of Glasgow. Within that frontier everything is more blurred than its edges. There is indeed a centre, the City centre, but it is backed on the north by some of the gentlest streets and most silent tenements that can be found in the whole area, and, apart from this central blob of tumult and business, and some sprawling suburbs, there are few distinctions. Residential areas meander confidently to the front door of industrial establishments. Slums and slum clearances lie like entangled lovers. Quietness collides with the sooty clank of traffic.[31]

Birmingham's reconstruction strategy similarly placed other priorities (road building, infrastructure and housing) over city centre development. Ever willing to indulge an urge to make and remake the city centre in a manner reminiscent of American practice, Birmingham Corporation readily entered into partnership with the private sector. Jack Cotton, a developer native to Birmingham, and Ravenseft Properties joined forces to develop the 3.5-acre (1.4-hectare) Big Top site adjacent to New Street Station destroyed by bombing in April 1941. With redevelopment including a 12-storey office block and a complex of retail units, the site represented the city's first major shopping development.[32] A further stimulus for commercial development arose as the city's engineers pushed the Inner Ring Road scheme forward. This had become part of Birmingham's planning policy in 1943, when land acquisitions started, but construction work commenced only in 1956–7. The corporation, acting on the policy of Herbert Manzoni's Public Works Department, deliberately made no plans for the city centre in case its stipulations disconcerted potential developers (see also Chapter 4). Instead, it sought to capitalise on the new scheme by offering developers sites along the line of the Ring Road, itself now effectively a limited access urban motorway.

At first, there was muted interest in those sites, but the potential benefits became clearer once work began in earnest on the first section of the Inner Ring Road from Horsefair to Moor Street. In 1957, John Laing and Son proposed an integrated building scheme to line the route of the section that became known as Smallbrook Ringway. Designed by a local architect James Roberts, it had echoes of London's Regent Street, including the Quadrant.[33] Roberts' scheme addressed the problem of elongated sites with no depth. It involved a continuous ribbon of building along the southern side, rising to five-storey height, with a similar development on the north side complemented by the Albany Hotel. The continuity of shopping frontage mirrored the Big Top development, although critics have varied in their response to its appearance. Whereas Gordon Cherry argued that it was architecturally 'conservative and rather undistinguished',[34] Elain Harwood considered it among the first examples of a new kind of speculative modernism: 'busy, curvaceous and altogether "pop" in its styling and easy admittance of signage, shop window displays and frequent alteration'.[35]

Whatever the aesthetic assessments, there is no denying the extraordinary nature of the strategy adopted by Birmingham City Council. The rationale of high-density urban motorways was to ensure free-flowing traffic, largely achieved by allowing only limited access and separating pedestrians from vehicles. The city entered a new phase of underpasses and flyovers, pedestrian precincts and subways. An early assessment in *The Buildings of England* praised the system for segregating movement systems on different levels through 'numerous and ingenious subways' that would prevent the Inner Ring Road from becoming 'an impenetrable barrier as so many Thru-ways have become in North America'.[36] Manzoni himself denied that it was an urban motorway, but 'a city street of novel character . . . a compromise between the ideal needs of traffic, shopping and commerce'.[37] Regardless of the exact definition, the decision to line this highway with offices and shops diverged sharply from conventional logic. The Inner Ring Road effectively combined high-speed movement with the corridor street. The management of the Albany Hotel, for instance, quickly recognised the need to replace the windows with double-glazed versions to exclude the overpowering noise of the three-lane dual carriageway situated immediately outside.[38] It was an extraordinary negation of the principles of pedestrian–vehicle segregation so cherished within Modernist circles. Rarely was the architect's ineffectiveness at exerting influence over road planning so clearly demonstrated.

## London

In many ways, London's experience replicated the piecemeal developments of the provincial cities rather than its own traditions of large-scale integrated development schemes or the grander conceptual approach suggested by the LCC's declaration of eight comprehensive redevelopment areas: Stepney-Poplar, Bermondsey, South Bank, Elephant and Castle, Bunhill Fields, Barbican, St Paul's Precinct and Tower of London.[39] The first major signs of publicly sponsored reconstruction occurred in the City of London. In 1952, its corporation launched the Golden Lane scheme in the Bunhill Fields CDA and, by the end of the decade, would commence extensive redevelopment to the north of St Paul's and at the Barbican.[40] The City, however, was undistracted by large responsibilities for rehousing the working classes and angled the projects that it did undertake to cater for middle-class workers wanting to live close to the City. Elsewhere, plans abounded but progress on officially sponsored reconstruction was limited. The LCC, for example, had initiated work on the complex 2000-acre (809-hectare) Stepney-Poplar Reconstruction Area, with its population of approximately 100,000, in line with the *County of London Plan* (1943).[41] It had tackled Neighbourhood 9 (Lansbury) as the living architecture exhibition for the Festival of Britain, with the Architect's Department preparing the layout and private architects designing the buildings. The intended integrated development of the eleven neighbourhoods in the area, however, never material-ised. The rebuilding process proceeded on a 'piecemeal fashion, as it depends on so many site factors',[42] with the result that here, as elsewhere, it rarely addressed the wider scale at which neighbourhood planning functioned. Apart from the most basic level, the housing provision rarely coordinated with local service provision let alone fitted together with other functions as part of a unified approach to rebuilding the city.

South of the River Thames, attention focused on the heavily bombed Elephant and Castle district of inner South London. Shortly after the war, the London County Council had designated this area as its Comprehensive Development Area 5. The ambitious aim for the 30-acre (12-hectare) site, situated around the major intersections of the roads from Westminster and the Waterloo and Blackfriars bridges, was to transform a lively but rundown district into the 'Piccadilly Circus of South London'.[43] As such, the scheme went through various versions included a 1951 scheme that proposed a multilevel intersection and combining the two underground stations, a scheme with a single level roundabout (1954), and the 1958 scheme (see Figure 5.2), which also involved architect–private developer competitions to design elements of the renewal project.[44]

The introduction of public–private partnerships – virtually unknown in town centre development before 1939 – was an important component of the scheme. Ernö Goldfinger won the commercial development competition for a brief that did little more than specify the need for a quarter of a million square feet of office space and add 'some minor height restrictions'.[45] This led to the construction of three office blocks connected by glass bridges, initially occupied by the Ministry of Health (Figure 5.3). The husband-and-wife firm of Paul Boissevain and Barbara Osmond, in association with the Willett group of companies, won the competition to build the shopping centre and broke with the precinctual trend favoured in the 1950s by creating one of Britain's first covered shopping developments. While neither architect nor developer had previously designed a shopping centre, the LCC's Planning Committee described the winning design as 'quite outstanding in its original conception of an arcaded multi-level shopping centre'.[46] Goldfinger subsequently completed the complex by gaining the commission to design the Odeon cinema in 1965.

The commercial arena provided a different picture, with the veteran American architectural historian Henry-Russell Hitchcock finding London in the midst of a building boom that 'reminds one of São Paolo or Toronto'.[47] The official end of the 15-year period of building controls in November 1954 had created a 'developer-friendly system',[48] which gave the private sector sufficient confidence in the longer-term outlook to commence the speculative redevelopment of the sites that property groups had assiduously, if often surreptitiously, accumulated.[49] The boom in office building then accelerated, as property developers and their architects acted on their steadily expanding knowledge of planning legislation (see Chapter 3). Richard Seifert, the arch exponent of this approach, commented that he originally made a point 'absorbing' the stipulations of the Town and Country Planning Act 1947 'rather than learning it'. Once the licensing system had finished:

i.2
Model of Elephant
and Castle
Redevelopment
LCC Planning
Department, 1958)

there was a vast amount of building to be done, there were clients who were anxious to get on with it, and there were not many architects who really were establishing their practices to meet a new world and a new situation. And that is what happened . . . it became known amongst the developers of the period that I was building up a reputation of knowing what I'm talking about and producing drawings which complied with the Act and gave them the best advantage of building on a site.

5.3
**The former Alexander Fleming House, Elephant and Castle (photograph August 2001)**

The returns certainly rewarded the time invested. Seifert's firm rode the tremendous demand for office blocks in the City. They designed 'maybe 700–800 of them, and perhaps 1000 buildings overall'.[50] In total, developers added over 41 million square feet (3.81 million square metres) of floor space through new buildings, rebuildings and extensions to central London's office floor space in the decade between 1954 and 1963.[51]

From the outset, the office boom created profound despondency among architectural commentators predisposed towards modernism. There were no official guidelines for design from central or local government. In central areas, the ministry advised planners to allow developers and their architects the maximum freedom commensurate with balance and harmony.[52] Initially, clients looked to architects to supply them with buildings in styles that expressed traditional solidity and grandeur (Figure 5.4). Surveying the results, J.M. Richards had written about

5.4
**Advertisement for Dorman Long (April 1958), depicting recent office developments in the city**

the City being 'on the brink of disaster', due to the prevailing poor choice of good design and an associated failure to consider the relationship of building 'to each other and to what exists' in the sense of carrying on and improving 'the best traditions of the City'.[53] Deploring the bulk of such buildings as much as their neoclassical design, Richards looked towards a more sensitive handling of sites through amalgamation and regrouping. If the habits of commercial rivalry prevented private owners from doing this, 'then the City Fathers, in the interests of their own reputation, should themselves embark on long range development on a large scale'.[54]

In the event, neoclassicism faded in favour of the simplified modernism and new materials that developers soon realised could supply good returns for conventional office development.[55] This encountered little resistance initially because until about 1957, 95 per cent of new offices were built on bombed land where no demolition was required.[56] From 1958, the appearance of further modern blocks meant replacement of the existing urban fabric. When these involved sensitive sites in the City or the West End, development could involve lengthy disputes – of which the most celebrated and least conclusive arose over the future of the Monico site at Piccadilly Circus.

The Circus itself had a relatively short history. Created in 1819, it lost its circular shape and became an 'awkwardly-shaped clearing' after the construction of Shaftesbury Avenue in 1886.[57] Nevertheless, it had developed into an important symbolic space that 'certainly in the minds of Commonwealth visitors' had become the hub of London's West End, but its bustling atmosphere was partly due to the heavy traffic that converged on the Circus for much of the day.[58] Any functional analysis of the road systems was bound to support the case for decisive action to eliminate this bottleneck. The Circus's character was also threatened by the fact that the surrounding land comprised four major sites and ownerships. At the start of 1954, these comprised the Café Monico, which belonged to Express Dairies, the Criterion site (the Crown Estate), the Trocadero (J. Lyons and Co.) and the London Pavilion (LCC). If major reconstruction occurred in any one of these sites, it would inevitably affect the appearance and atmosphere of the area as a whole.

The specific problem emerged in 1954 when Jack Cotton, in his first London venture, bought the Café Monico site on the north side of the Circus for redevelopment. Cotton then spent five years in negotiations with the LCC proposing a succession of schemes for this island site. Cooperation with the LCC was essential since, besides being the planning authority, it also owned an adjacent property that Cotton wanted as part of the development. For its part, the LCC looked to Cotton to purchase additional freehold properties so that it could implement much needed road realignments without having to find the funds itself. After obtaining provisional planning agreement in March 1959, the developer proceeded to demolish the existing buildings subject to retaining the façades overlooking the Circus and Glasshouse Street.[59] On 26 October 1959, a week after Cotton had received permission to construct the Pan-Am building over the tracks of Grand Central station in New York, he appeared to have triumphed again. The LCC planners indicated their readiness to grant final detailed planning permission to

Cotton's company, Island (Piccadilly) Development Limited and its financial backers, the Legal and General Assurance Company. The scheme involved a building containing shops, restaurants, a bank, exhibition rooms and offices, with a tower rising to 172 feet (52 metres) high for advertising display. Provision for the display accorded to the LCC's wish to have 'pleasing buildings by day and animation by night',[60] with the architects from Cotton's own firm (Cotton, Ballard and Blow) envisaging these displays integrated rather than superimposed on to the façades of the building. All that apparently remained unresolved were minor details involving parking space.

There is little doubt that the design would have gone ahead as planned had Cotton, buoyed up by his apparent success in London and New York, not called an ill-advised press conference to show off the plans and the model for this site at what he called 'the hub of the first city of the British Commonwealth'.[61] A chorus of objections followed from architectural critics, politicians, the Civic Trust and, belatedly, the Royal Fine Art Commission. Their criticisms centred on the massing and volume of the building and its lack of architectural merit for such an important site, with outrage directed at an inept perspective showing the building with a crane on top and a spoof advertisement for a soft drink on the front. To make matters worse, the drawing showed the retractable crane used for hoisting the advertise-ments into place with its arms fully extended, producing an effect justifiably described as that 'of an enormous fruit machine with a propeller mounted on top'.[62] The subsequent furore led the Minister of Housing, Henry Brooke, to call a public inquiry that opened on 16 December 1959. Besides the specific problems encountered at Piccadilly Circus, the key issue for the inquiry came from identifying the 'relatively new problem' that had emerged:

> Should the interest of a private developer overrule the interest of the community at large? Should Piccadilly Circus be replaced by Cotton pushing through a new design for his corner and the next man an unconnected design for his? Or should the private operators be forced to submit, with a particular property, to a comprehensive masterplan for a larger area?[63]

## 'Turn Again'

The findings of the inquiry heralded a stalemate that persisted through the 1960s, as will be seen in Chapter 6. At this point, however, it is important to note that the problem was not new to architectural critics, who had actively campaigned for improved standards of design. One example was the 'Turn Again' exhibition, organised by the MARS Group at London's Royal Exchange in July 1955. Unlike most initiatives associated with MARS, this event had relatively straightforward origins. Despite the Group's waning ability to mount any event not directly connected with CIAM congresses, there remained interest in staging exhibitions to convey the virtues of modern architecture to the public. After all, whatever its shortcomings, the MARS Group's previous effort – the 1938 'Modern Architecture' exhibition at the New Burlington Galleries – was still the most comprehensive statement of the philosophy of interwar British architectural modernism and, as seen in Chapter 2, continued to serve as a landmark for other events. The possibility of holding an exhibition featuring photographs of members' work had flickered into life in 1951, when contacts with the British Council had briefly aroused hopes that a MARS-designed exhibition promoting the best of British architecture might tour overseas. Despite negotiations, the MARS Group's Annual Report for 1951 recommended abandoning that project given the uncertainty of British Council support.[64]

None the less, the underlying idea of mounting an exhibition persisted. The report of the executive for the year ending 31 December 1952, surveying another bleak year of inactivity, mournfully concluded: 'The organisation of a MARS exhibition of the photographs of the work of members has been frequently discussed. Funds could be available if someone could be found to do the work.'[65] The subject resurfaced at the Annual General Meeting in May 1953, when the chairman (J.M. Richards) reported that 'the Group had enough money for an exhibition and that some show of the Group's activities would be of value [but] . . . it should be on a particular theme'. One suggestion was that the incoming executive should consider ways of arranging a touring exhibition assembled from the material submitted to the Aix Congress (CIAM IX).[66] Any exhibition, however, would need to have clear association with MARS. Shortly afterwards, the executive turned down a request from Peter Smithson, one of the promoters of the 'Documents 1953' exhibition at the Institute of Contemporary Arts, on the basis that

> the Group should not give money to assist an Exhibition that might not necessarily represent a MARS viewpoint, feeling that the money might later be used for an Exhibition which would be organised by the Group itself rather than one or two individual members.[67]

The eventual decision to stage 'Turn Again' stemmed from two developments. One was the continuing debate over the 'Heart of the City', which arose at CIAM VII (Bergamo, 1949), crystallised at CIAM VIII (Hoddesdon, 1951) and was surveyed in its conference volume *The Heart of the City*.[68] CIAM's enthusiasm for functional order had caused neglect of the conditions that generated vitality in the urban (civic) core. Questions arose as whether 'classical' functionalism had produced too narrow a definition of the building task and about the possible need for a 'new monumentality',[69] to give symbolic visual expression to the constitutive ideas of a community or to the social structure.[70] A meeting of the MARS Group's CIAM 10 Sub-Committee argued that the Athens Charter had produced static analyses that failed to take account of 'patterns of development, growth, or the positive activity of tradition' and also made no attempt to differentiate between different magnitudes in Urbanism'.[71]

The second development was that the return of Maxwell Fry and Jane Drew from India in 1954 provided volunteers to take the project further. Fry recalled that: 'When we got back from India, I learned that the Group had about £500. I said "spend it at once" – it came as a shock to me that there was actually money to spare.'[72] He and Drew jointly chaired a 20-strong organising committee, which drew together a core of those who had contributed to the 1938 exhibition (such as Misha Black, H.T. Cadbury Brown and Ernö Goldfinger), with newer members such as Michael Grice, Bill Howell, and Peter and Alison Smithson.[73] As specific duties emerged, John Bicknell, then newly graduated, assumed the role of exhibition organiser, Edward Wright prepared the poster and the exhibition typography, and Monica Pidgeon and Theo Crosby, drawing on the support of the *Architectural Design*, produced the souvenir brochure (Figure 5.5).

Set up in the courtyard of the Royal Exchange, the committee ran the exhibition as a free event that passing office workers might wander around during their lunch breaks. It comprised photographs and other illustrations, mostly borrowed or loaned by members, arranged in a set of display cases mounted in a Hills steel frame. Its aim was 'to draw attention to the low architectural standards of new buildings in the City and to act as a practical demand for bolder and more modern techniques'.[74] The title and the exhibition symbol of a cat, drawn by Nicholas Bentley and used in the publicity material, consciously evoked the City's own mythology. The present time, the exhibition asserted, was analogous to the point in the story of 'Dick Whittington' when the City's bells apparently urge the hero to 'turn again' and reconsider his actions given the promise that he was destined to become Lord Mayor. Opened at noon on 12 July 1955 by H.W. Seymour Howard, one of Whittington's distant successors, the exhibition invited visitors to rethink what was appearing in present-day London.

The case put forward by MARS was that the City of London had many problems: clogged up by commuter flows and the demands of motor traffic, threatened by uncoordinated development, and disfigured by the poor quality of new office buildings. In other cities, the response to new functional demands had

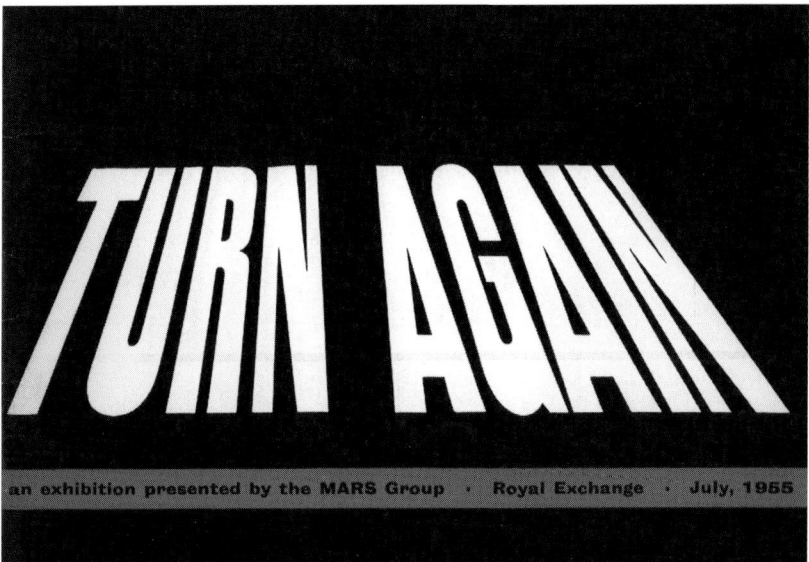

5.5
'Turn Again'
exhibition
brochure, MARS
Group (1955)

generated elegant new architecture as, for example, shown by Michael Scott's Dublin Bus Station (Figure 5.6), Mies van der Rohe's apartment buildings in Chicago, and stores, garages and restaurants drawn from practice in Italy, France and the Americas. Office buildings, however, took centre stage. Offices were not just utilitarian structures, but 'a challenge to create the future out of the present, out of what we are, and what we make for ourselves. A new office building is an act of faith'. Photographs of offices in New York, Rio de Janeiro, Milan and elsewhere reinforced this point. Elsewhere city authorities had encouraged the 'new materials of industry' – steel, aluminium, concrete and glass – to solve new problems in old ways, as well as finding new ways to deploy traditional materials. Yet while mechanisation set the pace,

> the architect plays the tune – humanising the machine – collaborating with nature converting the arid city to a symphony of geometry and natural form in which the scale of the common man is registered and his emotions find a place, in which the traffic-hunted pedestrian regains his dignity and finds peace of mind.[75]

5.6
**Dublin Bus
Station
(Michael
Scott,
1945–53)**

The time to affirm the transforming potential of modern architecture was at hand, despite repeated previous disappointments: 'This is the moment to *Turn Again*. When London rebuilds on the ashes of Hitler's fire, let us not be vanquished by our own past – the future lies within us.'[76]

The exhibition attracted around 14,000 visitors by the time that it closed on 30 July, after which it toured in reduced form to Manchester, Liverpool and Edinburgh.[77] Dubbed 'better late than never' by Denys Lasdun,[78] it supplied at least some domestic programme of MARS activities, covered its costs (unlike its 1938 predecessor), and was deemed successful in conveying its message visually.[79] Although some members felt that 'a lot of people got a lot out of it' and that 'it persuaded many people not to be afraid of modern architecture',[80] its impact on building policy was minimal. The sympathetic *Architectural Design* reported the 'fairly cool reception from the popular press' and suggested that the protest had probably come too late: 'the photographs relate immediately and poignantly to the world one encounters on leaving the Royal Exchange and walking past the many sites where an opportunity is being energetically lost'.[81] 'Turn Again' also represented little more than a footnote in the last rites of the MARS Group (see Chapter 10). Doubts even remained about its effectiveness as propaganda, especially in terms of the coherence of the case put forward. Although Trevor Dannatt felt that it gave the MARS Group a chance to 'offer another image, another philosophy of commercial building',[82] J.M. Richards, writing as *The Times* 'Architectural Correspondent', expressed his reservations:

> The photographs are stimulating indeed, but in allowing it to be inferred that the virtues of the style of architecture they depict are primarily aesthetic the MARS Group have failed to deploy their strongest weapon. London, by failing to take full advantage of modern building ideas and techniques, is in danger of losing not only its architectural charms but its reputation for efficiency and up-to-dateness, on which its prosperity rests.[83]

Once again, the Group's failure to agree underlying principles meant that another MARS exhibition ran the risk of being a style-only answer to significant urban problems.

## SPUR

Office development, of course, represented only part of the challenge for reconstruction. As the 1950s wore on, various groups of modern architects established further study projects and discussion groups as an expression of their concerns about the slow pace and confused strategies underpinning recon-struction. One such group emerged from the Association of Building Technicians (ABT), the architectural trade union to which many on the Left belonged. The ABT had organised a conference on 'Housing the City Dweller' on 24 January 1957 which, omitting 16 students, essentially brought together around 35 participants from the LCC and the London boroughs with a similar number of private practitioners.[84] Almost all were trained architects, although the attendance list shows that many then practised as planners. Not surprisingly, therefore, the conference's agenda went beyond looking purely at issues of housing to include the wider context. Initially generated by responses to a position paper published in the ABT's magazine *Keystone*,[85] it included discussion of the reasons for the shortage of building land, the logic and desirability of urban decentralisation, the possibility of developing new towns within cities, the strategy of urban renewal, and the appeal of 'thinking big'.

The success of this venture led to the establishment of a 'Continuing Committee' that might take the conference's discussion further. An initial draft statement, steeped in ideas derived from Geddes and Abercrombie, identified persistent urban problems and the difficulties of initiating comprehensive redevelopment within the prevailing financial regime. Housing emerged as the most pressing problem, but land shortage and the drawbacks of 'overspill' required 'more study and experiments towards raising the densities within the existing perimeter of our cities'.[86] The way forward, the committee suggested, lay in founding a council or committee for the promotion of city redevelopment, subsequently amended to the 'City Reconstruction and Planning Council'. This would be 'a body of the highest standing in the public estimation . . . whose objects would be to concentrate on the problems of city redevelopment and more particularly with those concerned with the centres of cities and living at high densities'.[87] Recognising that it was difficult to create such a body from scratch without wider backing, the group approached the Housing Centre Trust, based in London's Haymarket, as a potential home for the new council. Correspondence from May and June 1957 between the centre's secretary Margaret Solomon and Percy Johnson-Marshall, acting on behalf of the LCC/ABT group, showed the Housing Centre willing in principle to absorb this new enterprise into its structure.[88] In June, Solomon formally invited Johnson-Marshall to join the Housing Centre's General Committee to assist with the creation of a City Redevelopment Group and to define how it might fit in with the centre.[89]

Matters then proceeded slowly until December 1957, when the Housing Centre invited Lionel Brett to convene a Reconstruction Committee that might become an official part of the Housing Centre.[90] Politics influenced their choice of convenor. The Housing Centre, founded in 1934, was a centrist pressure group supported by voluntary subscriptions committed to 'the improvement of housing conditions by the dissemination of information and the building up of an informed public opinion'.[91] Its officials clearly required those invited to join the new group to be 'broadly based' and not 'people within what some of us feel is a rather narrow group of which he [Percy Johnson-Marshall] and his friends approve.'[92] By contrast, Brett, the future fourth Viscount Esher, was an acceptable choice. A well-established architect-planner with a Liberal background, he benefited from lacking direct association with the left-wing LCC/ABT group that had organised the 'Housing the City Dweller' Conference, even though he had attended that event. For his part, Brett quickly prepared an invitation to potential participants that laid out much of the philosophy for the still-unnamed new body. Its key elements reveal an approach that went well beyond housing, densities and land availability to address the essence of twentieth century urbanism, while studiously avoiding any rhetoric of class politics:

> It has for some time been agreed among the great majority of architects, planners and sociologists that a formidable concentration of factors – high living space standards, the high cost of urban land, family motoring, television etc. – are leading to a degree of disintegration that is a real threat to our physical environment and to our social solidarity. Left to itself, late twentieth century Britain could become a cheap version of Los Angeles, with all that implies in loneliness, monotony and mere ugliness. If the past and present picture of Britain as a network of cities, towns and villages in a verdant setting is to retain any validity, if it is to be positively desired and positively designed, it can only be by leadership, often in a direction opposite to that which blind forces would have taken.
>
> Many people realise that the crux of the problem is the reinvigoration of urban living. If the vicious circle of urban blight and suburban escapism could be broken, and life led back into the inner rings of our cities and towns, the social, economic and aesthetic gains would be incalculable. Individual designers and sociologists have been working on this problem for many years, yet strangely there exists no organisation, no anti-scatter society, no council for the renewal of urban England, to collect, coordinate and publish their researches or to make the case for a new type of urban life. The devoted work of the civic societies and the amenity societies must inevitably be mainly concentrated on symptoms, as and when they occur, rather than with the underlying causes of social disintegration. The only organisation which specifically existed to bring together the most creative research workers in this field has ceased to exist.[93]

The statement contains two significant elements. The first was the reference to 'anti-scatter'. What Brett envisaged transcended simple regeneration of the urban fabric in favour of a new approach that re-concentrated people back within the city. The second was the implicit allusion to the MARS Group. With MARS formally disbanding in January 1957 (see Chapter 10), there was again a place for an architectural discussion forum that also sought to undertake study group activities. It was striking that the new group when it formed would draw its support primarily from architects, despite consistently seeking a wider constituency from architects, town-planners, economists, real-estate developers and sociologists.[94] It was also noticeable that it should choose a structure similar to MARS, albeit with study groups coordinated by a general committee.

The group formalised its structure and relationship with the Housing Centre in February 1958, whereby it came under the aegis of the Housing Centre while retaining its own identity. Henceforth, the secretary of the Housing Centre also served as the secretary of the new group and the Housing Centre accommodated its committee and general meetings. Its terms of reference were 'to formulate the social, economic and planning conditions affecting present day urban renewal; to investigate prototypes and make proposals which meet those conditions; to publicise and popularise these proposals; and to appraise published projects.'[95] Members would join study groups devoted, respectively, to the structure of cities, social structure and employment, housing practice and densities, traffic circulation and utilities, the economics of urban renewal, and legislation and administration. The meeting that set up these study groups dismissed another suggestion for a group on 'the effect of new building forms on townscape' because 'this aesthetic aspect would come up continually in other groups'. All that remained was to find an appropriate name. Brett wished to affirm that 'cities were worth living in – that there was a quality about urban life which was better than suburban life and different from rural life',[96] and suggested 'The Urbanists' to indicate the nature of that commitment. His choice drew wry comment from George Grenfell-Baines:

> I am not happy about 'The Urbanists'. One thought suggests we might be a Concert Party, and another that we may be regarded as long-haired aesthetes. 'Ists' are always suspect and there is a tremendous amount of suspicion and resentment, particularly in the Provinces, of anything that smacks of dogma or uplift.

In its place, he suggested the 'Town and Country Renewal Association' or 'Association for Town and Country Renewal'.[97] Neither name received much enthusiasm, with Brett replying that he had abandoned his own suggestion.[98] Instead, the Group adopted Thomas Sharp's suggestion that it should be called SPUR (Society for Promotion of Urban Renewal).[99]

## Exhibition plans

The term 'urban renewal', which SPUR favoured over 'reconstruction', already had a recognised place in North American parlance. Title I of the US Housing Act 1949, for example, had established an explicitly named 'urban renewal programme' to accomplish slum clearance and area redevelopment. Under this, the clearance of entire neighbourhoods using federal funds preceded sale of the land for redevelopment by the private sector. This policy would prove to have significant racial overtones,[100] but that element, to the extent which it was known, impinged relatively lightly on the consciousness of proponents of comprehensive redevelopment at the time. Instead, they conceived of a programme that saw 'urban renewal' through the lens of rationalisation, revitalisation and efficiency. It sought to bring new taxpaying users into the core of the city in pursuit of economic regeneration in the central city. Urban renewal also stood for the 'rationalisation' of the physical design of the city and 'the rebuilding and preservation of its residential districts'. All actions would take place within the guidelines of a comprehensive plan for the city.[101]

Early meetings of SPUR occupied themselves with defining initial principles of urban renewal, conscious that British usage implied a 'social renewal' policy to accompany the emphasis on the renewal of the physical fabric of the city.[102] These deliberations soon gained added focus from an initiative sponsored by the RIBA. Its Town Planning Committee had decided in July 1958 to host a conference on City Reconstruction during May 1959 on the theme of 'The Living Town – a Symposium on Urban Renewal'. Arthur Ling, the instigator of this proposal and also a SPUR member, encouraged the committee to suggest 'that the Society for the Promotion of Urban Renewal at the Housing Centre might be interested in helping with the organisation of the meeting'.[103] The response recognised that the process had gone too far for SPUR to influence the agenda of the symposium, but considered that it might offer an exhibition to accompany the RIBA's conference for which SPUR would be entirely responsible.[104] George Grenfell-Baines, who also chaired RIBA's Town Planning Committee, confirmed the institute's willingness to see SPUR 'take a leading part in the Exhibition' and suggested establishing a joint action committee. Given that two of the three members running the symposium (Percy Johnson-Marshall and Eric Lyons) were similarly members of SPUR, this offered the basis for close cooperation between the two events.[105] By mid-October, the RIBA had invited SPUR to prepare a full-scale exhibition in the Henry Florence Hall to run alongside the RIBA's symposium on 'The Living Town'. The exhibition would seek to sell the idea of cities and towns as 'places which can be supremely worth living in . . . primarily to local authorities and the urban public'. To that end, it would analyse the qualities and defects of existing cities and towns and endeavour 'to put forward proposals for immediate action: technical, social, financial and administrative'.[106]

Reflecting on this initiative, Brett argued that the exhibition 'is the best chance SPUR is likely to have of justifying its existence and its ideas but to grasp it we shall need the support of every member'.[107] He then drafted an outline synopsis containing five sections.[108] The introductory section would examine the 'pleasures and horrors of urban living'. The second section, entitled 'diagnosis', would look at the perennial problems of 'the Heart of the Town', twilight regions and the fringes. The third section offered a new perspective on the 'seven pillars' of (urban) wisdom, with a table providing suitable examples (Table 5.1). The fourth section, seen as having considerable importance in establishing a credible case for urban renewal, dealt with 'lines of approach', subdivided into 'technical' (e.g. multilevel circulation), 'social' (e.g. 'living in high buildings, children in towns, and the social needs of special categories in the urban population'),[109] 'financial' (e.g. redistribution of values) and 'administrative' (e.g. reconstruction committees). The final section, called 'exaggerations', tentatively proposed making a case through the strategy of *reductio ad absurdum*, with slogans such as 'down with zoning' and 'a town is a town is a town'. Not all of the suggestions gained approval and, most notably, the final section disappeared, replaced by subdividing the fourth part. Elements of detail also changed. Responding to the selection under 'pleasures', for example, Walter Bor provided the cryptic note: '*add* Bloomsbury *delete* Birmingham'.[110] Nevertheless, the broad outlines of the synopsis remained as the guidelines for the exhibition.

**Table 5.1** Draft exhibition synopsis: Section 3 'Seven Pillars'

|  | Its opposite | Old | New |
|---|---|---|---|
| Convenience | Oxford Circus | Albany | Pimlico |
| Vitality | Letchworth | Soho | Coventry |
| Grandeur | Slough | Newcastle | Vickers Building |
| Liveability | Council estates | Chelsea | Basildon |
| Contrast | Preston | Edinburgh | St Paul's Precinct |
| Continuity | Kilburn | Oxford | Barbican |
| Universality | Dagenham | Norwich | South Bank |

Source: British Architectural Library, file BrL/4/1.

## Boston Manor

During a meeting of SPUR's General Committee in September 1958, the chairman drew members' attention to a special issue of the journal *Architecture and Building* on the 'Living Suburb',[111] 'which it was felt would also be a valuable basis for the exhibition'.[112] This was scarcely surprising given that it was a private project by individuals intimately involved in SPUR – the three senior partners in Chamberlin, Powell and Bon (CPB) along with two colleagues from the LCC Architects' Department (Graeme Shankland and David Gregory Jones) and Fred Millett (an artist and designer). Their scheme for the regeneration of Boston Manor, a somewhat run-down part of West London, was in many respects a throwback to the type of city design associated with the architectural schools in the late 1930s or 1940s. 'New Boston' was a hypothetical scheme for a real-world site that embraced the broad canvas of housing, employment, leisure and communications. What distinguished it from 'Tomorrow Town' and 'Zone', however, was that it was not a scheme for a New Town on a greenfield site. Alarmed at the extent of the overspill requirements of the nine major conurbations (Table 5.2), whereby the nine major conurbations alone would need to find housing for 1.5 million outside their boundaries, the authors proposed the comprehensive redevelopment of a suburb within the London region to create what was effectively a New Town within the existing urban area. The Boston Manor scheme discarded two touchstones of belief – prejudice against suburbia and against higher density – to produce a mixed development that would house 29,500 at 136 people per acre (336 per hectare) as against the existing population of 14,800 at 43–97 people per acre (106–239 per hectare).

The scheme for 'New Boston' involved a mix of six 30-storey blocks with four great quadrangles of six-storey terraced housing, two-storey housing around squares, low-rise flats and patio housing (Figure 5.7). As a close observer noted:

> Some of it reminds me of the work of Hilberseimer in Germany on courtyard housing. Courtyard housing actually appears as part of the

**Table 5.2** The overspill problem for the nine major conurbations

|            | **Population (1951)** | **Overspill population** | **Per cent** |
|------------|-----------------------|--------------------------|--------------|
| London     | 8,406,000             | 472,100                  | 5.6          |
| Manchester | 2,425,000             | 226,650                  | 9.3          |
| Birmingham | 2,237,000             | 203,600                  | 8.7          |
| Leeds      | 1,853,000             | 36,750                   | 1.9          |
| Liverpool  | 1,395,000             | 112,200                  | 8.0          |
| Newcastle  | 1,537,000             | 76,900                   | 6.0          |
| Sheffield  | 1,062,000             | 83,600                   | 7.8          |
| South Wales| 1,285,000             | 35,000                   | 2.7          |
| Glasgow    | 1,758,000             | 300,000                  | 17.0         |
| Total      | 21,958,000            | 1,546,800                | 7.0          |

Source: P. Chamberlin, G. Powell, C. Bon, G. Shankland, D. Gregory Jones and F. Millett, 'The living suburb', *Architecture and Building*, 1958, 33, p. 356.

mix. It wasn't quite as propagandist as the Ville Radieuse or things like that. It wasn't saying that you had to build high; it was saying that there was a need for an amalgam of different forms and heights.[113]

The town centre proceeded on somewhat grander lines than required for the population of the specific development. It partly took its inspiration from Vällingby in Sweden, a suburban district nine miles west of central Stockholm in which the city authorities had initiated a New Town project in 1954. Developed on four square miles of farmland purchased in 1930, the project proceeded on the so-called ABC (*Arbete–Bostad–Centrum* or Work–Dwelling–Centre) principle. As such, the plans envisaged not only accommodating 23,000 new residents but also providing work, shopping and service facilities for them and a surrounding population of 60,000 people.[114] A railway provided rapid connection with the cultural and retailing sectors of central Stockholm, with its town centre, built on a deck over the railway station. The deck contained shops and cultural facilities for the wider area, along with car parking spaces.

The version proposed for New Boston envisaged a triple-level centre built above London Transport's Piccadilly railway line that might serve a regional population, with 300,000 people living within a three-mile radius and a further 400,000 within an eight-mile radius. The centre would feature a garage and storage level, a shopping level and a roof garden level. At the west end of the complex, adjacent to Boston Manor railway station, was a market square and entertainment complex (including a small theatre, cinema, public lending library, restaurants and cafés). The plans for Hook New Town (Chapter 7) and the Barbican (London) – on which several of the participants in the Boston Manor study also worked – would eventually contain echoes of these ideas.

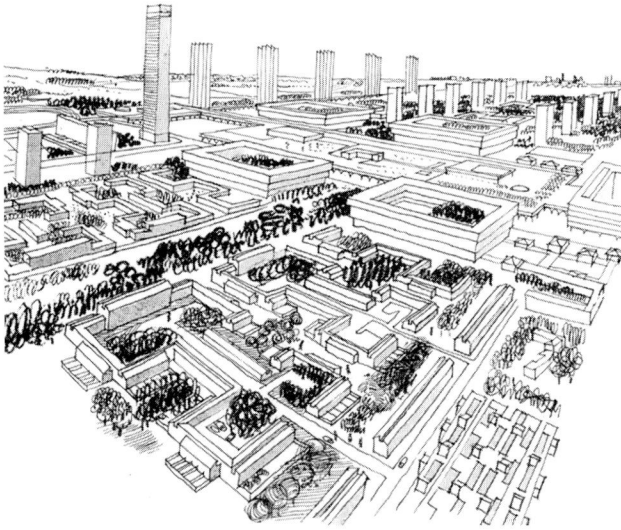

5.7
**Scheme for the regeneration of Boston Manor (1958): general view from the south-east**

## 'Better towns for better living'

The fluency and cohesion of the design for New Boston showed what was achievable when the preparation of a case for renewal involved only a handful of people and was unencumbered by the raft of complexities that surrounded the SPUR exhibition. Christoph Bon, the organiser, produced initial costings for the latter in November 1958 that set the cost at £1500. Various economy measures, such as the omission of film clips, reduced costs to £1170.[115] The scenario for the exhibition followed in February 1959, with accompanying sketches (see Figure 5.8).[116] As with the somewhat smaller 'Turn Again' exhibition, the displays largely involved photographs and illustrations, but the final policy section would include models loaned by members' practices. As the floor plan shows, the intention was that visitors would experience the sections in sequence, with the unfolding view of the displays mediated by the arrangement of the panels. The panels themselves comprised standard flush doors, an economic and effective basis for staging displays that could subsequently be demounted for touring. These could be freestanding or hung horizontally from supporting structures, as in the cross-section in Figure 5.8, although reporters at the exhibition later reported that this strategy had the disadvantage of 'the disconcerting number of legs one can see underneath'.[117] The tower supplied a visual focus, reminiscent of a tower block with large appended photographs.

Bon's scenario envisaged the exhibition starting with photographs showing a variety of town people engaged in their typical activities throughout the day (Area 1). Visitors could walk freely among these panels, thus identifying themselves with the situation. 'If possible, one or two large mirrors should be included to enhance this impression'. Area 2 comprised 'examples (large photos on continuous panels) symbolising some of the major defects and problems of today's towns'. Intended 'to be limited to a minimum', this part might communicate

5.8
**SPUR exhibition
scenario,
Christoph Bon
(February 1959)**

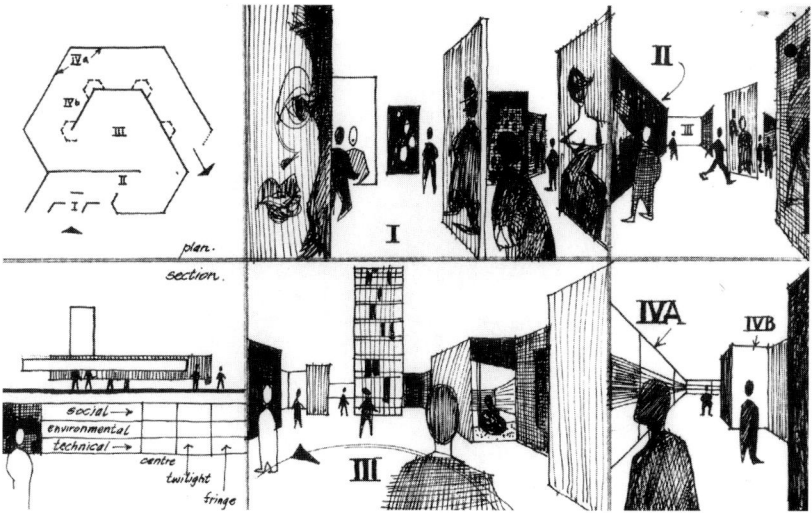

5.8
**SPUR exhibition
scenario,
Christoph Bon
(February 1959)**

such ideas as inconvenience, monotony, lack of open space, overcrowding, neglect, squalor, unpleasantness and disorder. Area 3 would communicate the idea of the city as 'a civilised meeting place'. This would be non-directional because 'one of the essential qualities of a town [is] that one can move when and where one likes. As far as there is any sequence in the illustrations, this can best be described as a "day in a town"'. From the open town square, the visitors moved on to the fourth area, 'The Way Forward'. This was intended to cover issues concerned with good visual design, 'a desire for compactness and walking scale', the conviction that single type zoning leads to monotony, the need for adequate open space, the importance of good husbandry of resources, and that 'roads should serve towns and not dominate them'. In design terms, Bon proposed composing the space 'rather austerely on a grid pattern' and differentiating each of the major headings (e.g. social, environmental and technical) by its own colour. Area 5 should contain:

> a statement of policy, recapitulating all important previous suggestions on what should be done and including references to a programme, the need for large scale experiments and methods of how to propagate planning proposals. A second large mirror, similar to that suggested in section I, might be placed at the end of the Exhibition in order to remind the visitor again that he is not only looking at these problems from the outside, but that they are his own problems as much as anyone else's.[118]

The exhibition lacked a name for several months. A General Committee meeting in January 1959 recorded that 'neither the "SPUR exhibition" nor "The Living Town" was regarded as entirely suitable.'[119] Only in March, when the need to start publicity activities became pressing, did the group eventually decide on the title 'SPUR Exhibition: Better Towns for Better Living'.[120] The main problem then was to translate the scenario into the final displays. Time was short, the organisers worked on a tight budget, and the study groups often wanted more materials included than could be comfortably accommodated. The demands of sponsors further complicated matters. Lacking its own funds, SPUR had sought funds from the construction industry and institutions such as the RIBA, Town Planning Institute and the Civic Trust. Most made no demands and relations with the RIBA, the main material and financial sponsor, provided few difficulties given the overlap of personnel concerned with the exhibition and the symposium. The Civic Trust, itself founded in 1957, was more intrusive in pursuit of its own agenda. Its financial support rested on provisos that the event must be accessible for 'the layman', that a version would be available 'so that its effect is not lost after the week or so that it will be on exhibition at the RIBA', and that the Civic Trust received mention in the descriptive matter.[121] As a result, its representatives repeatedly pressed their concerns about the exhibition's size, complexity, suitability for touring and appropriateness for a general audience. Perhaps out of deference to the Housing Centre's concern to achieve a broadly based reformist constituency for its projects, too, SPUR refused an offer of assistance from the newly formed 'Anti-Ugly Action' (Chapter 2) to help publicise the exhibition,[122] even though the two groups shared common ground.

Alarmed at the slow progress, Christoph Bon prepared a blueprint timetable,[123] which laid out the work necessary from 28 March through to the exhibition's opening on 21 May. CPB, rather than just Bon, took on the central tasks of organisation, despite concurrently being heavily involved in producing plans and models for the Barbican. CPB collected in the material from SPUR's study groups and from individual members and added additional linking materials, from which they prepared the panels. Brett prepared the text for the exhibition leaflet, which recycled large elements of previous statements of group policy. Hired consultants took on the remaining tasks of assembly and other technical work. The minutes of working meetings, however, suggest that discussions were often inconclusive. As late as 1 May 1959, the secretary wrote: 'It was almost impossible to write Minutes of our session the other evening, but I suppose one ought to have something on the book'.[124] Preparations lagged consistently behind schedule and there remained large gaps in the exhibition even at the time of the press viewing.

When formally opened by the RIBA's president Basil Spence on 21 May, the exhibition followed the agreed sequence of stages and had now reached some consensus on the conclusions that SPUR wished to impart to visitors. These centred on advocacy of multilevel circulation, 'exploiting the third dimension to liberate planning and architecture from the tyranny of the road pattern' and the building of new towns within cities.[125] The policy section offered models that hinted at a townscape comprising the familiar combination of modern buildings and capacious roadways, but in a disjointed manner that resulted from the exhibits being made for other purposes rather than being custom-built for the exhibition. The wall displays pleaded in small typeface for more funds for renewal, for the launching of experimental pilot schemes to test out unfamiliar and novel ideas for urban renewal, and for the establishment of a state-sponsored and financed National Urban Renewal Agency backed by local reconstruction committees.

## Towards a charter

The exhibition, of course, was only part of a larger event, albeit with overlapping personnel. The one-day symposium on 'The Living Town', chaired by William Holford, heard papers delivered by speakers with links to the LCC's experience (Johnson-Marshall, Ling, Matthew, Bennett and Richard Edmonds) and SPUR (Brett and Chamberlin), along with Sir Hugh Casson and David Percival (City Architect for Norwich). During the week of the exhibition, SPUR ran three discussion sessions on 'communities and neighbourhoods', 'public and private transport' and 'the big city'.[126] These components received good audiences and generated lively debate. By contrast, the exhibition evoked immediate and intense disappointment. Besides leaving the inevitable debts due to exceeding the budget, there were questions about the value of the exercise. Noel Tweddell, the Civic Trust's deputy director and also Chief Architect-Planner for Basildon, expressed his feelings forcefully in a letter to Brett:

> I must confess to being deeply disappointed. To think that after all that effort and money has gone into something which I fear will not advance the cause of architecture, or planning, or urban renewal is very galling. I hope I am not suffering from despondency – and therefore being too bitter. I'd easily list a host of things that I think were wrong with its presentation, no defined circulation, inadequate and unreadable captions, a confusing selection of photographs, no conclusions etc. It certainly leaves no memory with anyone I've talked to. But where do we go from there?[127]

This led to a spirited response from Brett, although shortly afterwards he confessed to Margaret Solomon, also a critic:

> I agree with all you say about SPUR generally, and about the Exhibition. I personally was greatly disappointed in it, but was too busy defending it against the Civic Trust to have time to criticise it to the designers, who in any case were in a state of collapse on the opening day. There were too many muddle-headed people involved, but what can one do but accept the devoted people who volunteer, whatever their findings, and trust them.
>
> My object in suggesting a general meeting was to let some air in and try to strengthen the non-architect contingent, since I am sure that economics is our Achilles heel, and is the key to the whole thing.[128]

In part, the problem lay in the lack of a defining vision. By coincidence, the same journals publishing accounts of the SPUR exhibition also carried reports and photographs of Chamberlin, Powell and Bon's model for the Barbican scheme – in one case, side by side.[129] The former inevitably suffered by comparison.

For the immediate future, the group repackaged the exhibition for touring purposes based around the principles of 'halving its size, increasing and clarifying its captioning, and redesigning the final section in a shorter and more telling form'. Ideas for longer-term activities included thoughts of a second exhibition on 'Conservation, Rehabilitation, Redevelopment' and for a 'stepping up of SPUR's economist membership and economic investigations'.[130] Yet the most pressing task remained that of filling the major gaps apparent from the contents of the exhibition. For all the words and effort, SPUR had yet to provide a working definition of what it meant by 'urban renewal' or to provide a convincing synthesis, despite the preponderance of architects among its members, as to what good practice in urban renewal might look like.

The task of defining 'urban renewal', and SPUR's aims in relation to it, became the group's major undertaking until the publication of the SPUR 1960 Report in February 1961.[131] It caught the mood of changing times. It was published in the same month, for example, as the Bow Group's pamphlet *Let our Cities Live*,[132] which dealt with the idea of creating 'improvement areas' to regenerate decaying urban areas and the need to widen the territorial basis of urban planning. SPUR saw urban renewal on a regional basis as covering the 'rebuilding of the obsolete tracts of our towns and cities and the creation of new towns within suburbia not only as social imperatives for their own sake, but also as safeguards against unnecessary inroads into the countryside'.[133] Its report addressed problems of density, the difficulties of central areas and smaller towns, renewal techniques, the support for new towns within suburban areas of existing towns, and the need for both local self-help and the foundation of a National Urban Renewal Research and Development Agency.

Specifically, the authors imparted scepticism about density and notions of single land-use zoning, noting that most density studies assumed 'homogeneity of land use which is unrealistic, and neglect the substantial economies that can be made by multiple use'.[134] It sought decentralisation, but only within the context of conurbations rather than decanting people and jobs out to other authorities as overspill. On central areas, the report rejected the American combination of freeways and suburban decentralisation seeking instead more homes in the centre and more jobs in the suburbs. Locally, it made sense to tie in urban developments with access to transport, with residential and office densities allowed to rise to a peak near public transport nodes. Crucially, however, there was complete faith in the value of urban motorways:

> the need for a greatly accelerated urban motorway programme remains, and it is vital that all new road works in central areas should be planned on the principle of vertical segregation, the number and use of the various levels depending on the traffic and pedestrian density in each case.[135]

It was a judgement that typified much of the thinking about the future shape of town centres as the 1960s opened.

# Chapter 6

# Heart and soul

**'Urban renewal' is a new phrase for an age old process – the redevelopment and improvement of buildings and even whole areas as they become outworn, outgrown or outdated. It is a slow but continuous process. In essence it is spontaneous and random. In the past it has sufficed to ensure that our towns and cities have become gradually adjusted to contemporary conditions. Today under the impact of rapid social and technological changes more conscious action is needed to guide renewal processes. The problems are complex. They are not confined to the largest towns; they will concern all towns in the years ahead.**

**Ministry of Housing and Local Government and Ministry of Transport[1]**

The changing economic climate led to renewed thinking about suitable approaches to the design of the central city. The above statement, taken from an advisory paper jointly published in 1962 by the two ministries most closely involved in remaking the city, showed that the rebranding exercise outlined in Chapter 5 was underway. Like other rebranding exercises, it spoke by definition to an older, tired agenda – in this case, the need for cities to respond to society's present-day needs while retaining their character and identity. What made the task qualitatively different from the past was the new agenda of technology and change. Although the authors' wording counselled respect for the city's historic character and paid lip service to rhetoric about the social purpose embodied in reconstruction, there was no doubt that change was the expectation or even the norm. It was assumed that the necessary change would come through adopting a scientific approach based on an expert and 'objective appraisal of the town centre as it is today'.[2] It would involve dispassionate assessment of the town's function in relation to others in the same region, its importance for those citizens that used it, its value as a shopping, commercial and social centre, and 'its civic character and architectural qualities'.[3] Change would exploit the opportunities available as 'an investment in the future', but renewal clearly rested on two premises: accepting public–private partnerships as a normal part of the redevelopment process and adopting radical rethinking towards the replanning of roads.

The former was already in progress, led sometimes by planners and sometimes by developers.[4] Public–private partnerships supplied opportunities for architects to design and build, often with considerable freedom of action within the scope of planning regulations (see Chapter 3), but did so on discrete projects governed by commercial considerations. The results already indicated problems when considering the wider picture. A cursory glance at the appearance and skyline of central cities throughout Great Britain suggested that planning permission was no guarantor of architectural quality and that 'co-option by commerce' was an eventuality for which the founding philosophies of modernism 'offered little guidance'.[5] Undoubtedly private sector participation in the rebuilding of town centres did generate important new sources of funding, particularly from the coffers of cash-rich insurance companies and pension funds. This was already a well-established procedure in the USA. In 1957, for example, the Prudential Insurance Company bought a 31-acre (12.5-hectare) plot on the south side of Boston's Back Bay district with a pledge to provide the city, then suffering from the flight of the middle classes to the suburbs and economic stagnation, with 'the world's largest integrated business, civic and residential centre'.[6] In Britain, the planning system did not allow the same scope for intervention that the American tradition of free enterprise readily permitted,[7] but development saw property groups, acting in collaboration with local authorities, take the lead in channelling the resources that the investment arms of the Legal and General, Pearl, Sun Life and the rest made available.

Inevitably, the piecemeal nature of such interventions did little to help create lively town centres that would serve not only as the core of the city but also as its heart and soul. Related to this, the wave of building activity occurred in an age that valued mass production for lowering costs and achieving efficiency but believed that flexibility could stem from imaginative, indeed endlessly flexible arrangement of the standardised parts. Application of these ideas to town centre design clearly excited the major construction firms, which readily sensed their opportunity to advertise their expertise in offering packaged deals for sale in a new and expanding market. Harry Vincent, the chairman of Bovis, spoke for the industry when he urged architects to 'think big' and 'build big'. He noted that the growth of interest in the renewal of town centres was seeing 'very large imaginative' schemes that might well incorporate 'a new town hall, public library and bus garage, all the present ones being removed and rehoused so as to create a proper precinct shopping centre'. Vincent recognised the prejudice against packaged deals but argued that they 'definitely provide for certain needs both in the public and commercial fields'.[8] Quite what comprised those 'needs' was a matter for debate. What remains incontrovertible is that the commodification of building into deliverable packages by the construction industry mediated the results when architectural modernism was translated into practice.

The second premise, the need for radical rethinking of road planning, was similarly already in progress. In June 1961, the Ministry of Transport had established a steering group for the study of the long-term problems of traffic in towns under Sir Geoffrey Crowther and a study group under Colin Buchanan to present a report to them. The resulting report,[9] published in 1963 and universally referred to as the Buchanan Report, became one of the most widely read planning documents of the 1960s. Walter Bor and Graeme Shankland, in charge of the teams responsible for planning the renewal of Liverpool, were sufficiently impressed by the report to announce that 'most, if not all, current Development Plans were obsolete and that a radically different approach was needed to deal with urban planning problems'.[10] As Peter Hall noted, it galvanised thinking: 'I know that I was obsessed, as were others, by the idea that "look, you do not know what is coming. Look at the Buchanan Report – a threefold increase in car ownership"'.[11]

There was effectively something in the Buchanan Report for most of the professionals concerned with urban renewal. It resonated with ideas favoured by highway engineers in local authority planning departments, particularly the notion that older urban cores could be opened up to accommodate modern traffic and communications flows on a wholesale basis.[12] Architecturally, too, it addressed key areas of concern. It embraced a wider conception of architecture, reflecting Buchanan's own view of architects as 'town-rebuilders'.[13] The report echoed modernist thought on functional order in road provision and multilevel circulation – an impression well conveyed by Kenneth Browne's accompanying perspectives.[14] Figures 6.1 and 6.2, for example, show the potential of complete and partial redevelopment schemes for an area of central London west of the Tottenham Court Road. Figure 6.1 depicts a machine-dominated space that celebrates the transforming potential of the car. Its multilevel arrangements, urban motorways, pedestrian movement at first-floor podium level, interchanges by lift and escalator, point blocks and slabs all fitted the thinking of the time – including the curious obliviousness to the resulting environmental conditions. Figure 6.2 matched these sensitivities in its depiction of the partial redevelopment scheme, albeit with the 'modern' here blending with the best of the past. The background depicts the Georgian splendours of Fitzroy Square, now largely reserved for pedestrians. The central part shows respect for this valued past by the way that the modern town houses retain the building line of their predecessors, but showing added functionality by their unusually heavily populated roof gardens. In the foreground, the pedestrian level rises to the upper levels predominant through much of the scheme.

Yet despite the attention and excitement, successive governments declined to implement the Buchanan Report's recommendations. Seen as too expensive 'by a fag-end Conservative Government', it subsequently appeared 'too minimalist in support of public transport by the incoming Labour administration'.[15] Instead, what occurred was partial application of Buchanan principles as town councils rethought the traffic arrangements and development potential of their central areas. The 1960s saw central area renewal or, at least, thinking about central area renewal as de rigueur, with local councils throughout Great Britain feeling the

6.1
**An impression of
the scheme for
complete
redevelopment,
looking along one
of the district
distributors
(Buchanan Report,
1963)**

need to prepare plans that looked ahead to a new and *different* future. Each issue of the professional journals for the 1960s gave prominence to another new crop of schemes for cities, larger towns, metropolitan boroughs, market towns and seaside resorts. *Official Architecture and Planning* for 1963, for example, covered town centre redevelopments in Blackburn, Bracknell, Cambridge, Canterbury, Dewsbury, Doncaster, Ellesmere Port, Fulham, Hammersmith, Kingston-upon-Thames, Leicester, Manchester, Margate, Salford, Shrewsbury, Stockport and West Kensington. In 1964, it was the turn of Bristol, Liverpool, Piccadilly Circus, Ramsgate, Sutton, Wath-upon-Dearne, West Bromwich, Wigan and Wood Green. These lists, of course, merely scratched the surface, presenting brief analyses of schemes that the editors thought worthy of readers' attention. The complete inventory was much greater, with one observer estimating that by early 1965 there were 'four hundred or more urban renewal schemes now at one stage of preparation or another'.[16] A substantial number of these schemes were never started. Most of the remainder were never fully implemented, but truncated in the early 1970s before completion as the climate of ideas surrounding urban redevelopment changed. Nevertheless, it was during these few years that the urban fabric changed more dramatically than almost any comparable period in British history.[17]

Behind the hectic activity lay local authorities at last beginning to use the powers available under the 1947 Act to declare Comprehensive Development Areas and then to apply compulsory purchase powers to demolish existing buildings, erase the road network and undertake complete rebuilding in the interests of the town as a whole.[18] The results shown on the plans were predictable. The typical future city

5.2
An impression of
the scheme for
partial
redevelopment
(Buchanan Report,
1963)

centre would see the imposition of single land-use planning. It would be bounded by a ring road and see gestures towards multilevel circulation (subways, pedestrian bridges and occasionally escalator systems). It would have multi-storey car parks and pedestrianised precincts. Shopping centres and civic centres would replace high streets and town halls. Towns from Sutton to Leicester were to have 'piazzas', as new squares and public meeting places were optimistically termed. New theatres and bus stations were also much in vogue. Historic listed buildings would be left as isolated islands, silent reminders of the town's past. Other buildings were judged unsentimentally in terms of their continuing functional value.

That, at least, was the rhetoric. In practice, what occurred depended on the policies and outlooks of the individual councils and, in particular, how eagerly they engaged in the clearance process. Some towns had longstanding plans for central area redevelopment or civic improvement, perhaps dating back to the interwar period or before, and made an early start in pushing modernisation ahead when resources became available. Other councils responded enthusiastically to the prospect of a new start with uncompromising, large-scale modernising projects that created an abrupt break with the past, but these seldom reached completion before the mood of the times irrevocably changed. Yet others acted more conservatively, doing relatively little other than to exercise a measure of development control over commercial office and retail developments. This variation, of course, would have long-term implications. As Paul Barker observed:

> Actual choices are involved, that is my point; it is possible even under those pressures to decide not to do it. . . . It was often those towns and

cities, run by councils unable to lift their eyes above the horizon that spared themselves the problems that councils, who prided themselves on having greater imagination, inflicted on their cities.[19]

This chapter samples this diversity. Its opening section starts the survey at the more cautious end of the scale by examining the experience of Portsmouth, a heavily blitzed city that delayed central city renewal until the mid-1960s. The next sections briefly survey a selection of provincial cities, highlighting how central area redevelopment normally brought major overhauls to the road system and large-scale shopping centres created through public–private partnerships. The civic realm of public buildings and civic centres, as the next section shows, proved more difficult. The intrinsically slow pace of civic centre development fell foul of changing resource availability and reappraisal of the architecture that left many planned large-scale and integrated civic centres unbuilt after years of preparatory work. The final sections focus on London, examining the variation in progress towards town centre renewal exhibited by the outer boroughs, before considering case studies that revealed the difficulty of redevelopment within the central city.

## Recovery from the Blitz

The centre of Portsmouth remained in urgent need of renewal at the start of the 1960s. Its proximity to the key wartime naval base on the south coast of England meant that it suffered severe collateral damage from blast and incendiary bombs. This not only caused physical destruction to properties, but also added the problem of loss of rateable value from firms that saw their premises destroyed. Early schemes for wholesale reconstruction foundered on grounds of cost given the termination of government special assistance to blitzed cities in March 1948 and the ruling local Conservative administration's unwillingness to commit large amounts of ratepayers' money to the rebuilding task.[20] In their absence came ad hoc developments that failed to tackle wider planning needs.[21] During the 1950s, commercial developers and the local authority widened and rebuilt the main shopping street (Commercial Road) with large stone-fronted stores and recon-structed the gutted Guildhall. A five-year plan unveiled in 1961 proposed further development of the shopping centre. A roundabout implausibly decked with 'trees, lawns and fountains' would dominate the Guildhall Square, 'surrounded by 80 shops, a departmental store, a multi-storey hotel, offices, flats, [and] a multi-storey garage'.[22]

Recognising that such development needed a master plan to provide a coherent basis for future policy, the City Council approached Lionel Brett (shortly to become Lord Esher) to act as consultant. In June 1963, he became Coordinating Consulting Architect for the scheme to redevelop the Guildhall and surrounding district. The designated area covered approximately 38 acres (15 hectares) bordered by the railway, South Brighton Street, Hyde Park Road and St Michael's Street. The commission quickly developed into something larger than just coordinating central area projects. A council minute from September 1963 made it clear that there had been second thoughts:

The Town Clerk stated that it was clear from the reaction of the Development and Estates Committee following Mr Brett's appointment that they were looking to him for something much more extensive than when the decision to make the appointment was first made. The Committee were hoping that Mr Brett would begin by making general recommendations with regard to the redevelopment of the area and that he would include in the scope of his report and recommendations not only the immediate area of the Guildhall itself, but also the surrounding areas.[23]

The district at the time still contained bombsites, with other areas showing the effects of prolonged planning blight.[24] Esher remembered the area around the Guildhall as largely derelict: 'Out in front of it was a kind of engineer's wasteland. Beyond was a wasteland with donkeys grazing on it'.[25] His colleague, Harry Teggin, elaborated on this:

> we were appointed to do a plan . . . from Commercial Road right round to the Law Courts. At the time that we were appointed, in front of the Guildhall were a public lavatory and a statue of Queen Victoria in the middle of a roundabout. And a hundred yards away there were gypsies camping on waste ground left over from the war. It had no focus. The Guildhall was built against the embankment of the railway and the Cenotaph was stuffed in between [it and] the embankment. . . . It had no personality at all.[26]

The first master plan, presented in March 1964 as a report with an accompanying model, laid out 'an appreciation' of the historical, functional and aesthetic aspects of the city centre and a first approach to the guidelines for the redevelopment. The plan and accompanying scale model visualised the Guildhall area as a pedestrianised space with a civic square, rather than the machine-defined space envisaged in the City Council's 1961 proposals. A wide flight of steps in front of the Guildhall would help to create a ceremonial space for the Navy, then Portsmouth's main employer. The council offices, contained in a curtain-walled glass building, would occupy two sides of the Guildhall Square.

The plan attracted favourable reaction, with contemporary reports stressing the intention to lend a 'continental touch' to Portsmouth, with open-air cafés and shops with canopies.[27] The City Council accepted these ideas in principle in May 1964, but began a local debate 'to decide on the next steps to be taken to carry the scheme a stage further towards a physical start'.[28] The Ministry of Housing and Local Government put the scheme to public inquiry in 1966, which approved the proposals, and confirmed a compulsory purchase order in 1967 for the purchase of properties. After site clearance, construction of the new road pattern began in 1969. Finance caused slower progress on the Civic Offices. Back in 1967, the City Council had explored whether to form a partnership with the private development company, Oldham Investments Ltd, run by the property developer Harry Hyams.

This had expressed interest in carrying out development, on the basis of a deal that included financing the civic office block with the council as tenants. When Oldham's terms made this out of the question, Esher sought to update the scale model as a way of interesting prospective developers.[29]

However, the plan itself was in need of updating given the passage of years. Esher's second version, published in April 1970, amended the first plan in light of changing requirements and circumstances, such as the construction of a six-lane urban motorway around the fringes of the area. It also set out the design parameters for the control of development into the 1970s. The plan (Figure 6.3) diverted city traffic round a new circuit, feeding three multi-storey car parks that provided approximately 3000 car spaces; these, in turn, connected to a new pedestrian network. The plan proposed pedestrianising segments of the central area and rationalising the pattern of land uses while stressing that 'the more they interpenetrate and interact the better'.[30] Architecturally, the prime focus was to retain vistas of the Guildhall's portico:

> The Guildhall area, until recently the only part of Portsmouth, except the Southsea front, where buildings above walk-up height had congregated, is now itself dwarfed by a background of huge anonymous housing blocks. It will need to make a powerful architectural statement if it is to hold its own as the heart of the City Centre.
>
> Fortunately the Guildhall portico on its noble flight of steps does this, and everything must be done to back it up.[31]

This suggested use of oblique views and surprise glimpses of the Guildhall's grandeur rather than axial planning based on the centre line of its façade. The latter style of planning had little appeal since it would

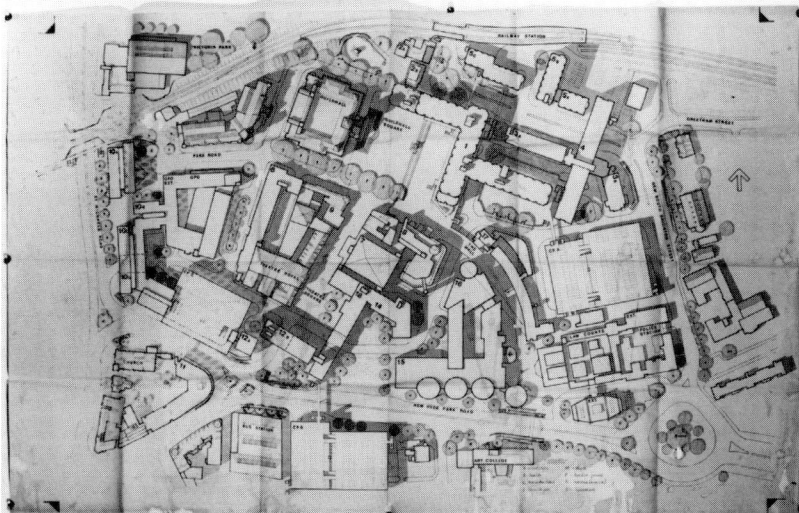

6.3
**Plan for Portsmouth Central Area (Bret▮ and Pollen, 1970)**

lead nowhere, be consequently unused, and show the Guildhall to least advantage. Much better to create a functional pedestrian route on the diagonal from the SE [south-east] corner of the Square in the direction of the Law Courts and the College of Art. This route should be gently curved on plan so that the pedestrian approaching from the SE is attracted by curiosity and rewarded by a surprise view of the great portico at a certain point in the bend.

An associated sketch (Figure 6.4), reminiscent of the Townscape school (see Chapter 12), illustrated this point. The Guildhall, 'the enclosing form' of the new seven-storey Civic Offices (for which Brett and Pollen received the commission), and the City Library (designed by the City Architect) flanked the pedestrianised Guildhall Square. Esher enthused over the conception:

This was the best job that we ever had and the buildings that we did were dark and, I think, very good of their kind. [The Civic Offices] occupied two sides of the square and on the third side, of the three that faced the old Guildhall was the new City Library, somewhat copied from Frank Lloyd Wright's great Guggenheim Museum on Fifth Avenue in that concrete manner – a deliberate contrast from our dark glass building.[32]

6.4
View towards the War
Memorial from the Guildhall
Steps

The plan set aside a large area adjacent to the Civic Offices for lettable office accommodation, with the intention of drawing in private developers. Tucked away near the station where building height was not an issue, this 'city-scale' development (Figure 6.5) could exceed the seven storeys of the Civic Offices and contrasted with the more intimate scale of other aspects of the scheme.

## Tricorn

The council trumpeted the resulting plan as now providing 'the last opportunity in any major British city to create a civic centre of the seventies built on the lessons learnt in the postwar years'.[33] Not all developments within central Portsmouth, however, came within the ambit of the city centre scheme. Portsmouth City Council had held talks with developers with a view to improving existing shopping areas or developing new ones in other parts of the central area. A notable example was the Tricorn Centre (Figure 6.6). Designed by Rodney Gordon and the Design Section of the Owen Luder Partnership for the E. Alec Colman Group, the Tricorn Centre occupied a roughly triangular 3.3-acre (1.3-hectare) site situated between Charlotte Street (a narrow side street containing market stalls) and a dual carriageway. Opened in 1966, the exterior finish of the Tricorn Centre in rough shuttered concrete matched the Brutalist idiom. Spiral access ramps at the ends of the complex served the two stacks of boat-shaped parking decks, staggered vertically and linked by crossovers.[34] In plan, the Tricorn comprised a pedestrian precinct with ground-level shopping around a central square (55 shops and a supermarket), a restaurant (later used as a nightclub), nursery, bowling alley and a public house. The first floor housed the city's wholesale fruit and vegetable market. The upper floors provided 490 parking places.[35] Its texture of dense, dark and maze-like interior spaces gave the

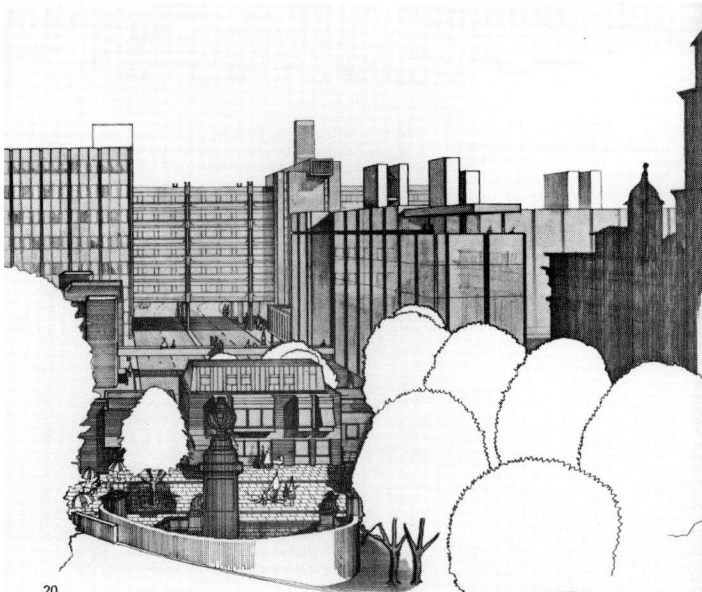

6.5
**Looking east along New Greetham Street from behind the War Memorial**

114

6.6
**Tricorn Centre,
Portsmouth
(Owen Luder
Partnership, 1968):
view of front
along Market Way**

scheme the feel of a 'casbah'. This term, first used by Owen Luder about the practice's unsuccessful entry to the Elephant and Castle Shopping Centre competition (Chapter 5), was picked up by press coverage, which described the Tricorn Centre as 'an exotic essay in reinforced concrete, using towers, pyramids and minarets to give it an Eastern feel – the character of the Casbah'.[36]

The Tricorn Centre followed a pattern for building concrete structures developed by the practice (see Chapter 3). For the exterior, Gordon based his design strategy in equal measures on aesthetics, economy and mistrust of the British construction industry. The key consideration was the poor quality of the shuttered concrete that most contractors could manage, a lesson that he had learned from working on an earlier project:

> One thing that I learned at Eros [House] in Catford [South London] was that . . . the contractors were going to build it and that they had never before built a major scheme of this kind. I realised that the quality of the shuttered concrete was certainly not going to be up to the quality of the South Bank, because we couldn't afford the specification to that extent. Therefore I learned that the more convoluted you made the shape, the less the inaccuracies of the pourer of the concrete are going to be noticed. So that there is an incentive to make it more dynamic and sculptural because the more convoluted you can fit things together, the less you are going to notice the raw quality of the material.[37]

The presence of the fruit and vegetable market on the first floor provided an opportunity for inclusion of further sculptural forms in providing access:

> The main task was to solve the circulation pattern. The inclusion of a wholesale fruit and vegetable market off the ground and putting it up a level and having car parking. So you had to have ramps. The most economic way of keeping as much land as possible at ground level is to make them circular. I would then sketch an idea and make them cantilevered and circular, and we would all work it up. The philosophy was mine but the expression was us.[38]

**115**

The Tricorn Centre opened in 1966 and won a Civic Trust award in 1967 for its 'exciting visual composition'. An authoritative contemporary review praised the centre for 'bustling with life' and admired its 'sense of place' predicting its future as 'a distinctive symbol of the town' that would act as 'a magnet within the area'.[39] Its subsequent troubled history, due to a mixture of poor location and constructional problems, lies outside the time-span covered by this book but Tricorn exemplified a contemporaneous approach to integrated structures that private and public sector alike used in renewing the central city. Bold decisions on large-scale clearance and renewal seemed to suggest, even demand, large-scale and imaginative solutions. Ideas of scale, enclosure, potent symbols and car-orientation were in the air as powerful spurs to innovation.

### 'This redevelopment way of life'
These thoughts resonated with developments in other provincial cities as local administrations commenced the long awaited tasks of central area renewal. Psychologically, there was a deep-rooted sense that this was a key moment in the lives of cities. City centres were the heart of urban life. Failure to grasp modernity and introduce change could leave central areas languishing, damage local businesses and condemn a town to second-class status in relation to regional rivals. By contrast, positive and uncompromising decisions could say much about its thrusting, progressive and dynamic nature. Civic pride and place promotion were at stake as well as the need for modernisation.

Newcastle upon Tyne had few peers with regard to linking renewal to wider agendas. Wilfred Burns, the City Planning Officer, placed timidity at the top of his listing of ills that beset 'this redevelopment way of life' and was keen to ensure that Newcastle's approach did not suffer from this failing.[40] Its earliest major expression, the 1961 *Plan for the Centre of Newcastle*,[41] envisaged a redevelopment that would 'accentuate' Newcastle's role as 'the centre for the North-East Region'. The plan, described by Basil Spence as 'the most adventurous ever created in this country',[42] proposed that 'the expanded and redeveloped shopping centre based on a new system of traffic free pedestrian routes should be served by underground and multi-storey car parks and be enclosed by a system of urban motorways'.[43] The plan allowed the continued access of cars to the central area from the urban motorway system, but with longer-stay car parks to help remove vehicles from central city streets (Figure 6.7). Limited use of a pedestrian deck around the new Central Library introduced a multilevel approach that would simultaneously help to create vehicle-free areas and speed up through-traffic. The plan allowed for the Eldon Square Shopping Centre (Chapman Taylor and Wilfred Burns, 1969–75), the partly completed All Saints Office Precinct (T.P. Bennett and Basil Spence, started 1969) and the Central Education Precinct. The last of these developments, an innovative means of bringing higher education into the central life of the city, emerged from the redevelopment of the district in and around Lovaine Place, to the west of Shieldfield. The destruction of this 'far from slum working-class area' said much about Wilfred Burns' priorities.[44] As David Byrne commented: 'Burns was ingenuous about "socially outworn housing". For him it

6.7
**Manners Street car park, Newcastle upon Tyne (photograph 2005)**

had a remarkable tendency to be located in areas where central area-related developments were going to be put.'[45]

The schemes implemented in the 1960s, however, were not necessarily new creations. The development of the Central Education Precinct and the extraordinary Civic Centre (Figure 6.8), for example, look like products of ebullient 1960s modernism, but were products of a previous generation's thinking. Like many towns and cities, Newcastle had longstanding ambitions to improve its civic buildings, which, in this case, surfaced shortly after the First World War. More formal plans dated back to 1934 when Robert Burns Dick proposed a Beaux-Arts design for Exhibition Park in 1934 near Barras Bridge. In 1945, the heavily modernist municipal *Plan for Newcastle* suggested the same area for a civic centre and academic precinct.[46] Although both these plans remained unrealised, the City Council did eventually chose Barras Bridge as the location for the new Civic Centre, moving the focus of municipal government away from its symbolic connection with the medieval town. Although built between 1960 and 1969 and with apparent echoes of Brasilia, the Civic Centre actually dates from designs produced from the early 1950s onwards by George Kenyon, Newcastle's long-serving City Architect. Not surprisingly, therefore, the building resonates with the Scandinavian influences popular at that time, with resemblances to the City Halls of Stockholm (R. Ostberg,

**117**

6.8
**Civic Centre,
Newcastle upon
Tyne (George
Kenyon, 1960–9)**

1911–23) and Oslo (A. Arneberg and M. Poulsson, 1931–50). Externally finished in Portland stone and Norwegian Otta slate, its quadrangular form around a central green space and its circular chapter-house-like council chamber suggest monastic influences.[47]

Glasgow equalled Newcastle's proactive approach to renewal, prompting leading observers to suggest that the acronym CDA really stood for Comprehensive *Demolition* Area.[48] The twenty-year programme announced in 1957 echoed the 'radical and reckless' approach of the 1945 Bruce plan (see Chapter 5),[49] without necessarily replicating its provisions. Approximately one-twelfth of the city's 60 square miles, comprising 29 separate areas, was designated for comprehensive redevelopment. Most were working-class housing districts in inner parts of the city and industrial areas along the Clyde, noticeably leaving the outer zones of middle-class housing almost untouched by clearance.[50] Although never fully completed, the projected scale of activity suggested turning the entire city into a building site, with a determined attempt to tackle Glasgow's endemic

6.9
Urban motorway,
West End,
Glasgow
(photograph
March 1976)

housing problem (see Chapter 8) and its perceived infrastructural deficiencies at one fell swoop. The creation of a motorway-grade Inner Ring Road around the northern and western flanks of the central area (Figure 6.9), including the construction of a new river crossing at Kingston Bridge (completed 1970), brought enormous changes to former areas of working-class housing like Woodlands, Garnethill and Anderston through which it passed.

Yet despite the extensive effort, implementation of clearance was slower than predicted. The necessities of detailed preparation, plan submission and approval, and complex compulsory purchase orders meant that in 1969, 12 years into the original 20-year development period, Glasgow had still sought the approval of the Secretary of State to commence work on only 9 out of the 29 CDAs.[51] With that elapse in time came the possibility of changing priorities. The eastern parts of the city, particularly Townhead, were spared large-scale destruction when it was decided to abandon the eastern and southern sections of the Inner Ring Road, despite link roads already being in place. Similarly, a proposal for vertical segregation of pedestrians and vehicles along Sauchiehall Street, pedestrianised at ground level with cars carried on an elevated carriageway, led only to some truncated spurs before eventual abandonment of the scheme (Figure 6.10)

Progress was patchy, with the extent of change often reflecting how early the scheme featured in the renewal programme. The Hutchesontown-Gorbals CDA, cleared for housing, witnessed complete transformation (see Chapter 8). The Anderston Cross CDA, designated in 1961, also saw active and sustained clearance. Previously a densely packed area of tenement housing with a busy train and tram interchange, it saw the population fall by 66.9 per cent from 21,457 to 9265 between 1961 and 1971.[52] Although large areas of land transferred from housing to circulation uses, most notably with the construction of the Inner Ring Road, the area gained an intended new focus in the shape of Anderston Centre (Figure 6.11). Designed by the Richard Seifert Co-Partnership for the Taylor Woodrow Group

**119**

6.10
**Road at end of
Sauchiehall
Street, Glasgow
(photograph
March 1976)**

(1967–73), the centre was an integrated scheme that, as originally proposed, contained car parking, services and a bus station under a deck which brought together thirty-three shops, two departmental stores, a 60,000 square feet supermarket, an entertainments centre, and three blocks of flats.[53] Poorly located in relation to the main shopping centre and unattractive to both shoppers and businesses, the department store and entertainments centre never materialised and the shops found trading conditions difficult. Large sections were demolished in the early 1990s.

Compared with the maelstrom taking place elsewhere, the area within the projected boundaries of the Inner Ring Road remained relatively unchanged, with the exception of the tenemented areas of Townhead and the Gorbals. In part, this was because attention and resources had focused so firmly on competing priorities, but also this reflected recognition that the centre already contained commercial buildings of a quality rarely seen outside London or Edinburgh.[54] Both considerations perhaps helped to deflect more radical pressures for swingeing renewal. A short-lived office boom in the early 1960s, encouraged by government office location policy, led to the piecemeal accumulation of undistinguished office blocks. Nevertheless, enough of quality remained for a report by Lord Esher in 1971 to declare that: 'A great many Victorian houses in their old settings and Victorian monuments in the city centre are built with more craftsmanship than we can hope to emulate or than the world is ever likely to see again'.[55] Assisted by this evaluation, policy shifted to rehabilitation and conservation. The West End became designated as a Conservation Area under the new Town and Country Planning (Scotland) Act in 1972, with the entire central zone following in 1975.[56]

## Birmingham

When I was first on the *New Society* as a staff writer I was writing about Birmingham, with which I have always had a fascination – very much not

6.11
**Anderston Cross, Glasgow, offices and council flats (opened 1967): pre-cast concrete panelled (Richard Seifert and Partners)**

a model city really. There were innumerable attempts, from the Chamberlain family onwards, to pull it up by its bootstraps. And, of course, that has continued since Manzoni/Borg era in terms of what they have done. . . . I thought there was something American about Birmingham, a spirit of get up and go.[57]

Birmingham's renewal policy, driven forward by the City Engineer's policy on road building (see Chapter 4), allowed the private sector considerable scope in determining the shape of development along the new routes. By 1960, the city had already seen major property developments along Smallbrook Ringway (the first section of the Inner Ring Road constructed). In 1958 JLG Investments Ltd, a local firm already associated with Laing's Smallbrook Ringway project, proposed a further and larger initiative in 1958 to the south at the Bull Ring. Given permission to demolish the nineteenth century Market Hall to create a larger area for development, the developers offered a scheme covering three interlinked sites that included a multilevel shopping centre, retail market, car park, offices and a bus station.[58] Although this did not go ahead, Birmingham's Public Works Committee accepted a similar scheme by Laing in 1960. This scheme, which proceeded without any direct consultation with Sheppard Fidler's Architects' Department, envisaged a traffic-free space bounded by high-density roadways. It would retain the city's existing general and fish markets and introduce a notable measure of pedestrianisation, but had little design or aesthetic control. The result was what one contemporary observer termed an 'ungainly cluster of buildings and roadways [where] all sense of rational control, discipline and care for good living appear to have been sacrificed to expediency and gain'.[59]

Prominent in that cluster was the Rotunda (by James Roberts, 1964–5), an iconic structure that survived, at the council's insistence, from the original scheme. This 24-storey, 280-foot (85-metre) high reinforced concrete circular tower at the junction with New Street (Figure 6.12) provided the city with a readily identifiable symbol, but one with little connection to its setting and notorious difficulty in finding tenants. The Bull Ring, named after a cattle market that received its charter in AD 1154, continued in two guises. One was as a traditional open-air market, held at a pedestrianised site near St Martin's Church, but uncomfortably below the level of the adjacent Inner Ring Road (Figure 6.13). The other, the Bull Ring Shopping Centre, constituted 'architectural surgery in a big way',[60] making few concessions to the urban environment on which it was imposed. Its design by Sydney Greenwood (in association with T. James Hirst) was freely adapted from work already carried out by James Roberts – to the point that architectural commentators cried foul play.[61] In essence, it comprised a covered multilevel mall on the lines of American retail developments although, by reason of its confined site, it was of more intricate design that its American counterparts.[62] Indeed, the need to concentrate activity in a smaller area than conventional in the USA helped to create an early example of a megastructure, in which a range of functions were brought together within the same container.

Megastructures, as Chapter 11 shows, were an important ingredient in the urban imagination of the Modern Movement in the 1960s, but the version adopted at the Bull Ring owed less to avant-garde theorising than to the economics of property development, in particular the desire to maximise available floor area. The scheme fitted an integrated structure to an awkward 4-acre (1.6-hectare) sloping site spanning the Inner Ring Road, comprising three separate parcels of land and sloping by 65 feet (20 metres) in cross-section. Having decided the cross-section, it was possible to make use of the slope by constructing a shopping centre on six levels; three of these were devoted to retailing and leisure services, one to car parking and access, one to delivery, and one comprised a ballroom. The designers integrated the circulation system, with delivery facilities and access

6.12
**Rotunda, Bull Ring, Birmingham (James Roberts, 1960)**

6.13
**Bull Ring open-air market, below the level of the Inner Ring Road (photograph 1975)**

corridors incorporated at the rear and a parcel delivery system to the parking areas. An early and short-lived experiment with valet parking saw attendants convey vehicles to the car park by lift. Walkways supplied connection with the bus station and, eventually, to New Street railway station. The introduction of subdued lighting and piped music was 'expected to relax walkers down to a profitable pace of 1.5 mph'.[63] Yet, as the developers quickly recognised, the centre had design and locational problems from the outset. Like Tricorn, the Elephant and Castle Shopping Centre (see pp. 84–6) or the much larger example of Cumbernauld's Central Area (Chapter 7), these problems were only briefly deflected by their supporters invoking the rhetoric of design innovation and place promotion.

Elsewhere in the city centre, the commercial boom continued to change retailing and office provision. Colmore Circus received a new cluster of offices, of which the most notable was the Birmingham Post and Mail Building (John H.D. Madin and Partners, 1960–5), with its 16-storey tower rising from a podium. Frederick Gibberd's practice designed the pedestrianised Corporation Square shopping precinct (1963–6) on an extensive site between Corporation Street and the Inner Ring Road. Another precinct opened directly above New Street station in 1970. In 1967, Birmingham joined the growing number of cities with tall communications towers. Designed by the Architect's Department of the Ministry of Public Building and Works, the 500-foot (152-metre) Post Office Tower (now the BT Tower) added a vertical feature to the city skyline. Interestingly, unlike its London counterpart's observation deck and revolving restaurant, there was no attempt to turn this into a tourist attraction: 'When the Birmingham tower was designed the idea of public access to the top was considered but dismissed out of hand. No one, they said, would want to go and look at the panorama of Birmingham.'[64]

By contrast with the frenetic pace of retail and office development, the city experienced enormous difficulty in devising plans for the regeneration of its civic centre, a project actively canvassed since the early 1920s. An open competition in 1926 produced a winning design by the Parisian architect Maximilian Romanoff considered too expensive for the city to implement. This was followed by an in-house design dating from 1934, from which only a single municipal office block (Baskerville House) appeared before the war.[65] A similar story of indecision and delay emerged from the period after 1945. Endless schemes involving civic and entertainment clusters came and went, with varying combinations of council offices, repertory theatres, exhibition centres, broadcasting centres, public squares, educational institutions and central libraries. It took until the early 1970s, with the opening of the new Repertory Theatre (Graham Winteringham, 1969–71) and the Brutalist cantilevered Central Library (John Madin Design Group, 1964–74) for the makings of a new civic cluster to become apparent (see Figure 6.14). John Madin originally envisaged the exterior of the Central Library as being finished in travertine marble and the library itself as part of a comprehensively designed civic complex set in landscaped gardens. On grounds of cost and arguably the attraction of a Brutalist aesthetic, the council left the exterior as precast concrete.[66] The surroundings, as Figure 6.14 suggests, long remained forlorn and neglected. Moreover, its location spanning the Inner Ring Road paralleled the experience of

6.14
**Central Library,
Paradise Circus,
Birmingham (1969–73)**

the Bull Ring, where the same road had bisected another important civic space. It again showed how, in the absence of a comprehensive and coordinated view, the Inner Ring Road was often not a ring road at all.[67]

By the early 1970s, the remodelled central city in Birmingham neared completion. For many observers, it represented the 'epitome of modernity',[68] demarcated by its new high-speed Inner Ring Road and new buildings (see also Chapter 5). Yet despite the enthusiasm for 'newness' that was forcefully expressed by the City Council,[69] and by visiting commentators,[70] many who knew the city expressed concern about the character of the transformed centre. Within the concrete collar of the Inner Ring Road (see Chapters 4–5), the realignment of many old routes and clearance of districts of traditional architecture had disrupted patterns of usage. The refashioning of commercial districts too often added undistinguished glass-fronted buildings leavened by a handful of architectural novelties in the shape of the Post Office Tower and the corrugated raw concrete signal box at New Street station. With the familiar disrupted, questions surrounded the quality that the American architect Kevin Lynch described as the 'legibility' of the city – the extent that individuals could interpret and organise the various elements of the cityscape into coherent mental representations (known as 'images').[71] Cities that were legible were ones that possessed strong images, a characteristic that arose when users could apprehend them as patterns of high continuity with interconnected parts. The legibility of the city, the argument ran, was also an important element in the urban experience.

To test these ideas, a group of researchers at Birmingham University conducted a study in 1971 with the assistance of the *Birmingham Post* newspaper. Entitled *City Scene*,[72] the study looked at the legibility of Birmingham's central area as measured by a mental mapping exercise. The results showed that the 'known' Birmingham essentially comprised three spatially discrete clusters of buildings and landmarks – or 'oases' as one respondent termed them. One centred on the major railway station and the adjacent Bull Ring. Another clustered around St Philips Cathedral and the city's two leading departmental stores. The third was the civic area around the Town Hall and the Central Library. Each comprised a mix of different periods, with little attempt to establish any harmony of visual appearance or scale among the component parts. Relatively little of the complex road pattern of the area emerged, other than four major cross streets, and nothing of its lower level of subways and the then-neglected canal basins. The central Birmingham of 1971–2 emerged as a confused space with no distinctive neighbourhoods and the old and new buildings rivalling one another for attention (Figure 6.15). It was a city of fragments loosely bounded by an Inner Ring Road.

## The allure of scale

Nottingham, in the East Midlands, offered variations on the same theme in terms of commercial architecture. After the war, the city allowed property groups a free hand in office development without overall planning strategy or substantive official architectural input, symptomised perhaps by the city appointing a Chief Architect only in 1964 and Chief Planner only in 1966.[73] One of the major opportunities for

development came in the early 1960s when British Railways made its long-awaited decision to re-route all passenger rail traffic through the city's Midland station and close Victoria station. This provided a 20-acre (8-hectare) development site in the heart of the city (Figure 6.16), bordered by the existing main shopping area to the south, the site of the proposed civic centre on its western edge and large areas of housing to the north and east. The 40-foot (12-metre) deep cutting that traversed the site immediately seemed a potential advantage rather than a drawback since it offered the intriguing prospect of a multilevel development. The joint developers – British Railways, as landowners, and Capital and Cities Properties as financiers – commissioned Arthur Swift and Partners as architects for the scheme.

Peter Winchester, employed as architect in charge of the project, recalled the excitement that the scheme afforded. He had had some previous contact with Nottingham through working for Basil Spence on the university contract, but was astonished at the design freedom that he received:

> Two of my co-distinction fellows from the Poly [Regent Street] were already with [Swift] and he said that we have a big scheme in Nottingham, would I do it? . . . Here is a space, four lines, do something. It was extraordinary.[74]

The attraction of the scheme was the ability to bring a redundant site to life with innovative design in a site of sufficient size to allow the construction of 'a city within a city'.[75] Winchester's starting point was analysis of the circulation pattern:

> From the movements of pedestrians across and through the site (the mass of people living to the east going to the town centre) and subsequent changes in the pattern influenced by the positioning of three basic elements (bus station, car parking and shops), a scheme develops which follows well-defined routes.
>
> The resultant form is a three-dimensional vertical and horizontal circulation network, thoroughly expressed in the form of spaces, ramps, banks of escalators, glass tubes and moving platforms, with elements attached specifically to them.

6.16
**Site for proposed Victoria Centre, Nottingham (aerial view, c.1960)**

This has led to a series of squares at the southern end of the scheme around which the shops are grouped into quarters with offices above the shops and flats above the offices, all overlooking the open squares; an entertainment centre is on one side with two department stores in the main corner entrance.

These squares lead into a covered parade which is the main route to the bus station. On either side of this are the shops on two levels and the majority of the vertical access points from car parks below and residential areas above.[76]

The scheme that Winchester and his team originally conceived in 1964 was a linear development in which the various components functioned as one building, with an aesthetic unity based on the use of glass (Figure 6.17). The design took inspiration from Sergei Kadleigh and Patrick Horsbrugh's 'High Paddington',[77] a glass-towered, vertical city scheme for a new settlement for 8000 people designed to occupy the air space over the railway tracks at one of London's main rail termini. As such, Winchester admitted to sharing the long apparent fascination that glass held for architects as a constructional material: 'I liked the idea of this [building], which contained everything. I liked the idea too of this glass city where the light constantly changed as you moved around it.'[78] The soaring interior spaces combined with the penetration of light into the deepest recesses (see Figure 6.18) aroused an enthusiasm verging on lyricism:

walking through, the sensations produced will be an ever-changing series of light and dark, like a day when the sun dodges in and out of the clouds. There will be fewer dogmatic definitions of spaces with walls and dark enclosures than usual, but rather a series of lights, semi-darks and brilliant lights blurred at the edges.

Architecture can be enchanting; it has only been made to look dull because of the nature of the materials previously used.[79]

Almost inevitably, as was the fate of most megastructural projects, the final version diverged considerably from this design. Retaining the Victoria Station clock tower as a souvenir of the site's past, Arthur Swift's eventual design for the Victoria Centre produced a conventional shopping mall with extensive car parking space.

The scale of intent behind such schemes paled into insignificance, however, compared with the plans for the renewal of central Liverpool. These came about as a result of a thoroughgoing process of reappraisal that the council conducted in the early 1960s into its housing provision (see Chapter 8), its rundown city centre, and its fading image – then a shadow of its prewar eminence as a North Atlantic gateway port and a vibrant manufacturing industrial city.[80] The legacy of problems included the decline of Liverpool's regional role, problems of accessibility, its dilapidated and outmoded urban fabric, unemployment, sectarianism, housing shortages and environmental degradation.[81] Concerned that redevelopment was not occurring as rapidly as in surrounding towns and recognising that matters could not be left to a small team in the City Engineer's Department,[82] the council created new administrative structures to handle the necessary work. In 1961, it retained Graeme Shankland as consultant for the city centre renewal. Shankland, formerly LCC planner in charge of the Elephant and Castle and South Bank and latterly part of the team working on Hook New Town (Chapter 7), had a long record of innovation as an architect-planner. The following year Walter Bor came from the LCC as City

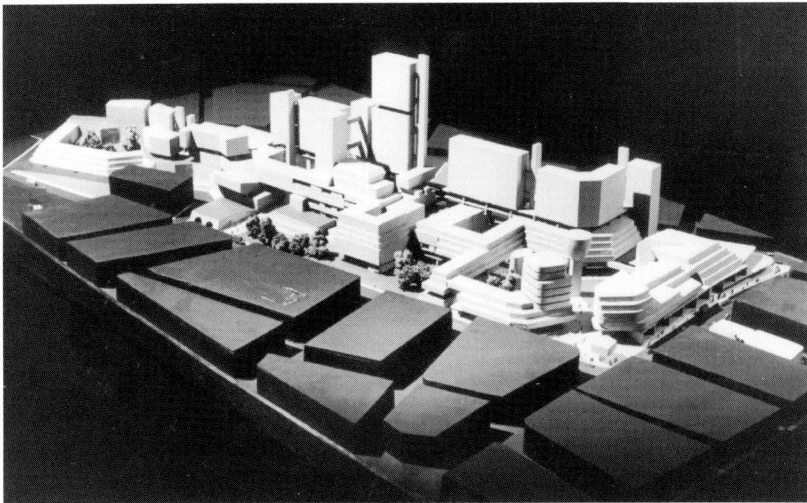

6.17
**Proposed Victoria Centre, Nottingham (Arthur Swift and Partners, 1965)**

**Interior of
proposed Victoria
Centre,
Nottingham
(Arthur Swift and
Partners, 1965)**

Planning Officer.[83] Each built up large teams. Liverpool, as a result, quickly received professional recognition that it, like Coventry and Newcastle, was a city that was 'trying to do things in a different way' and was a place that attracted quality staff.[84]

Shankland decided from the outset that the city centre should have a 'clear and memorable form' and that the local authority should not be afraid of clearance, suggesting 50 acres (20 hectares) between Exchange Station and Central Station as offering 'exceptional possibilities for continuous comprehensive redevelopment'.[85] Published in December 1965, the *Liverpool City Centre Plan* sought to grasp the sweeping ambitions underpinning those sentiments.[86] It aimed to integrate the city's various planning initiatives in a manner that aroused the highest hopes among apostles of large-scale urban transformation:

> The publication of the plan . . . is a major achievement in public relations; the complex process of planning is made clear and indicates that all aspects have been considered. The only question mark is not over Liverpool but over the nation – will the necessary minimal government financial aid be given to support the proud efforts of the city fathers and their highly skilled planning team?[87]

The city council proposed voluntarily discarding two-thirds of the buildings in the city centre as obsolete, apart from a small handful of buildings earmarked for preservation along with four conservation areas.[88] Office space would increase from 10 million square feet to 13.5 million (929,030 square metres to 1,254,190).

**129**

The heart of the commercial area would receive a new 'green square'. A small increase of residents from 660 to over 2500 would help to reanimate the city centre out of working hours, with the newcomers housed in tall flats.[89] The railways would be linked to a circular route with radials stretching out over Merseyside. The road system embraced 'the challenge of motorway age reconstruction',[90] with a new functionally based road pattern modelled on the findings of the Buchanan Report (see p. 107). This envisaged an inner motorway bounding the central area, with through-traffic excluded and extensive areas pedestrianised. Although this was scaled back, the city was nevertheless fragmented by multi-lane highways that severed the connections between the city and the waterfront and to the districts to the north and east.[91]

At the heart of the scheme was a proposal for a massive integrated Civic and Social Centre, itself an expression of the movement towards large, integrated developments that might bring local authority offices, entertainment facilities and law courts together in one complex. In 1963, Shankland and Bor had jointly recommended allocating a central area site for the new Civic Centre between the Municipal Buildings (which then housed local government offices) and the main legal and cultural area (containing St George's Hall, the Library, Playhouse Theatre, Museum and Art Gallery). The *Liverpool City Centre Plan*, published in 1965, had specified the city's requirements for the Civic Centre. This included housing the legal and local administrative functions, creating a symbol for local government and 'by including cultural and social activities in it, to humanise the image of local authority'.[92]

The commission for designing the centre went to Colin St. John Wilson against international competition. Wilson recalled:

> In the very week in which I set up my office for the first time in my house in Cambridge, I literally had three jobs . . . [an] experimental laboratory [the Biochemistry Laboratory at Babraham near Cambridge]; the house for Christopher Cornford; and I received a visit from Liverpool's city fathers and Shankland, in competition with Skidmore, Owings and Merrill [USA], and big firms from Italy [Gino Valle] and Holland [Jacob Bakema]. I packed this building with students, borrowing secretaries just to keep making typing noises on the day of the visit. And we got the job. What was quite interesting was the chap in charge of Estate Management at Cambridge said that it was the worse day of my life and that I would regret [it]. I said: 'Nonsense, can't you see that I'm walking on air. It's the most exciting new job in the whole country.' Ten years later, I declared that when I go to my grave, they will find 'Liverpool' carved between my shoulder blades.[93]

In their original outline study, the City Centre team had envisaged a low linear building, 'in order to make all offices accessible for the public', stretching anti-clockwise from the existing Municipal Buildings and largely filling the space between St George's Hall and the museums group. There would also be a public square, a new pedestrian mall and a precinct for the law courts.[94]

Wilson's thinking looked to larger, megastructural forms to bring these various functions together. Appearing in an auspicious month for new architecture,[95] his scheme adopted a pinwheel cruciform shape, with the central crossing comprising a public reception hall. This comprised a huge central atrium beneath a glazed roof that would have been one the world's first modern applications of this form of building.[96] The project sought to house offices for 4500 staff in 22 departments, along with social and cultural facilities, provision of 750–1000 parking spaces for cars and a centralised legal precinct.[97] Wilson also sought to include the potential for ordered growth at a variety of points. Summarising the design, he noted:

> The scheme had protected gallerias and an atrium in the centre and then growth over time, by multiplying elements. The basic theme was a kind of spiral. This was really rather Brutalist, quite bold stuff.[98]

Buildings of this type, however, involved complex sets of functional demands and circulation patterns which, given the numbers of interest groups involved, required lengthy planning and consultation periods. The conditions of the time, with changing thinking about design and resource availability, were not propitious for this type of enterprise. In the vast majority of cases, the window of opportunity quickly closed. As Wilson ruefully remarked:

> M.J. [Long] and I spent quite a lot of time up in Liverpool building up a huge brief, talking to people in all the different departments. We spent far too long, we were much too rigorous and we missed the boat.[99]

In this instance, the reappraisal process began with local government reform. The government's unwillingness to provide a £10 million subsidy to a project costing more than £20 million led Wilson to produce a smaller project for a £10 million budget, abandoning the pinwheel conception. The new version, unveiled in 1971, was 40 per cent smaller than its predecessor, provided offices for 2500 staff rather than 4500, and removed hotel, sports and conference facilities from the brief.[100] This emasculated version encountered local opposition and foundered in 1973, when a combination of ministerial rejection and changes in local political control killed the project. Like many schemes, weighty consultants' reports and three-dimensional models were all that remained to show what might have been.

## The London suburbs

The variations in the progress towards renewal seen more widely within Great Britain also manifested themselves within the London conurbation. The boroughs of Outer and Inner London, as they became in 1965 when the provisions of the London Government Act 1963 came into force, displayed a remarkable mosaic of activity as urban renewal sprang into life. The Outer London Borough of Croydon, for instance, had seen efforts to remodel the town centre that dated back to the Croydon Improvement scheme of the early 1890s. This sponsored the widening of the High Street and clearance of slum housing in the adjacent Middle Row district. The former county borough adopted further schemes in the 1930s and again in the

1950s. Where Croydon gained an advantage relative to competitors was the clarity with which its council grasped the demand from the office sector to decentralise from the centre of London but not move too far away. A successful campaign to gain a private enabling Bill led to the Croydon Corporation Act 1956, which allowed for the acquisition of land in the central area without having to refer compulsory purchases to the Ministry of Housing and Local Government.

Developments in the 1960s saw the creation of an approximation of what SPUR might have interpreted as a New Town within the London conurbation. A cluster of high-rise office buildings, especially near East Croydon station, combined with new roads, replete with underpass and flyover, and multi-storey car parks to form what *The Buildings of England* suggested 'suddenly became the most consistently modern-looking area in the whole of England'.[101] The addition of the Fairfield Halls (a concert hall, theatre and arts centre: Robert Atkinson and Partners, 1962), a new administrative centre (Taberner House, 1967) and shopping centre (the Whitgift Centre, 1969) completed the transformation. The net result proved highly effective in economic terms with 20 per cent of offices and 30 per cent of jobs that moved out of central London relocating to Croydon in the years 1963–70,[102] but gave architectural critics less pleasure. Despite looking 'thrilling from a distance and from the air', the lack of aesthetic control saw replication of a series of unrelated buildings without apparent coordination, with 'very few of individual architectural merit'.[103]

The thoroughgoing transformation of Croydon provided a point of reference for many other London boroughs. When Ealing in West London proposed a renewal scheme incorporating high-rise buildings and a flyover for through-traffic, community groups opposing the development used an illustration of 'the Croydon Flyover' on the front cover of their literature as a warning of the possible future urban environment (Figure 6.19). Further west, Uxbridge in Middlesex saw clearance schemes influenced by Croydon that resulted in the partial redevelopment of the town centre. Draft proposals for the town centre redevelopment published in 1961 provided for the eventual rebuilding of much of its High Street as a pedestrian precinct with shops, restaurants and markets, and the construction of a relief road to the south-west, leaving the old graveyard as a traffic island.[104] The slow progress of the redevelopment, however, generated the severe planning blight that was typical of both the period and the region. The postwar planning system placed the London boroughs in the position of large-scale estate managers, for which they were administratively ill equipped. Land acquisition always progressed faster than rebuilding, leaving empty pavements and void sites.[105] The long foreseen clearance in the Lawn Road area west of the High Street commenced in 1968, but caused a general rundown of services and building quality. Empty buildings in the High Street introduced a dilapidated note curiously at variance with its congested traffic and busy shops.[106] The shopping centre would be remodelled twice between the late 1960s and the early twenty-first century to compensate for problems stemming from the initial ill-judged redevelopment.

Local government reorganisation within the London region added further complexity to the renewal process. Wood Green in North London, for example,

6.19

**The Croydon Flyover: protest document against town centre renewal plans for Ealing (announced April 1968)**

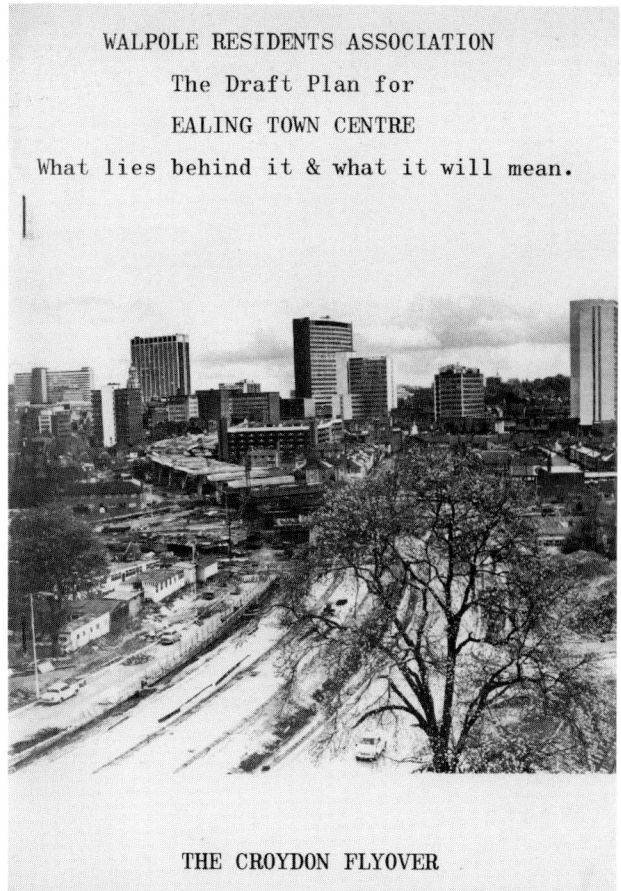

WALPOLE RESIDENTS ASSOCIATION

The Draft Plan for

EALING TOWN CENTRE

What lies behind it & what it will mean.

THE CROYDON FLYOVER

had held improving ambitions for its civic and commercial space that dated back to before the Second World War. In 1938, the council held a national competition for architects to present designs for council offices, auditoria, library and petty sessional courts on the site of the existing town hall. The outbreak of the Second World War caused postponement, but the council revived the winning entry by Sir John Brown, A.E. Henson and Partners after the war, albeit with amendments that omitted the courts and included public halls and a central library. As constructed, the scheme created the first large-scale town hall built in the postwar period. Built in stages in the years from 1955 to 1958, the reinforced concrete structure incorporated Home Office requirements relating to possible atomic bomb attack. The designer placed all the buildings on a podium with a common ground floor level to emphasise the linking of the blocks as a unified civic development, reached by terrace steps from pavement or car park.[107]

In many ways, however, the Civic Centre embodied the familiar problems caused by changing plans and aesthetics. The projecting rear wing on pilotis, planned as the south range of a courtyard with a public hall and library to the west and north, remained incomplete, with the library (1975–7) built on a different site in Wood Green High Street. In addition, although intended as a focus for Wood Green, the Civic Centre became somewhat isolated. The absorption of the Municipal Borough of Wood Green into the present-day London Borough of Haringey in 1965 changed the requirements for civic symbolism. This process was reinforced by development of the Wood Green Shopping City (Sheppard Robson and Partners, 1969–79). Situated a quarter-mile to the south and intended as a retailing focus for Haringey, the original design featured road diversion, a flyover, multilevel shopping, integrated parking and a complex network of upper walkways. The centre as built simplified this to a broad bridge with shops that linked a short stretch of upper-level shopping on either side of the existing High Road, which remained open to traffic.[108]

## Ilford

Ilford, then in Essex, provided a further instructive example of the ways in which a comprehensive renewal scheme became mired in developmental problems. In 1958, the borough council had started a comprehensive review of central area planning when proposing an extension to the car park behind the Town Hall.[109] The Town Planning Committee had proposed redeveloping the main civic and shopping area not just to alleviate congestion in the High Road and carry out modernisation, but also to make a statement about the town's progressive outlook and create a regional shopping centre that might match outer London regional rivals such as Croydon, Kingston and Bromley.[110] Its thinking was given an added stimulus by the announcement of plans by neighbouring Romford to redevelop its shopping area, which might serve as a major local competitor.

Plans for private developers to take over and develop the town hall site fell through. As it lacked a borough architect, the council commissioned Frederick Gibberd in 1961 to prepare a proposal for the comprehensive development of a new civic centre in association with H.J. Mulder, the Borough Engineer, Surveyor and Planning Officer. At the start of February 1962, Gibberd presented his ideas to the borough council, aided by a scale model. He stressed the possibility of providing an all-inclusive answer to renewal of the area, in which the 'motor car is banished from the shopping and civic scene'. The new civic centre and shopping area would occupy three blocks then occupied by the town hall, central library, a church, shops and around 150 houses. The scheme envisaged the High Road fronted by multiple stores backing on to a two-level centre, with the ground level itself devoted to parking space for around 1000 cars, storage and service space. The deck, roughly 12 feet (3.6 metres) above ground level and linked to the ground level by ramps and escalators, would house the new civic complex and a precinct for 45 smaller shops. The library with its multi-vaulted ('scalloped') roof was centrally placed between redeveloped shops and the civic square with municipal offices on the three sides. The council chamber, symbolically, was a separate freestanding structure, intended to symbolise independence.[111] Initial presentation of the scheme concluded with an astonishingly candid admission: 'The cost of the scheme, the most ambitious ever to be considered by the council, has not been worked out'.[112]

Notwithstanding the enthusiasm with which the council's representatives promoted it, the project stagnated. Almost at the time that they unveiled the proposal, uncertainty developed as to the configuration of the enlarged London boroughs after the creation of the Greater London Council (GLC). At that time, it was likely that the new borough would include Wanstead and Woodford to the north and possibly Chigwell, even further north. The suggestions of locating the new civic centre in the extreme south of the enlarged borough led to counter-proposals of alternative locations (perhaps at Gant's Hill, two miles to the north) or of going ahead with only the shopping redevelopment on the High Road site.[113] At the end of March, Alderman Harold Root announced a 'three-year pause' before the civic centre would start – a recipe for planning blight instantly recognised by the minority Labour group. At the same time, in the manner of a defiant gesture, the council instructed Gibberd to prepare a further scheme for the north of the High Road and to amend the original plan to facilitate pedestrian interchange between the two segments at first-floor level.[114] As if to insinuate this was insufficiently challenging, shortly afterwards the council's newly formed Town Redevelopment Committee announced that the Borough Engineer's Department had commenced 'detailed planning' of something far grander. The result was a highway engineer's dream. The new Ilford would be a town remodelled to take whatever developments in road transport could throw at it in the next 100 years, courtesy of a redevelopment that was

> so big, in fact, that the controversial Civic Centre plans are but a small part of the whole redevelopment.
>
> Within five years work will start on tearing out the heart of Ilford and replacing it with a heart so modern and far-seeing that it will last a century. Fly-overs, double-decker roads, shopping precincts, multi-story car-parks and blocks of flats – these will all blend into the mammoth redevelopment.[115]

Concerned perhaps by the resistance to and criticism of the more modest Civic Centre Plan, Alderman H.D. Cowan, the chairman of the Town Redevelopment Committee, switched to the offensive. Appealing to the nebulous concept of the 'public good', he cranked up the plaudits and moral justification for a scheme that would nevertheless proceed 'soberly and sensibly':

> We are engaged on a scheme for the improvement of our great town with the object of making it a better and happier place to live in.
>
> It is something which should excite the imagination of all who care for their town. It is a scheme of which no one need fear, as we have no intentions of being ruthless and the interests of everybody affected will be carefully and sympathetically considered.[116]

Clearly no one other than self-seeking or backward-looking individuals could resist its compelling logic.

Despite the polemics, it was hard to avoid the underlying sense that civic pride was pushing forward ever-grander schemes that bore little relationship to reality. A local journalist had noted soon after the publication of the original scheme that 'no one knows' whether Ilford would ever see the 'advanced civic centre envisaged by Mr Gibberd'.[117] It proved a perceptive observation. The council refused either to shelve the scheme or to press ahead with it.[118] Essex County Council, then required to vet the proposal, declined approval pending resolution of the Greater London boundary disputes. Legal problems, recognition that the scheme was too ambitious for the public purse and failure to attract private-sector partners produced years of delay. The passage of time eroded faith in the design and aesthetic principles incorporated in the plan. For the area's residents, there was a town centre scheme in the offing, but the starting date was continually postponed. The housing market in the areas directly affected by the scheme collapsed. In theory, it was possible to sell houses on the open market, but there were no purchasers for houses threatened with imminent demolition. The council's unwillingness to impose compulsory purchase meant that its obligation, as purchasers of the last resort, only matched site value (at a level set by its own District Valuer).

Acting within its legal powers, the council also engaged in tactics that increased the rate of property vacancy. Street repairs largely ceased and the physical and social fabric fell apart. Purchased houses were boarded up and selectively demolished rather than used for housing, creating a patchwork of temporary car parks. Those left standing were deliberately rendered unliveable by council workers stripping off all or part of their roofs. In the short term, this was justified by anti-squatter tactics. Ilford, as Colin Ward observed,[119] had become an important site of resistance to such tactics. The London Squatters Campaign, formed in November 1968, had moved homeless families into empty houses in the central area in the spring of 1969. The council, eager to reclaim the properties to provide additional temporary car parks, had engaged bailiffs whose own eagerness crossed the boundaries into unlawful violence. The result was favourable publicity for the squatters and a renewed national focus on homelessness,[120] but brought no significant change in policy. The strategy of pursuing the town centre scheme drifted into the shadows, other than instituting road improvements that pro-gressively carved the area apart. The purchased land awaiting development became temporary car parks of remarkable longevity (Figure 6.20). The subsequent non-implementation of the town centre scheme would leave a legacy of planning blight that clustered around the Town Hall – ironically still defiantly in place more than four decades after providing the stimulus for the ill-fated renewal scheme.

## Central areas

A similar picture of piecemeal renewal and abandoned schemes typified the Inner London boroughs. The LCC had tried to cling to elements of the *County of London Plan*, ratified by the 1951 Development Plan,[121] but general pressures for commercial development were antithetic to integrated urban renewal. The skyline changed rapidly after the relaxation of the building height restrictions, with towers springing

6.20
**The shape of the
future Ilford**

up wherever permissions were forthcoming. Ill-coordinated tall buildings, for example, fringed the Royal Parks. Describing the background to the Knightsbridge Barracks (Basil Spence, 1967–70), with its 320-feet tower overlooking Hyde Park, Anthony Blee noted that it was originally part of 'a cluster that was going to be built, where Bowater House is at Scotch Corner, top of Sloane Street. The fact [is] that the others didn't get built'.[122] He also noted that, on a whim, the minister had suggested doubling the height of the tower based on 'in for a penny, in for a pound', a suggestion that the practice had rejected because it was unnecessary to meet functional need.[123]

The progress of the Comprehensive Development Areas proved generally disappointing to those seeking coordinated change. The Elephant and Castle did little to justify the earlier hope that it might become 'the Piccadilly Circus of South London' (see Chapter 5). Badly conceived design coupled with poor location and difficult access plagued the shopping centre. Environmentally, the area became a traffic-infested nightmare. Although using comprehensive development powers, the LCC did not introduce radical rearrangements to the traffic patterns. Shop windows fronted on to busy roads. However appealing this might have seemed in the drawings (Figure 6.21), the reality was a noisy and polluted space, with the necessity of either crossing dangerous roads or using subways with an unenviable reputation for robbery with violence. The Stepney-Poplar Reconstruction left Lionel Esher, a sympathetic but disheartened observer, regretting the failure to buy land when it was cheap, the lack of an inter-authority management team, the failure to develop the areas designated as parkland, and the lack of a grand concept that 'could be apprehended, for better or worse, as a totality'.[124] The Barbican would eventually become a notable mixed development capable of drawing a middle-class population back to the central city, but endured an extended period in which non-architectural critics consistently panned the estate.

6.21
**Artist's impression of street scene at Elephant and Castle Redevelopment (LCC Planning Department, 1958)**

The South Bank had the advantage that the LCC owned large tracts of land, particularly around County Hall and eastwards towards Waterloo Bridge (including the former site of the Festival of Britain). A 1953 plan divided the area into 'upstream' and 'downstream' portions, with the upstream portion containing, *inter alia*, the County Hall extension, the Shell Centre, a proposed terminal for British European Airways (BEA), offices and the National Theatre. The plan envisaged multilevel circulation systems, with main access at ground level, basement parking and upper-level walkways. 'As with the other Reconstruction projects', Percy Johnson-Marshall observed, 'all kinds of problems emerged in endeavouring to turn the plans into reality.'[125] BEA built its terminal elsewhere and the County Hall extension provided an uneasy essay in updated Edwardian architecture: 'not classical in the same way, but it does maintain continuity'.[126] The massive Shell Centre (Easton and Robertson, 1953–63) received Portland stone facing instead of the desired 'graceful, glass-walled tower', inspired by Lucio Costa and Oscar Niemeyer's Ministry of Education and Health in Rio de Janeiro (1937–43). Johnson-Marshall noted that Robertson and Easton's design for the complex

> was a deep disappointment to us all. The bulk of the building blocks had been considerably increased, the considerable amount of open ground floor below the buildings had been filled in, while the architectural design went backwards instead of forwards for its inspiration.[127]

Soon afterwards, a 'cultural cluster' developed in a 21-acre (8.5-hectare) site centred around the Festival Hall – arguably the first attempted in the capital since the development of the grouping of museums and institutes in South Kensington after the 1851 Great Exhibition. The LCC Architect's Department designed the National Film Theatre (1956–8), located under the abutments of

Waterloo Bridge, with its Special Projects Group later responsible for the Hayward Gallery, Queen Elizabeth Hall and Purcell Room (1963–8). The much-delayed National Theatre (1965–76), designed by Denys Lasdun, completed the grouping.[128] Although the architectural detailing of the specific buildings lies outside current concerns,[129] the description of the cluster along with the Shell Centre as an 'essay in townscape' suggests an *ex post facto* view.[130] Completed at different times with varying interpretations of New Brutalist raw concrete, the complex achieved complete pedestrian segregation only by means of a maze of walkways and windswept flights of stairs (Figure 6.22). Peter Moro, one of the architects of the Festival Hall, considered there were mitigating attractions:

> For the visual excitement of turning a roof into a wall without changing material or finish or the petty intervention of a gutter, one has to accept a bedraggled look on a rainy day, possibly resulting in permanent staining. If one accepts this – and this building is probably strong enough to stand it – the skilful handling of the whole complex demands nothing but admiration.[131]

6.22
**Steps up to the South Bank walkway level, Waterloo, London (photograph August 1996)**

Beyond the ambit of the Reconstruction Areas, renewal schemes, inspired by aspects of the Buchanan Report, sprouted throughout the central areas. Digby Child, acting under the aegis of SPUR, offered a scheme for a two-level answer to congestion on Oxford Street, with pedestrians moved to a deck above the traffic. On a smaller scale S.A.G. Cook, Borough Architect for Holborn, proposed a 1:15 ramped crossing at the Holborn–Kingsway crossing with pedestrianisation at ground level.[132] During July 1965, for instance, reports by Leslie Martin and Colin Buchanan proposed schemes for the redevelopment of Whitehall that threatened to redevelop the area as a cohesive government precinct. This would include an up-rated road system that provided outer distributor 'primary routes' comprising four-lane dual carriageways and removal of through traffic from Parliament Square.[133] The plan's publication came just a day after that of Martin's scheme for the pedestrian precinct in Bloomsbury that would lead to the creation of the Brunswick Centre. At the same time, at least three major projects lay before the planning authority for the replacement of Soho's 'outmoded' narrow streets by the standard formula of wider roads and pedestrianised precincts. Powerful consortia planned to move into Covent Garden after the anticipated removal of the market, initially scheduled for Kings Cross and later for Battersea.[134] All saw architectural participation in schemes that favoured drastic surgery to the physical fabric to accommodate the car and replace the existing townscape of low-rise buildings and narrow streets with slab blocks and functionally differentiated through-routes.

## Causes célèbres

Predictably, many of these projects also spawned development sagas that lasted decades, although few achieved greater notoriety than the proposed development at Piccadilly Circus. This project, which Chapter 5 covered as far as the public inquiry, saw a remarkable volte-face by 1972. The inquiry witnessed the architectural establishment queuing up to make much the same points: namely, that the Circus had to be treated as a totality; that a single designer, possibly chosen through a competition, should take charge; and that the function of the Circus was as 'an arena for people, and only really required one fundamental character, that of enclosure'.[135] The LCC half-heartedly stood by its approval for the development, with Hubert Bennett arguing that a master plan for a complex entity like the Circus was unlikely, a view that contradicted the council's 1958 scheme for redesigning the area and countermanded the approach then taken at the Elephant and Castle.[136]

The process of reconsideration began when Colin Buchanan, appointed as the Ministry of Housing's inspector, delivered a report in May 1960 that rejected the submitted design. In inviting new designs, he stressed 'the need to reconcile the function of the Circus as a traffic interaction with its function as place thronged by pedestrians'.[137] The London *Evening News and Star* organised a competition for a new design with Maxwell Fry, Edward Mills and Noel Moffatt as assessors. The winning entry proposed a scheme somewhat reminiscent of the Bull Ring in Birmingham, replete with London's own rotunda.[138] Meanwhile, the LCC commissioned Sir William, later Lord Holford to prepare a comprehensive design for the Circus with pedestrianisation as its central theme. Holford accepted without enormous enthusiasm. He recognised the importance of the Circus but felt that the proposals were similar to 'hundreds of other applications of the same kind' that were 'not important or controversial enough for the Minister to call in'.[139] What was clear, he argued, was the nature of the dissatisfaction:

> Exactly what quality was about to be lost was never made clear, even during the long days of the Public Inquiry into the proposals for rebuilding the Monico site fronting the north side of the Circus. But there was no mistaking the general feeling of dissatisfaction with what was happening to civic design in the places where it is most in the public eye, namely in the centre of our cities.[140]

Holford's two preliminary schemes, put forward in 1961, took a wider view of the Circus than just the Monico site and worked with traffic flow diagrams prepared by the LCC's Chief Engineer's Department. There would be office blocks at the rear of the site, with the Monico building now to be designed by Walter Gropius and Richard Llewelyn Davies. The editorial in the *Architects' Journal* considered it 'a quite brilliant tentative scheme' for the area's redevelopment, 'praising the large pedestrian piazza above which rises a new London Pavilion, a series of shimmering hexagons for pedestrian circulation, cafes, bars and the like, interlaced with a weaving pattern of advertisements.'[141] Typically, the 'gaze' that architects, planners and officialdom trained on the existing Piccadilly Circus was unremittingly negative. Although admitting its cultural centrality, Holford's schemes seemingly treated the Circus less as an important symbolic space than as an encumbrance that interfered with the efficient functioning of London. The pedestrian piazza, with Eros as its focus, was dwarfed by the scale of the slab blocks grouped around the Circus. Any radical re-creation would need to combine respect for its appeal as a gathering place with the developer's demand for maximum floor-space and the traffic engineer's concerns for drastically improved arrangements for pedestrian movement and traffic flow.

In the event, the plan failed to appeal to the Ministry of Transport, which did not feel the traffic improvement merited a grant, or to the developers, who believed that the LCC, as the owners of the Pavilion, would gain an unfair advantage from that property having the best frontages and advertising space in the Circus. Holford prepared a second scheme, published in April 1962, that broke the larger blocks up into smaller masses, met the developers' requirements and 'looked as though it might constitute a civic space of a kind and quality scarcely built in Britain since the war'.[142] This eventually fell foul of the ministry's desire to increase the amount of available road space. Holford tried again in 1966, somewhat unenthusiastically suggesting a deck arrangement to achieve vertical segregation of pedestrians and traffic, but effectively removing the vitality of the traditional civic space. *The Times*, in an editorial entitled 'Piccadilly Forever', expressed weariness at the endless dance of schemes and committee machinations.[143] Holford's scheme provided the basis of developers' plans offered in July 1968, with a tower on the Criterion site now ramped up to 435 feet (133 metres). When this version foundered due to significant objections from groups concerned about the treatment of this important space and through the developers' claims that the scheme could not pay without additional office space, Westminster City Council worked on yet another scheme. Published in October 1972, it effectively rejected the key principles of comprehensive redevelopment and recommended retaining the existing shape, layout and atmosphere of the Circus. Henceforth policy centred on limiting the traffic and conserving the buildings as heritage.

This lengthy, costly and ultimately abortive episode was far from the only cause célèbre from this period that cast light on the complex interweaving of politics, planning and architecture in urban renewal. The development of the central and inner areas of London, always likely to attract the spotlight of public attention, threw up other instances where development processes significantly failed to yield the intended outcomes. Many sought to conduct renewal schemes on a basis of public–private partnerships, combining major surgery to the road systems and ancillary land uses with provision of civic space, the desired amount of commercial retail and office space and landmark buildings. Centre Point was a notable example. This 398 feet (121 metres) tower block erected at St Giles' Circus, at the junction of Charing Cross Road and Oxford Street, owed its origins to a complex public–private agreement. The LCC had decided in July 1956 to build a traffic roundabout and improve the road layouts, but found its way blocked by the property holdings of Beatrice Pearlberg's Ve-ri-best Manufacturing Company. Acutely aware of its inability to undertake the project from its own funds with so many competing demands, the LCC sought a private sector partner to help it finance the scheme. The resulting arrangement saw the Oldham Group purchase the necessary properties and donate the freeholds to the LCC, which promptly handed the site back on a 150-year lease at a fixed rent. Hyams's architects, Richard Seifert and Partners, then produced a series of designs for the tower, associated buildings and a public square. Figure 6.23, for example, shows one of the interim designs, with Figure 6.24 illustrating the tower block as built.

For all its potential attractions as a sleek addition to London's skyline in an area of predominantly low-rise buildings, Centre Point soon gained notoriety. The Ministry of Transport announced changes to the traffic flow pattern for the area that, though not implemented, made it seem that the traffic roundabout that motivated the scheme was redundant and that the developers and LCC had collectively sold the scheme on a false premise. Moreover, there was an impasse on letting policy. The developers maintained that they were prepared to offer it only as a single building but, since no suitable occupant was forthcoming, the building stood empty for many years. There was widespread suspicion that they had done their sums carefully and had calculated that Centre Point was more profitable if kept empty, given the sharp rise in rents, rather than tie its value down to a particular rent level. The concrete-and-glass tower therefore became a powerful symbol of the workings of property speculation. Architectural modernism's co-option into the world of property development led to guilt by association. In addition, Centre Point also represented an illustration of William Holford's observation that postwar redevelopment had provided few examples of the 'planned and furnished places of resort which the city has traditionally provided'.[144] Instead of a public square had

.23
Initial perspective
for the
development of
Centre Point,
London (Richard
Seifert and
Partners, *c.*1960)

come a windy and noisy traffic-dominated space that offered little to civic life. Certainly, very little had appeared in London to match the architectural quality or open space provision that had accompanied the development of Mies van der Rohe's Seagram Building on New York's Park Avenue.

Implicit recognition of this point lay behind the proposal to develop a square at the Mansion House in the City of London. The developer Rudolph Palumbo had commissioned William Holford's practice to work on a scheme for a site to the west of London's Mansion House, for which Palumbo was steadily acquiring premises.[145] The realisation that sensitive sites required outstanding designs if they were to stand any chance of approval led to commissions for prestige architects. In 1967, Palumbo commissioned Mies van der Rohe to work with Holford on the design. The site offered considerable challenges. It required a building of sufficient distinction to be located in the immediate vicinity of the Mansion House (Charles Dance, 1739), the church of St Stephen Walbrook by Wren and Vanbrugh (1672) and Lutyens' Midland Bank (1936), with the added complication that any tall building would compete with views of St Paul's Cathedral. It also presented the problem that one of London's underground railways ran diagonally in a tunnel across the site, preventing the erection of tall buildings without the prohibitive costs of bridging over the line.

**143**

6.24
**Centre Point as built (Richard Seifert and Partners, 1959–66)**

Holford's team had previously produced a scheme that placed an octagonal building on the site. This offered little public space and perpetuated the severe problems encountered at the nearby major traffic intersection. Mies looked to produce a scheme reminiscent of his design for the Seagram Building in New York, which combined a tall glass-and-bronze building with a new public plaza. The Mansion House scheme would have provided a new foreign branch headquarters for Lloyds Bank (the client), an underground shopping concourse with direct access to the underground railway station and landscaped public square. Peter Carter, who worked as project architect for Mies on this scheme, described Mies's design procedure as working through small-scale site models, then simple mock-ups of shapes to represent buildings, followed by experimentation with different configurations and positions for the building. 'At least a dozen fully worked out and amazingly different schemes were tried in three dimensions and then rejected, until the final scheme came about.'[146] The positioning of the building to the west of the site, partly a response to avoiding the underground railway line, provided a new public square, which would have been 'about the size of Leicester Square'.[147]

An exhibition of the scheme in the Royal Exchange attracted 30,000 people, who mostly provided appreciative comments, and the Court of Common Council of the City of London agreed in principle to the project on 22 May 1969, but did not grant planning permission 'at this stage for a development which would leave for a considerable period an incomplete square'.[148] The requirement for 'continuous staged operation' meant that nothing could go ahead before the acquisition of all the properties and stalled the development.[149] With no recourse to compulsory purchase, the developer (now headed by Palumbo's son Peter) took until July 1982 to reactivate the application, by which time he had purchased 12 of the 13 freeholds and 345 of the 348 leaseholds on the site. By this point, however, the corporation's letter of intent was out-of-date. Palumbo's ensuing efforts to revive the project in the 1980s and its eventual replacement by James Stirling's postmodern building at One Poultry are a subject for the third volume. For the mean time, regardless of the merits of the scheme, Mansion House Square showed yet again the limits as well as the opportunities for modern architecture. Chapter 7 reveals that the same could occur even when architects thought that they had a free hand.

# Chapter 7

# Second generation

**All the while – like a jeweller fashioning precious metal – I hammered the cross-sections and shaped landscape to forge an urban morphology.**
**Geoffrey Copcutt[1]**

Although attention during reconstruction and renewal focused on the major cities, to which the New Towns 'were only a small appendix',[2] the latter nevertheless offered the chance to see what might happen when architects were presented with a clean slate. This opportunity came in the 1950s when two separate groups of planners and architects came to work on schemes for New Towns: one was built and the other cancelled at the planning stage. Both schemes allowed their designers to look again at the design policies of the first generation of New Towns, designated between 1947 and 1950, and to reconsider the conventional handling of traffic, density and layout. Their reformulations led to striking departures from previous practice. Both devised plans that abandoned the typical cellular arrangement of neighbourhood units that had underpinned the Mark I schemes in favour of cohesion and compactness. They embraced commensurately higher densities than their predecessors, looked to modern design rather than back to Arts and Crafts or vernacular traditions, and even accepted limited use of multi-storey buildings (Figure 7.1). Traffic planning also sharply diverged from earlier precedent. Pre-Buchanan and strongly influenced by American experience, their planners applied ideas for handling large throughputs of traffic to create a town *engineered* – a verb commonly applied at the time – for the motor age.[3] They both also offered determinedly modernist town centres, known initially to their design teams as 'Central Areas' rather than town or city centres. These were envisaged as single multi-storey complexes, with car parks and service areas at ground level linked by stairs and lifts to shops, offices, leisure facilities and dwellings above.[4] As originally designed, they gave rise to what still have claims to illustrate the most comprehensive vertical separation of pedestrians and vehicles seen in town centre design anywhere in Britain during the postwar period.

7.1
**A different type of
New Town
landscape,
Cumbernauld
(photograph 1979)**

The earlier, and built, scheme was at Cumbernauld in Scotland. Cumbernauld, designated in late 1955, was Britain's fifteenth New Town and the only one created in the 1950s. Occupying 'an unpromising moorland ridge fifteen miles north-east of Glasgow',[5] it owed its rationale to the appalling housing problems facing Scotland's largest city (see Chapter 5). Cumbernauld, however, was always much more than just overspill housing with requisite amounts of industry and services thrown in. Catching the flood tide of architectural innovation, the combined architecture and planning team in the Development Corporation had the time and freedom to pursue a plan contemporaneously described as 'epoch-making'.[6] As that plan evolved, it had a major impact on the team working on the second and unrealised scheme, intended for Hook in Hampshire. Unlike Cumbernauld, Hook was not part of the official New Towns programme, but a private New Town project for the London County Council. Initiated in 1958, the scheme had reached only concept planning stage before it was abruptly cancelled in 1960. As such, it would have remained little more than a minor footnote in New Towns history had it not been for the LCC's decision to produce an extensive report to ensure that the effort invested was not completely wasted. The result was an extraordinary text that would explain better than any other available source the philosophy behind not only Hook but also Cumbernauld, from which its designers had drawn considerable influence.

This chapter looks at both schemes, focusing specifically on the ideas behind their Central Area design and implementation of those ideas in the case of Cumbernauld's town centre. It opens by recognising that the key decisions underpinning the design of Cumbernauld's Central Area were enmeshed in the circumstances that lay behind its designation as a New Town, drawing attention to its locationally challenging site and the principles underpinning its housing layout and circulation patterns. The second section provides connection with the scheme for Hook (Hampshire). The third section follows on from the discussion in Chapter

6 by providing a detailed analysis of the megastructural town centre – one of the few such structures that ever made the transition from paper vision to built form. The final section, in turn, makes links with the ensuing chapters, both in the sense of the flowering of creativity of the 1960s and the more fundamental reappraisal to come.

## 'A high degree of amenity'

The original decision to build a New Town at Cumbernauld stemmed from the decade-long debate between the Scottish Office and the City of Glasgow over the relative merits of population retention within the city's boundaries and overspill to other authorities (see Chapter 5).[7] Cumbernauld-Condorrat, a site approximately 2.5 miles (4 kilometres) south-west of the area eventually designated, was one of four locations considered as possible sites for Glasgow's New Towns in the 1946 Clyde Valley Regional Plan, along with East Kilbride (North Lanarkshire) and Bishopton and Houston (Renfrewshire).[8] Despite the plan describing Cumbernauld as having a 'high degree of amenity' and being 'at sufficient distance from the centres of population to be free from dust and smoke', it was regarded as the least attractive of the four options.[9] Besides steep ridges and deep valleys, the area bore the scars of industrial dereliction, with the remains of coal and fireclay workings and the added complication of further areas earmarked for continuing extraction. By contrast, East Kilbride had no such problems and was quickly designated as a New Town in 1947.

The extent of Glasgow's housing crisis, however, ensured that more was required. The initial preference was for a second New Town at Houston, which received Cabinet approval in December 1949. Initial plans were prepared,[10] but powerful local opposition supported by Hector McNeil, the Labour Member of Parliament for Greenock and subsequently Secretary of State for Scotland,[11] caused delays. The change of national government to a Conservative administration, initially hostile to New Towns policy, placed a temporary brake on proceedings pending a policy review.[12] When the New Town proposals for Glasgow were again seriously mooted in 1954–5, the opposition to Houston had strengthened. Sir Robert Grieve, once a senior technical officer in Abercrombie's team on the Clyde Valley plan and later Chief Planning Officer at the Scottish Office, recalled that the agricultural lobby had thrown its weight against development at Houston:

> I was there at the designation inquiry, and I remember how we were faced, by then, with a growing agricultural lobby – a really powerful lobby, pressing that New Towns shouldn't be built on the best land. This had led people's attention towards the Cumbernauld site, which was on an open, hilly setting. But because of mineral subsidence between there and the city, and the presence of coal strips all around, there was only a small area left to build on.[13]

The agrarian arguments decisively tipped the scales, despite recognition that this was the least favoured site. A Draft Order by the Department of Health for Scotland in 1955 allowed for a parcel of 8000 acres (3237 hectares) to be centred on Cumbernauld.[14] This would then act as a reception point for 50,000 people, 40,000 of whom would come from Glasgow's housing lists. Crucially, however, the proposed designated area overlapped the county jurisdictions of Lanarkshire and East Dunbartonshire. Although prepared to accept industry, Lanarkshire County Council had no wish to relinquish land for other purposes and opposed the New Town designation. Choosing not to delay matters further through protracted negotiations, the Scottish Office decided to press ahead. As established by the New Town (Cumbernauld) Designation Order (9 December 1955), the New Town proceeded on the segment of just 4150 acres (1680 hectares) that lay in the detached portion of Dunbartonshire (East Dunbartonshire). The loss of the Lanarkshire land had two implications. First, it meant that the railway line to Glasgow was now peripheral rather than central to the designated area. Second, the Dunbartonshire land contained most of the topographically difficult and industrially blighted terrain. The site was designated primarily because the county council concerned had little interest in it for any other purpose.[15]

After review, the development team led by the Chief Architect and Planner Hugh Wilson (appointed in October 1956) decided that development would centre on an oval-shaped area of around 930 acres (376 hectares) dominated by the hogback Cumbernauld Hill. Roughly 1 mile (1.6 kilometres) wide and 2.5 miles (4 kilometres) long, the hilltop rose approximately 260 feet (80 metres) above the surrounding area.[16] However development proceeded, the steep gradients on either side of the main ridge would create problems, although the nature of those problems as they impacted on Cumbernauld's future citizens would depend on issues such as the chosen population density, the location of the principal housing areas and the positioning of the town centre.

The question of density provided an initial preoccupation. The government raised the initial target population of 50,000 to 70,000 in 1959, which carried clear implications for the size of the town. Rather than pursue the lower population density for housing areas that characterised the first generation of New Towns as seen at East Kilbride (32 per acre; 79 per hectare), the initial residential density selected for the town was 95 persons per acre (234 per hectare), which would rise to 120 persons per acre (296 per hectare) in later parts.[17] This was done as part of a strategy to devise a more compact town than found with the lower, quasi-suburban densities more typical of the Mark I schemes. Coupled with that strategy came abandonment of the neighbourhood units adopted by those schemes, which Hugh Wilson decried as emphasising 'pseudo-village-greens' and as encouraging residents 'to look inwards to the local centre instead of visualising the town as a whole'. This, it was said, worked 'to the detriment of the creation of civic pride which should be one of the advantages of a medium-sized town'.[18] Rather, 'urbanity' was the key, defined as representing 'a way of life in which the concept of the town as a meeting place plays an important part'.[19] The exact meaning of that idea in both conceptual and operational terms was open to question:

> We used to debate the principle on which Cumbernauld should be based in a pub in the old village. There was a kind of thing that was appearing in architectural journals, almost like a holy writ. It meant that the kind of

> garden city idea, which is really what East Kilbride was built on, the good
> old garden city idea, wasn't good enough and we had to have a higher
> density and more 'urbanity'. This had something to do with playing about
> with the two words 'urban' and 'urbane', and it was exhibited really in
> that little development which looks like the little fishing village, you know
> tight, against the wind.[20]

Given that the town was to be seen as a single entity instead of an agglomeration
of individual neighbourhoods served by their own centres, it was decided 'to create
instead a compact urban integration whose people have to look to the town centre
for virtually all their services'.[21]

The town centre would need to take account of two sets of flows. First,
it had to be readily accessible to all parts of the town by foot. Second, it needed to
occupy a nodal position on the road network to allow speedy and efficient
movement of people and goods to and from the centre. The location of that town
centre, then, was crucial to the functioning of the town. The Preliminary Planning
Proposals, published in late May 1958, envisaged a T-shaped Central Area in the
valley immediately north of the railway station and rising to a point below the crest
of the hill. The text promised a 'multi-storey' town centre, with people and vehicles
on different levels and perhaps a measure of enclosure against the elements,[22]
although there was as yet no specific suggestion of bringing all elements of the
town centre together in megastructural form.

Hugh Wilson, however, remained convinced about the importance of
using the hilltop, seeing Cumbernauld Hill as the focus for a nucleated and compact
settlement. He had expressed that preference when originally interviewed for the
post of chief officer in 1956 and returned to this option, which he saw as an
opportunity to design a settlement with a dramatic image.[23] More prosaically, using
the hilltop site for the Central Area also positioned it at a point that was
geographically central to the residential areas.[24] This would permit Cumbernauld to
be a pedestrian town, in which no dwellings would be more than three-quarters of
a mile from the shops, with full separation of pedestrians and traffic, and an
advanced highway system that supplied speedy access to the centre for deliveries
and people travelling from a distance. Yet it was immediately realised that this was
a problematic location for a town centre. The site was narrow and elongated, which
placed limitations on the chosen design in terms of the disposition of roads and
buildings. Any pedestrians visiting the city centre on its hilltop would have to cope
with the stiff gradients on the way there regardless of the direction from which they
approached. There were also microclimatological problems. The south-west to
north-east lineation of the central ridge coincided with the direction of the strong
and frequently rain-bearing prevailing winds. Development along the crest of the
ridge had to take into account probable wind channelling and might require
the construction of substantial windbreaks, something that would have been
unnecessary if the alternative valley site had been chosen.

Several of the development team continued to press for the valley
site for the centre rather than placing it on the hilltop, but the wider strategic

considerations for the design of the town swayed the decision in favour of the latter. The undeniable disadvantages, however, would require considerable ingenuity even to ameliorate. That opinion was shared by the architects and planners working on the scheme for Hook.

## Hook

It was an authoritative appraisal since the story of Hook paralleled, informed and complemented that of Cumbernauld. The Hook proposal, as already noted, was an initiative of the LCC and stemmed from attempts to tackle the housing problem of inner London. In the mid-1950s, lack of undeveloped land within the administrative county of London and the national government's unwillingness to allow the LCC to use land in the suburbs called for drastic action. As Young and Garside noted:

> Denied access to its own suburbs and the Green Belt, and with New Towns and Town Development schemes proving slow and cumbersome, the LCC was looking further afield for overspill sites. Early in 1954, the Ministry of Agriculture expressed concern that the LCC was 'scouring the countryside' and considering areas of good agricultural land for development. In the next two years a policy of 'direct action' gained momentum at the LCC and pressure was brought to bear on the minister for the approval of a site for the LCC's *own* New Town, specifically for the reception of population and industry from the Administrative County. Sites which the LCC considered included Ringwood, Newtown (near Newbury), Wootton Underwood (near Aylesbury) and Tadley (near Aldermaston).
>
> Attention finally turned towards Hook in Hampshire.[25]

In the face of opposition from the Conservative government, which was not then prepared to countenance any other New Town besides Cumbernauld, the LCC's powerful Joint Development Sub-Committee, under its chair Evelyn Dennington, decided to press ahead with the Hook scheme and seek a private Act of Parliament, if necessary, rather than use the New Towns Act 1946. To implement the scheme, the committee established a development group under the leadership of Oliver Cox and, eventually, Graeme Shankland. Cox assembled a multidisciplinary team of 15 to work on the project. They included planners and engineers as well as architects, with the choice of Michael Ellison as landscape architect stemming from advice given by Peter Youngman, who was actively working on the landscaping at Cumbernauld.[26] His choice of Graeme Shankland as part of the team took several months to accomplish, since Shankland was initially under a cloud within the LCC over his association with the Boston Manor study (see Chapter 5). As Cox recalled:

> I needed a planner that I could work with on this. I was asked if there was anyone that I could suggest and I suggested Graeme Shankland, who I knew shared my views about planning. I also knew that he had been very impressed with the more recent development of Sweden's

new suburbs. The tram line goes out, there is a big station and the New Town [Vällingby] created. I knew Graeme was not going to be acceptable at the start because he was *persona non grata*. He, David Gregory-Jones and 'Joe' [Peter] Chamberlin had been responsible for the Society for the Promotion of Urban Renewal [SPUR]. They had done a study of Boston Manor, which had got on [BBC television]. The people who lived around Boston Manor had assumed that the LCC was responsible for this. They got on to Isaac Hayward, who was the Leader [of the Council]. I have no idea what he said, but he carpeted Graeme Shankland and David Gregory-Jones and told them that they had misbehaved. I said, however, that I am not going to do it unless I have Graeme Shankland and the team that I wanted. In the end, I had a team . . . from all over the departments. Because they came from many different departments, the Chief Architect Hubert Bennett could not claim that he could be responsible for a team that included the Chief Engineer's men, who was a senior officer to the Chief Architect. So the Clerk of the Council took over our team and we moved from the Architect's Department into the Clerk's Department.[27]

The team, which blended planning and architectural skills, readily admitted the strong influence that Cumbernauld, effectively two years ahead in planning terms, had on their thinking. As Cox observed: 'Hugh Wilson called us "the boys", Graeme [Shankland] and me, at that time, because we were continually watching what he had been doing at Cumbernauld and were very much guided by that.'[28] That intellectual debt became readily apparent with the publication of *The Planning of a New Town*.[29]

That, in itself, was an extraordinary event since it was effectively an obituary. Faced by resistance from Hampshire County Council and continuing government displeasure, the LCC had abruptly cancelled the New Town project in 1960 in favour of Expanded Town schemes at Basingstoke, Tadley and Andover. No construction work ever materialised. Cox had immediately resigned on principle. A critic described the council as having sold 'its birthright for a mess of cottages'.[30] The LCC, however, recognised that the amount of effort and resources invested in the project justified publication to avoid the complete wastage of the development work. It therefore

decided to publish this report on the studies and first plans for the proposed new town, in the knowledge of their usefulness in its own subsequent work in dealing with the problems of town expansion elsewhere, and in the hope that they may of similar assistance to technicians and students everywhere who are, or may be, concerned with new and expanding towns and the problems they involve.[31]

Nonetheless, Elizabeth Dennington was careful to add in her 'Introduction' to the report that the findings 'cannot be held to represent accepted Council policy'.[32]

The plan mapped out the design and layout of a clustered, walking-scale city located in a valley. It too embraced the car as a central parameter of planning. Its functionally organised road system embodied assumptions about hierarchy of flows and the need for pedestrian–vehicle segregation. At its heart lay a multilevel town centre intended to serve as a genuine focus for the gathering community. The upper level comprised a pedestrian deck featuring shops and a market area (Figure 7.2), with the blandishment to 'Read *The Scotsman*' making a wry reference to the debt to Cumbernauld. Beneath this came parking and servicing level (Figure 7.3). Although a present day view of the latter illustration might suggest the inadvertent replacement of utopia by dystopia, with a portrait of a semi-subterranean and noisy environment polluted by idling buses in the rolling fields of Hampshire, the report captured the scheme's appeal:

> The central area at Hook must inevitably be a complex mechanism. It is planned to provide the main focus of the town's social life and be the centre of specialised amenities and services for the local and surrounding population. Difficult problems of servicing, of the delivery and dispatch of goods, of people arriving and departing by bus, car or on foot, and moving about from one part of the central area to another must be resolved. The needs of these various functions could best be met if pedestrian and vehicular traffic were completely segregated. This could only be achieved in the central area by keeping all pedestrian movement on a platform, raised to a sufficient height to enable a network of roads to service the area from beneath and to cover the necessary car parks.[33]

The platform would cover the network of roads, allowing pedestrians and vehicles to coexist in the same geographical location but without conflict. As the authors observed, the scheme allowed 'pedestrian movement to be planned without the

7.2
**Hook New Town proposals: market area on pedestrian deck (1961)**

7.3
**Hook New Town
proposals: ground
level bus stops
with ramp,
escalator and lift
to pedestrian deck
(1961)**

need to equate it with design-speeds and turning-circles of vehicles – movements which have long proved incompatible and which are responsible for so much of the chaos in our towns and cities today'.[34]

The Hook report achieved national and international attention, running to four reprints between 1961 and 1965, and being sufficiently convincing to prompt coach parties of visitors to tour the area vainly looking for signs of the new town's construction. The Hook report also provided a far more powerful visual exposition of the key ideas than anything in the comparable literature from Cumbernauld. Oliver Cox was keen to recognise the project team's intellectual debts:

> We respected Ebenezer Howard and we respected very much the work of Unwin in the Garden City movement, although people on the housing side more than those on the planning side. You could see that these men had an idea which was very much related to people. It was a sociological thing. In planning terms, the work at Cumbernauld was an inspiration. We went to all the New Towns. One reason why the Hook book was the best seller that the LCC ever produced is that it did contain a summary of what we found interesting in the other New Towns that were being built. There was a great deal of emphasis in the Hook book of how you decided what sort of housing and where, and how you programmed it and how the town developed. It was very much based on the principles of transportation being developed at Cumbernauld, later applied at Runcorn by Arthur Ling. . . . it was basic to the planning of Cumbernauld, Runcorn and Hook. You wind your services through the place that is its centre as many times as you can, so that the centre really is a centre.[35]

The key difference in thinking lay in the site chosen, especially in terms of its implications for the location for the town centre. Influenced, as noted above, by Vällingby, the town centre plan made full use of the configuration of the site. At Hook, the centre would have occupied a small valley allowing the top deck 'to be placed like a lid over the valley'. As shown in Figure 7.4, this arrangement saved excavation for roads and car parks needed at the lower level and would have allowed pedestrians to walk down or along it instead of having to walk upwards as would happen with location on a hilltop.[36] It was a damning indictment of the location of Cumbernauld's Central Area, without actually mentioning it by name. Cox later elaborated explicitly on the report's implicit criticisms:

> The problem of Cumbernauld was that taking a centre and placing it on top of a hill was totally wrong. We looked for an opportunity to build a centre in a valley so that you could sink down and go over the top without making people walk higher and higher. We were right about that, although I think that assuming that people were going to walk now looks wrong.[37]

## The Central Area

There was no specific template for town centre design available from the earlier New Towns either to reject or to use for inspiration. Some of the smaller Mark 1 New Towns, such as Hatfield and Bracknell, had existing shopping centres that were modified or extended to suit the new needs.[38] The larger ones, with the exception of Hemel Hempstead, had shopping centres planned and built on new land, and thus from scratch.[39] Most were designed around standardised shopping units in low-rise buildings, with vehicular access for both shoppers and delivery. For example, both the previous Scottish New Towns, East Kilbride and Glenrothes, had a principal street running through their centres from which pedestrian ways diverged.[40] Only gradually did they and the other New Towns adopt wholesale pedestrianisation in the manner pioneered by Stevenage, where the shopping centre was designed as traffic-free from the outset.[41] Pedestrianisation, of course, did not affect the fact that the conceptions underpinning the design of these centres remained firmly rooted in the social and economic conditions of the late 1940s and early 1950s. By the end of that decade, the New Town planners at Cumbernauld were already looking for something commercially different even before deciding that it should be architecturally different.

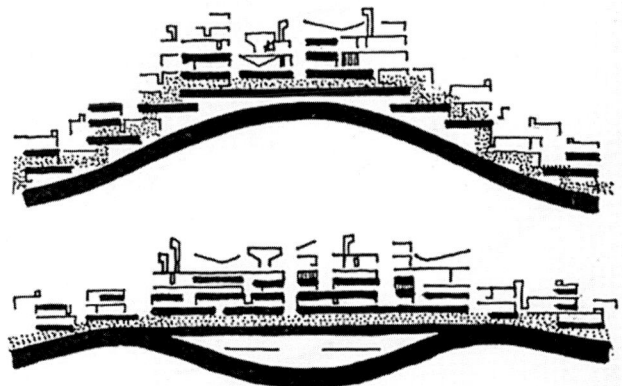

7.4
**Town centre situated in a valley site compared with a town centre on a hilltop (1961)**

The task of designing the town centre design devolved to a small interdisciplinary group led by Geoffrey Copcutt, who arrived in 1958.[42] Trained in Edinburgh,[43] Copcutt had received a degree of international attention by featuring in the first issue of the magazine *Zodiac*,[44] as well in national journals,[45] as one of Britain's most promising young architects; an accolade thought to have been important in his appointment to the Central Area portfolio.[46] His avant-garde credentials fitted the innovatory ethos that pervaded the Development Corporation at this time and it is clear that he, in turn, was captivated with the scale of the scheme and the unique properties of the hilltop location. The design work itself took roughly three years to complete. An early priority was to clarify what cross-section might take best advantage of the topography. Derek Lyddon suggested that makings of the cross-section appeared relatively early in proceedings:

> We started off with the main spines of the town going along the hilltop, therefore you have to get pedestrians on top and therefore that is the level of shopping. It almost started in my recollection with that simple cross-section.[47]

At the same time, the development team initiated major studies of potential transport systems and retail provision.[48] The former tested the assumptions behind the initial road proposals and led to radical alterations, whereby the principal radial roads were redesigned as urban motorways with grade-separated interchanges linking into the distributor or ring road systems. The latter study posed basic questions about the nature of shops, foreseeable changes in retailing in light of rising living standards and the growth of private car ownership, regional influence, number of workers in the town centre, and car parking provision.[49] Besides these studies, the senior officers paid extensive visits to the USA to study regional retail centres and to developments in Britain that addressed similar problems. For example Andrew Derbyshire, then in charge of developing the multilevel Castle Market shopping centre in his capacity as Assistant City Architect for Sheffield, recalled a visit in 1959 that showed that Copcutt clearly recognised similarities with his own scheme:

> I remember when I was at Sheffield, Geoffrey Copcutt had in mind a megastructure with a multiplicity of functions and I had the same thing in mind when I did Castle Market in Sheffield. I remember he came along to look at it because I was ahead of him. He said that this is exactly what I am trying to do, but I am on a much bigger scale than you . . . I have a whole town centre and you only have this market.[50]

## Implementation

Description of the Cumbernauld Central Area as a 'megastructure', however, immediately requires a word of caution. The scheme preceded the invention of the term in 1964 and bore little direct reference to the short-lived craze for megastructures in the 1960s (see Chapter 11). Rather, its origins reflect the way in which traffic engineering and the commercial logic of property development appeared to coalesce with architectural innovation. The Preliminary Planning Report argued that the town centre should be 'one huge multi-storey building, to be built in phases',[51] and that it was necessary 'for the design and structure of the town centre, the buildings and facilities they will contain, to portray and amplify this concept'.[52] Efforts to give shape to the future town centre in three-dimensional form continued throughout. Copcutt explored different ideas primarily through his favoured media of scale modelling in card (pocher), paper or plywood.[53] Copcutt worked primarily through scale modelling. While a compulsive visualiser who drew good sketches, he was a relatively poor draughtsman and tended to work by supplying ideas from which others produced line drawings. Alec Kerr noted:

> Copcutt was always accompanied by a 10 inch roll of tracing paper, 20 yards long. On this, he produced loads of ideas and basic sketches which could be taken forward by others more able to execute line drawings with the type of attention to detail that this demands.[54]

The early versions produced by these methods exuded a tangible excitement for the possibilities of building on this site: one example showing shopping and other central uses under a vast ramped canopy of housing, using the profile of the hillside to bring the closest possible connection between residents and the facilities of the town centre. In this arrangement, people would live in and, if possible, over the centre.[55] By stages, however, this gradually transmuted into a multi-storey structure arranged in a series of decks; again the analogy with the neat layered functionality of ocean liners that had resonated in modernist thought since the 1920s. People might still live over the centre, but only in penthouse flats.

By January 1962, a prototype scheme envisaged shopping located on three levels, with other communal uses above, surmounted by three ranges of penthouses.[56] The layout in the centre included two squares, civic buildings, a hotel and spaces for entertainment buildings. By this stage, any significant use of the railway down in the valley had faded from the picture and the vision was entirely road-based. The whole edifice would be placed over a one-way system of roads, with separate lanes for different types of vehicles and car parks. In the words of the Buchanan Report, which took a special interest in Cumbernauld, the plan for the Central Area was

> of linear form, built on a deck *above* the approach road. The idea of an inner ring road encircling the central area has completely vanished. The shops and business premises are to be built on the deck with a number of dwellings on the top again. Thus cars, buses and service vehicles are brought very close in, *underneath* the shops, but in very close proximity thereto, and complete separation of vehicles and pedestrians is obtained. . . . Ground space is saved, and the bleak parking and service areas are drawn in out of sight.[57]

The passion for innovation continued, with the Central Area Group conducting feasibility studies of various innovative methods for handling traffic and circulation.

Although none was subsequently adopted, these included tracked magnetic-levitation systems, parcel pick-up schemes and gravity parking.[58] Evidence gained from the studies of regional shopping centres in the USA helped to refine the pattern for retail provision, but brought home the uncomfortable fact that American shopping centres were enclosed, whereas that at Cumbernauld was largely open to the weather. Windbreaks were clearly necessary. The landscape architect's report advocated 'as much shelter planting as possible';[59] another consultant recommended abandoning the proposed 45-foot-high artificial earthen mounds at each end of the structure in favour of long high buildings with air gaps beneath, which wind-tunnel testing suggested might be more effective.[60] In the event, neither adequate planting nor windbreaks were implemented.

The initial intention was to build the Central Area in five phases, scheduled to fit in with the planned expansion of the town's population, although the precise content of the later stages were listed as 'provisional with regard to detail' and in this respect 'subject to continual modification'.[61] Any development in phases inevitably faced the problem that the whole must add up to the sum of the parts and the parts had to be built with the complete structure in mind. By the same token, it was perfectly possible that any initial phase of building might not make complete sense until the megastructure was completed – something that might take 20 years. Building in this way meant there was a fundamental choice for Phase 1: either to build a complete deck horizontally across the entire site or divide it into sections, with some parts inevitably coming to blank ends until later phases were built. After debate, the decision was made to adopt the second strategy which, as Whitham points out, had important implications for the image of the emerging town:

> The decision to construct a slice, though later seeming a recipe for near-disaster, forged the image of Cumbernauld and secured the remarkable skyline which in some views seems a man-made extension of the hill-top.[62]

Plans and models for Phase 1 were unveiled in late November 1962. Figure 7.5 shows an aerial model, combining urbanity with rurality by strategically placing a flock of sheep grazing in the far distance; Figure 7.6 uses different lighting to convey an appealing night view. The scheme had been considerably simplified from the earlier version, for example, with the principal shopping elements placed on one deck, at the level of the ground on the north side, with an additional deck at one floor below on the south side. Yet despite the manifest complexity involved in fitting the decks to the hilltop site, Phase 1 comprised just two basic elements. As described by Glendinning,[63] the larger segment comprised the main commercial, administrative and housing block, located to the south of the dual carriageway: in profile it represents 'a gigantic, squat, tiered structure progressively stepping up from south to north, and crowned by a range of penthouses' Figure 7.7). By contrast, the second element was a spur to the north that directly continued the main shopping concourse for a short distance across the dual carriageway. There

7.5
**View (c.1962) of model of first stage of Central Area development, as seen from the north-west. The main spine carriageway at ground level can be seen beyond the hotel and bank buildings; note the flock of sheep grazing at the top of the picture**

7.6
**View (c.1962) of model of first stage of Central Area development, illuminated as night-time**

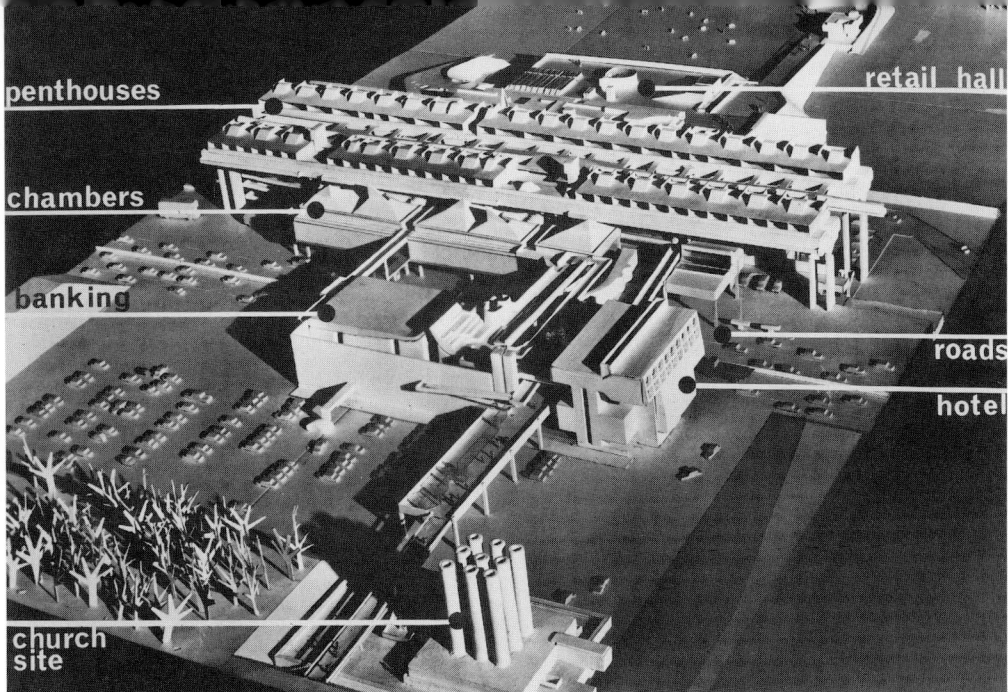

penthouses

chambers

banking

church
site

retail hall

roads

hotel

were also sites adjacent to the north-west, where other agencies would build St Mungo's Parish Church and the seven-storey 'Golden Eagle' hotel (Figure 7.8).

The keynote was flexibility. Copcutt described the scheme as comprising 'demountable enclosures'.[64] Where components of the building ended abruptly, this was frequently to signify a temporary stage before the next sections were constructed and thereby to illustrate the megastructure's vaunted characteristics of plasticity and extensibility. Its future managers might rearrange its interiors or expand in planned fashion, either within the structural grid or in spaces beyond. In a remote future, if certain central area functions declined, the centre could become 'a giant vending machine through which the motorised user drives to return revictualled'. In language that would become a familiar part of megastructuralism, this was 'a drive-in centre', 'a vast terminal facility', where levels 'interpenetrate', forms 'erupt', sections are revealed to the 'mechanically propelled' visitor, and advertising presents a 'kaleidoscope'.[65] Playfully, too, Geoffrey Copcutt added a landscape view with the future town centre in the background and a large American gas-guzzler car in the foreground. Its registration plate was 'GC 1963'.

The chosen aesthetic for the centre comprised the angular geometries and unfaced concrete of New Brutalism. This departed from the aesthetics of the scheme that appeared in the early models and did not receive unanimous support, as an unpublished essay clarifies:

> The early models of the centre showed an almost sculptural approach to architectural form and as this plastic quality developed it was felt by some that the underlying philosophy was more attuned as a monument to individuality than to the production of well arranged enclosed space capable of being manipulated in a variety of ways to accord with changing methods of retailing and central area use. Here . . . changes were introduced in an attempt to achieve a simple architectural statement with a strong framework which would be capable of

7.7
**Photograph of Cumbernauld Central Area, Stage 1 (c.1980), showing penthouse deck in greater detail**

7.8
**View of
Cumbernauld
Central Area, with
the now-
demolished
Golden Eagle
Hotel (photograph
April 1976)**

absorbing the many diverse elements of the centre contained in what is essentially a single building structure. In the process there were many sincerely and strongly held views and team working was stretched almost to breaking point.[66]

Latching on to New Brutalism, with its characteristic blend of design preference and sociological presumption, would bring new ideas to the table. Some may have seen use of concrete at Cumbernauld as a cheap way of providing texture (see Chapter 5),[67] or as an inevitable result of the government requiring that the centre be built as cheaply as possible,[68] but there was an image inseparably linked to New Brutalist buildings that designers found compelling. New Brutalism was uncompromising, pioneering, forward-looking and expressed modernity. Those values seemed eminently suitable for the megastructure that was due to appear regardless of the tensions that using this aesthetic might have aroused within the design team.

Construction of Phase 1 progressed relatively smoothly, notwithstanding the sudden bankruptcy of the contractors Duncan Logan and the early departure of the key staff – Hugh Wilson left in October 1962, although he remained as consultant, and Geoffrey Copcutt in February 1963. The British government, although still Conservative, had abandoned the ambivalence of its predecessors towards the New Towns. Indeed the Scottish Office now gave both financial and moral support to what was regarded as a showpiece to kick off a second generation of New Town building, even to the point of encouraging the development team to take risks and make a bold statement.[69] Phase 1 of the Central Area was built between 1963 and 1967, by which time the town's population had reached 27,000 people.[70] The scheme proceeded according to Copcutt's plan and chosen aesthetic, but was implemented by his successors Philip Aitken and Neil Dadge. Although the Cumbernauld staff contributed working diagrams, the contractors, who had been hired on a 'design and build' basis, handled the detailing.

The opening of Phase 1 attracted worldwide interest, with articles appearing in the professional press in many countries.[71] The Institute of American

Architects chose the opening of the Central Area for the inaugural presentation of its R.H. Reynolds Memorial Award for Community Architecture, which Cumbernauld had won against competition from a short-list that also included Vällingby (Sweden) and Tapiola (Finland). The commendation contained a citation of the Central Area as a 'town centre designed for the millennium'.[72] *The Times*' correspondent spoke of the centre's 'ambitious scope and scale', although stating that it was 'almost too imposing for the relatively scattered groups of housing surrounding it and separated from it by open space still to be built on.'[73] Frank Schaffer compared the '£15 million multi-deck building' to a luxury liner, even if it had 'long ramps . . . rough grey concrete and lack of trees and grass' and threatened high costs of building and maintenance.[74] Osborn and Whittick were willing to pass a preliminary judgement that the centre promised 'much that is unusual and impressive', while suggesting that 'more warmth and less wind will be common wishes'.[75] The reviewer for the *Architects' Journal* concluded that, 'its final worth and justification exists in the powerful identity it gives to those who live in Cumbernauld. They do not believe, not even the critical, that they have been given something which is second rate'.[76] Furthermore, 'it has, already, a bookshop' – clearly an index of worthiness. Whatever the problems of microclimate, detailing and construction workmanship: 'all this is nothing against the positive contribution it will make to those who live in Cumbernauld new town and to those of us whose concern is making new environments fit for this century'.[77] Against this, the architectural historian Patrick Nuttgens gave a guarded response that tempered qualified approval with a carefully worded catalogue of reservations. For all the positive talk, such as the centre being 'one of the most impressive sights in town planning today', the criticisms catch the eye, for example:

> it is sometimes coarse and verging on the megalomaniac; here and there it ignores simple needs in favour of some private aesthetic. And yet with ironic justice it is the occasional pieces of pure architecture that in the end are the most irritating aesthetically, communicating a lively sense of the unnecessary. . . . The next phase . . . must inevitably correct what appear at a superficial glance to be major faults.[78]

His comments presaged an uncomfortable future. Phase 2 (1968–72) was the last part built integrally to Copcutt's original design and with similar aesthetics, albeit with a 'marked dilution of the visual ferocity of the previous phase'.[79] This phase almost completely swallowed up the previous phase's northern spur across the dual carriageway. It was built up against the side of a sharp slope at the north and consisted of a single block, aligned north–south, and between three and four storeys high. Its lowest levels were occupied by what was once the north car park of Phase 1. Its upper storeys provided additional office space and shop units. The sense of being a town centre was addressed by including a small market hall. This contained 'gaily cluttered kiosks and signs, set beneath the original coffered ceiling'[80] – a reminder of the urbanity that was one of the megastructure's initial selling points.

## The folly on the hill?

The reputation of megastructures collapsed astonishingly quickly in the 1960s, leading to criticisms that they were 'monumental follies'.[81] Certainly, to view Cumbernauld's town centre in its own time is to see in microcosm the hopes and problems that attended modernism in the practice of creating and recreating town centres. Although the depressing future that lay ahead for this scheme after 1972 lies beyond the scope of this text, there were abundant signs by that stage that it faced fundamental problems. In an official press release from 1968, the Development Corporation's Information Office had praised the Central Area's pedestrian–vehicle segregation for providing relaxed conditions for shoppers:

> This is a pedestrian shopping centre, and the success of such centres elsewhere has proved that people like to shop away from the noise and danger of motor roads. The hectic struggle in crowded streets is replaced by the pleasant conditions in the vehicle-free areas where shoppers can stroll and chat.[82]

Yet Ferdynand Zweig, in his study of social life in Cumbernauld carried out just two years later, provided a list of comments about the town centre that were almost entirely negative.[83] Although Zweig declared himself unwilling to draw conclusions from such reactions, Neil Wates – whose firm had sponsored the report – had no such qualms. In his Preface to the report, he argued that, despite the planners' intentions of making this a walking town, the people 'turned their backs on the centre and drove elsewhere to socialise'.[84] By 1969, following Frank Lloyd Wright's ideas about the potential role of the filling-station as an agent of decentralisation, critics were wondering whether two conveniently situated filling-stations might replace the inconveniently located town centre as a shopping focus.[85] That, of course, applied only to those with cars. Those without were confronted, in the words of another contemporary commentator, with a 'dirty, windy megalith of piled-up shopping ledges, which now crushes into insignificance the mothers who push their babies up endless ramps to get to it'.[86]

Those intimately concerned with developing the centre recalled the way that problems compounded. Dudley Leaker, Hugh Wilson's replacement as Chief Architect and Planner, had noted that 'the climate of high hope and financial backing changed before the second stage had a chance to get started and before the right quality of materials and finishes could be applied'.[87] Cost cutting had left a legacy of poor quality work and finishes. The bankrupted contractor, Logan, had left no records of major elements of design, such as with regard to the steel reinforcement in the main concrete structures.[88] The concrete finishes soon began to show signs of being unable to cope with water percolation. The microclimate proved every bit as inclement for users as forecast, requiring enclosure to make conditions more hospitable. Potential developers had found the centre unattractive internally and externally. Phase 3 would show that even the much heralded extensibility was a myth, with any significant change to the centre's concrete carapace proving uneconomic and disruptive.[89] Particular problems surrounded the deck principle. Looking back on his own experience at Sheffield's Castle Market in relation to

Cumbernauld, Sir Andrew Derbyshire remarked how costs and inflexibility undermined the entire logic advocating the megastructure:

> This effort of producing large tightly structurally defined buildings, I now regard it as a hopeless mistake. If everything is bound up so closely with everything else, if for instance the mechanical ventilation system is so closely integrated with the structure so that all the air ducts have a structural purpose, then nothing can change without the whole building being pulled down, which is what in fact is going to happen. It was, in fact, incredibly inflexible . . . because the pedestrian deck was fixed. . . . Vehicles underneath, people on top, but it was a very expensive investment compared with doing everything at ground level. When money ran short, as it invariably does, everything had to drop back to ground level.[90]

Yet there were always countervailing influences that worked against the scheme that were not specifically related to it being a megastructure. These included the initial locational choice (Cumbernauld not Houston); the amount and quality of land left after the loss of the Lanarkshire portion; choosing the hilltop site; failing to tackle its inherent problems adequately (especially the decision not to construct proper windbreaks); and the inability of the construction industry to deliver results of sufficient quality.[91] To these should be added the problems of undertaking a project with a 20-year or greater time horizon in the light of changing economic and cultural circumstances. We saw in Chapter 6 how opinion turned against large civic and social centres, often lightly discarded after many years' preparatory work. The fate of Cumbernauld's town centre, in many ways, was an extension of this trend. Although started with some optimism, official willingness to back the town centre scheme evaporated, with a commensurate diminution of resources. This was particularly so after the financial crises of the late 1960s and early 1970s placed general pressures on major capital projects in the public sector.

The resulting cost-cutting adversely affected constructional work across the sector, but was particularly serious for unconventional buildings using materials like concrete, which demanded exacting standards of workmanship if they were to function effectively. The net result was that, iconic though Phase 1 and the reduced Phase 2 might have been, they were not the full megastructure but just 'a tiny wee bit of it'.[92] Yet whatever extenuating circumstances are raised, the fact remains that substantial parts of this expensive and experimental town centre were already failing within a decade of construction. Certainly, Copcutt and his Central Area Group relished the opportunity 'to forge an urban morphology',[93] for what they conceived as the emerging society and undoubtedly drew on their own values, as much as their studies of functional need, to design the town centre. Their wish to have the freedom to implement their creativity rather than build in more conventional ways created problems, as did their naïve faith in technology to solve problems. It is a conclusion that anticipates the gathering force of the reappraisal that constitutes the findings of Chapter 12.

Chapter 8

# The pursuit of numbers

Our civilisation is a different one than we've ever had and naturally our architecture has to be different to go along with it. We hear talk if we try to do something that we're going too far, but if we look back a little ways, no one ever went too far. No architect, composer, anyone ever went too far. It seems to me that anything we can do now, and that we need to do now, and can actually do now is not too far. It's part of what we are capable of in our own civilisation. No matter how different it may seem to the so-called cultural lag.

Bruce Goff[1]

On 6 July 1957, the International Building Exhibition opened in West Berlin's Hansaviertel-Tiergarten district. Better known as 'Interbau', a contraction of its German title *Die Internationale Bauausstellung Berlin*, architectural journalists quickly hailed it as the most important architectural exhibition since the war.[2] It included, *inter alia*, a Congress Hall (by Hugh Stubbins), an industrial exhibition held at the permanent Berlin fairground near the Radio Tower, and eight national pavilions in the adjacent Tiergarten showing national approaches to building and construction technology.[3] At its heart was a model settlement, which rebuilt war-devastated Hansaviertel as a modern residential district for 3000 people. This development, of course, provided much-needed housing, but it was also a display of work by a group of international architects. The organisers had invited 48 architects from Western Europe, Scandinavia and the USA to work on buildings for the settlement, especially seeking designs that might 'stimulate new ideas on housing, particularly flat-construction, and that these ideas would be adopted outside Berlin'.[4]

Interbau was a product of Cold War ideological hostilities. In 1951, the authorities in the eastern sector of the divided city of Berlin decided to rebuild the

Stalinallee – the former Frankfurter Strasse and the route by which the Red Army had entered Berlin in 1945 – as 'the first socialist street in Europe'. Described as a 'curious fusion of baroque ideas and socialist housing',[5] the reconstruction, directed by Hermann Henselmann and Richard Paulick, aimed to produce a 'showpiece of social housing and amenities in the face of scarce resources',[6] in the shape of a six-lane highway flanked by well-constructed and, for the time, generously serviced slab blocks of flats. As a response, the authorities in West Berlin decided to undertake a permanent international housing exhibition to emphasise their rival ideological connections with the liberal-democracies of West Europe. Directed by Otto Bartning, President of the (West) German Architects' Association, the exhibition eventually bore the slogan *Wir wohnen gern modern* ('We like to live modern'). Preparations began in earnest in1953. Keen to avoid the civic monumentality of the Stalinallee, the Hansaviertel was dispersed in a green park,[7] and was a mixed development that illustrated the full repertoire of modernist dwelling forms from 'skyscrapers to bungalows',[8] rather than an exercise in multi-storey living.

It proved popular with British visitors. This was, after all, the era in which deputations from British municipalities went to continental Europe in search of helpful examples to guide practice. It was also an opportunity to find buildings by a substantial number of famous international architects gathered together in one place. As one observer noted:

> What excited you were the names: Corb, Gropius and the rest. These were gods and they were all here in one place. . . . I went in them all, taking in one after another. It wasn't all finished either. It was show architecture; even it was intended as a permanent fixture.[9]

At the smaller end of the scale, Wassili Luckhardt, F.R.S. Yorke, Arne Jacobsen and Hans Scharoun showed low-rise experimental terraced houses or detached villas. However, it was the larger blocks that caught the eye. Walter Gropius, working in Germany for the first time since 1934, collaborated with TAC (The Architects' Collaborative) and Wils Elbert to design a nine-storey block of flats. Alvar Aalto's eight-storey block was his first permanent building in Europe outside Scandinavia. A similar structure by Oscar Niemeyer and Soares Filho had a separate lift tower that connected with the main building only at the fifth and seventh storeys – an arrangement that perplexed some observers and irritated its new tenants.[10] Eugène Beaudoin and Raymond Lopez amazed the correspondent of *The Times* by designing a block of flats that grouped the main fitments for kitchen and bathroom together, allowing tenants to arrange the remaining floor area according to their wishes.[11] Le Corbusier revisited his *unité d'habitation* project with a typical 17-storey slab. Deemed too large for the Hansaviertel site, the organisers allocated it to a site at the Reichsportfeld in the Charlottenburg district, roughly four miles west of the main exhibition area.

In many ways, Interbau readily drew comparisons with its iconic predecessor Die Wohnung ('Dwelling'), the exhibition that Mies van der Rohe had organised at Stuttgart in 1927. Die Wohnung was also a broadly based exhibition of modern design – including displays of domestic appliances, furniture, kitchen-ware and building technology – but, like Interbau, was best remembered for its model settlement, the Weissenhof Siedlung. The Weissenhof was an earlier product of a collaborative endeavour by modern architects, drawing the efforts of an illustrious cast from all over Europe. Its key achievement was to offer a sense of the convergence of modernism around the International Style alongside an assertion of difference from conventional architecture. Nevertheless, there were two major differences between these events.

In the first place, the status of modern architecture was much different than in the late 1920s. The Weissenhof was an island of modernist innovation in a hostile architectural environment. By 1957, critics argued that Interbau offered little that was 'technically . . . new',[12] and merely revealed a broad consensus that 'modern building materials are international and functionalism has imposed a pattern'.[13] Indeed, the battle of political ideologies barely extended to the architecture. Although the redesign of the Stalinallee featured a monumentalism not seen at Interbau, the architecture shown at Interbau was not significantly different from that shown at the Stalinallee.

Second, the Weissenhof and Hansaviertel differed in the message that their architects wanted to convey about the patterns of living that accompanied the new architecture. In 1927, the architects sought to convince the onlooker that this new architecture promised to improve the lives of its residents and, in so doing, offered real hopes for social change. By contrast, Interbau was preoccupied with production. The exhibits, of course, retained the semblances of the social agenda, but enough had already been said and written to take the social benefits of modern living, rightly or wrongly, for granted. What the present situation demanded was new housing in quantity. Despite being show architecture, Interbau supplied urgently needed housing to a city and nation still struggling to cope with rapid population increase caused both by natural demographic growth and the flood of refugees arriving from the German Democratic Republic. Accompanying literature pointed out how the emerging settlement might illustrate such general topics as 'town planning, urban units, housing, architecture, superstructure, building methods and rationalisation'.[14] These were emphases of concern, to greater or lesser degree, for many other European nations as they similarly tackled the need for more housing.

This chapter follows this orientation, concentrating primarily on the production of housing and, specifically, how those responsible for the housing looked to high-rise flats and industrialised building methods when attempting to meet their targets. The first part provides context about British housing policy during the 1950s and 1960s. Although not seeking to provide a comprehensive overview, for which a large literature is already available,[15] it highlights the influence of the state in a decentralised system through operation of its subsidy regime and its powers of persuasion. The next section considers aspects of variation arising from the local scene, containing a brief survey of the public housing strategies of three provincial British cities. These, in their differing ways, show how housing policies unfolded, especially with regard to deployment of high-rise flats. The ensuing sections examine the parallel progress of the drive to deploy industrialised building methods. They consider the particular advantages that these methods allegedly offered, the commercial pressures that ensured their propagation and the role of official sanction. The final section briefly considers the myths of production and notes the neglect of the living conditions in the new public housing estates.

## Housing the nation

Whereas town centre renewal had scarcely begun by 1954 (see Chapter 5), the housing drive led by the local authorities was already in full swing. The year ending in December 1953 had seen the local authorities in England and Wales approve over 195,000 new dwellings for construction, a level of building that consumed just over 80 per cent of total capital expenditure by local authorities (£399 million out of £493 million).[16] In 1954, there were almost 310,000 housing completions, comprising 220,924 houses built in the public sector against 88,028 by private developers (then only just emerging from the restrictive effects of postwar building controls).[17] Government strategy consistently aimed to provide a favourable environment for the private sector, but primarily centred its attention on council housing – which, in the decentralised system established for housebuilding, it could influence but did not directly control.

When examining the role of the local authorities as providers of housing, attention invariably centres, first, on the changing aggregate levels of provision and, second, on the relative position of flats versus houses as part of the annual totals. Starting with the former, the situation changed with remarkable speed during the 1950s and early 1960s, usually following changes in the subsidy regime. Following a radical policy shift in 1955 in favour of private sector initiative, the Conservative government temporarily stopped playing the 'numbers game' that made the production of public-sector housing into a political commodity (see Chapter 1) and abandoned the favourable terms under which housing finance was dispensed. Instead of having access to the reduced rates offered by the Public Works Loans Board,[18] local authorities now had to borrow money on the open market which, it turn, greatly diminished the amount available for construction projects. Concerns about the cost of the housing drive to the Exchequer led to the abolition of the general needs subsidies altogether under the terms of the Housing Subsidy Act 1956. So rapid was the decline in the public sector that the rise in private sector house building failed to compensate.[19] In 1961, there were only 98,466 houses built in the public sector against 170,366 for the private sector.[20]

Central government progressively backtracked in the early 1960s, especially when it appeared that this level of performance in council house build-ing might have electoral consequences. Reviving the 'numbers game', the Conservative government brought back a general needs subsidy in 1961, while at the same time backing the higher standards for housing laid down by the Parker Morris Report.[21] Sir Keith Joseph, the Minister of Housing and Local Government, actively pushed for an increase in housebuilding. In February 1962, the government affirmed the target of 300,000 houses per annum. The 1963 White Paper raised that to 350,000, with the minister increasing it to 400,000 by October of the same year.

When Labour came to power in 1964, it upped the ante still further to 500,000 dwellings per annum by 1970, with 50 per cent in each of the two main sectors. There was, however, no coherent philosophy on behalf of the state as to how to achieve this vast increase in production other than to adjust the subsidy regime and to advocate industrialised building methods, particularly in the public sector.

This infatuation with numbers extended to the highest levels of government. Richard Crossman, Sir Keith's successor at the Ministry of Housing and Local Government, reported on a discussion during a private meeting with the Prime Minister Harold Wilson in May 1965. In it, Wilson emphasised his personal commitment to a 'magnificent housing drive' that would yield up to half-a-million houses a year by 1970:

> We'll make housing the most popular thing this Government does. We won't build another single mile of road if a cut-back is necessary to get that half-million houses a year.[22]

With this degree of support, Crossman and his immediate successors pressed ahead. Fuelled by buoyant private-sector housing completions, which exceeded 200,000 in each year between 1964 and 1968, and high levels of completions for public-sector housing, the target briefly looked in sight. Yet after the headline figure reached 414,000 housing completions in 1968, the production of housing went into steep decline. Changes in the subsidy system that now discouraged the building of high flats, local elections in 1967 and 1968 that saw the return of cost-cutting Conservative local councils, and an economic crisis that demanded transparently visible reductions in public expenditure produced major cuts to the public housing programme.[23] The targets for housing were therefore quietly, but enduringly, dropped.

Table 8.1 shows that conventional houses still dominated in 1953, the peak year, representing 77 per cent of the total local authority approvals for new housing against just 23 per cent for flats of all types. Significantly, high-rise flats represented only around 3 per cent of the total at this stage, but over time the relative balance shifted decisively in favour of flats. That process had already began in the interwar period, most notably with the Housing Act 1930, sponsored by the Labour Minister of Health Arthur Greenwood. In seeking to ensure optimal use of expensive inner city land, the Act provided a special subsidy so that local authorities could build flats on expensive sites to maximise the number of dwellings provided. The Act's provision adjusted the subsidy according to the cost of the land, which gave greater funding with increasing height of the building. Postwar measures retained such provisions, but with the subsidy scales for building height enhanced in 1946 and 1952. More fundamental changes came in 1955–6 when, as noted above, Treasury concerns about housing expenditure saw the reduction and then abolition of the general needs subsidy. The expensive-sites subsidy was replaced by a much smaller one based on acreage, with subsidy introduced in November 1955 that increased progressively according to building height. The aim was to compensate local authorities for the higher construction costs associated with having to supply lifts and 'shift from brick to more expensive building materials'.[24]

**Table 8.1** Local authority approvals by building form, 1954–72

| Year | Houses | Flats | High-rise | Total |
|------|--------|-------|-----------|-------|
| 1953 | 149,904 | 38,749 | 6,730 | 195,383 |
| 1954 | 133,004 | 39,797 | 8,932 | 181,733 |
| 1955 | 97,365 | 31,606 | 8,044 | 137,015 |
| 1956 | 82,031 | 31,677 | 8,011 | 121,719 |
| 1957 | 72,964 | 31,992 | 10,009 | 114,965 |
| 1958 | 58,591 | 32,113 | 11,369 | 102,073 |
| 1959 | 66,099 | 37,583 | 15,109 | 118,791 |
| 1960 | 58,256 | 36,372 | 15,685 | 110,313 |
| 1961 | 53,213 | 33,428 | 17,107 | 103,748 |
| 1962 | 54,535 | 35,502 | 18,871 | 108,908 |
| 1963 | 58,835 | 39,109 | 27,500 | 125,444 |
| 1964 | 65,861 | 45,675 | 35,454 | 146,990 |
| 1965 | 78,250 | 49,067 | 34,953 | 162,540 |
| 1966 | 81,959 | 46,292 | 44,306 | 172,557 |
| 1967 | 85,211 | 45,025 | 39,309 | 170,545 |
| 1968 | 76,133 | 47,559 | 30,616 | 154,308 |
| 1969 | 56,731 | 40,253 | 15,217 | 112,201 |
| 1970 | 56,461 | 37,879 | 9,740 | 98,080 |
| 1971 | 46,460 | 38,419 | 8,004 | 92,883 |
| 1972 | 37,458 | 34,062 | 5,692 | 77,212 |
| 1973 | 48,141 | 36,531 | 2,970 | 87,642 |
| 1974 | 63,184 | 47,021 | 2,794 | 112,999 |
| 1975 | 70,173 | 32,336 | 1,484 | 113,993 |

Source: P. Dunleavy, *The Politics of Mass Housing*, Oxford: Clarendon Press, 1981, p. 41.

This principle of rewarding higher buildings with greater subsidy remained in force until 1966. Although, as the next section makes clear, this subsidy regime 'in no way can be said to have "caused" the high-rise flat boom',[25] it did create a climate of encouragement for such buildings – particularly on non-expensive sites[26] – and was a factor in ensuring that flats overtook conventional houses as a component of social housing in 1963 and held that position until 1968. This transformation stemmed less from deployment of low-rise flats, which remained remarkably constant in absolute terms up to 1975, as to the increase in production of high-rise flats. Compared with only 3 per cent in 1954, tall flats accounted for 25.6 per cent of approved starts in 1966. As Table 8.1 indicates, the situation altered rapidly in the course of a remarkable 11-year cycle. It began with a frenetic growth, with approvals rising 66 per cent to stand at 172,557, the highest since 1954. Thereafter, the cuts in public expenditure, combined with specific resistance to system-built flats, led to a rapid decline. The 1972 total of 77,212 approvals represented only 44 per cent of the level recorded six years previously. For tall flats, the decline was even more spectacular, comprising 7.2 per cent of housing approvals in 1972 and 1.3 per cent in 1975, when just 1484 units were produced compared with 44,306 nine years earlier. These figures alone provide eloquent testimony to the underlying problems confronting a once-vaunted component of British public-sector housing provision. Indeed, the revival of interest in building conventional houses (over 61 per cent of the total by 1975) reveals the degree of retreat to the traditional mould, as interest switched to housing improvement and conversion.

Four further points are important when interpreting the trends that underpin national housing statistics. The first concerns the central government's attitudes towards building high flats. Throughout the 1950s and early 1960s, there were signs that clear distinctions were drawn between higher density (needed to compensate for lack of building land) and high-rise flats (for which there was no imperative). There was acceptance in some quarters that tall blocks could act as a twentieth century visual equivalent of a church spire, adding interest to the skyline and texture to the townscape. It was the strategy, for example, behind Frederick Gibberd's design for a 10-storey block at The Lawn (Harlow) or Arup Associates' 17-storey Point Royal (Bracknell), both of which added a vertical feature to otherwise low-rise New Town surroundings. As Dame Evelyn Sharpe (then Deputy Secretary to the Ministry of Housing and Local Government) stated, for example, in a speech to the RIBA symposium on High Flats in 1955:

> from the point of view of the urban scene, high dwellings interspersed with low and middle-sized dwellings are really a thing of beauty. There is nothing it seems to me more appalling, more deadening in the urban landscape than a uniform mass of low buildings covering acres and acres.[27]

However, she avoided conflating aesthetic considerations with strategic thinking about density: 'I know . . . that one does not save as much land by building dwellings in high flats as some people think'.[28] Official thinking retained scepticism about this form of dwelling. Several years later, although the authors of the Ministry of Housing and Local Government's publication *Flats and Homes 1958* were at pains to stress their unwillingness to recommend one type of building against another, their carefully assembled evidence clearly suggested restricting the number of high blocks deployed in any given mixed development scheme.[29] During the early 1960s, the ministry's Research and Development Group led by Oliver Cox pushed forward its support for industrialised building without corresponding support for high-rise flats. The key areas of support for the latter, as we shall see later, came from a powerful alliance of the larger local housing authorities and the construction industry.

Second, the local authority housing drive began several decades before the long-overdue reorganisation of local government under the London Government Act 1963 and the nationwide Local Government Act 1972. In 1963, there were almost 1450 local housing authorities in England and Wales and a further 232 in Scotland,[30] operating within territorial boundaries that, although overhauled by the Local Government Act 1888, often dated back to the sixteenth century or well before. Although town councils sought to extend their boundaries in order to make sense of the results of nineteenth and twentieth century urbanisation, they frequently found themselves short of land within their jurisdictions on which to build. This, coupled with the endemic planning preference for containment to prevent urban sprawl, fashioned a 'land trap' for the cities. One way round it was to resort to 'overspill', whereby major cities decanted applicants from their housing lists under arrangement with other local authorities, although this meant accepting a loss of population and inevitably local income. The other response to the 'land trap' was to undertake 'massed building of Modern flats'.[31] Frequently, these two options were used in tandem but, in the 1950s at least, the desire to rehouse within the city boundaries provided a stimulus for building high. Besides facing severe problems of central area renewal (see Chapter 6), for example, Portsmouth suffered severe land shortage. Hence, when proposing placing 12-storey blocks in a central area of Portsmouth in 1959, Alderman Day argued:

> The chief concern in Portsmouth, where we have so little land at our disposal, is to make sure of its economic use. We appreciate the difficulties. But we also appreciate that if too many people go outside the City boundary, Portsmouth will become a less economic unit.[32]

The sentiments that he expressed prevailed, with the first of 38 tall blocks approved in 1960.

Third, house-building was conceived narrowly in terms of the production of residential units. Broadly speaking, the state aimed 'to break the back of the "postwar shortage" as quickly and cheaply as possible' and that policy persisted through into the 1960s.[33] The nature of the subsidy regime supplied funding for housing, but generally treated the associated infrastructure and social capital as normal local provision to be met from the rates. This narrowly defined approach compromised the broader concept of 'dwelling' that typified much of the interwar Modern Movement's thought about housing. 'Dwelling' emphasised resituating housing back into its broader context, thereby integrating provision of homes with the services necessary to support modern urban life, particularly through the creation of neighbourhood units (see Chapter 7). Although most often associated with New Towns, the neighbourhood unit concept also seemingly offered prospects for the reconstruction of housing areas in existing cities. Kenneth Campbell, for example, noted that idea was 'very strong indeed'; there was a real sense that 'the neighbourhood would be the urban small town'.[34] A key attraction, particularly when translated into formal neighbourhood units, was the combination of physical design and sociological elements. Neighbourhood planning offered a 'kind of pattern logic . . . [that] seemed such an obvious and clear thing.'[35] Early acceptance of the concept occurred in Hull, which used neighbourhood units in early reconstruction. Bilton Grange, completed in September 1955, housed almost 10,000 people in 2550 houses in a development that included a community centre, churches, 5 schools and 18 shops.[36] The LCC, as seen in Chapter 5, had attempted to apply neighbourhood unit principles in the Stepney-Poplar Reconstruction Area, but with limited success. Open spaces came under constant threat from building rather than for use of the community. Small parcels of land in industrial areas were re-zoned for residential purposes, offering an unsympathetic environment for housing. In the London Borough of Newham, for example, two isolated tower blocks appeared in the middle of a sea of industry at Barnwood Close in Silvertown – a decision approved as fitting the neighbourhood vision by the Borough Architect T.E. North and the chairman of the Housing Committee, Councillor Kebbell.[37] It was, however, far short of anything that might offer the cherished platform for the emergence of genuine community life that was inherent in the neighbourhood unit concept.

Fourth, there was the question of slum clearance – the emotive issue that attracted many architects towards modernism in the first place. The 1930s had seen the modern flat juxtaposed with the slum and gain moral authority from that juxtaposition. Slum clearance, however, languished until the mid-1950s, given the priority accorded to general housing need. Various cities had attempted their own small-scale programmes,[38] but these were unable to keep pace with the continuing deterioration of substandard working class housing. There were, for example, 847,000 designated slum dwellings in 1954 compared with 472,000 in 1939 (although admittedly the classificatory criteria had changed).[39] Hence, despite local authorities clearing 900,000 dwellings and rehousing more than 2.5 million people in the years 1945–68, most of whom moved into social housing, large pockets of decayed and substandard housing remained. Liverpool, for example, had 92,000 unfit dwellings in 1965, Manchester 55,000 and Birmingham 42,000.[40] These statistics, of course, need treating with care. Cullingworth,[41] for example, observed:

> To those who know Lancashire there is something odd in the fact that though 43 per cent of the houses in Liverpool are estimated to be unfit, the proportion in Manchester is 33 per cent; in Oldham 26 per cent; in Salford 24 per cent; in Bolton 10 per cent and in Stretford 0.5 per cent. It is true that Liverpool and Manchester have appalling conditions, but they are not so markedly different in proportion to those in some of the other towns.

## The local picture

Such differences, of course, were inevitable given the decentralisation of decision-making for housing. Local authorities were required to accept and implement the state's current housing priorities, but their officers were free to exercise their 'expert' judgement to act on the situation as they saw it. On occasion, as Chapter 6 suggested, an appraisal might reflect the ambitions of the councils that employed them. A council's declaration that an area was a 'slum' could circumvent other planning requirements and affect the levels of compensation required. Such designations could help smooth the way for undertaking clearance and redevelopment, especially in boroughs short of land or keen to remodel their town. The internal politics of the town hall also contributed diversity. Housing was notoriously an arena in which campaigning councillors, especially those chairing housing committees,[42] and assertive 'production-minded officers, engineers, architects, town clerks',[43] could make their mark. Private sector architects, in particular, understood the importance of finding such people when working on local authority housing projects: 'Once you find people who are enterprising then you latch on to them. . . . [All] you needed [were] just a few protagonists.'[44]

Perhaps the most important local variation, however, came from the choices about the mix of housing types chosen in support of social housing goals. For smaller authorities, the choice revolved around conventional houses and low-rise flat provision. At the other end of the scale, the LCC was the first to develop a coherent programme for building multi-storey flats. Having steadily built flatted estates with stairs and gallery access throughout the late 1940s when housing came under the Valuer's Department, the LCC turned to more adventurous prototypes after the return of housing to the architects in 1949–50.[45] Around 50 blocks of 11 storeys and above were under construction by 1955, including the landmark estates at Ackroydon (Princes Way, Wandsworth), Alton East (Portsmouth Road, Wandsworth), Alton West (Roehampton), Loughborough Road (Lambeth) and Bentham Road (Hackney). In these years, the LCC predominantly deployed tall buildings as part of a policy of 'mixed development', which had roots in Forshaw and Abercrombie's *County of London Plan* (1943).[46] Whitfield Lewis, the council's Principal Housing Architect, described the advantages of a policy that balanced high blocks, four-storey maisonettes and two-storey maisonettes, allowing larger families to be housed on or near the ground with a private garden and resonating with the picturesque architectural sensitivity. He observed:

> The broad sociological advantages of such a policy are obvious but there are other equally important factors. As well as creating valuable open spaces within a layout, the use of high blocks in contrast with low development gives the variety and interest which is so sadly lacking in those schemes of uniform 5-storey blocks which we all know so well.[47]

Over time, this line of thought was challenged. Martin Richardson, who joined the LCC in 1956 and later participated in the design of the system-built estate at Morris Walk (see p. 189), attacked the principles underpinning mixed development. Reacting against what he saw as its inherent eclecticism and apparent disorder, Richardson observed:

> In this approach, in default of any inherent, structural, organisational relationships between the buildings, aesthetics in the head-on-one-side, flower arrangement sense come into their own. Massing, enclosure, verticality, horizontality; all the terminology of 'civic design' is called upon in a hopeless attempt to impose order on an approach which had no intrinsic order.[48]

The mixed development model, however, proved popular elsewhere in the 1950s. *Birmingham*, one of the more enthusiastic of the early providers of high flats, followed mixed development strategies when land was available, even though the earliest experiments with flats were on restricted inner city sites. The city council had taken its first steps in the direction of developing multi-storey flats with the unsuccessful three-storeyed Garrison Lane scheme (1927), widely criticised at the time for the small size of the flats, absence of communal facilities and failure to maintain the environmental quality of the surrounding area.[49] Better results followed the development of the St Martin's flats at Emily Street in 1939.[50] This four-storey scheme, constructed on a slum clearance site, appeared despite local resistance and gave Herbert Manzoni's Public Works Department grounds for arguing that residents soon became satisfied with their new homes. This helped to promote a consensus that recourse to flats was the only way to rehouse people in the city's high-density central wards.

After the Second World War, an early start was made on rehousing in the 267-acre (108 hectare) Duddeston and Nechells Redevelopment Area. This early nineteenth century 'walking suburb', housing around 19,000 people, was originally proposed for clearance in 1936–7 but the work was postponed at the outbreak of war. Subsequently cleared in 1948, the site was rebuilt as a mixed development that included construction of four brick-finished 12-storey blocks (designed by S.N. Cooke and Partners). Constructed around a steel frame and including a Garchey waterborne waste disposal system and a central heating plant, the tall blocks proved extremely expensive and were not repeated elsewhere in the city. Instead, Manzoni's Public Works Department continued to commission much simpler, 6-storey Y-shaped blocks such as those built by Wimpey at Tile Cross in the city's eastern suburbs.[51] These blocks, actually completed before the Nechells towers, were typical of those which the incoming City Architect, Alwyn Sheppard Fidler dismissed as 'mud pies' with 'very little architectural quality about them – a set of pattern book designs'.[52]

By 1957 over 100 blocks, mostly of 6–8 storeys, had already been constructed within the city boundaries, with many more planned or under construction. In the same year, the City Architect's Department resolved to provide one-third of all dwellings in the central areas in tall blocks of flats, another third in multi-storeyed maisonettes (usually two-storey family maisonettes, built one above the other in blocks of four or six storeys), and the remainder in individual houses (including old people's bungalows).[53] Over time, use of maisonettes declined, while the typical height of the high-rise blocks progressively increased. In 1958 12-storey blocks returned to favour. The following year, heights reached 14 storeys in the suburbs and 16 storeys in the five central redevelopment areas or 'New Towns' (Duddeston and Nechells, Highgate, Ladywood, Newtown and Lee Bank: see Figure 8.1). This did not mean that there was an inevitable switch to a greater proportion of dwellings in high-rise flats.[54] Worries about tenant reactions to high blocks, with continued preferences for houses-with-gardens, and the city council's concerns about the demonstrably higher costs per dwelling of the higher blocks, led to a *decline* in the commission of multi-storey blocks between 1959 and 1963.

Commitment to the principle of building high, however, remained strong among the city's design professionals and was imminently boosted by the government-promoted industrial building drive. After considerable study, it was decided that the cost of the structural frame was 'out of proportion' to the total cost of the dwellings and that increased use of industrialised building was necessary. New tendering arrangements, illustrated by those for the mixed development estate at Millpool Hill (Figure 8.2), looked for designated contractors to make use

8.1
**Lea Bank
Redevelopment
Area (1968)**

of precasting and prefabricated components.[55] At much the same time, Sheppard Fidler decided to campaign for dramatically increased output by turning to industrialised building methods. Impressed by Liverpool's contract with the French firm Camus, Fidler pushed for a similar agreement with sufficient scale to yield significant economies of scale and greater speed of production. While significant resistance within the council steered the decision towards home-grown British systems rather than Camus, these developments presaged a brief but spectacular episode in the city's housing history centring on industrialised building methods.

In this regard, Birmingham became a 'river of productivity', representing the heaviest user of system-building of any provincial city.[56] This applied to both low- and high-rise dwellings. Output soared from 2542 completions in 1964, to 4036 in 1965, 4728 in 1966 and a remarkable 9033 in 1967.[57] Around 83 per cent of this peak output was system-built, with the city concentrating on only three systems: No-Fines (Wimpey, 1660 completions of flats in 1967), Bryant (1044 completions of low-rise housing) and Bison Wall-frame (contracted by Bryant from Concrete Ltd; 1530 completions of high-rise flats). In addition, 1030 houses were completed using four rationalised traditional systems.[58] Many of these developments proceeded on the basis of 'package deals' with large construction companies, by which design and production services were included at a set price. The underlying principle saw the corporation specify the numbers of dwellings required at each site and obtain what its officers regarded as the best tender. Outline design briefs might be given, but architects and structural engineers working for the sponsor of the system, rather than the local authority, effectively designed the building.[59]

With regard to multi-storey flats, the boom of approvals peaked in 1964 when 59 per cent were for high-rise flats, although the resulting completions did not reach their zenith until 1967. Approvals for tall flats and their completions fell steeply after those dates, but the cumulative impact was already impressive. By 1974, there were 464 blocks of 6 storeys and above within the city boundaries,[60] with the tallest measuring 33 storeys in height. Adoption of industrialised building methods undoubtedly allowed production levels that were unachievable with

8.2
Millpool Hill Estate, Birmingham,
Block C from the north-east (1958)
(architect: A.G. Sheppard Fidler)

conventional house-building techniques, but the fixation with output left many other problems. Inadequate landscaping and management quickly became apparent in many estates. Contemporary reviewers, for example, described the mixed development estate built on the site of the former Castle Bromwich airport as making 'imaginative and well organised used of a difficult site',[61] but later observers castigated the poor implementation of the plan and the inadequate management of the estate. Moreover, despite Birmingham's commitment to the sensitive landscaping of housing areas to create 'a happy environment',[62] the results soon proved tawdry. One later writer, describing its 'anonymous and forlorn appearance', commented:

> an almost flat site did not help, but there is a desperate lack of planting, the tall blocks, all named with airfield connotations, rising from an open, windswept, litter-strewn green sward . . . the whole environment [is] a dreadful testimony to impoverished planning and management.[63]

*Glasgow* would prove a more than equal provider of high flats, leading Glendinning and Muthesius to label it the 'shock city . . . of the Modern housing revolution'.[64] No city had more large-scale high-rise estates under development by the late 1950s and between 1961 and 1968 roughly three-quarters of housing completions within the city took that form.[65] Although Glasgow did not commission its first high-rise flats until 1952, an eight-storey block of one bedroom 'bed-sits' (Crathie Court) at Partick, the city was no stranger to building high given its tenement tradition. A substantial part of its housing provision, particularly in the 1950s, proceeded in tenemental form at four large out-estates within the city boundaries and, even in the 1960s, small tenements remained the dominant form of residential property. The intense policy debate which had raged between proponents of overspill and redevelopment options since 1945 (see Chapters 5 and 7), gained further impetus after declaration of the 29 Comprehensive Development Areas (CDAs) in 1957. The designated areas contained 118,500 houses, 29 per cent of Glasgow's housing stock,[66] of which 80,700 were for urgent demolition.[67] The sheer scale of the necessary renewal favoured some retention of overspill in the short term, given that it was impossible to replicate the housing densities of some areas in terms of modern housing.

In the medium term, however, the city turned to a forceful strategy of building high-rise flats on any available site. In 1956, a joint working party from Glasgow and the Scottish Office had considered the possibility of building multi-storey blocks of flats in the city.[68] A foretaste of the scale of redevelopment came with the Hutchesontown-Gorbals CDA, which had a national reputation as 'Britain's most publicised slum'.[69] The designation of the CDA in February 1957 tackled a mixed development district that covered 111 acres (44 hectares) and housed a population of 26,860 at a density of 459 persons per acre (1134 per hectare). The plans foresaw all 7605 houses being demolished and industry relocated in industrial zones elsewhere. The resulting residential area would house 10,179 people at a net density of 164 persons per acre (405 per hectare).[70] The remaining 62 per cent of the population required rehousing outside the area. Tom Brennan, who carried out a survey of the area in 1957–8, found that two households out of three stated that they would prefer to stay in improved housing in the Gorbals rather than move.[71] That option, however, was not on offer, leading Brennan to suggest that the most enthusiastic proponents of redevelopment

> hope that not only will it result in the renewal of the fabric of the Gorbals but also that it will wipe out, with the old buildings, some of the features which earned the Gorbals its unenviable reputation; and, perhaps too, that it will purge of guilt the city which allowed the old conditions to prevail for so long.

The blocks used for rehousing in Hutchesontown-Gorbals varied between 8 and 20 storeys. Although Archibald Jury's Architect's Department designed a small sector of housing as 4-storey maisonettes (Area A), overload on the city's architectural staff led the corporation to commission well-known private practitioners for the two larger segments of the site. Robert Matthew designed a group of four 17-storey blocks and a mixture of 2–4-storey blocks for Hutchesontown-Gorbals B (Figure 8.3). Basil Spence's Edinburgh office (Basil Spence, Glover and Ferguson), with Charles Robertson as project architect, designed housing in Brutalist idiom for Hutchesontown-Gorbals C (Figure 8.4). Spence's original scheme envisaged a single 20-storey megastructural spinal building, mounted on colossal pilotis, which contained services and shops as well as dwellings. The design visualised the flats as 'cross-over maisonettes' with substantial inset communal balconies. This feature led certain commentators to greet the plans with an enthusiasm that equated it with the Seven Wonders of the Ancient World:

> Five years from now – if Glasgow Corporation give financial approval – the name of the Gorbals will be on the lips of the world's leading architects, but no longer as that of Britain's most painful and publicised slum. Their eyes will be looking up and taking in a picture of one of the most progressive social and architectural experiments this country has seen: a staggered 20-storey block, jacked up on spreading concrete stilts, containing 400 houses and 1280 inhabitants, with a suspended garden, or patio, 10ft by 22ft, attached to every house.
>
> Mr. Basil Spence . . . claims that this 'spine' of the new Gorbals will be unique. He sees the 'hanging gardens' as a perpetuation of the green, for his aim in replanning the heart of the Gorbals has been to recreate a community spirit – 'to get the suburban life of houses and gardens high up,' as he put it.[72]

In the event, Spence's lightly pronounced, and quickly discarded, sociological anticipations remained rhetoric (see also Chapter 9). Despite retaining the visual ferocity of the design, the scheme was built as two blocks and the lavish facilities

were cut back. It was an early symptom of the approach that typified Glasgow's programme of building flats in the next 15 years. Prestige developments like those designed by Matthew and Spence were expensive and slow to implement. By contrast, Wimpey had gained a commission in 1959 to build three 20-storey towers in the Royston Area A redevelopment in the Garngad district of the city.[73] Containing 351 flats, they were completed in just eight months, seemingly showing the unlimited potential of industrialised building to boost output in a short span of time. Suitably convinced, the Housing Committee unleashed the most concentrated multi-storey building drive experienced by any British city, with high flats accounting for nearly three-quarters of all completions in 1961–8, compared with less than 10% for all other years between 1945 and 1974.[74]

Favouring speed and economy of output, the corporation enthusiastically sanctioned high blocks in all manner of locations – suburban, inner city gap sites and patches of brownfield land (Figure 8.5). As with Birmingham, many projects proceeded on the basis of 'package deals' with large construction companies. There was no stipulation that the appointed developer must use tall blocks, but the numbers involved 'often made difficult any pattern other than 100% multi-storey blocks'.[75] The council were also partial to the grandiloquent gestures often attached to very tall buildings, to the extent that Glasgow developed more of this type of block than any British city outside of London. By 1971, it had built 208 tower blocks containing 20,836 flats, primarily to house those displaced by slum clearance.[76] Of these, almost 140 blocks measured 20 storeys or more, with two sets of blocks soaring to over 30 storeys. The first comprised two 31-storey towers at Bluevale Street (Gallowgate), approved in 1963 and containing 348 flats. The second comprised a close packed cluster of eight steel-framed blocks at Red Road in Balornock, consisting of four point blocks, two tower blocks of 31 storeys and two slabs of 26–8 storeys (Figure 8.6). Designed by Sam Bunton and Associates and built by the city council's direct labour organisation, Red Road collectively supplied 1350 flats, with the estate therefore housing a population of nearly 4700 in just 21.5 acres (8.7 hectares).[77]

Later, the Red Road flats became famous for their social problems. Vandalism was already endemic in the blocks with the largest flats before the estate

3.5
Gap-site location,
Glasgow East End
(photograph
September 1981)

8.6
**Red Road flats,
Balornock,
Glasgow
(photograph April
1977)**

reached completion. In the short term, too, they also proved a poor advertisement for industrialised building. The steel frame and asbestos cladding panels proved a difficult combination to assemble with speed. The first block took two years to construct rather than 'twenty weeks' and the entire estate took nearly seven years to complete: 'in a continual state of crisis, improvisation and structural redesign, and locked into the wider context of the institutionalised chaos of [direct labour organisation] work practice'.[78] Economies led to under-provision of lifts for buildings of such height, which meant long waiting times when the lift was in use and frequent breakdowns at other times due to overuse. Provision of communal facilities was similarly poor. Public transport services remained woefully inadequate for a population with low car-ownership. Sam Bunton's description of the Red Road flats as 'public building without airs and graces' gained inadvertent and unwanted connotations as a result.[79]

The problems at Red Road, however, had little impact on the city's enthusiasm for high-rise flats which reached a peak in 1970 (21.8 per cent of provision of public sector dwellings) and continued into the mid-1970s, when the final contracts worked through the system. Glasgow's housing became transformed by flatted developments in gap sites, scattered throughout the city's former industrial districts, and in larger clusters. Sighthill, built by the Scottish-based firm Crudens, was typical of the latter. Crudens had previously designed Cranhill, an estate with three 19-storey tower blocks and five 5-storey blocks in Glasgow's outer ring.[80] The goodwill gained from that helped in gaining the four commissions for the much larger Sighthill between 1963 and 1967. Sighthill was an unpromising site close to the city centre, bounded, *inter alia*, by a cemetery, industrial land and transport routes and had suffered severe environmental damage. Described as 'a vast chemical dumping ground, which would require huge reclamation work', it was noted that sites 'like this were far more an engineering than an architectural matter'.[81] The resulting development, which housed a population equivalent to that of a small town, comprised ten massive 20-storey slabs in Zeilenbau alignment, a 5-storey deck-access block, and some 1- and 2-storey houses. Collectively, these supplied a total of 2280 dwellings. There was no doubt, however, that this was mass housing with little finesse. As George Bowie, then Crudens' Chief Architect, recalled when reflecting on the experience of developing Sighthill:

Because of massive financial constraints, the design frills disappeared bit by bit. And bit by bit, you got used to graffiti, vandalism – the heart slightly got knocked out of the original vision! To me, the scale of Sighthill seems really too harsh.[82]

A similar tendency to develop uncompromising, repetitive slabs also emerged in *Liverpool*, albeit after a slow start. While having a tradition of building blocks of flats stretching back to 1869 with the opening of the 3- and 5-storey walk-up St Martin's Cottages, Liverpool had only spasmodically experimented with multi-storey flats. In 1954, the city sent a fact-finding deputation to North America, 'to see for ourselves what living conditions were really like in American publicly aided multi-storey projects.'[83] The visitors were not entirely enamoured with what they saw in New York (Figure 8.7), particularly the very high densities (300 persons per acre; 741 per hectare) imposed at Parkchester, but remained determined to take positive messages from what they saw. Ronald Bradbury, the City Architect and Director of Housing, wrote:

> The effect upon the deputation of this vast scheme, with its terrifically high density, was very great indeed. In one sense it was frightening because it was so different from those which one had seen before. But whilst one could not conceive a development of this kind proving entirely satisfactory, nevertheless it did cause one to wonder whether or not we are making the maximum use of our small stock of land available for redevelopment in our central areas.[84]

Clearly, nothing the committee saw deterred them from pursuing the path of introducing high-rise flats as a component of its social housing provision. Faced with a grave shortage of building land and, like Glasgow, anxious to resist resorting

8.7
Packing of high-rise blocks in Lower East Side, Manhattan (1979)

to overspill, the visitors were prone to identify the more positive aspects of what they saw. Thus, even Parkchester had some redeeming factors with its 'five main lungs of open space' described as 'quite pleasant and well laid out' in spite of the blocks being 'very tightly packed around them'.[85]

Policy in Liverpool, a city that regularly oscillated between Labour and Conservative control, rested on a complex alliance of executive and administrative forces. The constant presence until his death in 1966, however, was Ronald Bradbury. The former City Architect for Glasgow, Bradbury headed both the Architect's and the Housing Departments until 1963 (when J.W. Boddy became responsible for housing). Bradbury presided over a strategy that wholeheartedly implemented very high-density high-rise development using slab blocks, without much use of the mixed development of houses, maisonettes and flats seen in London and other cities.[86] Moreover, Bradbury's office repeatedly defied accepted wisdom on the diminishing marginal returns on increasing the height of blocks, by adding more storeys to those already authorised and ignoring land-use restrictions if found inconvenient.[87] The policy began in 1954 with approval for Liverpool's first postwar multi-storey block, the 10-storey Coronation Court, on the Sparrow Hall Estate (Figure 8.8). Designed by Bradbury and built by Costain, it was 330 feet (100 metres) long and 100 feet (30 metres) high – large enough to dominate the approach to the built-up area of the city via the East Lancashire Road.[88] It was the first of 67 tower blocks constructed in Liverpool in the period up to 1974.

8.8
**Coronation Court, Liverpool (advertisement, 1958)**

System-building made a decisive contribution to that total. It was a return to dimly remembered roots. The city had pioneered housebuilding from precast reinforced concrete slabs at the start of the twentieth century with the Eldon Street dwellings (1904–5), built to the design of the City Engineer, John Brodie (Figure 8.9).[89] In June 1962, Liverpool City Council sent a deputation to Paris to inspect products of the Balency-et-Schuhl, Coignet and Camus building systems, along with the factories in which they were produced. It decided that the Camus system had the best track record, with over 50,000 flats already built in France by these methods and in blocks of up to 21 storeys. After negotiations, Liverpool entered into an agreement in early 1963 for 2486 dwellings and 1206 garages to be built by Camus methods over five years. As a result, the Unit Construction Company (the British licensees) built a prefabrication factory at the Kirkby Industrial Trading Estate capable of building room-sized panels for 1000 dwellings per annum.[90] The problem, however, was that the city lacked land on which to erect the commissioned blocks. Development therefore took place wherever sites were available, a mismatch of land and development strategy that symbolised concerns about the organisation and efficacy of Liverpool's housing drive.

As a result, the city requested advice on industrialised building techniques from the newly formed National Building Agency (NBA) at the end of 1964. The request came from a personal approach from Bill Sefton, the new Labour Leader of the Council, who had decided that housing policy was not meeting its objectives.[91] The NBA decided that the problem required a wider approach that looked at the context for industrialised building rather than the techniques to be used and expanded its brief to cover the city's housing policy and programme – a decision that caused apoplexy among the mandarins of Whitehall (see p. 198ff).[92] The ensuing report noted that the current rate of slum clearance barely kept pace with 'the rate

8.9
**Picture of concrete slabs leaving Cobbs Quarry, Liverpool, by steam traction engine (July 1905)**

of generation of new slums' and recommended a three-phase clearance pro-gramme.[93] The first (1966–72) would tackle clearance of the worst 33,000 inner city slums, the remaining 3500 prefabricated bungalows and would accommodate 2800 from the Housing Register. Using accelerated slum clearance as a means of freeing land, it was recommended that 3000 dwellings should be built between 1966 and 1972 by traditional methods and 2400 by industrialised building techniques. The report recommended that an external consultant should advise on the planning and phasing of the housing programme, work which the NBA 'would be happy to undertake'. The report noted the 'shortage of architectural staff', but felt that private architects might be allocated sites for development, provided that they received 'precise terms of reference'.[94] Notably, the report made no specification about whether the industrialised content should be flats or houses, but merely made recommendations as to the size of the dwellings in terms of number of bedrooms.

Although resisted by Liverpool's Housing Department, which saw the report as limiting its power over its programming function and traditional autonomy,[95] the city accepted the NBA's target for the seven years up to 1973. The programme, however, merely escalated the production-led housing drive to parallel the large-scale and transformative approach to urban renewal already shown in the proposals for the city centre (see Chapter 6). It involved around one-third of the city's 47 square miles, including nearly all of inner Liverpool. By 1972, despite its slower start, Liverpool's 20 per cent of council housing in high-rise flats was little different from that of Birmingham (21 per cent).[96] Seen from any vantage point, the new housing reshaped large swathes of the city. Areas of closely packed housing in areas such as Everton and Toxteth were swept away by slum clearance projects,[97] yet there was little sense that the replacement environments accorded to any preconceived plans about the city's visual appearance or skyline. Throughout the history of architecture, tall buildings had been special buildings and the Modern Movement's thinking in the past had always stressed the need to situate such buildings sensitively, with emphasis on proportion, perspective and composition. Now in Liverpool, as in Glasgow, development depended on site availability. When a larger area was available for development, it was possible to develop substantial numbers of high blocks, as in Everton where the clearance of terraced streets saw placement of clusters of blocks on the slopes of the ridge that runs through the area. Elsewhere, development proceeded wherever sites could be found for the pre-ordered blocks. High output was achieved, but seldom had the design and deployment of tall buildings been treated so casually.

## Industrialised building

The key phase of construction for high-rise flats in the 1960s coincided with the government-sponsored turn towards industrialised building, although their coincidence was not inevitable. High-rise flats could be built without recourse to industrialised building, as many existing examples readily showed. Equally, there was no reason why adopting industrialised building methods automatically led to the construction of modern housing, let alone high-rise flats. Use of systems had soared in the early 1950s when the immediate postwar housing shortage prompted a rise in systems from 13 per cent of local authority housing projects in 1951 to 24 per cent in 1954,[98] but high-rise then barely figured in the equation. Indeed, the most successful building systems in 1960s Britain were those versatile enough to be used in estates that contained a mix of low- and high-rise elements.[99] Further confirmation that the adoption of industrialised building did not necessarily mean high-rise flats came from the fact that system building still contributed 19.6 per cent of local authority completions in 1976, by which time use of high-rise structures for council housing had dwindled away to nothing.

The sheer number and diversity of the authorities responsible for housing ensured that patterns of implementation of both industrialised building and tall flats were uneven. Some smaller provincial cities followed a similar pattern to the larger cities considered above. In Leicester, for example, the number of council houses built by industrialised building methods rose from 21 per cent to 42 per cent between 1964 and 1967, of which the majority were tower block flats.[100] By contrast, other smaller towns and cities, including the New Towns, rarely sought approval for multi-storey flats for social housing,[101] although later New Towns such as Cumbernauld and Livingston made extensive use of industrialised building methods. Even those authorities that might later seem avid enthusiasts for high-rise flats adopted such structures at different speeds. Manchester, for example, initially resisted the trend. For much of the 1950s, the city showed a preference for mixed development using low-rise flats and conventional houses, accompanied by a vigorous policy of moving residents to overspill estates at Heywood and Langley (Middleton) in the north, Hyde in the east and Worsley in the west.[102] It was not until the 1960s that the city turned to both high flats and industrialised building methods, although then doing so with an enthusiasm seemingly borne of wishing to compensate for lost time.

The short-lived convergence between the methodology of industrialised building and the specific building form (high-rise flats) in the 1960s reflected, *inter alia*, the implications of land and labour shortages, the belief that high flats represented a potential 'technological shortcut to social change',[103] and an interpretation that saw construction of tall flats in significant clusters as yielding maximum economies of scale.[104] Active central government promotion of industrialised building was also vital. While this came without specific support for high-rise buildings, these gained significant backing from key local authorities (the providers of social housing) and from a construction industry that urgently needed orders to justify its investment in plant and equipment. The industry also adjusted its selling strategies, through the creation of affordable package 'design-and-build' deals, so that even local authorities that lacked a substantial architectural staff might aspire to such structures as part of their housing provision. As George Bowie recalled with reference to some smaller Scottish towns:

> If you were a councillor and you went trotting down to Glasgow or London, or were taken on a trip to the Interbau experimental housing area in Berlin, and saw impressive multi-storey blocks, prestigious buildings, you'd say: 'We must have a few of these!' You'd get places

like Buckhaven and Methil: there's only one reason why there are multis there. They'd say: 'If Kirkcaldy and Dunfermline can have multis, by God we're gauny have a couple too!' In many respects, the builder would be happier building two-storey houses.[105]

## Deploying systems

The deployment of systems, as a specific form of industrialised building, had occurred over a lengthy period of time. A 1934 Ministry of Health initiative to examine the efficacy of system-building for flats, for example, saw Leeds import the Mopin system from France for the slum clearance site at Quarry Hill, Leeds (R.A.H. Livett, 1935–8). The LCC, the only local authority to have had anything approaching a developmental programme, had conducted occasional tests of industrialised building during the 1950s. In 1953, the Architect's Department began an experimental building project with a private contractor (Laing) for the Elmington Estate at Picton Street, Camberwell, described as 'probably the first estate in the country laid out to suit the path of the travelling crane that built it'.[106] In December 1956, Hubert Bennett reported that the savings in construction time and cost were less than anticipated, but that further schemes would develop the lessons of the Picton Street Experiment. These included modification for flats of the precast large-panel Reema system, devised by British architects Reed and Mallick in 1948. This presaged the qualitatively different approaches of the 1960s, but not on the pattern that later emerged:

> This was systematic building, but it was not yet a building system. The size, dimensions and articulation of units was architecturally determined and not productivity determined.[107]

Moreover, even with an authority interested in developing new housing prototypes and building methods, the links with the past in the mid-1950s were stronger than sometimes imagined. Peter Carter, for example, recalled that the development of the Bentham Road estate offered a curious blend of innovation and tradition, a 'wonderful [modern] structure' combined with nineteenth century heating:

> We did the Bentham Road scheme, which was essentially two horizontal blocks of the 'mock-up' maisonettes and a number of low-storey buildings: two-storey buildings for elderly people, a terrace of four-storey maisonettes and also a children's play space (which was great fun to design because the site sloped). The thing that we were most conscious about was that the site, which had been bombed, had a row of two-storey Georgian terraced houses on one side and then Victoria Park. So people in the high buildings, they were eleven-storey maisonettes – the ground floor was open and then there were ten storeys . . . basically five lots of maisonettes piled on top of one another. . . . It was fascinating to watch during its construction; it really was a twentieth century technology, which was terribly ironic because that building had fires and chimneys . . . going up eleven storeys – can you believe it?[108]

It was not, indeed, until the early 1960s that the LCC moved on a stage in its thinking about industrialised building. The immediate spur was severe labour shortage. Hubert Bennett reported in 1962 that the workload of staff at the LCC's Architect's Department had increased by 11 per cent between 1959 and 1961, whereas the numbers of architectural staff had fallen by 13 per cent, due particularly to the better pay prospects in the private sector.[109] Five days after presenting his report, Bennett announced his proposal for 'improved staff productivity and greater speed in building by bringing the Danish Larsen and Nielsen system into London'.[110] This form of system building involved manufacturing large prefabricated concrete panels off-site, putting them in place *in situ* by means of tower crane, and bolting the sections together to construct the block of flats. The arrangement involved a private sector partner in the shape of Taylor Woodrow-Anglian, a company jointly owned by Myton Ltd, a subsidiary of the building contractor, Taylor Woodrow, and Anglian Building Products Ltd, a subsidiary of Ready Mixed Concrete Ltd. Anglian would operate the fabrication plant at Lenwade, near Norwich and contracted to build the dwellings, although the conceptual design remained with the LCC architects.[111] A delegation from the Housing Committee visited Copenhagen and reported its satisfaction with the potential of the system.

In April 1963, the LCC signed its first contract for the erection of factory-made housing units under licence from Larsen and Nielsen,[112] with 562 dwellings at Morris Walk, Woolwich. At the time, this was the largest industrialised housing contract in the country. Morris Walk comprised 47 three-storey blocks with 6 flats each and 7 ten-storey blocks with 40 flats each. The LCC and its successor, the Greater London Council,[113] would diversify their suppliers of system-built housing while looking to 'ensure continuity of orders for whatever industrialised methods of building construction it decides to employ'.[114] Nevertheless, the Larsen and Nielsen system remained the leading system. Looking ahead, this was an ill-starred decision. In May 1968, the partial collapse of a Larsen and Nielsen block built by the London Borough of Newham, the 22-storey Ronan Point in Custom House,[115] cast serious doubts on this particular system and led to expensive strengthening measures.

Further comment about that occurrence and the associated public debate is in Chapter 12. At this point, it should be emphasised that the type of arrangement entered into by the LCC in the early 1960s caused few anxieties within the architectural profession per se. The proposal to turn to industrialised building clearly came from the architects and was framed with an eye to maintaining design standards. The LCC's own record of innovation gave grounds for reassurance that the architects' contribution to housing projects would not be diluted by commercial pressures from contractors or manufacturers. In other circumstances, however, things might not be as positive. A report by the RIBA in 1965, for instance, identified the value of industrialised building in saving time on repetitive tasks such as standardising detailing from one building to another, economising on the number of working drawings required, reducing the need for site supervision and improving cost planning. Nevertheless, the authors added, somewhat apprehensively, that 'the greatest advantages [of industrialised building] seem to accrue to those who have initiated the industrialisation'.[116]

Quite simply, it was readily apparent by 1965 that public sector architects frequently did not initiate the process. When initiated by contractors, the prime advantages of industrialisation tended to be on saving construction time, reducing site labour, cutting down the number of operations carried out on site and circumventing restrictive practices. Design was seldom the prime consideration. When initiated by manufacturers or suppliers of systems, the major benefits of industrialised building comprised a share of a housing market potentially worth millions of pounds over a period of at least a decade, provided it was possible to keep production lines running at somewhere near optimal output. This led to powerful commercial pressures to sell system-built housing to local authority clients, to reduce costs and maximise throughput to achieve economies of scale and profitability. Standardisation and repetition of identical units, with a minimum of site-specific design, seemingly offered the clearest route to achieving that goal. As Kenneth Campbell noted:

8.10
**Aldbridge Street, with Aylesbury Estate, Southwark (1967–77) under construction**

> By definition industrial production involves capital investment in plant which must be amortised. In most concrete systems a large part of this plant is in the form of heavy moulds, each of which can produce a single type of component or, with more or less simple modification, a restricted range of components. Therefore a sufficient run of such elements must be obtained before the moulds can economically be scrapped or remade.[117]

In the same way, it made best commercial sense to develop in a way that allowed the most efficient deployment of heavy building machinery in one place: a consideration that again tended to favour building concentrated blocks of high-rise flats rather than widely scattered low-rise.

The results were often painfully clear in the finished product, of which the Aylesbury Estate in the London Borough of Southwark is a poignant example. Later to become a byword for social problems and recommended for complete clearance in 2005, Aylesbury was the largest social housing estate of its type in Europe when completed. Designed in 1963 by Derek Winch for the Metropolitan Borough of Southwark and subsequently revised by the London Borough of Southwark's architects under Frank Hayes, Aylesbury was constructed between 1967 and 1977. The estate covered 64 acres (28.5 hectares) and supplied 2434 dwellings for 8000–10,000 people.[118] Aylesbury replaced streets of low-rise and substandard terraced houses (Figure 8.10), with a pedestrianised estate of slab blocks, ranging from 4 to 14 storeys, with networks of internal walkways. While the prefabricated dwellings were recognised to be spacious and well equipped, the estate revealed design and structural problems from the outset. Open space was in short supply, especially since an adjacent park never materialised, although the smaller slabs were grouped alternately around garage courts and grassed areas.[119] Attempts to capitalise on industrialised building methods saw the taller slabs constructed in extremely long lines to allow construction to proceed economically from tracked cranes. This led inevitably to repetitive and monotonous façades (Figure 8.11). The conclusion that form followed 'crane-ways' was hard to avoid.

8.11
**Elongated façade of Aylesbury Estate, Southwark (1967–77) under construction**

Regardless of built forms, however, manufacturers and suppliers were not necessarily effective in achieving their aims of production economies of scale. In the first place, they failed to help themselves by maintaining an extraordinary number of different systems and opening relatively small-scale factories. John Laing Construction Ltd alone offered five different systems in 1963 – Jespersen, Sectra, Easiform, Laingwall and Laingspan – with no less than three specifically recommended for high flats. In the same year, Concrete Ltd produced its Bison Wall-Frame system for high flats at no fewer than five factories: Hounslow, Tilbury, Lichfield, Leeds and Falkirk.[120] The possibility of obtaining production runs likely to yield significant cost reductions per unit was remote. Second, the industry faced a difficult client base. The multiplicity of clients often made 'it difficult to establish the large or continuing building programmes which industrialised methods require'.[121] Third, manufacturers readily accepted the local authorities' tendency to place small orders for industrialised buildings with several different firms, usually in the hope that they might achieve repeat business later, and catered for requests for small variations in design that invariably led to greater costs in working diagrams and modifications to production lines. This produced the ironic result that the industry failed to achieve fully the economic benefits associated with standardisation, but the variations introduced were of such small visual significance that they did little to counter the accusation that 'rationalisation and functionalisation' stripped architecture of its 'poetical content' and produced mundane buildings and dull environments.[122]

The result of these difficult trading conditions led to 'cutting corners' to lower production costs – 'the whole thing was a disaster, not because it was run by architects but because it was run by the Valuers, who were saving their pennies'[123] – and contributed to sustained hard selling. The major architectural and building journals of the time swelled in size due to their advertising content and special supplements about industrialised building. New and often short-lived professional journals, such as *Interbuild* and *Industrialised Building: Systems and Components*, specifically targeted the growing market. System builders, building contractors, component manufacturers, structural engineers, raw material suppliers and others used public relations and direct approaches by sales teams to tout their wares to design professionals and senior political figures in the local authorities. At this point, an endemic weakness assumed greater significance. The decentralised system established for housebuilding worked on a degree of trust and with an absence of system-wide auditing and lack of accountability for decisions that now seems astonishing. Expenses-paid visits to the sites of production factories in continental Europe, involving senior architectural staff and members of housing committees, were freely arranged. Hospitality and gifts were freely dispensed. Other forms of largesse, sometimes crossing the dividing line into corruption, served to win the support of local dignitaries and design professionals (see Chapter 12).

## Official sanction

Central government was perhaps the most intriguing force behind the advocacy of industrialised building and, to a lesser extent, high-rise flats. Although the state's role in the disaggregated housing market was to subsidise and persuade rather than directly intervene, its sustained support for industrialised building played an important part in propagating the technology. First, from a macroeconomic perspective, introduction of industrialised building addressed the general question of productive efficiency by seeking reform to an industry renowned for low productivity. Second, and more specifically, it was believed that industrialised building could ramp up production of housing without significant increase in the supply of skilled labour – the key constraint on existing supply. A.W. Cleeve Barr, Chief Architect to the Ministry of Housing and Local Government, summarised the essential attraction of industrialised building in this context:

> What we can expect from the industry is speedier building, a greater volume of building from the same labour force, and in the long run, better quality building from factory-made components, with higher standards in terms of heating, insulation, draught-proofing, equipment and services generally for only a little extra money.[124]

Yet, as Cleeve Barr also observed, there was little conviction in central government circles that such housing would prove more cost-effective: 'the actual costs of housebuilding are unlikely to come down, but as a result of industrialisation, I would hope for better value for money'.[125] At best, they could create structures that might reduce costs, such as encouragement to form regional consortia of larger authorities 'with major programmes to pool and with highly-qualified staffs'. By late 1963, for instance, the formation of such groups in Yorkshire (Hull, Leeds, Nottingham, Scunthorpe and Sheffield) and the Midlands (Coventry, Derby, Dudley, Leicester, Smethwick, Stoke-on-Trent, Walsall, West Bromwich, Wolverhampton and Worcester) and putative groups in London, Merseyside, North Lancashire and South-East Lancashire involved 37 authorities accounting for 11 per cent of the housing programme.[126]

Predictably, the breadth of support for industrialised building in government encountered the problems of cross-ministry approaches in the arcane world of Whitehall. Broadly speaking, the most significant support came from the Ministry of Public Building and Works and the Ministry of Housing and Local Government. The former, for example, had appointed Sir Donald Gibson to the new post of Director-General of Research and Development at the Ministry of Public Building and Works on 5 November 1962. Gibson, City Architect for Coventry during its reconstruction (1938–55), had served as County Architect for Nottinghamshire between 1955 and 1958, where he oversaw the development of the Consortium of Local Authorities Special Programme (CLASP) system for prefabricated school-building. More recently, as Director-General of Works at the War Office, he had designed the first War Office building using the CLASP system, which extended its use from three to four storeys.[127] Gibson's new post was to coordinate the activities of groups within the ministry and 'throughout the Government service' with regard to 'new and rapid methods of construction', with specific responsibility to 'standardise the use and production of building components to the greatest possible extent'.[128] His appointment seemingly symptomised official determination to push industrialised building methods through:

> at that time, Donald Gibson was Head at the Ministry of Works and was in the position of promoting construction policy. A pretty strong message came round that prefabrication was the only way to produce the buildings that the country needed within the price and the time available. There was a lot of political support for a programme based on prefabrication.[129]

The Ministry of Housing and Local Government had its own architects working on industrialised building, although they had little direct input into the business of constructing housing. The main group worked under Oliver Cox, the Deputy Chief Architect, in the Research and Development Group. Cox had long experience of the development of system-building through his various appointments prior to moving to the ministry in 1960. He had begun his career in the school-building programme at Hertfordshire County Council and then joined the Development Group at the LCC Architect's Department, where he had helped to evaluate the large-panel Reema system. Having moved to the ministry after the denouement of Hook New Town (see Chapter 7), he had participated, among other things, in the development of the Adaptable House for the 1962 Ideal Home Exhibition (two terraced houses designed to Parker Morris standards for a building cost of £2000), the 5M version of the CLASP system for four prototype houses built at Gloucester Street, Sheffield for Sheffield City Council, and adaptations of the 12M Danish Jespersen system at St Mary's Oldham.[130] The work at Oldham, in particular, involved a 16-acre (6.5-hectare) site in the cleared St Mary's ward, close to the city centre, to serve as a working textbook of how to put into practice the official Parker Morris housing standards.[131] Looking back on this work, Cox observed:

> We tried a steel frame system (5M), which was not very successful – we built at Sheffield a small group with which we had awful problems. The CLASP people said to us that we would never be able to do it at the prices that we were aiming at because the scope in school building is so much bigger . . . and they were right. So I am afraid that failed there, but there was pressure from the government, especially Sir Keith Joseph, who was very keen to get system building going, like in Germany and France. We studied them and then used a Danish system, which was 12M, the Jespersen system, pre-stressed concrete. We built an experimental scheme. The ministry wanted a demonstration project, but we said that was not the purpose. We must be allowed to make mistakes, which we did. They thought that was terrible. It was not a popular idea that you did what you thought was right and, if it went wrong, you made a public statement about it so that other people did not do the same thing. That never got through to the administration.[132]

The reference to Sir Keith Joseph alludes to the fact that industrialised building gained significant Cabinet support following Harold Macmillan's 'Night of the Long Knives' reshuffle in July 1962, with the appointment of Geoffrey Rippon at Public Building and Works and Sir Keith Joseph at Housing and Local Government.[133] Both had connections with the construction industry: Geoffrey Rippon was a director of Cubitts, while Keith Joseph was the heir to Bovis, which his father Samuel had developed into one of Britain's leading house-building companies. Both also had specific remits to promote industrialised building as part of reinvigorating the housing drive, to the extent of contested overlap. At least one observer noted the need for 'reconciliation of Mr. Rippon's expanding empire at Public Works with the ambition of Sir Keith Joseph at Housing and Local Government'.[134]

Shortly after taking office, Sir Keith Joseph started to map out a future in which industrialised building took a key role alongside traditional building. Although never a believer in widespread use of high-rise flats, he looked to higher-density developments and industrialised building to boost housing production. Systemic problems, however, existed in terms of the 'entirely uncoordinated' nature of supply and demand. His initial task was to hold discussions with relevant parties to examine the conditions necessary for the successful introduction of industrialised building systems.[135] He acknowledged that these could imply standardisation and repetition, but sought to counter the negative aspects of this observation:

> There is, in fact, no reason why houses built by industrialised methods need be any more standardised than housing built by traditional methods. In all housing schemes there is a large amount of repetitive work, and there is ample scope for variety of plan, finish and appearance in projects using standardised components. Indeed, the use of these components, while setting its own discipline, opens up new opportunities for skilled and imaginative design.[136]

The change of minister to Labour's Richard Crossman after the general election of October 1964 made no significant difference to advocacy of industrialised building. Crossman had no previous knowledge of the construction industry but, in the words of his private secretary John Delafons, had a penchant for 'taking up ideas, articulating and enlarging them, formulating policy and organising someone else to do the work'.[137] Industrialised building was one such idea. Crossman's diaries are full of private as well as public passions for the potential of industrialised building. For example, he wrote about 'the most exhilarating time' that he had when meeting the ministry's Research and Development Group, 'a brilliant group of young men and women actively at work developing two methods of system-building, 5M and 12M'. Crossman was particularly interested in their work at Oldham (see p. 194), believing that they should think bigger in the interests of improving prospects of profitability:

> I asked why it was only 750 houses they were building at Oldham: why not rebuild the whole thing? Wouldn't that help Laing, the builders? 'Of course it would,' said Oliver, 'and it would help Oldham too.' 'Well, why don't we do it?' 'It depends on the Minister.' And Whitfield-Lewis, the

Chief Architect, smiled, and I said, 'Why shouldn't we? Why shouldn't we assume that instead of doing one little bit of the centre of Oldham we should use the whole 300 acres and have a real demonstration that our system-building can work and really does reduce costs? Let's see that one piece of central redevelopment is really finished by us.'

I drove back to the Ministry (it's only just round the corner) warmed and excited. I'm going to insist if I can that we should persuade Oldham to let us do the whole thing; there's no doubt that Laing would be delighted because they will be mass-producing for a longer continuous run, so that costs can be cut.[138]

Crossman retained these enthusiasms, even though the question of large-scale interventions in urban renewal, like that of profitability, remained stubbornly difficult to achieve. Sending a message to a conference on industrialised building that he was unable to attend towards the end of his time as Minister of Housing and Local Government, Crossman stressed that the basic problem remained the need 'to combine good design with efficient production'. His message was upbeat and optimistic: 'Much thought, skill and money have been put into developing industrialised building systems for flats and houses and in production terms we are already seeing the benefits'. Nevertheless, he warned his audience that organisational change was also necessary:

To reap the full benefits of industrialisation we must look on the whole building operation from start to finish as an integrated process. We must increasingly give thought to rationalising and industrialising site works and substructures.[139]

Part of that reorganisation should also address the quality of local authority architects, about whom Crossman was also not over-enamoured. Reflecting on visits to Leeds and Sheffield, he noted: 'What they need more than anything are architects of genius and they haven't got a single one.'[140] A few days later (15 January 1965), he recollected:

In describing my visit to Oldham in this diary I tried to indicate how important industrialized building is to us. Since I wrote that, the Prime Minister has committed us to industrialized building, and I see nothing to lose if we make the local authorities turn over to it since conventional architecture is so terrible it couldn't be worse. If we are going to do this, the agency through which we have to work is the National Building Agency.[141]

## The National Building Agency

The agency to which Crossman referred presents an instructive example of both the problems and confusions of giving direction to the industrialised housing drive and of the architect finding a place in this evolving area. The NBA originally came about as a result of an initiative by the Conservative Geoffrey Rippon at the Ministry of Public Building and Works. Rippon's initial task on taking office was to implement the main findings of the Emmerson Report,[142] which had examined the chaotic state of the building industry. In a speech delivered in October 1962, he announced his general intention to work towards bringing a measure of coordination and rationalisation to the construction industry, with a specific commitment to industrialised building:

> I further intend to promote, so far as it lies within my power, greater standardisation of materials and components; the improvement of the numbers and quality of personnel at all levels of the building industry; more research into economy in building and practical problems and more effective dissemination of technical information.[143]

Rippon believed that more was necessary and worked towards the establishment of an independent organisation to promote industrialised building across the sector. Confidential documents from January 1963 show him proposing the creation of a Central Building Agency which would seek:

> (a) to obtain economies of mass-production in the manufacture of building components by standardisation,
> (b) to make the building process itself more efficient and less costly by the adoption of systems which permit more cooperative operations, call for less skilled labour, involve less outdoor work, or less 'wet' processes,
> (c) to improve the standard of design.[144]

He compared such an agency with a New Town Development Corporation, although 'concerned with construction only and *not* with the acquisition of land or with the subsequent maintenance or management of property'.[145] The agency would effectively be 'a large design office' preparing site layouts and detailed designs, obtaining tenders, placing contracts and supervising work. He continued:

> By virtue of undertaking schemes for a large number of authorities, it would be able to group the work into substantial contracts and apply industrialised methods of building to them, thereby improving the speed and efficiency of the national building programme. . . . The agency would need to employ a first-rate professional staff with experience in the housing and industrialised building field but I also envisage it having power to employ consultant architects.[146]

More ambitious in scope than anything previously mooted, an accompanying note from Rippon suggested that the Central Building Agency could provide 'the means of securing the transformation of the slums of Stepney, the Gorbals and Liverpool'.[147]

Such an agency would have dramatically increased the role of central government in housing, with considerable implications for the engineering and architectural professions. Predictably, it was soon apparent that this proposal, which senior civil servants mischievously labelled the '*Centralised* Building Agency' (with all that implied in Cold War parlance), had 'not been welcomed in Whitehall'.[148] The Minister of Health and others expressed the 'strongest doubts about the political wisdom of establishing such an agency'.[149] Orchestrated by the redoubtable Dame Evelyn Sharpe, the Ministry of Housing and Local Government conspired against the intrusion of an independent agency into its affairs. Discussions with the building industry also encountered resistance from those that, not without reason, saw their interests threatened. Their objections centred around disquiet at interference in client–supplier relations, more general threats to the operation of private enterprise, and concern about any testing involved.[150] When Rippon finally launched the idea in public in June 1963, the unnamed building agency had already become emaciated. It was now an advisory and collaborative body that would offer assistance to bodies, such as smaller local authorities or the newly proposed housing associations. Rippon also carefully emphasised: 'I would not suggest that such an agency should itself act as a contractor or displace the client's own architect.' Rather, its first function would be to

> collate orders into the necessary volume and to ensure that this was done on a large enough scale so that authorities in any part of the country could join in and benefit from the orders placed in other parts of the country.[151]

Opposition continued within Whitehall primarily motivated by mandarin concerns about the creation of a body that operated independently of specific ministries. As late as mid-November, a senior civil servant at the Treasury suggested that the agency would duplicate functions for which 'adequate arrangements already exist or are being created by the Departments concerned for the fostering of industrialised building for schools, hospitals and high flats'.[152] Finally, and almost at the end of the informal consultative period, the new body gained the name of 'National Building Agency' instead of the Central Building Agency or Sir Keith Joseph's counter-suggestion of the 'Building Order Agency'.[153]

The RIBA provided responses of behalf of architects to the establishment of the new body. As late as 5 December, less than a week before the White Paper that launched the new body, the RIBA retained its characteristic cautious ambivalence about the whole subject of industrialised building (see also Chapter 4). The president, Robert Matthew, stated that the organisation had 'no official view' about it, other than to state that members had misgivings about the position of smaller private practices, that relied on work from local authorities and about fee scales. The minister in reply stated that the agency would respect the position of architects and that it was not the intention to 'deprive private architects of a fair living'. He also informed the RIBA's representatives that the NBA would not carry out research and development and that membership of its board would 'contain people who reflected all the major interests concerned' but would 'not be chosen as representatives of particular organisations'.[154]

Rippon placed formal proposals for the NBA before Parliament in a White Paper on 10 December 1963. Stripped of its powers for radical intervention, the new body would assist the 'industrialisation of building', mainly by helping public and private clients to organise their demands into larger contracts and giving independent advice. Despite the Whitehall intrigues, the NBA remained outside direct ministerial supervision and funded by grant-in-aid and revenue from private and public sector clients – never likely to be a recipe for long-term security or continuity. Its scope remained limited. It was not a direct labour organisation and any hopes that this would be a major contributor to architectural or engineering research were quickly dashed. There was, at most, a possibility that in 'a few exceptional circumstances . . . the Agency will provide a full design service'.[155] It had no statutory responsibility to carry out testing programmes or make even formal interventions in the manner of the Development Group at the Ministry of Housing and Local Government. Its recruitment base was also limited owing to 'the tightness of professional staff', since it was regarded that 'the Agency should not seek staff itself on a scale which would seriously deplete staffs of local authorities, etc.' but would instead 'look for staff on secondment'.[156]

The NBA commenced its uncertain future in May 1964 from offices in Portman Square, London and in Edinburgh. Its Board of Directors scrupulously represented the major professional interests with a stake in industrialised building and was thereby doomed to replicate the usual frictions between engineers and architects. The chairman, Thomas Prosser, was formerly managing director of the Liverpool engineering firm, William Thornton and Son, while its deputy chairman was A.W. Cleeve Barr, formerly Chief Architect at the Ministry of Housing and Local Government. Its staff, which grew to 150 in 1968, reflected the prevailing professional demarcations, with the larger London office having an Architectural Division and an engineering-based Operations Division. There were suggestions that the NBA might open more regional offices 'in parallel with the Ministry of Housing and Local Government', but this received a barbed response from the architects at that ministry. In a memorandum from October 1964, Whitfield Lewis commented:

> On the matter of the National Building Agency being associated with our regional offices, I am in full agreement but doubt if they have the staff to implement the idea. If they attempt to recruit on such a basis they will probably denude us of more staff![157]

Seeking to retain the initiative, he suggested giving the NBA 'some definite assignments', including 'the organisation and servicing' of two emerging consortia in Southern England (South-East Essex and the South Coast), provided that they 'accept 5M as the basis for work and not attempt to substitute their own proposals, or a proprietary system'.[158]

As the working relationship unfolded, it became clear that the NBA was achieving little in its consultative and evangelistic role. Its early development was marred by funding problems and demarcation problems with existing ministries, particularly Housing and Local Government. In January 1965, it took charge of the technical appraisal of new techniques and systems of building for the public sector, would help when requested to arrange industrialised building contracts, and offered an advisory service on project management.[159] Moreover, positive statements as to how the NBA's existence might profit the housing drive started, somewhat belatedly, to emerge: 'The Chairman of the Agency said that the agency's ultimate object was to achieve a production of 100,000 system-built houses a year. They believed that a figure of 50,000 a year was possible almost immediately.'[160] Somewhat remarkably, the figure of 50,000 excluded 'such labour-intensive and near-traditional systems such as Wimpey's No-Fines and Laing's Easiform',[161] presumably because they were not seen as sufficiently innovative applications of the technology. The commentary on the state-of-the-art made sombre reading:

> Wimpey were in a class of their own; eight other firms were major producers; and some forty companies had viable systems but on present production methods could only expect to market a total of 5,000 dwellings a year between them. Thus of the 110 systems which were referred to in a directory to be published by the NBA next month [January 1965] only 49 . . . had in fact been built in more than 10 units.

In response, the NBA resolved to cut the number of systems recommended to local authorities to 'around a dozen'.[162] What was necessary was not the establishment of new enterprises, but better use of the productive capacity in which many firms had invested 'over the past two or three years in the anticipation of obtaining housing orders which have so far failed to materialise'.[163]

The ensuing years saw continuing problems in defining the NBA's role. Close liaisons with the work of Ministry of Housing and Local Government architects led to the building industry expressing concerns in early 1966 about the NBA's independence in appraising the systems in which they had a major financial stake.[164] Having reconsidered these arrangements, the government changed the NBA's role in May to concentrate on housing and transferred departmental responsibility for the NBA to the Ministry of Housing and Local Government.[165] In early 1967, serious thought was given to winding up the agency due to 'acute internal disharmony within the NBA and the difficulty of finding a suitable role [for it]'. In 1968, Treasury disquiet about lack of 'adherence by professional staff to an inherently sound costing and accounting system' and more general anxieties about low morale prompted further questions about the NBA's future.[166] Yet the most significant problems followed the downturn in housing in the late 1960s to 'a limited, possibly dwindling field of activity' and the 'tapering off' of work on system building.[167] Regardless of the value of its expertise in appraising systems and assisting the spread of industrialised building methods to smaller local authorities, the NBA struggled to make any real impact in the key task of addressing over-capacity in the building industry with regard to competing systems. When asked in 1967 about a 'situation where a multiplicity of systems inevitably produced small runs', Cleeve Barr expressed his hopes that the issue of the NBA's appraisal forms would reduce the number of systems and result in longer runs, but felt compelled to add: 'But in the event, market forces will prevail'.[168]

## The myths of production

It was an unavoidable conclusion. During the years of the housing drive, the chances of making substantial profits prompted many firms to remain in the market. They were fully aware of over-capacity in the industry and recognised the oligopsonistic nature of the market, with much depending on the purchasing decisions of a handful of larger local authorities. Nevertheless, there were enormous potential returns for the firm that invested in the right system, as with Wimpey No-Fines (Figure 8.12).[169] Few foresaw the extent to which the market for public-sector housing would tail off in the early 1970s, when dramatic rationalisation took place. Production lines fabricating large panels for system-built high flats quickly closed. More versatile on-site systems and other aspects of industrialised building fared better. Industrialised building had existed long before the government decided that it was the key to a technological advance that would cut the Gordian knot of housing need. It continued to find a niche after the public-sector housing drive had dwindled away.

Viewed in retrospect, there is no doubt that industrialised building, coupled with the high-rise boom, briefly delivered a major increase in the number of dwellings completed. The productivity gains were never as great as anticipated and the resulting buildings occasionally suffered serious flaws, but the state-sponsored housing drive did allow a sustained slum clearance campaign. At the same time, industrialised building failed to deliver cheaper housing, with the comparison between housing and, say, mass production of cars always likely to be simplistic. The government's hopes that industrialisation would set an example of good practice that would diffuse through the construction industry were sadly disappointed. Although modern flats undoubtedly provided a healthier environment than the erstwhile slums, it was highly debatable as to whether industrialisation supplied functionally superior buildings when compared with conventional housing. Finally, whether or not housing built by industrialised methods enjoyed the approval of its residents depended on the skills of the designer, the build quality and the overall planning and reputation of the neighbourhood – exactly like any other form of housing. It was simply another form of building technology, not the inexorable embodiment of the march of progress.

The quality of the new estates, however, deserves further comment. It was perfectly understandable that provision of housing by local authorities was given moral imperative by the requirement to supply homes, that most basic of human needs, to homeless people and those living in poor conditions. Speed clearly was of the essence. Nevertheless, even as the housing drive gathered pace in the mid-1960s, it had become clear that municipalities throughout Great Britain were supplying 'no frills' housing estates – monotonous system-built schemes of tall slab or point blocks crammed into small plots of land rather than the 'city in the park'. Although local authorities like Sheffield showed great pride in their new housing estates as an indicator of municipal achievement (see Chapter 9), others allowed them to languish on the social as well as physical margins of the city. Council estates simply looked like council estates and were stigmatised in a process of 'moral depiction'. They had a 'big entrance, everyone sees everyone going, no private

gardens and no civilising too much. You are part of an estate.'[170] This tendency was not confined to local authorities. The ministry's St Mary's Estate at Oldham featured exteriors that suppressed 'all hint of the single home . . . beneath a rigid uniform of 12M-Jespersen window bands and precast units resembling a technical college or flatted factory'.[171] The reviewer's conclusion was that the architects were more interested 'in exposing their white aggregate than in expressing the multi-coloured individuality of the tenants'.[172]

The result was that in England and Wales, if not Scotland, where multi-storey living was more common, modernism became indelibly associated with social housing and with being the dwellings of those who had no choice. Although there were exceptions, as with the City of London's estates at Golden Lane and Barbican with their increasingly middle-class professional residents, modern flats had become the dwellings of those with few other options in the housing market. Those with the means to exercise choice headed for the suburbs. This social labelling, coupled with growing recognition of design and constructional problems, dealt devastating blows to the reputation of a form of housing intimately connected with architectural modernism, even if architects were far from being the only ones responsible for propagating such housing.

Architects themselves were not oblivious to what was happening. Reflecting on his experience of working at the LCC in the late 1950s, Rodney Gordon recalled the conditions facing his colleagues in the Housing Division:

> Corb realised with the *unité d'habitation*, that if you were going to take people up out of their environment, then you had to take the

environment up with them. So they put in laundries, swimming pools and kids' nurseries up into the building. What was happening when I was at the LCC was that the Valuer suddenly realised that you could build a lot more houses provided that you only built the housing. This is one of the fallacies about high-rise buildings. . . . It was this cheapness of divorcing housing from the social amenities that were really required in a high-rise – the pubs, the coffee bars, the crèches – which would make living so much easier and more dynamic inside the building, but this would never happen. We were screaming about this at the time, that you can't divorce people from the environment, but it was not up to us, it was up to the Valuer.[173]

A significant number of commentators began to question the results in contributions to symposia and in articles in the professional press. For example, Martin Richardson, by 1965 the Development Architect to the Yorkshire Development Group and an important voice in the world of industrialised building, lamented:

why are we so repelled by the average council estate? Do blocks of flats really look like factories or barracks, are they really soulless, arid; can we dismiss these criticisms as showing a lack of courage in facing the realities of the present – can we insist that were we brave and progressive enough we would see how lovely these prismatic boxes really are?[174]

Two years later Ivor Smith, co-designer of the iconic Park Hill flats in Sheffield, commented in similar vein in a lecture to the RIBA:

Up and down the country housing estates are still being built with no regard for sun or view and without concern for privacy and human movement. Towns and villages are being wrecked. All that you know. . . . What is baffling is how it can possibly be true that about 65 per cent of all new building in this country is now designed by architects. What is worrying is the wide difference of opinion among architects themselves, not only on how these problems are to be tackled, but more essentially on what is a desirable result.[175]

Yet these remarks must be seen in context. At that point, they were not counsels of despair. Majority opinion, even in the summer of 1967, retained its belief in the historic mission of modern architecture. Like others, while questioning the direction being taken in the public housing sector, Richardson and Smith believed that there were sufficient instances of good practice to give hope for the future. The next chapter considers some examples in which architects attempted to find an architecture that would improve the way of life on offer to the working class groups for whom social housing predominantly catered.

# Chapter 9

# With social intent

In the majority of [western nations] the large family dwelling with the burden of the upkeep of a garden is an anachronism. The labour-saving flat on the other hand, all on one level and equipped with modern conveniences including lifts, refuse chutes, and a private balcony, and with the companionship of families and children nearby, is in many ways the ideal remedy for melancholia and boredom. Near at hand is the garden, not a demanding 'patch' surrounded by fences and needing constant attention, but a large spacious and well-maintained park-like area giving a unique sense of freedom.

Rolf Jensen[1]

Architects share a sense of social purpose and believe that their work as architects may potentially improve society. Unfortunately, a serious lack of intellectual discipline becomes evident within the profession when the designer confronts social theory. For example, there are expectations among architects that physical design exerts an impact on the patterns of social life among the users and will directly and deterministically affect the way that people behave. As a profession, architects suggest that people are shaped by the environment created for them.

Henry Sanoff[2]

Although published in 1966, Rolf Jensen's words could have been written any time from the mid-1930s onwards. Paraphrasing Le Corbusier's lofty theorising from *La Ville Radieuse*,[3] the former Director of Housing and Borough Architect for North Westminster, London (1947–56) was essentially reiterating the Modern Movement's long-cherished beliefs that providing housing was not just about constructing dwelling units. Modern design, from that standpoint, also stood for social transformation, seeing particular forms of dwelling as capable of inculcating particular lifestyles. That view had encouraged the deployment of flats as an important idea in itself and had stimulated experiments with size, configuration, layout, access and innovative service provision as part of efforts to build on the progress made in developing modern social housing. The end-products varied, but the underlying goal remained much the same – that better housing really could deliver a better society. Experience of the new housing estates, however, had dented that view. First, as shown in Chapter 8, preoccupation with numbers had led to emphasis on standardisation and repetition as the keys to delivering target figures and reducing housing lists, but at the expense of the social facilities provided for the new residents. Second, it had occurred to some observers by the early 1950s that redevelopment might also have removed certain *valued* characteristics of the pre-existing urban environment.

One such element was the patterns of association that people forged through street life. During the 1950s, concerns that architects had neglected the importance of the street when designing rehousing schemes led to new radical innovations that reconfigured buildings and circulation patterns. A second element was the private garden. A small plot of resident-controlled space, even if only a small backyard, was recognised to have particular value for child development and for adding a degree of informal flexibility to everyday life. When the opportunity arose, architects looked for ways to address these two perceived deficiencies, searching for ways to incorporate them in a wider project that used modern design to recapture traditional virtues.

Unfortunately, their attempts to improve matters did not always fare better than that which they were criticising. One significant problem, as Henry Sanoff (p. 204) suggests, was that architects had only vague notions of what they were trying to achieve and, given the social gulf between architects and the typical residents of council housing, they had even less grasp of the real needs of those they sought to help. Although readily receptive to the works of writers and theorists who offered ideas that looked promising, they seldom had more than the haziest notion about how the process of social transformation would take place aside from properties somehow inherent in the new architecture. In addition, architectural projects take a considerable time to proceed from initial sketches to final built form. As individuals with well-developed skills of visualisation – able to think years ahead to foresee how a particular complex structure would fill a space currently occupied by something completely different – they can often devise structures that remain remarkably consistent over time (especially if their clients were attracted to the initial concept). By contrast, their views about the relationship between design and user often shift restlessly as new thinking that looks promising is absorbed, with greater or lesser reliability, from architectural sources or from the social sciences.

This chapter proceeds in light of these comments. Its first section identifies three sociological characteristics that architects had in mind when they talked about the benefits of the new architecture, namely, social equality, the new sociability and community. The ensuing sections consider case studies which detail how these ideas motivated attempts by architects to address what they regarded as the social needs of the user. These start with Denys Lasdun's development of 'cluster blocks' in public housing schemes in London. Later sections deal with 'streets-in-the-air' schemes, ranging from their conceptual development in entries for the Golden Lane competition (1952) and implementation at Park Hill (Sheffield, 1954–61) through to the Smithsons' Robin Hood Gardens in London (1966–72). The final sections deal with the growing conviction in the 1960s that high density need not mean dispensing with the traditional pattern of making private gardens available to residents.

## Social reconstruction

The starting point for most architects' thinking about society came from the weight of ideas accumulated by the Modern Movement since the 1920s, which looked to the future with a sense that architecture could deliver a new world that was healthier than the old and freed from conflict, greed and social inequality.[4] With the passage of time, new layers of theory accumulated while other ideas faded. Nevertheless, three basic themes found expression, to greater or lesser extent, in the work of those who continued to address the social agenda of modernism.

The first was *social equality*. This, it was assumed, came as a product of design and layout. The traditional townscape readily expressed inequality through the way that developers parcelled out space. Its most carefully demarcated relationships of spaces and solids were reserved for the wealthy – large town houses with squares delimited with iron railings or detached villas set in their own grounds surrounded by walls and symbolic barriers. Superior access to space and differentiated dwellings were the norm and acted as ready symbols of a hierarchical order. The poor, by contrast, received much smaller amounts of living space, often with little demarcated exterior space other than the minimal backyards made available by the sanitary concerns of housing legislation. The Modern Movement reconceptualised space in an egalitarian manner by the mass building of blocks of self-contained flats, identical save for the necessity of catering for different sized households. Stripping architecture of ornament and unnecessary stylistic devices removed the opportunity for external displays of ostentation and expressed a transparent honesty. The working classes could live in flowing open spaces like those at the other end of the social spectrum, since the areas around the flats, in theory, belonged equally to all who lived there.[5] With no one categorised by the appearance of their home or the perceived status of their neighbourhood, design could counter some of the traditional bases of inequality and raise the self-image of the residents of the new dwellings.

The second theme may best be called the *new sociability*. Owing something to social thought from the time of the New Objectivity (*die Neue Sachlichkeit*), this meant more than just providing labour-saving devices in the home and supplying communal facilities efficiently, although these were certainly part of the matter. Rather, it was hoped that the functionality offered by such innovations would impact on life style and aspirations. Time freed from drudgery by domestic gadgetry was time available for other purposes, such as spending time with family or friends, playing sport or even engaging in self-improvement. Creating communal facilities such as canteens, sports clubs, shops and the like within estates provided opportunities for contact and association. These contacts, especially when building on shared interests, could act as the cornerstone for developing warm social relationships.

The third and related theme was *community*. Almost all of those that participated in the process of creating new housing schemes happily invoked images of the vibrant communities that would fill the estates. Community formation, indeed, would be an affirmation of the quality of the new residential environments. This proposition, however, rested on two casual assumptions. First, it assumed that the incoming residents of these estates, especially those being housed after slum clearance schemes, would find those environments to be places where they could readily establish community. Second, it was assumed those being rehoused through comprehensive redevelopment had lost little of importance when clearance took place since, by implication, the physically blighted slum was also socially blighted.

New research relating to the second of these assumptions gave grounds for fresh thought. Studies of social relations on both sides of the Atlantic indicated the complex family and rich community life sometimes found in established working-class districts of cities.[6] Although the authors of such studies might still recoil from the appalling physical conditions of life in those areas sufficiently dilapidated to be labelled 'slums', they recognised that there was no automatic correlation between physical and social blight. The rundown physical fabric, therefore, might sometimes mask a vibrant communal life that could offset the undeniable deprivation suffered by residents of such areas. In reaching such conclusions, these studies emphasised the value of street life, and of informal neighbourly contacts in shaping social and community relations. Given, however, that the areas hosting such social life were scheduled for imminent clearance, the major issue was how these valued qualities might be transferred to new estates by sensitive design (see also Chapter 12).

For architects addressing questions of community in relation to flatted estates, the most significant issues revolved around the method chosen for gaining access to the dwelling. Reduced to basics, there are three ways to give access to flats that are aggregated into multi-storey blocks: stairs (or lifts) with corridors off landings; internal corridors off stairs or lifts; and external balconies.[7] Each has its advantages and drawbacks. The multiplication of lifts and stairs implied by access off landings is often preferred in that it reduces noise and provides privacy, but the expense of duplicating lifts or staircases means that it tends to be used primarily for more exclusive dwellings. Interior corridors allow access in a manner that does not affect the exterior design of the building and had gained acceptability by association with Le Corbusier's *unité d'habitation*, but are dark and make surveillance difficult. External balconies provide a relatively cheap solution to the problem of access, but give little privacy, darken the rooms below and behind them, and clutter up one elevation of the building.[8] The balcony solution was often taken to be the least preferable of the three options – the hallmark of the interwar walk-up block – but might have possibilities if the balcony could somehow be scaled up into the equivalent of a street. Each of these options would be carefully considered as part of efforts to create housing with social intent.

## Cluster blocks

The concept of 'clusters' became significant in architectural theory in the mid-1950s. The idea came from a paper written by Kevin Lynch in April 1954. Lynch analysed the form of cities, which he regarded as the characteristic physical manifestation of civilisation,[9] arguing that cities possessed size, density, grain, outline and pattern, with the people living in the city shaping these properties and being shaped by them. Grain was an assessment of the actual structure of a city. Acting on a typology reminiscent of CIAM's fourfold functional classification, he argued that 'grain' referred to the sorting out and segregation of different uses (living, working, recreation and communication). Unlike CIAM, however, Lynch saw advantage in their juxtaposition rather than separation. He argued that a city with a fine grain will see these uses stirred together in small parcels. Those with broader grain see them segregated into larger units, with the consequence that residents face longer hauls from one thing to another. A public library, for example, may have little patronage if isolated in a civic centre. Lynch, therefore, recommended an approach in which each use is studied to find the minimum cluster – the unit of natural aggregation – that gives functional efficiency (best use for the city's facilities).[10]

Lynch's ideas, of course, had no basis in empirical research, but had an intuitive appeal to those looking to understand the networks and connections that underpinned social interaction. Their number included Denys Lasdun whose practice, Drake and Lasdun,[11] was commissioned by the Metropolitan Borough of Bethnal Green (London) to design a 'cluster' block of flats at Usk Street in 1952. Construction work started in 1954 for an 8-storey block, with a further commission in 1956 from the same borough for a 16-storey version at Claredale Street (Figure 9.1). Lasdun had the idea of disaggregating the slab block into four component point blocks around a central services and circulation spine; an innovation that might give the advantages of access off landings without the costs of duplicating lifts and stairs. The dwelling units themselves followed the partiality for maisonettes already exhibited by the LCC, allowing division of interior space into an 'upstairs' and 'downstairs' in the same manner as a conventional house. Lasdun emphasised that this organisation of interior and exterior spaces followed genuine attempts to come to terms with what the future residents were used to and wanted:

> These were people who came from little terraced houses or something with backyards. I used to lunch with them to try and understand a bit more about what mattered to them, and they were proud people. They kept pigeons and rabbits in their back yard and hung their washing there. . . . And as a result of those contacts I didn't have flats. I said no, they must have maisonettes, two up and two down, or whatever it is, because this would give them the sense of home. And from those conversations, they wanted a degree of privacy. They said: you know, we're not used to being in a great sort of huge block of one of thousands. So the thing was radically broken up, this building, into four discrete connected towers, each semi-d on a floor, each a maisonette, so that

they were moving into homes not so very different from what they were used to, updated on sanitary stuff. . . . And even in the lift shafts in the middle, on alternate floors, were mini-backyards where no function was given. They'd have to find out what they wanted – if it was for drying clothes or whatever. It was an attempt to get some of the quality of life retained as distinct from being treated like a statistical pawn in a great prism. And they were very appreciative of this in the end and this distinctly touched me.[12]

Lasdun's designs, however, were emphatically not driven by field observations. In part, they had precedent in the shape of the infants' wing of Drake and Lasdun's design for Hallfield School, Paddington (1951). There, four low classroom units clustered around a communal courtyard, an arrangement that offered advantages in terms of circulation and in creating 'intimate spaces in scale with the children'.[13] The earliest descriptions of the Usk Street commission contained no sense that serious social intent underpinned the design of cluster blocks. Indeed, at the outset, there was neither mention of the term 'cluster' nor any attempt to provide a specific sociological rationale for the new development. Rather, the aims of the design were 'to eliminate the necessity of escape stairs' and also isolate 'the noise of public stairs, lifts and refuse disposal from the dwellings'.[14] The Usk Street block could

9.1
**Keeling House, cluster block, Bethnal Green (Denys Lasdun, 1955–9)**

also concentrate on larger maisonettes rather than having to juggle the layouts of different sized flats within the same block, because the adjacent development at Kirkwall Place by Yorke, Rosenberg and Mardall concentrated on smaller dwelling units.

With the passage of time and the indulgence of sympathetic journalists, the claims for the building steadily grew. By 1956, Lasdun had absorbed Lynch's ideas about grain and cluster. The second scheme at Claredale Street was offered as an answer to the problem that this, like many other slum clearance projects, had a restricted and irregular site. By way of compensation, it was claimed that the cluster block arrangement offered specific advantages with regard to identity, environment and quality of life. More specifically, it would

> reduce the apparent mass and repetitive content of the building by creating within it recognisable visual groupings . . . allow the environment to penetrate the body of the building and be experienced from within . . . [and] separate the core with its services and communal amenities from the dwelling areas which remain private and quiet.[15]

Their design, it was argued, 'tries to take into account not only the broader question of city re-creation but also how people are to live in high blocks'.[16] Lasdun himself would later refer to Keeling House (Claredale Street) as 'an immensely important building socially'.[17] His argument that the arrangements of the flats as two-storey maisonettes somehow made the block seem more like houses in the sky would not have seemed unusual at the time, because this idea already had its precedents in the LCC architects' designs for public housing schemes. Few would also have questioned the idea that the sense of privacy was enhanced because the narrow towers of the cluster block avoided long access balconies, although they might have raised an eyebrow at the description of them as being only 'short ones of garden-path scale' or that having two flats per floor of the individual towers was equivalent to being semi-detached.[18] Rather more fanciful than the homeliness of the suburban analogy were the claims about the relationship of the block to the conventional street. Seen as the antithesis of the *unité d'habitation*'s 'public corridor' system within a slab block, the cluster block apparently embraced the idea of a 'vertical street':

> the Claredale Street cluster-block . . . is intended to be read as a type of vertical street of stairs, lifts, services and public spaces (which could be shops under a more liberal legal dispensation) flanked by two-storey, two-maisonette units of semi-det scale.[19]

As so often in modernist thinking about the domestic environment, the 'cluster concept' appealed because it simultaneously addressed design and sociological elements: the former because its designers asserted that the thin towers did not visually affect the grain of the surrounding neighbourhood; the latter because it shows promise in possessing domestic scale in the component parts of these towers and maintaining something like the pre-existing sociological groupings of the streets that gave the original urban grain to the district.[20]

The addition of this form of sociological imagery appeared in incremental instalments, but progressively rewrote the rationale for these buildings. An arrangement originally explained as seeking to reduce noise to tenants and avoid unnecessary expenditure on staircases had changed, in the course of six years, to represent a logical response to community needs. Tall, thin towers joined to a central core were now described as homely, visually unobtrusive, and helping to perpetuate the area's original social structure. In the process, Lasdun had effectively subsumed the cluster block into his subsequent argument that architectural creation required a clear understanding of the relationship between order and diversity as a key to finding an architectural language that 'is in tune with what ordinary people want'.[21] The results were reassuring and quoted with approval in the architectural journals, but not everyone agreed. Bill Murray, a housing manager then working in Bethnal Green for the LCC, wrote in his diary in June 1959 about the poor finish of the block and the 'dark and nasty' staircases. On 23 April 1961, he recorded his reactions to a television interview given by Lasdun about the cluster blocks:

> See on television the architect who designed the ugly Bethnal Green Council Claredale Estate blocks. And he seemed quite proud of them! He described it as a cluster block which recreated the intimacy of people's living conditions in the houses where they lived. What a load of tommyrot! The block is ugly and I cannot see how it can be regarded as otherwise. But obviously all eyes do not see the same. As for recreating relationships, he has been listening to those potty people who make surveys of family life in East London. I have met some of them. Quite nice but not really with us. Just dreaming of concocting a thesis. They ought to have to work and deal with people on housing. It's a different matter to formulating theories about family patterns.[22]

At much the same time, Ed Cooney of the Institute of Community Studies carried out a survey of privacy in Bethnal Green housing, which included Keeling House. Cooney noted the wind eddies and gusts attributable to the cluster block layout, which whistled around the access galleries and bridges to the lift shaft. Far from being places to congregate and talk, they were spaces to move through quickly, especially during the colder months. The net result was that people on the same floor but in different blocks rarely got to know one another. This 'vertical street' turned out to have four isolated culs-de-sac per floor.[23]

## Streets-in-the-air
Lasdun was not the only architect looking for ways to design modern housing in which predominantly working class communities might feel at home. Another

group of architects worked on the idea that it was possible to introduce surrogates for streets into flatted estates, most notably through the notion of 'streets-in-the-air'. This had a variety of possible antecedents. The *rues galéries* suggested by Fourier's drawings of the architecture of the Phalanstery, the methods of interior communication as at the Galeries Lafayette in Paris, the catwalks of Sant'Elia's *Città Nuova*, the fifth-storey podium in Ludwig Hilberseimer's *Hochhausstadt*, or the Narkomfin flats in Moscow arguably provided earlier prototypes.[24] In the postwar period, planners in London had envisaged an elevated system of footpaths in the 1953 plan for the South Bank arts cluster (see Chapter 6), which eventually opened in 1967, and the Corporation of the City of London had progressively extended its use of walkways 20 feet above ground level, with plans for a 32-mile network within the Square Mile.[25] Applied to housing, Le Corbusier's work clearly supplied sources of inspiration. His project for the *îlot insalubre* number 6 in Paris (completed with Pierre Jeanneret, 1936–8) gave precedent for outside walkways, whereas his use of 'public corridors' at three-storey intervals in the *unité d'habitation* at Marseilles supplied a prototype of interior streets.

These themes clearly influenced entries to the City of London's 1952 competition for housing at Golden Lane,[26] albeit not the winning submission by Geoffry Powell or the three runners-up but two unplaced entries that employed Corbusian-inspired deck access ideas. The first was by Alison and Peter Smithson. Their entry, rendered in photomontage and line drawings, envisaged an eleven-storey elongated slab development with three levels of pedestrian or 'street' decks. The second, a deck-access scheme by Jack Lynn and Gordon Ryder, would eventually gain attention because it provided the inspiration for the seminal Park Hill development in Sheffield.

Although the Smithsons were widely seen as key figures in 1950s modernism for the design of Hunstanton school, their participation in the Independent Group and leading the movement that split and reconfigured CIAM (Chapter 10), they were not 'rabid modernists'. As Trevor Dannatt suggested, 'I think that they had a much deeper sense of architecture. I don't think that there were many architects of that time who had historical interests; the Smithsons were good in that respect.'[27] This was clearly manifested in their approach to housing. They did not idealise the street in the unquestioning manner that many on the left of British politics adopted when confronted with manifestations of working class life, but felt it was worth 'looking back further to its roots' in order to understand processes of social development and, in particular, the 'problem of identity in a mobile society'.[28] The Smithsons argued that working-class districts had preserved the vital relationship between people and the street: 'children run about, (the street is comparatively quiet), people stop and talk, dismantled vehicles are parked . . . you know the milkman, *you* are outside *your* house in *your* street.'[29] A decade later, Jane Jacobs would reach quite different conclusions from such thinking (see Chapter 12), but the Smithsons saw this as a springboard for modern design. For them, the street deck functioned socially in the same way as a normal street. With Golden Lane in mind:

There are three levels of 'streets-in-the-air', each level we call a 'deck'. Off each 'deck' live 90 families and their group activity is concentrated in two crossings at the street intersections, these crossings are triple volumes contrasting with the single volume streets and inviting one to linger and pass the time of day.

Vertical circulation is possible at crossings and street ends (which are similarly triple volume). A new dimension has been added to the life of the street.[30]

The placement of refuse chutes at crossing points would allow informal neighbourly contacts while carrying out an essential function – rather after the manner of casual meetings at the village pump.[31]

The resulting schemes had resonances of contemporary movements in the social sciences. In terms of form, their sketches suggested the 'wiring' diagrams of early systems theory or cybernetics, with their elements, nodes and lines of connection,[32] but are almost certainly too early to have drawn significant influence from that source.[33] Rather more likely is that, in tune with contemporary thinking about neighbourhood design and service provision, the Smithsons took it for granted that social life had a hierarchical structure and needed provision of a hierarchy of spaces for it to function properly. The deck, like the street, was an extension of the house. Networks of street decks, joined together, gave connectivity to the district. In turn, districts 'in association generate the need for a richer scale of activity which in their turn give identity to the ultimate community (THE CITY)'.[34] The street played a particularly valuable role in socialisation. In it, 'children learn for the first time of the world outside the family; it is a microcosmic world in which the street games change with the seasons and the hours are reflected in the cycle of street activity.'[35] This positive characteristic of the street was forgotten in many housing developments but would be revived by the street decks: 'It is the idea of street and the reality of street that is important – the creation of effective group-spaces fulfilling the vital function of identification and enclosure, making the socially vital life-of-the-streets possible.'[36]

This hierarchical approach was related to the theory of Urban Reidentification that the Smithsons had proposed at CIAM IX (see Chapter 10). A token of the schism within CIAM, it started with an appeal to turn away from that organisation's 'hitherto functional theory' and for a renewal of the 'house–street relationship'.[37] Later reworkings subsequently developed this into a full-blown theory,[38] which argued that allowing people to re-establish their traditional spatial hierarchy of associations would help the inhabitants of the new housing estates to feel quickly at home. In due course, the Smithsons became uneasy about such group concepts as 'house, street, district, city (community sub-divisions)' or 'isolate, village, town, city (group entities)' on the grounds that these were 'too loaded with historical overtones'. In their place would come 'cluster' meaning a 'specific pattern of association',[39] although the Smithsons stressed that it was a tentative term that was useful only until a better one arrived.

These speculative sociological notions, along with the 'rough poetry' of New Brutalism,[40] provided keystones of the theories and projects that the Smithsons would develop further at CIAM X and through Team X. In 1957–8, for example, they reworked their ideas about the 'cluster city' into a plan that won joint third prize in an international open competition for the Berlin Hauptstadt (in collaboration with Peter Sigmond).[41] The competition looked for a design for the reconstruction of the entire city centre, ignoring the borders of the zone controlled by the East German authorities. The Smithsons matched that spirit by complete disregard for the scale of the city. Their plan worked in terms of two interconnected levels that separated pedestrians and vehicles. Cars remained at ground level in low speed straight streets. Pedestrians moved free from vehicles on an upper level pedestrian net, like a constantly growing cobweb, along walkways often more than 330 yards (300 metres) wide and 1.8 miles (3 kilometres) long.[42] The proposal would leave the historic spaces of the ruined city at ground level, moulding the new city around them. The deck would be punctuated by series of numerous, but comparatively small high-rise buildings. The future centre of Berlin would have an inverted profile: 'instead of the city being the apex of a building-height-and-density pyramid, the high buildings form a wall at the periphery and the centre itself is low with a single symbolic visual "fix" at its centre.'[43] The 'wall' at the boundary would comprise offices and housing. It was, arguably, closer to the scale of megastructural developments than the intimacy of scale once argued for 'streets-in-the-air'.

As private practitioners, the Smithsons had little opportunity for involvement in building public housing, much less for showing how it might slot into the wider urban context. In 1964, however, they received a direct commission from the LCC for a site in Tower Hamlets (Manistry Street). That scheme, eventually named Robin Hood Gardens, provided 213 flats in two extended slab blocks enclosing a green courtyard area:

> We made a project with two blocks to shelter the site from the two main traffic arteries by planning the buildings on a so-called kipper principle; that is you put all the noisy things on the outside – the living rooms and the walkways – and you put all the bedrooms and things on the inside, where you can open the windows into the space. That is the classic case of being non-ideological. Though the principle of connectivity seemed to be most important thing in 1952, when the real situation comes and the noise is unbelievable, that becomes more of a prime consideration.[44]

That departure from earlier thinking marked a perceptible change. In many respects, the grand scheme was essentially the same: 'The realisation of it, the date of handing it over to the client, was 1972, but the idea was adumbrated . . . in the Golden Lane competition of 1952 and then more work was done in 1954.'[45] Perhaps caught up by their personal history in this field of innovation, the Smithsons fell back on a mid-1950s raw concrete Brutalism even though, a decade later, they now favoured a gentler aesthetic.[46] It was a tacit admission of the extent that the rationale for application of Brutalist aesthetics had degenerated into style preferences.

Other elements of the paper plans of the past were less easy to recapture. This was a housing development on an awkward site, delivered under cost restraints. The prime social and circulation functions of the 'streets-in-the-air' had disappeared. The main intended arena for neighbourhood socialising was now the central courtyard rather than the streets-in-the-air, with the Smithsons evoking imagery of life in London's Regency squares rather than East End streets in support of their design.[47] Moreover, the failure to interconnect the 'streets-in-the-air' showed a movement away from the idea of a creating a prototypic model for a future multilevel circulation city back towards the familiar use of access balconies.

## Park Hill

The other entry to the Golden Lane competition relevant here led indirectly to one of the most celebrated public housing schemes built in the postwar period, namely, at Park Hill, Sheffield. Now working in collaboration with Ivor Smith, Jack Lynn had refined his ideas about deck access in relation to a site at Rotherhithe in south-east London. In particular, Lynn and Smith had taken on board the Smithsons' idea about the importance of 'street corners' for the formation of social life, including such activities as shops, pubs, play areas and laundries in their scheme.[48] The design came to the attention of the new Sheffield City Architect, Lewis Womersley, who recruited Lynn and Smith for his staff (see Chapter 3). Although both were inexperienced, they would imminently become responsible for designing one of the largest and most intensely scrutinised public housing schemes of the period.

The district of Sheffield initially proposed for development was Norfolk Park, an area of farmland around ten minutes' walk from the city centre. After preparing an initial deck access plan, the hint that the government would restart the slum clearance programme caused a change of policy in May 1953. Norfolk Park was left for a decade, being developed in 1963, with a mixture of low-rise maisonettes and 15 tower blocks. Attention switched back to the inner city. The choice for development was the Park district, notorious for its crime rate and poor housing (primarily back-to-backs). This was a challenging site, situated to the east of the city centre and sloping 210 feet from the Midland railway station up to Skye Edge. Part had already been redeveloped in the interwar period using conventional low-rise flats, but the rest was mainly occupied by back-to-back housing and prefabricated temporary bungalows.[49] Womersley expressed his enthusiasm for the possibilities that the site presented:

> I was tremendously excited by the dramatic topography of the city and I felt that the opportunities which the site afforded had been completely lost by covering all these hills with small two-storey houses. I saw the possibility of replacing these with towers of flats on hill-tops with open space as a foreground to them so that in their redevelopment people could see the transformation that had been brought about.[50]

Housing developments, therefore, offered the chance to make statements about modern life as well as provide dwellings, but the hilltop developments also apparently looked back to an older prototype much loved by architects:

The careful exploitation of this topography – the building up of hill-top architectural compositions – is gradually producing something of the fascination of the Italian hill towns. It is simulating; exciting![51]

Plans for renewal proceeded on the basis of redevelopment at high density to retain easy access to workplaces for the existing community. An initial plan dating from July 1953 saw the creation of a scheme for 2000 new dwellings, for both the low and hilltop portions of the site, with the alignments of the buildings following the current street pattern since, for reasons of economy rather than social continuity, the council wanted to use the existing roads and services. Over the next two years, that stipulation was relaxed in light of the poor condition of the roads and amenities. More important perhaps, the site itself was split into two portions divided by a development of conventional walk-up flats built between 1936 and the outbreak of war in the triangular plot between Duke Street and Bernard Street. Working on the two sections in sequence made financing and project management easier,[52] although it delayed the time when the new tenants could return from the outlying housing estates to which they had moved during the complete clearance of the site. Budgetary constraints necessitated the maximum use of structural repetition and 'minimal finishes',[53] the normal euphemism for rough-cast concrete. Even when new, visiting journalists commented on the 'grimness' of the architectural details and surface finishes. At best, some might note, albeit unconvincingly, that they are 'not unsuited to the character of a northern industrial city'.[54] The new residents did receive the Garchey system of refuse disposal and oil-fired district central heating systems, although the latter served a functional need by obviating the need for fuel deliveries and storage.[55]

Park Hill, the first phase of development, occupied the steeply sloping western portion of the 32-acre (13-hectare) site (Figure 9.2). Designed by the team from the City Architect's Department, with Lynn and Smith as project leaders, construction was handled by Sheffield's direct labour organisation between 1957 and 1961. The estate, referred to as a 'pedestrian precinct',[56] provided 995 dwellings in a mixture of flats and two-storey maisonettes. The buildings were in serpentine sections, resembling scorpions' tails, interconnected by the streets-in-the-air. These were placed at three-storey intervals, with the locations at which they switched from one side of the block to the other supplying 'street corners' and places where the service lifts were situated.[57] Although essentially elevated walkways, they were given names (Rows) that were used in the postal address. At 12 feet (3.5 metres) wide, the decks could accommodate hand-wheeled milk trolleys or similar light, electric powered floats. The roof level throughout Park Hill was at a constant height, with the height of the blocks varying with the slope of the land. As seen in Figure 9.2, this meant a difference between 14-storey blocks at the northern end of Park Hill and 4 storeys along Talbot Street in the south. Using the topography, therefore, all the streets-in-the air apart from the top-most ran out to ground level at some point.[58] Hyde Park, the second and larger phase, was constructed from 1962 to 1965 on the brow of the hill (Figure 9.3). It contained 740 flats and 582 maisonettes. Its vertical dimension, with blocks up to 19 storeys, complemented the horizontal emphasis of Park Hill.[59] Kelvin, a related deck-access

9.2
**Park Hill flats,**
**Sheffield**
**(1957–61)**

site located in the Don Valley about a mile north-west of the city centre, completed Sheffield's experiments with this form of public housing.[60]

Alongside the ideas for development of the design came the constantly shifting sociological justifications offered in support of radical changes to the conventional domestic living environment. The case made in favour of the decks was that they would assume the social character of conventional streets and act as an extension of the home. Being covered from the elements and free from vehicles, the decks would be ideal places for 'daily social intercourse – for the conversation of adults and for children's play'.[61] The decks were places along which prams could be pushed and milk trolleys wheeled. The milk trolleys assumed a disproportionate importance, as they had with the Smithsons' schemes. Quite apart from the importance of the fresh milk for public health, the repeated references to daily milk deliveries evoked a standard sight in any city neighbourhood. The image seemingly testified to the normality of the deck solution – socially as well as functionally similar to a regular city street.

In 1961, shortly after Park Hill had opened, the corporation's own trilingual (English, French and Russian) guide to Sheffield's modern housing showed that thinking about social and communal life had moved on. The architects, it was claimed, had taken steps to encourage 'a sense of domesticity and identity for the residents' and to prevent this from becoming a 'vast inhuman building block'. These ranged from the banal – different colours for the facing bricks for the different decks and for the front doors 'with the intention of helping the families to feel that they are part of a smaller community within the development'[62] – to the cerebral – increasing the area of the spaces between the blocks as the height of buildings increased northward down the slope to supply an experience of 'a completely different character and scale . . . as one progresses through the scheme'. As with

the Smithsons, however, it was the decks that bore the brunt of the social theorising. The frequent changes in direction of the blocks broke up the decks into shorter lengths, each of which would gain its own 'street' character. The 'decks' would implicitly play a key role in socialisation, by creating an intermediate step in the expansion of the child's spatial range. Although repeating the familiar argument that the street was an 'extension of the dwelling', there was apparently now a notion of an expanding spatial range of experience at stake here:

> The child's earliest play needs are in general catered for inside the flat or maisonette, where with its large private balcony he can play in safety. Later on, the decks extend his range on a level with his front door. Later still, when sufficiently confident to roam further, he can use the various play areas at ground level.[63]

A lengthy, reflective review of Park Hill by Jack Lynn on 1965 noticeably filtered these ideas. It opened with a comparison between managerial and back-to-back housing, then recognising the improvements made by Victorian by-law housing, seeing the terraced row as an expression of the 'new urban democracy'.[64] The arrangement did not force the householder into any special relationship with neighbours, but allowed the other ingredients of a happy neighbourhood, the local pub, corner shops, workshops and agencies to develop naturally. The design for Park Hill had tried to preserve a situation where the street allowed maximum freedom of movement and association rather than the 'socially retrogressive' designs for 'forms of collective houses imported from other European countries'. In this regard, Lynn perceptively condemned the 'tower' or 'point' block for interposing a 'no-man's-land' between the front door and the open air:

> It is an ambiguous space, being neither public nor private and, as such, it can make a positive contribution neither to the life of the individual family nor to the social life of the community. Worse than that, it has an inhibiting effect on both.[65]

The streets-in-the air retained their role as safe channels of movement and forums for meeting, but supposedly engaged the walker in a conscious aesthetic experience:

> The layout of pathways, ways under and through the building forms are designed to exploit the pedestrian's capacity for abrupt changes of

direction and level with all the excitement of rapid contrast in space and light experience which this can bring. Gradual changes of level are used too, so that there is always a choice, in moving about the site, between steps and a ramp, the fast and slow way, to suit varying mood or differing ages.[66]

Lynn enthused about children using the 'whole site area as their playground' and about them using the ramps for roller-skating and go-karting – views that other residents might have found less than desirable. The places where the ground footpath system met the street decks were heralded as lively places where people would meet and stop to chat. Lynn ended his analysis of Park Hill with a lyrical account of walking through the complex that was heavily permeated with an architect's sensitivity to the changing spatial sensations offered by the scheme. As one walked northwards through the project, the decks became progressively higher above ground level without the pedestrian necessarily realising it. Then came sudden moments of revelation:

> but, surprisingly, the ground itself moves further and further away and gives the impression of one having become very securely airborne. This feeling is strengthened when, rounding a corner, the deck leads through the width of the building and suddenly there below is the rest of the city across the valley and beyond, a broad sweep of open view with a horizon of farm and moorland.[67]

Park Hill had thereby achieved the Modern Movement's aspiration of bringing the town and country closer together. 'Walking in the city' had seemingly acquired 'some of the quality previously found only on the fells or on cliff tops by the sea'.[68]

These sentiments would eventually ring hollow as the weight of other problems bedevilled the estate's future. In the initial phases, however, the results seemed encouraging enough to support the innovative arrangement of buildings and access routes and to recommend the deck-access principle as a prototype for replication elsewhere. Park Hill was unusual in that efforts were made at the outset to ensure that community formation was not simply left to the alchemy of architecture. Its population received similar attentions to the first arrivals at the New Towns, where the development corporations often appointed welfare officers to oversee the removal and settlement of incomers and help their adjustment to their new environments. The first tenant at Park Hill was Joan Demers, a housing welfare officer, who assisted other tenants to move in and helped the formation of community associations. A survey of 20 per cent of the residents that Demers administered in 1962 found that initial tenant response to the location and the street decks was dominantly positive.[69]

At first, Park Hill enjoyed qualified critical approval. A commentary four years later by A.E.J. Morris found plenty to admire in the 'unity and strength' of the basic concept, but noted problems of soundproofing, graffiti, vandalism to the lifts and breakdowns in the service infrastructure.[70] In November 1967, Park Hill would receive a rare accolade from the groundbreaking and caustically critical 'Housing and the Environment' issue of the *Architectural Review*, which described it as 'the finest achievement of the 'fifties in community building, primarily because it tackled the problem of access'.[71] Nevertheless, failings were noted. The lifts were reported as being frequently dirty, despite daily cleaning, and, when not out of commission, likely to generate such long delays that people preferred to walk. The author then quoted statistics, not previously highlighted from Joan Demers' survey, which said that only 9 per cent of respondents mentioned the value of being able to stand on the decks and look at the view and a mere 4 per cent remembered that the deck made it possible to stand and socialise. As the writer noted: 'This discounts a good deal of romantic nonsense about the decks being a hive of activity; as any visitor knows, they are not'.[72] If true, there could be few bleaker or more wounding conclusions about features on which so many hopes had been pinned. Later commentators unquestioningly quoted these figures with approval.[73] Yet curiously, they and the conclusions drawn did not appear in Demers' report and were either misinterpreted or concocted to support a hypothesis. It was a foretaste of one aspect of the process of reappraisal to come.

## High density

In just the same way as architects had second thoughts about the handling of circulation and access in modern housing, so too had they started to rethink the question of how to handle high-density development. This had emotive connotations, given that population density had occupied a key role in planning for residential areas since the mid-nineteenth century. Nevertheless, questions were being raised about the value of existing approaches by the early 1960s. Muriel Smith, community development officer for the London Council for Social Service, for example, argued that the concept of density was meaningless. She argued that what the tenant

> likes or dislikes about living in any of these conditions has little to do with density; it has to do with architectural design and layout, with social amenities, housing management, transport and proximity to work, the size and structure of his family, the rent and such intangible factors as whether he likes his neighbours and how much or how little he misses relatives and friends from his former environment.[74]

This type of thinking led in two related directions. The first suggested that high-density schemes should be contemplated, especially where they gave the advantages of retaining population close to the city centre, provided that design offered a high-quality living environment in which the essential communal facilities were not skimped.[75] This view gained support in government circles. In 1962, for example, Sir Keith Joseph wrote a foreword to a Ministry of Housing and Local Government planning bulletin that challenged local authorities to review their housing density policies. His case was that it was impossible to find enough extra land given that '[over] the next 20 years we are going to need at least six million more homes'.[76] Higher densities were essential to make housing available where it was needed.

This was exemplified by the eight-year controversy over the World's End estate, built on an 11.2-acre (4.5-hectare) site adjacent to the Thames at Chelsea (London).[77] Supposedly named after a remark by Charles II when his coach became stuck in the poor roads of the area and perpetuated in the name of a tavern on the King's Road, World's End was an area of dilapidated terraced housing that had suffered considerable damage during the Blitz. It also represented one of the last substantial areas available within the Metropolitan Borough of Chelsea for clearance and social housing. The council had completed the adjacent Cremorne Estate as flats in low-rise slabs (Armstrong and MacManus, 1949–56), staying within the density figure of 136 persons per acre (336 persons per hectare) laid down by the County of London Plan. The borough decided, however, that it could not clear its substantial waiting list for council housing if it redeveloped World's End at that figure. The Borough Engineer prepared a scheme in 1962 for a higher density estate, which was rejected by the LCC. This was partly because the LCC still regarded such densities as carrying connotations of Victorian overcrowding, although the proposal also faltered for lack of architectural merit and the potential visual impact on the riverfront.[78]

Given that the government was clearly willing to countenance schemes of above 200 persons per acre, the council decided to prepare another proposal in collaboration with Eric Lyons and Partners. Eric Lyons had successfully contested the LCC's policy against higher-density developments at a planning appeal at Blackheath in 1961,[79] and had gained a reputation for quality in housing design through the SPAN estates. Adopting the strategy described previously when his firm handled larger contracts (Chapter 3), Lyons acted in association with H.T. Cadbury Brown, John Metcalfe and Ivor Cunningham to produce the design presented in 1965. This included eight tower blocks interconnected with a pedestrian podium, with traffic movement at ground level and underground car parking. After this scheme was sent back for amendment, the Metropolitan Borough of Chelsea's successor, the London Borough of Kensington and Chelsea, finally obtained approval for the scheme in 1967 with building work starting in 1969. The prime reason why the scheme gained acceptance was Lyons invoking the proviso from the Parker Morris Report that 'solutions involving the dual use of land may be preferable when 100 per cent provision of parking and surface access is attempted'.[80] The estate was therefore designed at two levels, with the housing raised on a deck, below which were two levels of parking. The accepted scheme provided 765 flats at a net density of 270 persons per acre for the site as a whole. The blocks ranged from 5 to 14 storeys, with amenities including an 18-unit shopping centre, a Methodist church, public house, youth club, community centre and a primary school. Originally planned as Brutalist concrete with precast cladding panels, the designers turned to brick facing in line with the mounting reaction against concrete finishes, even though this produced some constructional problems for the tall polygonal blocks.[81] The design also sought to humanise the appearance of the scheme through landscaping. A number of 'newel posts' filled with earth and extending down through the two parking levels allowed full-grown trees to be planted. The decks were turfed over to 'complete the illusion of natural parkland'.[82] Construction finally started in 1969, with the estate reaching completion in 1977.

The second question about high density was whether it meant that high-rise buildings were obligatory, apart from the most constrained sites. The higher construction costs per dwelling of flats in high-rise blocks were well known. What had become clear at the start of the 1960s was that high densities of 136–200 persons per acre (336–494 per hectare) could be achieved without recourse to high buildings. In a review, schemes that Walter Bor identified as illustrating that point were Eric Lyons' designs for SPAN housing at Highsett, Cambridge; the Brunswick Centre in Bloomsbury (London, 1959–72), originally designed by Leslie Martin and Patrick Hodgkinson but only partly built to their design; and the winning competition entry by John Darbourne for a housing estate at Lillington Street, Westminster.[83] The last-mentioned scheme and the further developments of its basic premises by the Darbourne and Darke practice at Marquess Road, Islington merit further analysis.

## Flats *with* gardens

Westminster City Council represents one of the few boroughs that receive continuing credit as a client for postwar social housing. In 1947, Philip Powell and Hidalgo Moya established their practice by winning an open competition for the 30-acre (12-hectare) Churchill Gardens Estate on Grosvenor Road. Churchill Gardens replaced an area of terraced housing that had suffered considerable bomb damage with a mixed development of taller (9–11 storey) slabs in Zeilenbau alignment and lower rise blocks. Started in 1950 and completed in 1962, the scheme was notable both for the quality of design, which included district heating, and for achieving a density of 200 persons to the acre (494 persons per hectare). At the end of 1960, the council announced a second housing competition. The 12-acre (4.8-hectare) site, initially known as Lillington Street, was an area of terraced housing off Vauxhall Bridge Road awaiting clearance. It comprised three streets of stucco-fronted houses 'dilapidated in places but scrubupable and quite cosy; a Victorian church, by appointment to Pevsner, to be retained; provision for schools and other special buildings to be made'.[84] Space had to be left to accommodate proposed road widening along Vauxhall Bridge Road. The remaining 9.5 acres (3.8 hectares) was for redevelopment as housing, which the competition's rules specified should be a mixture of smaller one or two bedroom dwellings (between 60 and 75 per cent of the total) and the rest larger dwellings. Additional provision included three children's playgrounds, a tenants' social hall and car parking with 350 spaces.[85]

The council set the competition deadline for 10 July 1961, with Philip Powell acting as assessor. Ten days later, Powell's report recommended John Darbourne as the winner from 68 submitted entries. Darbourne had studied architecture at University College London and had worked for two years for Eric Lyons and Partners before moving to the USA to study for a Masters in Landscape Architecture at Harvard University. Acting with the encouragement of the head of department Dan Kiley and the Japanese landscape architect Hideo Sasaki, Darbourne prepared the plan for Lillington Street as his Master's thesis. His scheme differed from the mixed development pattern favoured by the LCC and replicated by many other competition entries, which routinely put forward an assortment of tall towers and lower slabs. Darbourne's design blended together three-storey terraces and eight-storey maisonette blocks, with the 136-foot-high (41-metre) spire of G.E. Street's red-brick Gothic Revival church, St James the Less, remaining the major vertical feature (Figure 9.4). The scheme featured extensive landscaping, retaining existing trees wherever possible and grassing over the roofs of the parking levels.

After winning the competition, Darbourne returned to Britain to open a practice with Geoffrey Darke (see Chapter 3). Their practice, Darbourne and Darke, initially operated from an office in the top floor of a flat in Churchill Gardens, with Darbourne himself living in the lower level. After six months surveying the site while the council completed the necessary land acquisitions, the practice prepared the designs for the first phase of the scheme, working in conjunction with Westminster's Director of Housing, E.J. Edwards. The first phase of the scheme was built between 1964 and 1968, with two further phases following between 1967 and 1972. The resulting scheme, as it eventually developed, was distinctive in three respects.

First, it achieved a density of 218 persons per acre (538 per hectare) without recourse to buildings over nine storeys and the monumentality associated with tall blocks of flats. This was achieved by a system of interlocking maisonettes with deck-access 'streets' in eight-storey and four- to six-storey blocks, along with three-storey houses that combined maisonette and roof-garden bed-sitters. The brick-paved streets occurred twice in the eight-storey blocks and once in the six-storey blocks.[86] Clearly, the density reflected the client's need for housing and the borough's shortage of building land, but the architects were happy to equate density with urbanity. While accepting that overcrowding brought obvious disadvantages, they believed that higher densities could improve life by making the neighbourhood more compact and its facilities more accessible: 'If you can't get that density, then the prospects of getting that urban way of life are reduced.'[87]

9.4
**Lillington Gardens (Darbourne and Darke, 1961–72), with St James the Less**

Second, at a time when architects had turned to precast concrete cladding for exteriors, the estate used brick facings throughout, with concrete banding and dark asbestos slate sheets for roofing (Figure 9.5). The inspiration for the slates came from the original aesthetics of the neighbourhood, whereas the model for the dark red brick came from seeking to match that used in St James the Less. The decision to use the brick, purchased from Guildings kiln in Hastings especially for the purpose, now appears proto-conservationist. However, in this instance it would have been perfectly possible to use concrete or stucco for finishing the exteriors, given that the flats 'replaced rendered Regency-type housing in Pimlico itself, with lots of plasterwork'.[88] The decision to use brick cladding largely rested on the practice's view that recognised the unsuitability of unfaced concrete for the British climate:

> We [the practice] did do concrete, but not in housing work. This uses a local brick. Certainly we grew up with Corb and he was building in a country where concrete looked right. In England it always looked mucky – that was our view – and it doesn't mature well. The right bricks and the right detailing made a big difference. The Brutalists didn't want to face up to that. We were embarrassed at the time to be called vernacular traditionalists; it was something of a black mark, in that you weren't part of the revolution. You were reneging. Yet we had an eye for what buildings might look like in 50 years' time. If you look at them [concrete buildings] now, they look awful. The climate, the pollution in the air ruins anything, but concrete is worse.[89]

9.5
**Lillington Gardens (Darbourne and Darke, 1961–72), Phase 3 showing materials and gardens**

There was also an element of functional rationality in the decision. Despite wariness of being labelled 'traditionalists', there was a sense of using materials that could complete the job cheaply and effectively:

> You use the materials that are appropriate and sometimes brick is appropriate. . . . I was always wary of rendering; replacing it is very expensive. We didn't want precast concrete. Natural concrete, if it is any good, will be expensive anyway. To show the aggregate happily and make it an acceptable finish is actually more expensive than brickwork. Barbican concrete isn't ordinary; they built it in concrete and then bush-hammered it to get the finish that they wanted. That costs a fortune. You can't just opt out of providing an acceptable finish and brick seemed like the only way to do that. Even with brick, you can get the mortar over the face and the joint out of place, but even done poorly it is just about acceptable. That is not the case with concrete.[90]

The third distinctive feature of the estate lay in eventual provision of private gardens. The first two phases of Lillington Gardens proceeded broadly according to Darbourne's original plan. These relied on the conventional pattern of flatted housing with communal gardens, which a critic referred to as 'landscape designed only to be looked at'.[91] Further consideration, especially in light of reaction to tower block estates, led to second thoughts. Despite the prejudice against private gardens to which the epigram by Rolf Jensen testified, new plans for Phase 3 caused Lillington literally to justify the 'Gardens' tag attached to so many council housing estates. By the time of the third phase, the practice had devised a complex spatial design whereby flats intended for families were interlocked scissor-like in pairs in such a way that each flat had access to a private garden. Although described as no more than a 'pocket-handkerchief 320 square feet',[92] the gardens represented an important element in the design. Their purpose was not yet controlling space in the manner recommended by Oscar Newman's defensible space hypothesis (see Chapter 12), but rested on an informal theory of child development. The architects believed that the child's need for play spaces changed over time. In early years, playing under supervision inside the flat or on the balcony was sufficient, but within a short period there was a need for further outdoors provision:

> Parents were reluctant to allow their children to play at ground level when the home was several storeys up, so children went deprived. This led us to endeavour to provide a small outdoor space [garden] for each family dividing where the children can play safely near the parent, until old enough to venture further.[93]

As a source of greenery, gardens might also help to reconnect the domestic environment with the natural world. Finally, they offered a measure of privacy from the gaze of passers-by, although not necessarily from neighbours given that the scissors arrangement meant that each flat looked down into someone else's garden below.

Lillington Gardens gained and continues to receive positive commentary from architectural critics. Like Park Hill, it escaped the root-and-branch condemnation meted out to public housing schemes by the *Architectural Review*'s November 1967 'Housing Issue' (see Chapter 12). It gained credit for 'the individuality of the grouping of the dwellings', although lost points for the treatment of buildings alongside the Vauxhall Bridge Road and 'the fashionable imposition of massive brick facings' that resulted in 'overwhelming institutional unity'.[94] A 1972 review of the completed scheme talked about Darbourne and Darke having 'achieved the seemingly impossible' in managing to achieve high density and making private gardens available to families.[95] Lionel Esher, for example, noted how the scheme seemed to give hope 'that the reign of concrete and the rule of repetition could be ended'.[96] Yet the architects may well have been fortunate in their client's willingness to sponsor quality social housing and in the surrounding environment in which the development took place. The same principles applied elsewhere did not necessarily produce the same results.

This was illustrated by Darbourne and Darke's subsequent project for the London Borough of Islington at Marquess Road (1966–77). Directly commissioned by the Borough Architect A.E. Head, who was personally familiar with the practice's work, the task involved provision of 1185 dwellings on a 28-acre (11.3-hectare) site in Canonbury at a density of 200 bed spaces per acre. The site was even more problematic than Lillington Gardens in terms of existing buildings and site constraints. These comprised a noisy and high-density boundary road (Essex Road), a major thoroughfare (St Paul's Road) that bisected part of the site, and the Channel Islands Estate, a 286-dwelling housing estate including two tower blocks completed by Islington Borough Council in 1956. The area also contained Sir Charles Barry's St Paul's church and was adjacent to the New River, for which Darbourne and Darke gained a further commission to produce a landscaped linear park.

The planning of the estate at Marquess Road involved fundamentally changing the road pattern, removing some roads and narrowing others. The result was to produce a largely pedestrianised estate, fitted sympathetically around existing developments. The plans for housing represented an evolutionary development of the third phase of Lillington Gardens. There was immediate scepticism from a socialist group on the Housing Committee, which reacted against what it saw as gentrification and wanted to retain the rigid standardisation of earlier social housing schemes.[97] The practice, however, eventually gained acceptance of a scheme in which 60 per cent of the flats, intended for families, gained a private garden. The bulk of the site, therefore, was three-storey blocks of family maisonettes with gardens at ground level, above which were smaller flats intended for older people. The latter had their own walkways, here described as 'roof streets' with space for planting.[98] Car parking was below the blocks, with servicing by authorised access over primarily pedestrianised 'mews streets'.[99] There was extensive landscaping and creation of squares along the pedestrian routes. In Geoffrey Darke's words:

> The point is that we took a chunk of London, in Islington, knocked it down and built again. All those effectively had a little yard, a little space, something to give light to the windows. To take them away and construct 40 storey blocks of flats, seemed the wrong approach to us. The gardens became a very strong argument. We were being challenged all the time, the politicians were saying they wanted us to buy flats in deals with Swedish contractors, building with these pre-cast systems. We were saying that was wrong. We were packing in the ground; they were leaving lots of wind-blown spaces. Our gardens protected things a bit; what they had was great ghastly open spaces. That is a fundamental argument. We were opposed to the pressure from elsewhere to build in a certain way.[100]

Marquess Road was completed well after the end of the period covered by this volume. Initial critical commentary praised the estate as a 'great success'. Its spaces were compared with 'academic quads', the street widths were 'generous', the scale 'friendly', and the planting was 'attractive'. The estate, seen from the perspective of the early 1970s, was 'a paragon of domestic felicity' seen alongside 'the giant towers of misguided postwar dreamers'.[101] Yet architectural design alone does not create thriving estates. Despite the success of the basic ideas at Lillington, Marquess Road was not a repeat. The estate would experience problems with regards to the roofing, cladding, walkways and water percolation. The pedestrianised spaces, dark passageways and maze of routeways through the estate proved to be a policing nightmare, with the estate becoming regarded 'by the council, tenants and police as a hostile and confusing environment in which crime and the fear of crime had taken hold'.[102] A key part of the problem for the architects was that the barriers restricting access were frequently locked open. This was seen as resulting from poor communication and management, in that neither the police nor the housing managers seemed to understand the nature of the access system, but the architects also recognised their responsibility:

> They [the Council] didn't know what they were getting. They took it but they didn't know what they were getting. We designed what we believed with our heart and soul that we were helping the housing problem, but no one knew what we were doing. All our objectives were for ourselves, really.[103]

That conclusion is one that points to a stage of reappraisal to which we return in Chapter 12. Before considering that subject, however, it is important to introduce another strand of argument. At the same time as the town centre renewal and the housing drive reached full speed, new strands of thinking emerged which informed and challenged architectural modernism, nationally and internationally. It is to these issues that the final part of this book now turns.

Chapter 10

# Succession

The gist of the situation is not merely that official policy has nearly caught up with SPUR policy, but also that SPUR committee members are now too senior, busy and geographically scattered to form an effective ginger group.

However rather than merely expire, it is obviously better to pass the torch to a younger generation, if there is one.

Lionel Brett (Lord Esher)[1]

By 1962, SPUR had managed four years of exhibition and other propaganda activities (see Chapter 5) before patently running out of steam. Formed by a group of senior architect-planners to provide a forum to campaign for attention to the then-neglected topic of urban renewal, the organisation faced a variety of problems. Changing government policies that gave greater priority to urban renewal posed questions as to whether the group, as presently constituted, remained necessary. The programme of events had become sporadic and perfunctory, with meetings poorly attended and group projects resting on the initiative of a handful of members. SPUR also faced the inevitable problem of succession. The first flush of enthusiasm had receded and many of the original members had ceased to be active participants often, like Graeme Shankland or Percy Johnson-Marshall, through moving to major public sector jobs away from the organisation's base in London. Others had become embroiled in the growing wave of renewal projects and could not spare the time. Ted Hollamby, a committed stalwart of many architectural pressure groups over the years, had written to apologise that his work on the LCC's Thamesmead project had caused his attendances to be

> so disastrous this last year, but my time and energies have been completely absorbed by work on the vast project at Erith (50 million pounds) which has been my 'Swan-song' to the LCC. I undertook to complete the design and get it through the Committees by the end of this year, and this I have done, but at some cost to all my other interests.[2]

Those who remained active found the weight of administration involved in servicing the group's programme an increasingly onerous chore. In these circumstances, they faced the choice of either proposing disbandment or of finding others to take over.

During the spring of 1962, a possible new line for revivifying SPUR had come through contacts with the Architects' Action Group (AAG). The AAG had wanted SPUR's support in its campaign over the powers to be allotted under the reorganisation of London government. SPUR had made a conditional offer to contribute to the expenses of the exhibition that it was hoping to hold, but was hesitant over the likely politics of the group. Mindful about the Housing Centre Trust's political stance, the General Committee had second thoughts. It withdrew its offer of support for 'a show regarding matters on which its members' views were themselves divided without some further assurance that the exhibition would be handled in a statesmanlike manner and would be on a technical rather than a political level'.[3] However, it seemed possible that there were prospects worth exploring with a group that described itself as 'composed largely of the younger, and we like to think, more progressive members of our profession for whom a forum for discussion on issues involving architecture has been found lacking within the established professional institutes and societies'.[4]

This point arose again when the proposal that SPUR should dissolve itself was put to an open annual meeting of all members at the Housing Centre on 4 December 1962. The chairman noted: ' The gist of the situation is not merely that official policy has nearly caught up with SPUR policy, but also that SPUR committee members are now too senior, busy and geographically scattered to form an effective ginger group.'[5] Yet rather than simply recommend immediately dissolving the group, he reported on a confidential discussion with the chairman of the AAG, Jeremy Mackay-Lewis, about forming a new committee to further SPUR's work. The existing committee agreed to serve for a further year to launch a major new research project, albeit on an unspecified subject and to ensure, 'if a good handover can be arranged, to pass the torch to a new generation'.[6]

Brett's scepticism about this arrangement was expressed in a letter to Donald Insall, who had just joined the General Committee: 'it will be interesting to see whether we are able to attract a younger crowd, or whether societies of this kind are a slightly obsolete conception'.[7] Another letter to Mackay-Lewis continued that theme, beginning: 'I don't know whether you have had a chance to give a thought to SPUR since Christmas, or whether you are finding with all your other work the project of the AAG combining with SPUR is beginning to seem a little unrealistic.'[8] The reply seemingly justified his doubts: 'Apathy seems to have overtaken the Architects' Action Group which in fact has not met since I first met you last summer!'[9] Although Mackay-Lewis maintained an occasional correspondence, by October the outcome was clear:

> Although I had every intention of putting much more time into the formation of a new committee for SPUR I am afraid that I have not achieved as much as I hoped in this direction.

> Most of us who were interested in forming a SPUR committee have been putting a lot of our spare time into the Architects' Discussion Group and the Junior Liaison Organisation of Architects, Builders, Engineers and Quantity Surveyors. This has tapped off much of the energy left for SPUR.
>
> As I realise you want to make a decision about the future of SPUR at your next committee meeting, I must regretfully say that I have been unable to form a committee that is prepared to put in the time and energy required to make a real success of SPUR.[10]

Besides betokening the end for SPUR, which formally disbanded at the end of 1963, Mackay-Lewis's letter also supplied a telling commentary on the problems faced by other architectural pressure groups, both British and international, at the end of the 1950s. Chapter 2 noted the problems of continuity that architectural associations were having, other perhaps than professional accreditation bodies and trades unions. Unlike the interwar or early postwar periods, architects now had abundant work. The public sector, in particular, was having trouble recruiting skilled practitioners. Discussion groups or pan-artistic collectives tended to have a short lifespan, given that preoccupations with solving problems arising from the real world gave architects less reason to spend their time and energy engaging in propaganda or hypothetical exercises. Moreover, there was the issue of *raison d'être*. While those committed to socialist causes might have a shared political basis around which to found an association, the shift in the material and intellectual climates questioned why it was necessary to cluster together at a time when modernism occupied a hegemonic rather than marginal status. This posed a major problem not only for newer groups, but also for longer established associations that sought newer members to replace their steadily ageing leaderships.

This chapter proceeds in light of those comments. The first section deals the disbandment of the MARS Group in 1957. The next section considers the last full CIAM Congress at Dubrovnik (CIAM 10, 1956), the emergence of Team X (Ten) and the disillusion of CIAM in 1960. The ensuing section uses the activities of Team X to pose questions about the continuing trajectory of the avant-garde after the 1960s. It notes how Team X carried the imprimatur as the successor to CIAM but that status perhaps gave rise to unreal expectations about focus and authority.

## Ceasing to be

If judged only by the size of the membership, the MARS Group in the postwar period appeared to be thriving. Although, for varying reasons, formerly prominent members such as Coates, Yorke, Lubetkin and Chermayeff no longer contributed to the group's activities, membership was substantially greater than in the interwar period. For example, compared with the 1930s when membership stood at 70–80, the group had 117 British and 25 overseas and visiting members on 1 January 1956, with additional unlisted student affiliates.[11] MARS also had a much larger presence in CIAM. The group had successfully organised the sixth and eighth congresses at Bridgwater (1947) and Hoddesdon (1951) respectively, and its younger members were taking the lead in organising the programme for CIAM X at Dubrovnik (1956). Yet changing circumstances meant that CIAM activities were increasingly the sole focus of activity. As the officially accredited national group that sent delegates to CIAM congresses, MARS had an undeniable function that would last as long as CIAM retained that structure. Quite simply, if MARS did not exist, a substitute was needed to take its place. That function apart, the group seemed progressively to lose direction. Attempts to contribute to debate over architectural competitions or education scarcely raised a ripple in the outside world.[12] The 'Turn Again' exhibition received a polite reception, but lacked cutting edge in its protests about office redevelopment. Part of the problem was felt to be age. Most of the core leadership that had established MARS in the 1930s were born around the turn of the twentieth century: Wells Coates in 1895, Maxwell Fry in 1899, F.R.S. Yorke in 1906 and J.M. Richards in 1907. Equally, part of the problem lay in redefining the group's role. To revivify its agenda, MARS needed to escape from its past as a pressure group for a then-unrealised future and create a new sense of purpose linked to the idea of modernism as a continuing project. The group took the decision in June 1953 to admit younger members to the group and participate fully in its activities, for which Bill Howell in particular had campaigned since the Hoddesdon meeting in 1951.[13] There had been conscious efforts to add a younger grouping to its Executive Committee, which had occurred without the atmosphere of schism associated with CIAM (see p. 236). Executive committees from the period between 1953 and 1957 retained older members such as Ove Arup, Godfrey Samuel, H.C. Cadbury Brown and Ernö Goldfinger, but had recruited a cadre of younger architects from the public and private sectors.

It made little substantial difference. The younger members clearly saw MARS membership as their passport to participation in CIAM congresses, in which they were passionately interested. MARS itself was of little relevance. They did not seek, for example, to impose their views on MARS projects like the 'Turn Again' exhibition, even though Theo Crosby, Bill Howell, and Peter and Alison Smithson were on the organising committee. Unlike CIAM, therefore, few MARS members believed that a clash between the generations had much to do with the group's demise. For Cyril Sweett, the problem was the declining expectations placed on members, which he attributed to the group having shed most of its aspirations for maintaining exclusivity through dropping entry requirements during the war.[14] Maxwell Fry supported that position. He considered that the 'calibre of people involved' had declined in the postwar period, with the membership 'no longer dedicated . . . to put in the effort necessary for research but were more wanting to join a club that gave them the right sort of stamp'.[15] J.M. Richards, another founding member, felt that it simply faded away because its original purposes had been achieved and its 'ideas had become part of the common currency of the architectural profession'.[16]

The ending of CIAM's formal organisation at Dubrovnik and the termination of the national groupings (see p. 240), therefore, removed the only convincing reason for the MARS Group's continuance. An Executive Committee meeting in November 1956 decided to close the group. Rather than talk of disbandment or dissolution, the note said simply that 'the MARS Group should cease to be from midnight of the 28th January 1957'.[17] After a party designed to give it 'a proper send-off', MARS was formally wound up and trustees appointed to handle its remaining assets (financial and archival). After canvassing the membership to see if they wanted the return of the funds, it was decided instead to retain the money for any 'worthwhile cause'. In the event, it sponsored the writing of a monograph on Wells Coates (who died in 1958). This commission in itself proved surprisingly traumatic. The commissioned writer defaulted and only the threat of legal proceedings gained the safe return of the papers so that another author (Sherban Cantacuzino) could eventually complete the task.[18]

The safekeeping of the MARS Group's records proved even more problematic. The two three-drawer filing cabinets that contained the group's meticulous minutes were entrusted to the Building Centre. Lacking 'the same archival interests in those days',[19] these were absent-mindedly lost in the early 1960s, believed simply discarded as waste material. Regardless of any assessment of MARS' importance as an architectural pressure group, the Building Centre's action effectively destroyed records that traced the path of the British architectural Modern Movement over almost a quarter-of-a-century. Its only potential compensation, as Trevor Dannatt wryly noted, was that at least 'it had given art historians something to do'.[20]

## CIAM

If MARS had a problem of ageing, that faced by CIAM was a dimension worse because it became an intrinsic element behind clashes within the organisation. Regardless of real ideological differences, especially over the approaches associated with the so-called Athens Charter,[21] the principal antagonists explicitly identified themselves by age. On one side, were the generation that had pioneered the work of CIAM, whom some have referred to as the 'Old Masters'. By the mid-1950s, they were already at or beyond the normal retirement age for other professions. Walter Gropius and Sigfried Giedion were born in 1883 and Le Corbusier in 1887. Only Sert (1902) was born in the twentieth century. On the other side stood those who the older generation laconically referred to as the 'Young Turks',[22] a group who had entered CIAM since the Bergamo Congress (CIAM VII, 1949).

Addressing the conflict primarily in terms of age, however, has potentially misleading aspects. The forces of conservatism were often members of what might be termed a 'middle generation', with many of the older members not inherently opposed to change. What often concerned the latter more than change per se was the lack of clear-cut detail in the proposals that the 'younger' members, especially Team X, would make. As for Team X, co-opting age in support of their argument made a powerful impact, but the fact was that their views did not necessarily appeal even to younger members who had participated in CIAM congresses:

> Their arguments were getting more and more rarefied; indeed if you talked to the Smithsons it became harder and harder to know what they were talking about. It was as opaque as their architecture. When I was

a student that style of debate was enormously stimulating and absolutely relevant, but when I got involved in practice and had to work within the constraints of budget and time, it became less relevant.[23]

Moreover, even when able to exert influence over the congress programme, as at Dubrovnik (1956), not all contributors of their own generation saw things in the same way. Those differences, however, were either ignored or, as noted below, airbrushed out of a history largely written by participants in the struggle.

The makings of the clash arose out of the congresses of the early 1950s. Peter Smithson, who first attended a CIAM Congress as a MARS delegate to the Hoddesdon meeting in 1951 (CIAM VIII), described the hierarchical nature of the organisation at that time:

> I went with Bill and Gill Howell to that meeting. It was then that we saw for the first time people like Corbusier and Gropius and so on in the flesh. They were almost two generations removed and had had time to become mythical.[24]

Noting that he did not speak to them personally:

> it was like all clubs, very hierarchical. There was a second generation of people, who formed an inner circle . . . and their role was to protect the masters. There were others, like John Voelcker, who we knew a lot more, who were there as students. We made contact with them. Jacqueline Tyrwhitt buzzed about trying to see that everyone was treated properly. But we had not formulated a position at that point; we were actually just observers.[25]

At that stage, they had no position for or against, but that had hardened by CIAM IX (Aix-en-Provence, 1953). As noted in the previous volume,[26] the leadership of CIAM had initiated moves at Hoddesdon to involve the new generation of architects. Sigfried Giedion,[27] for example, addressed the generational problem in a manner that stressed assimilation of difference:

> Today we look for the coming generation to continue the work that has been begun and to develop it with their own imagination. Among the most talented members of this coming generation one finds an ever stronger rejection of rationalism and narrow specialisation. It is in line with the character of CIAM that it regards the coming generation as an aid and not as a threat.

The leadership, however, backtracked at a CIAM Council meeting in Paris (May 1952). CIAM IX, they had decided, would be treated in the same manner as previous congresses, returning to the theme of *La Charte de l'Habitat*. There might then be a period of transition until CIAM X, with increasing attention paid to the work of younger architects.

CIAM IX turned out to be a watershed. A group of younger members, led by the Smithsons, John Voelcker, Jaap Bakema and Aldo van Eyck produced contributions clothed in the discourse of disjuncture. This, of course, had always occupied a special place in modernist thought. The emergence of the architecture itself was linked to the upheavals and dislocations that followed the First World War. As such, modernism constituted a distinct and conscious break with all architectures of the past apart from a carefully selected lineage of favoured antecedents. Not surprisingly, then, the same style of analysis was much favoured when the Modern Movement apparently faced a schism of its own in the mid-1950s. While paying lip service to ideas associated with the Athens Charter as having value in restoring 'principles of order within our cities',[28] the future members of Team X contested the idea that the organisation could move forward to a new Charter from that point. Instead, the organisation needed to return to first principles. The first principles that they had in mind concerned 'human association' – precisely the theme, somewhat opportunistically, that the Smithsons were concurrently developing in relation to their 'streets-in-the-air' schemes (see Chapter 9). The Smithsons later summarised their position as follows:

> It seemed that through the very success of CIAM's campaigning we were now faced with inhuman conditions of a more subtle order than the slums. The planning technique of the Charte d'Athènes was analytical of functions. Although this made it possible to think clearly about the mechanical disorders of towns, it proved inadequate in practice because it was too diagrammatic a concept.
>
> Urbanism considered in terms of the Charte d'Athènes tends to produce communities in which the vital human associations are inadequately expressed. It became obvious that town building was beyond the scope of purely analytical thinking; the problem of human relations fell through the net of the Four Functions. In an attempt to correct this, the Doorn Manifesto proposed that 'to comprehend the pattern of human associations we must consider every community in its particular place'.[29]

The 'Manifesto' to which they alluded was a short document written during a CIAM meeting that Rolf Gutman, Denys Lasdun and André Wogensky arranged at Doorn (The Netherlands) at the end of January 1954. While attending, Peter Smithson, Voelcker, Bakema, van Eyck, Hans Hovens-Greve and Daniel ('Sandy') van Ginkel wrote a discussion document that offered a way forward from the Athens Charter.[30] Thinking particularly of the failings of that supposed charter when faced by the 'heart of the city' debate, the manifesto proposed focusing on human associations, studying every community as a 'particular *total* complex'. To make that feasible, the group proposed a Scale of Association ranging from isolated buildings, villages, towns and cities to 'enable us to study particular functions in their appropriate ecological field'. Illustrating the idea by imposing the scale of association on the 'valley section' devised by Patrick Geddes, it was suggested that CIAM could make progress by establishing working parties to study human association '*as a first principle* with the four functions as *aspects* of each total problem'. In short, therefore, the Doorn group sought to place their agenda at the heart of future CIAM activities.

The first bulletin of the MARS Group's CIAM X Committee, reporting on a meeting held under the chairmanship of Denys Lasdun, discussed how the Doorn report might be taken forward.[31] The sub-committee, which contained the core of the future British leaders of Team X,[32] provided its own commentary on the manifesto, offering a bleak example of how the functional design was not enough: the 'Housing Project at Drancy satisfied the functional code of the Charte d'Athènes. The Germans saw fit to use this project as a concentration camp'. Predictably, the bulletin added an admonition that all matters affecting CIAM X 'must be dealt with through this Committee. This is essential for coordination.'[33] A larger sub-committee meeting revealed more of the underlying disagreement about what might feed into a rewritten charter. Arthur Korn, for example, believed that the Athens Charter remained a valid framework for analysis, since it was concerned with the interaction of the four functions, whereas Ernö Goldfinger considered it a mechanical framework that had nothing to do with the human spirit and John Voelcker that interactions 'were academic if the functions themselves were irrelevant to Urbanism'. As one unnamed participant enigmatically commented: 'The Athens Charter is one side of the line and life is on the other. It is poetry which has not come off.'[34] These early discussions focused more on dissecting the failings of the Athens Charter than on exploring the advantages of ideas suggested by the Doorn Manifesto, but absorbed the essential idea that architectural work needed 'means of survey which do not destroy the Life of Human Associations'.[35]

Already asked to supply feedback to a four-point questionnaire issued by CIAM's Secretariat in advance of the Council (CIRPAC) meeting in Paris on 30 June 1954, the MARS Group made representations to support its discussions about the Athens Charter. It sent a six-point letter to the CIAM Secretariat proposing, in line with the Doorn Manifesto, that CIAM considered the study of human association as a first principle with the four functions as aspects of each problem. Tellingly, its last point recommended that it 'should not be assumed until the problem has been studied by the Congress that the end product will in any literal sense be a *charte de l'habitat*'.[36] A reply by Giedion, already in search of allies over the future activities of CIAM, thanked the group for its response to an earlier circular producing 'the most constructive of all the replies' he had received and promised to put it before the meeting, to be held at UNESCO headquarters.[37] There was no record, however, of a reply with regard to the MARS Group's strictures about human associations.

The Paris meeting divided between those that believed that producing a charter was an urgent necessity (Emery, Lods, Tyrwhitt, Honegger, Giedion), those that believed that there was already enough material produced since the Charter of Habitat was first raised at Bergamo in 1949 to do so (Steiger, Wogensky, Roth), those that believed that there was enough for a draft for discussion to be placed before CIAM X (again Emery), and those that believed that, at best, CIAM X could come up with some first proposals (Le Corbusier, Sert). In the event, this last view prevailed, with the congress theme to be 'The Problems of the Human Habitat: first CIAM Proposals – Statements and Resolutions'.[38] Recognising the possibility of new sources of energy, the meeting 'entrusted to a group of younger members the task of developing the ideas of Doorn and submitting a suggestion to the Council for the orientation and organisation of CIAM X'.[39] These individuals formed the committee for CIAM X, then scheduled for Algiers in September 1955. Its members were listed under their national delegations, with the first named person acting as liaison for the group: The Netherlands (*Jaap Bakema*, Aldo van Eyck), England (*Peter Smithson*, Bill Howell, John Voelcker), Morocco (*Georges Candilis*, Shadrach Woods, Richards) and Switzerland (*Rolf Gutman*, E. Neuenschwander). These, along with a handful of others, would form the nucleus of Team X. In September, when the CIAM X Committee met in Le Corbusier's office in Paris, they received reports by the Moroccan group that made references to Equipe X (Team X).[40]

### 'We were the terrorists'

The development of Team X would cause lasting controversy. Based around a small group of English and Dutch architects and subsequently joined by a handful of others (see Table 10.1), it only gradually coalesced into a recognisable grouping, so much so that the various founders of the group tended to have different versions of the point at which it formally emerged.[41] From the outset, its members drew criticism for being relative newcomers who had taken over the planning of CIAM X with determination to have their own way. Jane Drew, for example, expressed a common grievance:

> My chief objection to them, and not just them, was the way that they jumped on to the CIAM bandwagon, having done nothing and setting up what was called [Team] Ten. . . . I thought that it was colossal cheek.[42]

Certainly, there was a sense that a wind of change was blowing through a body that, possibly through its concern to re-establish itself after the cataclysm of war, had become hidebound by its own bureaucracy and structures. For younger members looking forward to participating in CIAM X, there was a sense of difference: 'We were not MARS or CIAM though; we were the alternatives, we were the terrorists, Team X'.[43]

Yet despite freely availing themselves of the discourse of disjuncture, the development of Team X was a torturous affair. The 'emergence' of Team X from CIAM, a favoured word when describing the succession process,[44] occurred almost imperceptibly over more than five years. Although it is argued that especially 'the English youngsters were eager to abandon the CIAM organisation and set up their own platform',[45] this was only overtly expressed after the Dubrovnik Congress. Team X members freely recognised the value of continued connection with a body that retained enormous prestige through its connections with the pioneers of modernism. The Smithsons, with their well-developed historical sensitivity (Chapter 9), were certainly not immune to the attractions of clothing their projects in the

**Table 10.1** Major non-British participants in Team X

| Name | Born | Birthplace | Major architectural training |
|------|------|-----------|------------------------------|
| J.B. Bakema | 1914 | Groningen, Netherlands | Amsterdam Academy of Architecture, Netherlands |
| Georges Candilis | 1923 | Baku, Azerbaijan | Polytechnic, Athens, Greece |
| Giancarlo de Carlo | 1919 | Genoa, Italy | Polytechnic Institute, Milan |
| Aldo van Eyck | 1918 | Driebergen, Netherlands | Eidgenössische Technische Hochschule, Zurich, Switzerland |
| Daniel van Ginkel | 1920 | Amsterdam, Netherlands | Elkerlyc Academy of Architecture and Applied Art, Lage Vuurse, Netherlands |
| Shadrach Woods | 1923 | Yonkers, New York | Practice (Georges Candilis) |

prose style and iconography of the heroic age. For their part, the erstwhile leaders of CIAM showed a continuing, if steadily diminishing, willingness to participate once the succession process had started. That persisted, as we shall see, even after the apparent demise of CIAM after Dubrovnik.

By December 1954, the committee for CIAM X had prepared instructions to contributors in their Draft Framework 5.[46] The document reflected on the lessons learned from Aix. The Doorn Manifesto, now said to have been drawn up 'with the encouragement of the Council', had tried to determine why the analytical methods of the Athens Charter were not producing better results. What followed was close to a disavowal of that charter:

> The meeting decided that analysis by means of the Athens 'Four Functions' (Living, Working, Recreation and Circulation) although it had proved a useful tool for clarifying the mechanical disorders of towns, was proving inadequate when faced with actual construction or reconstruction. The meeting decided that the reason for this was that such an analysis was failing to make creative use of the forces of Human Association, which must be the basis of urbanism.[47]

After clothing CIAM's new endeavours in the language of human associations and observing that the Aix meeting had spent more time in thinking about a charter and too little on the nature of 'Habitat', the document gave instructions to participants. The unpopular *grilles* would again be used as the format for exhibiting materials. A letter written by the Smithsons, Howell and Voelcker in reply to earlier criticisms of a document by the Dutch Group made a crucial point about the differences of approach between Team X and CIAM. In studying 'Habitat', Team X wanted to go beyond the study of form to reveal fundamental groupings:

> We have seen flats and houses and all that goes inside them, what we want to know is how to put them together. Our aim is simple, to discover archetypal groupings of dwellings which are as vital for our society as were squares, streets, kraals, etc., in other societies.[48]

Against CIAM's acceptance of architecture as a 'mediated representation', Team X sought 'a primal language in which form and meaning would be one'.[49] It was a fine-tuned approach unlikely to work well with a multicultural and multilingual association like CIAM.

Gradually the preparations for CIAM X were taken over by the problems of the venue. As late as 15 June 1955, Emery wrote to delegates to supply details about the congress, still scheduled for 10–19 September.[50] Although senior figures in CIAM continued to offer support, the unrest that presaged the Algerian War of Independence made this impossible. Instead a meeting of delegates took place during 8–10 September 1955 at La Sarraz in Switzerland – the chateau where CIAM was founded in 1928. The minutes record the exchange of ideas between 'the Delegates and Team X' as if separate bodies; there was no sense of the latter being a limited life grouping established to arrange a congress. The meeting revised the theme for CIAM X to 'The Habitat: Problem of Inter-relationships. CIAM's First Proposals, Statements and Resolutions'. In light of the subsequent concerns of Team X about who should attend CIAM meetings, the minutes contain a terse note:

> The attention of the Groups is called to the fact that the quality of their individual members cannot be controlled by the Council of CIAM nor by CIRPAC. It is a matter that rests squarely on the shoulders of the Delegates of each Group, who are also responsible for the quality of the work produced at the Congresses.

All that was added was that groups 'should exercise the *utmost severity* in admitting new members'.[51] The meeting rescheduled CIAM X for the second half of July 1956. Although the Portuguese group (Group Porto) issued an invitation to meet in Braga, the delegates decided to take up the earlier offer from the Yugoslavian delegation to meet in Dubrovnik.[52]

The summary of a talk by Sigfried Giedion on the 'task of CIAM',[53] issued in translation with the minutes, was laden with veiled scepticism about the suggested direction for the congress. Giedion began by recognising the problems connected with the human habitat in 'periods of transition, such as our own time'. Thinking ahead to how a congress might tackle this complex subject, he stressed the need for organisation and clarity. He argued that a congress 'which has the Habitat as its theme, with all its manifold implications, must first of all establish a method of work, a method of investigation, and a method of procedure'. The notion of 'interrelationships is among those that *could* [my emphasis] provide a structure for CIAM X', but then provided a lengthy list that was 'by no means comprehensive' about the underlying variables. He also stressed the need for 'great care in the actual presentation of material'.[54]

Team X's reply tied together the emerging agenda of CIAM with the changes taking place within the organisation. Their statement of November 1955, issued with a translation of Giedion's talk, opened with a light paraphrase of Giedion: 'The members of CIAM herewith admit that we find ourselves in a transitional period, during which the relations between people and things are fundamentally changing.'[55] Their commentary continued by stating that it was 'impossible for Team X to mention those relations, decisive for Habitat. They can only be defined after CIAM X'. Grumpily, the statement observed that: 'A short typed specification of the work may be useful to oblige the CIAM X secretariat.' An appendix, pointedly labelled 'as agreed by Team X and Giedion at La Sarraz', summarised the requirement that participants should prepare four grilles, which outlined the problem, the general solution, the detailed solution and a statement of principles. Perhaps the most striking point about the statement was the extent that it firmly resisted any call to be more prescriptive:

> The *design*, however, will be the first consideration for the Congress work. If the form defined with a design is correct, the relations in it, such as those between the houses and also those between houses, shops, schools, workshops and play-spaces will be understood intuitively.
>
> In addition, it may prove necessary to study the relations concerned in the procedure to develop 'habitat' e.g.
>
> the relationship of the scheme to the detailed plan;
>
> the relations between the town-planner and architect;
>
> the relations between town planning–architect and tenants.
>
> With the Congress work it ought to be established what kinds of relations will be decisive for the modifications of form in architecture and town planning. This will only be possible, however, if with their designs, the groups show understanding of the fundamental changes of relations in our time.
>
> The 10th Congress can only be an initial contribution to approach this problem.[56]

Any thoughts of devising another charter, or even the making of a charter, had been abandoned. An ensuing Team X document watered down the presentation requirements, saying that any group that wanted to display 'analytical studies or other material IN ADDITION to the 4 panels . . . is free to do so, but it must be understood that it may not prove practicable to exhibit this material alongside the 4 panels.'[57]

This casualness and lack of expectation of outcome failed to impress Giedion. An open letter to all CIAM groups, delegates and members from CIAM's general secretary attacked the underlying approach, especially the lack of careful scrutiny of the expected new material. Above all, he criticised the lack of commitment to produce a new charter:

> Everyone expects from CIAM that the Xth Congress has to produce at this occasion a document on habitat, similar in quality to the *Charte d'Athènes*. In contrast to other organisations CIAM, according to its goal and structure, has the right and obligation to express its opinion not involved in any other than objective viewpoints. The visual material and other contributions collected during the last Congresses contain practically everything that we need to prepare the *Charte de l'Habitat*.[58]

For his part, Le Corbusier recognised that CIAM had reached the point at which decisions had to be made about its future. Recognising the inevitable, he sent a letter to its president, J.L. Sert, containing a message that he wished to place before CIAM X, albeit in his absence.[59] This recommended dissolving the commissions and sub-commissions inaugurated at Bergamo and to clear the way for the metamorphosis of CIAM by passing it on to 'those of 40 years in 1956, the only ones qualified *to act* in the new phase of CIAM'.[60] For Le Corbusier, the activities of the organisation up to 1956 constituted 'First-CIAM'. At Dubrovnik, it should be succeeded by 'Second-CIAM'.

The Congress at Dubrovnik (3–13 August) would lack the finality of the ending of MARS. At one level, it was business as usual. Participants prepared a total of 35 grilles, with the MARS Group contributing eight and the Dutch groups six. These were discussed at sessions in the normal way. Moreover, the new agenda was apparent but did not dominate proceedings. It has been argued, for example, that the MARS Group's grilles 'were all based on the notion of creating community by means of the concept of "cluster"',[61] but that essentially adds a retrospective coherence to their exhibits. Certainly Denys Lasdun's Bethnal Green cluster blocks and the Smithsons' five studies exploring scales of association fitted that description. By contrast, Peter Carter and Colin St. John Wilson, for example, prepared a vertical city with echoes of Ludwig Hilberseimer's concepts and projects of the 1920s. Peter Carter recalled:

> The project that Sandy [Wilson] and I put together for Team X . . . was a stratified idea. It was not Venice, but Venice with its separation of pedestrians from traffic was very much a stimulation for that concept; in fact, we had a picture of Venice on our panels. We were allowed four panels, so we did a perspective showing people walking around on these different levels with traffic taking place at a lower level.[62]

Wilson's recollections were of a 'loose zoning of vertical strata', proposing a mixed-use five-storey podium structure with tower blocks above, parking beneath and traffic segregated into wide highways. The scheme included a roof-level helicopter station.[63] Jim Stirling, never destined to play much of a role in Team X, seemingly through the opposition of the Smithsons,[64] showed three proposals for linear villages. These were scarcely ahead of their time in terms of building materials (traditional brick or load-bearing masonry construction), but did have mono-pitched roofs and an ingenious plan in which the houses were interlocked.[65] Peter Ahrends, then a graduating student from the Architectural Association, showed a project for a forestry settlement in Scotland. As with most CIAM congresses, exhibits reflected a diversity of theoretical positions on modern architecture and urbanism, from which the ideologically inclined could draw whichever conclusions they favoured.

Yet, at another level, Dubrovnik was quite different from what went before. It was the last of CIAM's sequence of numbered congresses, marking the end of '28 years of action, myth-making and reminisence'.[66] CIAM X was dominated by recognition that change was imminent. Many of the older members stayed away, including Gropius, Cornelius van Eesteren, Marcel Lods and Le Corbusier (who delivered his message by proxy). The meeting began with Sert reading out Le Corbusier's message and general assemblies that debated the future of CIAM, albeit with little consensus about the organisation's future form. The resolution of these discussions led to the establishment of a Reorganisation Committee, composed of Pierre-André Emery, Rogers, Roth, Bakema, Howell, Peter Smithson and Shadrach Woods.[67] The old organisation of officials, ruling council, and working groups would disappear, with the existing council and CIRPAC formally ceasing to hold office at the end of 1956. The name CIAM would be replaced if 'the problems, aims, and technique of work seem too dissimilar from those of 1928'. What appeared in its stead depended on Team X: 'Complete liberty being given to it'. As a last gesture, Sert continued to pursue the mirage by gaining the meeting's consent to having the *Charte de l'Habitat* completed at Harvard. The report ended defiantly: 'It is intended to go on studying the structure of communities come what may.'[68]

## Otterlo and after

The dual existence of CIAM and Team X did not end at Dubrovnik. The lack of any decision to disband CIAM meant that it could persist as long as Team X found that linkage useful. The result was that CIAM retained a presence alongside Team X for the rest of the decade. September 1957, for instance, saw a meeting of the Reorganisation Committee and the new CIAM Council at La Sarraz, the organisation's founding home. A Second Declaration of La Sarraz committed the CIAM 'to study social and visual inter-relationships and to draw conclusions of practical use' – an aim so vague that it failed even to mention architecture. In keeping with that aim, the new organisation was subtitled 'CIAM: Research Group for Social and Visual Relationships'.[69] Crucially, its congresses and other meetings would no longer draw its delegates from national delegations, but from invited individuals. Although phrased in the egalitarian terminology of allowing participation without respect to 'nationality or race', this meant that participation rested on the ruling council's predilections. Another problem comprised what to call the next congress, scheduled for Otterlo (The Netherlands) in September 1959. Although logically it was 'CIAM XI' if that link was retained, that name seemed to infer that it was simply a continuation of the old pattern. As that was unacceptable, the new congress was named CIAM '59 to signify the start of a new series. Otterlo would also see the end of the transition process initiated at Dubrovnik, with the coordinating committee handing over responsibility to a new working party at the close of the congress.

The only remaining problem in advance of the Otterlo meeting was to produce a new official history. It was a notable feature of Team X activity that its leaders periodically wrote and modified the history of the perceived struggle in light of their current outlook. Prior to the congress, the Otterlo participants received a pre-publication issue of the Dutch architectural magazine *Forum*, in which Jaap Bakema sought to provide 'a comprehensive evaluation of CIAM and to give direction to the whole Otterlo confrontation'.[70] In it, Bakema used the writing of history to mount an attack on CIAM's erstwhile establishment. Making extensive textual references, he sketched the way in which CIAM had become hidebound in structure and increasingly governed from Harvard. Expressing doubts about the value of continuing with the preoccupation with the *Charte de l'Habitat*, Bakema argued that the congress should concentrate on 'concrete problems and submit concrete examples'.[71]

Held in the Kröller-Müller Museum, the somewhat derided CIAM '59 was considerably smaller than previous congresses. The Otterlo meeting was shaped by its new leaders' contention that CIAM, nominally with 3000 members, had become so large that it had become diffuse.[72] Instead the Coordinating Committee invited just 43 architects, compared with the 250 who had attended Aix. They presented their work in sessions spread over the first six days, with work displayed as panels on the museum's walls. Judged by any standard, the meeting produced notable architectural exhibits that indicated the changing state-of-the-art. Early megastructural design was readily apparent. *Inter alia*, the British-born but Swedish-based architect Ralph Erskine exhibited plans for ideal Arctic settlements, which embraced 'continuous faceted buildings' to maximise energy efficiency in a harsh climatic environment.[73] Kenzo Tange, the Japanese Metabolist, showed his scheme for Tokyo City Hall and the Kagawa Prefectural Office, as well as Kikutake Kiyonori's ideas for a new city built on reclaimed land in Tokyo Bay. The new development would house an additional 10 million people in a series of giant cylinders interlinked by a double transport spine.[74] New town planning was represented by van den Broek and Bakema's project for North-Kennemerland and by Georges Candilis, Alexis Josic and Shadrach Woods' project for the new town being constructed for the French Atomic Energy Commission's workers at Bagnols-sur-Cèze. From the more symbolic end of architecture's repertoire came Giancarlo De Carlo's shops and apartment buildings for Matera, the poverty-stricken town made famous by Carlo Levi's memoir,[75] and by Oskar and Zofia Hansen's design for the Auschwitz Monument. It was a rich and varied fare that would have done justice to any CIAM Congress.

The most apparent disagreements came courtesy of what Giancarlo De Carlo called the 'termite of history'. The Italian group's emphasis was to deal with history 'not as preset forms to be copied but as the essential premise for understanding the present and a way for the architect to insinuate himself into the circuit of contemporaneity'.[76] This point came to the fore when the Smithsons displayed their London Roads Study, an unsentimental pre-Buchanan Report scheme that would only 'keep the things which are urbanistically and constructionally valid'.[77] The record of subsequent discussion between Peter Smithson and Ernesto Rogers suggested that Smithson, under persistent pressure from Rogers, did not believe that Soho with its narrow streets came into that category. Ernesto Rogers' presentation of the Torre Velesca (see Figure 2.3) drew counter-criticisms from Peter Smithson for the historical referents that he detected in the building.[78]

The seventh day of the congress began with a talk by Louis Kahn, followed by rapporteur commentaries and analyses of the meeting's contents. The final day saw discussion of CIAM's future. The exact nature of what followed remains contested. The conference volume, edited by Oscar Newman, is a model of opacity, even within a book that a critic described as 'likely to disappoint even the few *illuminati* it was destined to interest'.[79] Newman, a recent architectural graduate from Montreal's McGill University, had been asked by Bakema to edit the conference volume from the tapes, even though he had not personally attended. His introduction scarcely hints at the controversy involved in arriving at the seemingly momentous decision not to continue in any formal manner, aside from establish a framework ('Post-Box') to maintain contacts:

> Fearing the organisational congealment which incapacitated CIAM in its later days, it was decided that no formal structure be given to the Otterlo group, nor any officers be appointed, beyond the creation of a 'Post-Box' for the purpose of maintaining communications between colleagues and of gathering and disseminating information and material pertinent to the aims of the Otterlo meeting.[80]

Alison Smithson,[81] in an impressionistic account, was more forthcoming:

> Last evening, extremely heated meeting in bowling-alley of hotel; the middle-age group pleaded for CIAM to be kept on the road for them; yet no offer from them to take over the organisation of meetings for the grey men of Europe; we withdrew to bed.

To conclude matters, the core of Team X posed for photographs with the enormous sign proclaiming 'CIAM' that had adorned the entrance to the museum. The superimposition of a memorial crucifix and wreath underneath the acronym pronounced their prey officially dead.

It was not quite the end of CIAM. Those who resented the organisation being declared dead without much consultation protested that CIAM still had a part to play. Kenzo Tange, alluding back to the clash between the Smithsons and Rogers, placed the 'Utopian view of Team X' alongside the 'escapist fatalism of the Italian group . . . as being only a partial grasp of reality, and both seem likely to result in widening the rift between humanity and technology, which is reality itself'.[82] Tange believed that CIAM still had a future in promoting the cause of modern architecture, at least in areas of the world outside Europe. The final rites came with an exchange of letters in 1961 about abandoning the name CIAM. In putting their side of the story, four key CIAM figures (Sert, Gropius, Le Corbusier and Giedion) wrote that: 'Repeated attacks on the leadership and policies of the previous CIAM meetings and congresses made in various publications by members of Team 10 caused us to give this short account of the past activities of CIAM.'[83] They proceeded to analyse the twists and turns in Team X's position, the lack of proper consultation in refusal to use the name CIAM further, and its continuing relevance to contemporary architecture even if it had 'fulfilled its initial task as far as Europe is concerned'.[84] Bakema replied, complaining about the Japanese and Italian delegates failing to remain for the last day's proceedings ('the decisive moment for organisation matters') and stating that in his opinion CIAM could 'continue where it likes and Team X can never dissolve CIAM as long as there are members who like to continue'.[85] Ever conciliatory, and perhaps hopeful that there might be 'the opportunity to work for some months for your School [Harvard] . . . in 1963 or 1964', Bakema wrote to Sert in June 1961 suggesting an 'Otterlo II-meeting' for September 1962 to promote 'decisions about international architectural research contact'.[86] He continued:

> Then the reality will be:
> 1.  there is still a framework called CIAM
> 2.  there is a communication-centre called BPH [Post Box for the Development of the Habitat]
> 3.  there came some new smaller groups like Team X is [sic].

Bakema also proposed that CIAM would turn into a 'Communication-centre (in the sense of a Post-Box)' at Otterlo-II.[87] Nothing came from this suggestion, but Bakema, at least, remained mindful of the existence of a remnant CIAM. True to that position, he could still be found in 1975 writing circular letters that carefully differentiated between whether recipients were 'CIAM' or 'Team X'.[88]

Team X itself maintained a programme of activities until 1981. Judgement on them tends to be coloured by continuing comparison with CIAM, which is wholly unrealistic. CIAM was an internationally constituted movement drawing its support from national delegations, each of which had a right to participate. Team X opted for a different approach and, in the process, mirrored that of avant-garde groups elsewhere. Its work centred on a small core of activists, who increasingly saw themselves as the Team X 'family'. They included the leadership of Team X (Bakema, the Smithsons, Candilis, Giancarlo de Carlo, Aldo van Eyck and Shadrach Woods), with a dependable cast of associates (Ralph Erskine, Jerzy Soltan, Brian Richards, Alexis Josic and, in the earlier years, John Voelcker). Meetings were by invitation and deliberately kept small. Team X held a further 16 meetings after the demise of CIAM between 1960 and 1977; 7 of those meetings had fewer than 10 in attendance. The largest, at Urbino in 1966, had 25–30 participants but that, in itself, was a cause of contention. Team X had struggled to decide the character and size of its membership.[89] The organiser, Giancarlo de Carlo, found himself caught between the wishes of van Eyck, who wanted a more inclusive invitation policy, and the Smithsons, who felt that participation should be limited to people that could submit works 'relevant to the topic set for discussion'.[90] The Smithsons responded by not attending the meeting. Efforts to heal the rift led to a meeting in Paris in February 1967 to achieve a 'restatement of convictions', which would take the form of a re-edit of the *Team 10 Primer*, originally published in *Architectural Design* in 1962.[91] It also gave the editor the gratuitous opportunity to erase John Voelcker's name from the original list of authors.

Personality problems, of course, were also a perfectly familiar feature of CIAM activities. The competition between the French and German delegations for leadership of CIAM in the early days and Le Corbusier's machinations over the Athens Charter showed the operation of naked self-interest. The outward appearances of collaboration in the interwar years concealed major disagreements and personal rivalries. Team X's tactics were scarcely different in that respect. Moreover, as their own voluminous studies and recent independent scholarship show, the activities of Team X meetings through the 1960s present an impressive inventory of architectural thinking with an unmistakable utopianism tempered by a constant willingness to work through real world projects. The 1962 Royaumont meeting on 'urban infrastructure', for example, focused discussion on communication and large-scale urban renewal, dealing with the role of the architect at larger scales of design and the problems of integrating new infrastructure into the existing context. Equally, at the 1971 Toulouse-Le Mirail meeting, the delegates placed the comparative spotlight on a range of ambitious housing schemes produced under the aegis of the Welfare State.[92]

Yet, it is reasonable to reflect on what was lost. CIAM supplied a unique forum in which an increasingly diverse assemblage of delegates came together periodically to discuss architecture and urbanism. A small group of European architects had taken over this organisation, abandoned its mechanisms and structure, and then established a new framework of invited meetings within which they primarily talked to themselves – even if that occurred without a predetermined plan. With hindsight, the same result could have been achieved as an extension of the Doorn meeting, without the need to dispose of CIAM.

In Team X's defence, CIAM may well have been moribund, as the lack of resistance to the takeover might signify. Moreover, although the Athens Charter had the enormous attraction of offering a straightforward way of analysing cities and planning for their future, it was badly flawed in its analyses and unlikely to be salvaged by the incremental addition of another charter. Team X, unlike many other avant-garde groups in the 1960s maintained an element of engagement with the real world in the sense of requiring a 'critical reading of context'.[93] Their agenda addressed the Athens Charter's deficiencies and offered concepts that might serve as new foci for discussion. These included the 'cluster concept' with its implications of multiple centres of intensity and polycentric growth, and the framework of 'scales of association'.

The problem, however, was that while these conceptual tools offered the prospect of returning debate to first principles, they lacked the requisite clarity to serve as the basis of that debate. While CIAM existed, there always remained a possibility that its international dialogues would bring issues of central importance to the future of modern architecture into stark relief, as was shown even as late as Otterlo with the clashes over the historic environment. Although CIAM had lost its way in the 1950s, its demise effectively closed the last prospects of finding an international platform for the self-critical focus on practice that modern architecture so urgently needed, and lacked, in the 1960s.

# Chapter 11

# Late-flowering modernism

**If you can remember anything about the sixties, you weren't really there.**
**Paul Kantner[1]**

If the activities of Team X and others merely constituted eddies that were 'detectable at the edge of the modernist tide' during the mid-1950s,[2] then by the mid-1960s the flow of projects from the avant-garde had assumed a quite different order of magnitude and turbulence. In one sense, these were symptoms of a familiar restlessness. Given its history as a radical movement that had long cherished its avant-garde credentials, there was unease at the practice of modernism steadily coming to occupy the middle ground of architectural thought which, like middle age, was something to be avoided. At precisely the time when reconstruction and modernisation gathered pace, architecture experienced a period of radical innovation but not one that had much to do with the everyday world. Charles Jencks, deploying a military rather than marine analogy, saw British architecture in the 1960s as a 'scarred battlefield . . . saturated with the shellholes of polemic'. The architect proceeded as the avant-garde did in any battle, 'as a provocateur', who 'saps the edges of taste, undermines the conventional boundaries, assaults the thresholds of respectability and shocks the psychic stability of the past by introducing the new, the strange, the exotic and the erotic'.[3]

The passage of time has been unkind to the judgements behind such sentiments and the language used, suffused as they were with notions of counter-culture and revolution in the arts, but they symptomised a broad feeling that thinking about the modern city had become monotonously obsessed with function and utility. They were also permeated by fears of the demographic crisis, which then seemed close to home as well as of concern to the developing world. One forecaster suggested that the British population might rise from 53 million in 1964 to as much as 85 million by 2004.[4] Putting some substance on these abstract statistics, Peter Hall noted in 1966 that this meant:

> Eight and a half million more people by 1980, 20 million more by the end of the century: for this cause alone, the need to build a town the size of Bournemouth, or Wolverhampton, or Bolton every four months to the year 2000.[5]

Homes, then, were required in large quantities in a country that already had a high density of population. Could this be achieved in the old ways or, as the problems of the housing drive were suggesting, were radically new forms of habitation necessary? Could the appropriate numbers of people be accommodated without severe impoverishment of the living environment? Might we not relax the rigidity of architectural and planning restrictions and allow the appearance of new urban forms, wholly dissimilar to conventional cities?

The standard response looked to architectural creativity to supply answers. Buoyed by an atmosphere of confident expectancy about the availability of resources and about the possibility of social progress through technological advance, new thinking appeared that extolled the art of the possible. If it could be thought, the idea ran, then it could be built. Individuals and small groups laboured, sometimes over many years, to reinvent the city, *inter alia*, spiritually, aesthetically, politically and spatially. Instead of multilevel circulation systems, entire cities could be multilevel. They could be super-concentrated or global in extent; underground, surface, raised, flying, floating or submarine; fixed or mobile; consumer-oriented or proto-environmentalist. A small amount of this thinking would directly influence practice, for example, as seen in the plans of certain second generation New Towns or in experimental designs for leisure centres or housing schemes. Much of the rest remains known today primarily through the efforts of exhibition curators who lovingly present visionary architecture to new audiences as emblematically capturing the spirit of the 1960s – in varying measures confident, optimistic, counter-cultural, rebellious, uncompromising, frivolous and profoundly imaginative. It was work that often sought to blur the boundaries between utopian speculation and serious proposals for practice. In some circles, it was fostered by a sense that pursuit of the fantastic might reveal truths hitherto obscured by convention. As a survey from 1960 noted:

> occasionally one might even feel that these so-called freakish ideas are concerned with something much more fundamental – and perhaps much more important – for the architecture of the future than the exquisite over-refining of accepted and already perfected forms.[6]

When looked at another way, that type of advice was an invitation to place the normal canons of criticism in abeyance. Who, for instance, could say in advance what was far-sighted and what was far-fetched during a period of rapid change? The result, in many cases, was a recipe for indulgence.

This chapter examines the continuing freewheeling progress of modern-ist thought as it unfolded in the 1960s through into the early 1970s. It opens by considering the basic options that avant-garde thinkers considered when rethinking contemporary approaches to urbanism and spelling out new visions for the future city. We then look in detail at the tendency to think big, examining the brief passion for megastructures as the recipe for dealing with large-scale problems at one fell swoop. The final section takes stock of efforts to map the plurality of modernism in the early 1970s, showing the strains encountered by attempting to constrain the abundant plurality of modernism within the overarching framework of a singular 'Modern Movement'.

## Possibilities

Revisiting thinking about possibilities for future cities from the late 1960s quickly reveals diverse voices pressing to be heard. Table 11.1, for example, shows a selection of twelve commentaries dating from 1968–70,[7] which deal in varying ways with questions involving urban form and urban society. With regard to urban form, they occupied all positions from high-density cities that retained a sharp boundary between city and countryside and low-density urban realms theoretically extending up to planetary size. They included cities that were high- and low-rise, dispersed and concentrated, mononuclear and polynuclear. With regard to society, they occupied all positions from the classic dystopian science fiction vision of human existence in the urban anthill to the hedonism of life in an alluring leisure-oriented post-industrial future, and from consumerist freedom to environmentalist sacrifice.

Within that diversity, two not-so-new models re-emerged as foci for architectural experiment. The first saw processes of decentralisation achieving a qualitative boost from developments in communications technology, rising affluence, increased leisure and exercise of choice. Under such conditions of 'explosive' urban expansion, the dynamics of growth might be accommodated by channelling new development into designated corridors or linear strips. Such thinking reactivated interest in linear city plans, one of the Modern Movement's favoured prototypes. Pioneered by the Spaniard Arturo Soria y Mata in the 1880s, linear city ideas had inspired such projects as N.A. Miliutin's schematic plan for Stalingrad, Le Corbusier's Montevideo and Rio de Janeiro plans (both 1929) and Algiers Plan (1930–1), and the MARS plans for London.[8] Their main attraction had always been transport efficiency and the potential for close contacts between city dwellers and the countryside. Their main drawback was that, beyond a few prototypic applications, they had never enjoyed much appeal as the recipe for a complete town.

The second model was the megastructure. Already broached at several points in this book with regard to specific examples from practice,[9] megastructures comprised large multifunctional urban complexes containing transient smaller units adaptable to changing needs.[10] As such, they could include anything from open-ended linear grids to huge single enclosing structures. Like linear cities, they had a considerable pedigree. Megastructures had appealed to the urban imagination of early modernists, as exemplified by Antonio Sant'Elia *Città Nuova* or Ludwig Hilberseimer's *Hochhausstadt* (Skyscraper City). One of the best summaries of

**Table 11.1** The future city: the view from 1968–70

| Forecaster(s) | Urban form | Urban life |
|---|---|---|
| Banham et al. (1969) | Deregulated spread | Freedom of expression, mobility |
| Calder (1969) | Spatial spread of city, 'frightening' urbanisation | Post-industrial society, leisure orientation |
| Cook (1970) | Celebration of possibilities of new architecture; megastructures | New lifestyles, affluence and consumerism, mobility |
| Cowan (1970) | Megalopolis England, spread of suburbia | Increased mobility, affluence, consumerism, increasing leisure and educational opportunities |
| Cox (1968) | Explosive growth, spread of the 'secular city' | Accelerated mobility, dehumanisation |
| Doxiadis (1968) | Ecumenopolis | 'Planetisation' of urban culture |
| Eells and Walton (1968) | The 'explosive city' | Urban culture varies with adaptation to population pressures and technology |
| Knight (1968) | Vast, high-density, high-rise cities; sharp divide with countryside | Dystopian visions of cities as physically and socially blighted |
| Lewis (1969) | Polynuclear cities | Wired society |
| McHarg (1969) | Organic restructuring of city, restoration of nature into city, abolition of sprawl | Society in ecological balance, better use of leisure time |
| Soleri (1969) | Urban implosion, creation of megastructures | Society in ecological balance, arcology |
| Whyte (1968) | Greater concentration, higher density | Leisure orientation |

Source: Adapted from J.R. Gold, 'The city of the future and the future of the city', in R.L. King (ed.) *Geographical Futures*, Sheffield: Geographical Association, 1985, p. 94.

their supposed advantages appeared in Paul and Percival Goodman's *Communitas*. Proposing a complete city in an air-conditioned cylinder 1 mile (1.6 kilometre) in diameter and 385 feet (117 metres) high, they argued:

> Let us . . . take the bull by the horns and make of the many large buildings one immense container: (1) the intermediary streets vanish; (2) the through driveways now carry out their function to the end, bringing passengers and goods directly to stations in the container, without two speeds and without double-loading for trucks and trains; and (3) the corridors are transfigured, assuming the functions of promenade and display which the streets performed so badly.[11]

The Goodmans also identified the potential energy savings involved:

> In the entire downtown there will now be only one exterior wall and roof that is rigid, instead of many thousands. There is only one wall and roof

to lose heat and cold. Lighting, ventilation, cleaning, etc. can be handled on a uniform system, at least cost.[12]

## Linear cities

In many respects, the re-emergence of linearity stemmed from an analysis that foresaw not just the spatial spread of the major conurbations, but also the emergence of huge megalopoli, formed from chains of functionally interrelated metropolitan areas.[13] In the case of Great Britain, for example, Peter Hall had projected a 'dispersed city' future for the affluent South East England in his book *London 2000*.[14] For Hall, parallels with southern California readily came to mind. The Los Angeles region, in particular, offered a possible prototype in the form of a new low-density, extensive (sub-)urban realm based on the private car.[15] While recognising the different social and cultural patterns that applied,[16] he suggested how that model might offer clues to the future of the London region. The book ended with a portrait of the life of a family (the Dumills) who lived in the fictional New Town of Hamstreet in Kent (which bore resemblance to the much-admired scheme for Hook: see Chapter 7). Although living 61 miles from central London, the Dumills were 'representative' Londoners. Hamstreet was not as an outpost of the distant city, but a fully integrated part of the city-region.

Linear city theorists applied that form of analysis at varying scales. In *A Town Called Alcan*, for example, Gordon Cullen and Richard Matthews produced a series of studies (sponsored by an aluminium manufacturing company) that saw business potential in the development of New Towns. They identified four possible candidates for 'Circuit Linear Towns'. Three were new cities, designed around peripheral road systems designed to take fast-moving traffic (Solway, Solent and Redrose); the fourth showed application of the same principles to London. Cullen's sketches depicted high-density settlements, embracing the characteristic picturesque perspective of the 'Townscape' school (see Chapter 12). The Solway scheme, for example, envisaged six communities scattered at intervals along the shores of the remote Solway Firth, linked into a circuit running from Carlisle along the north and south shores of the Firth and connected by a road running across the top of a long-proposed, but never built, barrage. The 'high-density townscape' of the communities constructed around the Firth 'would be in dramatic contrast to the great spaces outside' (Figure 11.1).[17] Redrose, situated between Liverpool and Manchester, would be a new settlement developing at the meeting place of four circuits. The intention was that it would draw the old towns 'into a new life' and convert 'the amorphous Green Belt into four interconnecting green places' (Figure 11.2).[18] Its city centre, shown in Figure 11.3, saw shopping facilities on a pedestrian deck above the traffic access level, with regional government offices in the background (Figure 11.3).

The Alcan studies remained discussion projects, but linear city ideas influenced the thinking of consultants working on the plans for several of the second generation New Towns.[19] The 1971 plan for Irvine New Town, on the Ayrshire coast, was developed in collaboration with Hugh Wilson, late of Cumbernauld, acting as consultant. The plan envisaged growth along 'community routes'. These were seen

11.1
View of the interior of one of the new Solway Firth communities (drawing from 1964)

11.2
Plan of Redrose showing the city centre and its tangential circuits (drawing from 1964)

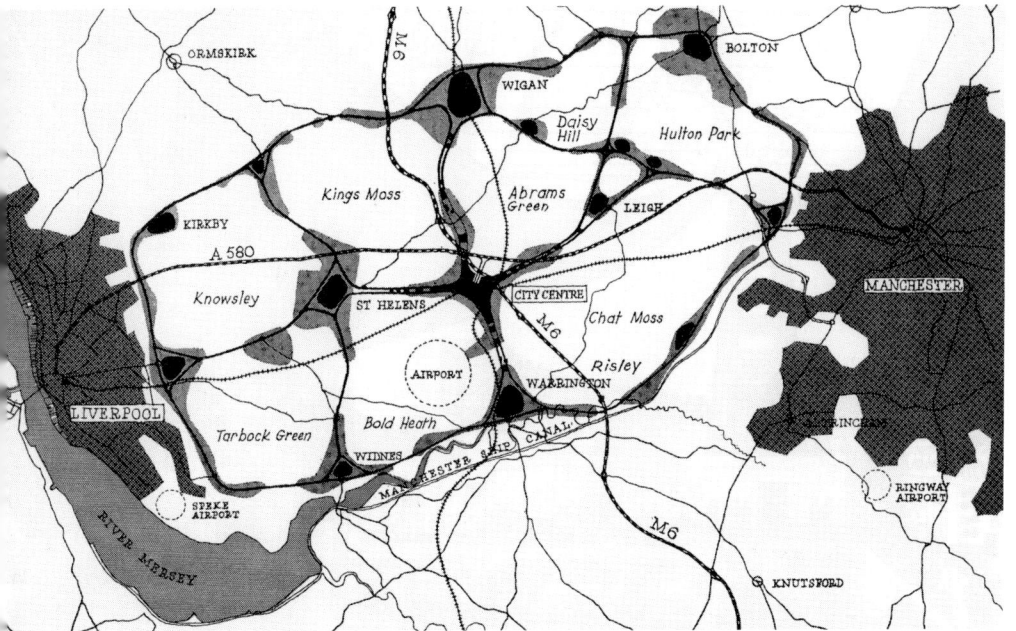

11.3
A view of the covered shopping centre of Redrose, raised above traffic access. The regional government offices are in the background (drawing from 1964)

as the focus of the surrounding development, with social, educational and other facilities located at public transport stops. The community routes would allow a cellular pattern of growth, adding new cells when more were needed, and linking directly with the Central Area. This structure, an ambitious design with hints of Cumbernauld (Figure 11.4), would eventually create a 'comprehensive, linear central area from the existing centre of the burgh to the coast'.

Linear city principles also influenced the plan for the Central Lancashire New Town, based on the three existing centres of Preston, Leyland and Chorley[20] – a scheme intended to tackle both overspill and urban restructuring in mid-Lancashire. The plan employed a triple-spine approach, with a central public transport route (similar to the community route principle employed at Irvine) and parallel high-speed motorways. These spines of development were linked in to the existing towns in the area, with employment distributed along the chain to try to alleviate the journey to work (Figure 11.5). Andrew Derbyshire, who worked on the Master Plan for RMJM (the consultants), noted that the commission had initially come through contacts with J.D. Jones, then deputy permanent secretary at the Ministry of Housing and Local Government. Jones had liked the practice's plans for the university campus at York because

> it was indeterminate. You could stop at any point and [it would] be viable. It was not radial or concentric, which is very inflexible. Once you have filled up the middle, you have had it. He liked the combination of repeated groups, which were coming together to form a unique whole. He thought that this was the way to do the second generation of New Towns, which were all based on existing communities.[21]

11.4
**Model of linear town centre for Irvine New Town (1971)**

Application of a similar philosophy to Central Lancashire was intended to produce a city that could grow along its axes and acquire over time the character of a polycentric unit. Its advantage again lay in its indeterminacy, with the linear city principle not relying to the same degree on the initial plan being correct in all aspects as might be the case with a more conventional design:

> There are diagrams in the report that compare the concentric city with the distributed city and demonstrate that the concentric city has no flexibility and no potential for growth and no uncertainty attached to it. It works at a certain finite size, smaller than that it isn't viable and bigger than that it doesn't work, you can't do it. We proposed the polycentric city as being the answer to coping with this problem of uncertainty and flexibility. The future can never be prophesised, so produce something which can respond.[22]

Indeterminacy and city expansion on ever-extending axes would prove popular themes. Peter Cook's design for 'Plug-In City', with its megastructural underpinnings, is discussed in the next section, but it too incorporated linear city principles. Plug-In City was a framework for an open-ended urban corridor. Starting around London, it would expand north through the Midlands towards Lancashire and south-east across the English Channel to France.[23] The theme of international scale was taken perhaps to its apogee in the work of the Greek architect Constantinos Doxiadis. The creator of the self-styled school of 'ekistics' (essentially

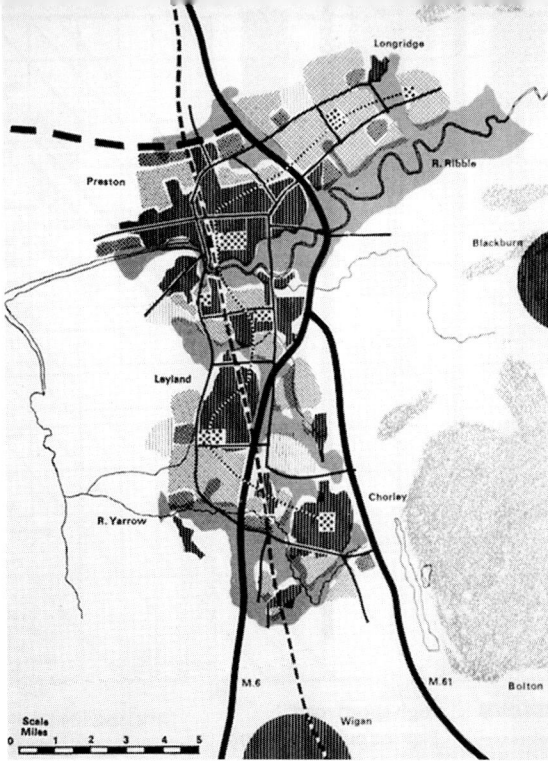

11.5
**Plan for Central Lancashire New Town, showing the three-strand structure applied to Preston-Leyland Chorley (1967)**

a science of settlement building), Doxiadis's ideas combined acceptance of the dynamics of metropolitan growth with a planner's desire to channel growth into specific channels. At the global scale, the final stage in urban evolution would see the coalescing of the world's linear cities into the single world urban system that he called 'ecumenopolis'. This would occur within approximately a century, with the world's population then at 12 billion.[24] Working on that assumption, Doxiadis focused on the need for planning the axes between the major urban areas, with the creation of new centres where necessary. Given that the car was an inevitability, Doxiadis envisaged full pedestrian-vehicle segregation, using 'underground conduits' if possible. Urban development would take place along perpendicular axes, containing cellular residential units, no more than 2 kilometres square, the maximum comfortable walking distance.[25]

## Non-plan

Despite dealing with the subject of ecumenopolis, which in the hands of science fiction writers normally called forth dystopian accounts of urban life, Doxiadis retained faith in *planned* linearity to deliver pleasant living environments. Linear city principles sought through planning – whether using strips, corridors or grids – to direct the established dynamics of road-based radial expansion. Towards the end of the 1960s, a distinguished group of writers posed the question as to what might happen if *no* controls were exercised over such developments. Their thoughts appeared in the essay 'Non-Plan: an experiment in freedom', published in the journal *New Society* in 1969.[26] 'Non-Plan' was the work of the architectural and design historian Peter Reyner Banham, the architect Cedric Price, the geographer Peter Hall and the magazine's deputy editor, Paul Barker. It was conceived by Barker and

Hall 'out of despair of what was happening in late '60s planning and architecture'.[27] Planning was identified as representing a

> whole cumulation of good intentions . . . the only branch of knowledge purporting to be some kind of science which regards a plan as being *fulfilled* when it is merely *completed*; there's seldom any sort of check on whether the plan actually does what it was meant to do, and whether, if it does do something different, this is for the better or for the worse.[28]

Official architecture was judged dreary and sometimes dysfunctional:

> The purpose is to ask: why don't we dare trust the choices that would evolve if we let them? It is permissible to ask – after the dreariness of much public rebuilding, and after the Ronan Point disaster – what exactly should we sacrifice to fashion.[29]

The idea, then, was to hypothesise what might happen if controls were removed, taking as examples three 'rural tracts whose apparent despoliation was guaranteed to cause most offence'.[30] The list was Constable Country (East Anglia: Banham), Montagu Country (Southern Hampshire: Price), Lawrence Country (East Midlands: Hall), with Barker providing a contextual overview.

The resulting publication drew on the established interests of the writers. Banham and Hall shared a belief that 'we [had] to learn from the freer forms of North America'.[31] Hall, as noted above, applied that logic to the emerging geography of South East England. Banham noted that most urbanists tended to see Los Angeles as either an 'impenetrable mystery' or an 'urbanistic disaster-area'. Instead, as argued in various articles in *New Society* and later in his book *Los Angeles: the architecture of the four ecologies*, the city might be 'instant architecture in an instant townscape', but there was 'a comprehensible, even consistent quality to its built form'.[32] Indeed, he argued that it might well offer clues to the urban environment appropriate to a post-urban age.[33] For his part, the architect Cedric Price had developed a thread of 'indeterminacy' in his approach to architecture. Responsible for unrealised projects such as the 'Fun Palace' (1961–4) and the 'Potteries Thinkbelt' (1963–6), Price offered a view in which the architecture was informal, flexible, unenclosed and impermanent, but applied to very precise and detailed locations in order to allow 'the immediate and future consequences of the proposals to be closely examined'.[34]

Drawing on these distinct but complementary interests, 'Non-Plan' provided a series of snapshots of dynamic growth in small parcels scattered throughout the regions. Lawrence Country would see growth, 'more scattered and less geometrically tidy than our present planners would like' diffused over hundreds of small villages and towns, with low-density strip development along main roads after the North American pattern. Constable Country, somewhat moved to a portion of ex-urban Essex and Hertfordshire, would see expansion around a new airport complex with 'infilling and backfilling' of communities. Montagu Country would see the spread of a pleasure zone, to become one of the main 'play-and-live' edges of the London region. Besides the spread of mobile homes, there might be 'high-level, tree-top chair rides through the [New] Forest and convoys of computer-programmed holiday houseboats'. Fawley oil refinery would offer *son et lumière* displays. Additional marine-related activities might include floating grandstands, large retractable marinas and a nudist colony within a giant dome.[35]

Part-conjecture and part-tease, *Non-Plan* gave expression to important undercurrents in the 1960s. It aimed to counter the uniformity and dullness imparted by the hand of planning and official architecture. The formula favoured dismissing the constraints of the past, considering alternatives, and thinking small. It thought of architecture in terms of conventional form unconventionally applied, favouring liberating individuals to choose their personal environments and to see what happened when those choices aggregated together. In doing so, its visual code remained that of the ex-urban environments of the western states of the USA; seen as not as amorphous and placeless, as later writers would assert,[36] but as bright, colourful and empowering. As such, *Non-Plan* provided one reading of trends that stressed flexibility and choice. Other readings of much the same trends, however, could lead in wholly different directions.

## Megastructural thinking

On 28 April 1967 the Universal and International Exposition, better known as Expo '67, formally opened in Montreal. Had all gone according to plan, it would have been the greatest display of megastructuralism seen in the 1960s. The original scheme, devised at a symposium held at Montebello in western Quebec in May 1963, was for a showground based on a megastructural grid with services and a linking mechanized circulation system. The underlying motive was to use architecture as a way to remove the national rivalries inherent in international expositions and which, as the Canadian organisers correctly surmised, would shortly be on display at the 1964 New York World's Fair. Instead Expo '67 would organise the exhibits within the framework of a unified structure, thereby symbolising unity and dispensing with the outward signs of competing national identities. 'Theme pavilions' would explore central ideas, with three different levels of communication system allowing themes and sub-themes to be explored in greater or lesser detail.[37] Movement would link to visitors' interests and enable them to move quickly through sections that held little attraction, but slowly when they had greater interest.

This idealistic schema was eventually rejected, less because of the 'hesitant conservatism' of the government-sponsored group established to run Expo '67,[38] than through the problems manifested by the structure and what it represented. It quickly became clear that the complex site, then partly under reclamation from the St Lawrence River, would make it impossible to complete a vast and complex set of integrated megastructural grids in time and to budget. Moreover, as was so often the case with megastructural plans, the proposers ignored simple realities. National governments invest considerable sums to build large prestigious pavilions to act as advertisements for their nations; they had little to gain from financing an event that chose to blur national advantage in the interests of international solidarity. Gilles Gagnon, the architect chiefly responsible for implementation of the master plan, illustrated the theme of national interest by reference to the behaviour of the French and British. These nations, to his amusement, had received adjacent plots. Basil Spence, the architect of the British pavilion, kept altering the design on the basis of the latest reports about the design of the French pavilion:

> They [Britain] wanted to have the biggest pavilion on the site, because Canada was a former colony of England [sic] and because of the Commonwealth. France next door had a pavilion that was getting bigger, adding more floors; it was getting higher than the British one. The British decided to do this truncated tower so that it would be higher than the neighbours. And they kept detrunking the thing to make it higher and higher and higher. It was a kind of folly.[39]

The resulting national pavilions, however, did still ensure that the fair caught the flood tide for megastructures. Most represented megastructures-as-spectacle, in which the container became as much part of the show as the exhibits. Frei Otto's West German Pavilion, for example, comprised an experiment in suspended structures, with a tent-structure in which eight masts and cable-nets supported a translucent membrane. The Dutch Pavilion featured similar principles, with a building suspended in a cage of aluminium tubing. The American Pavilion was a geodesic dome designed by Buckminster Fuller. Measuring 76 metres in radius and tall enough to enclose a 20-storey building, it comprised an inner hexagonal steel skeleton, an outer triangular steel exoskeleton and an acrylic membrane to keep out the elements (Figure 11.6). Although an imposing structure and the chosen design

11.6
**Buckminster
Fuller's American
Pavilion, Expo '67**

for a pavilion from Canada's superpower southern neighbour, the acrylic membrane made it a profound fire hazard. Preferring to avoid a diplomatic incident, the building was permitted to go ahead but made subject to 24-hour fire-watch. In the event, the fair passed off without problems, but the underlying analysis proved correct. In 1976 a unsupervised welder working on the frame caused a fire which led to the entire acrylic membrane being burnt off in a twenty-minute inferno.

The national pavilions, however, were simply structural containers for exposition exhibits. A more rigorous test of the viability of megastructural principles was the apartment complex designed by Moshe Safdie as the 'living architecture' exhibit. Known as Habitat '67 (Figure 11.7), the design was a megastructure based around interconnected A-frames. This gave the resulting structure a pyramidical shape, again predictably claimed to be analogous to a Mediterranean hilltop village. Prefabricated units were clipped to the frame to create a three-dimensional structure that maximised the external exposure of the dwellings – each of which looked out in three or four directions – with external walkways replacing internal corridors.[40] As originally conceived, Habitat '67 would have been a vast complex, consisting of 1000 flats with accompanying commercial facilities, rising to 22

11.7
**Habitat '67 (Moshe Safdie)**

storeys. The size of the development was predicated by the economics of prefabrication. A factory to produce the prefabricated units was built at one end of the pier. The apartments, complete in all details, would roll out of the factory and be transported into place by tracked crane. Once in the right location, the units were attached to their allotted place on the frame. Covering the costs of the factory and ancillary facilities required a sufficiently large production run. This, however, was never likely to occur. Over time, Habitat '67 was reduced to a pilot project of just 158 dwellings rising to 12 storeys – a figure never even remotely likely to make the development economic.[41]

Expo '67 encapsulated in microcosm much of the excitement and drawbacks of a genre that briefly captivated the imagination of architecture's avant-garde before the underlying vision collapsed under its own grandiose absurdity in the 1970s. Megastructures came in three different, albeit overlapping, types, exemplified respectively by Habitat '67, the national pavilions and the original conception of the Montebello symposium. The first type used advanced technology to create large-scale structures that offered striking new ways to handle existing tasks. The second were large shells, somewhat akin to the circus's Big Top. They were designed to present and *provide* spectacle and, as such, were not necessarily subject to the rule that the same function could often be fulfilled at a much lower cost by means of a different type of structure. The third were massive integrating structures, which sought to offer flexibility and endless extendibility. These were generally considered subject to no limits other than the confines of imagination and included plans for entire cities within geodesic domes, immense urban grids, continental-scale cities and even complete extra-terrestrial cities in geostationary Earth orbit.[42] Huge in ambition and primarily conceptual in design, they had a habit of not only rarely being built but also being unbuildable.

All these expressions of megastructuralism had appeared by 1964, when Fumikomo Maki coined the term as an *omnium gatherum* to fit the burgeoning development of massive integrated schemes.[43] To Maki, a mega-structure was simply a large frame that housed all or part of a city. Four years later, by which time 'megastructure' had ousted rival terms such as 'omnibuilding',[44] the term had acquired additional defining characteristics, now treating the city as an 'open web or network',[45] structured according to some internal dynamic and able to expand externally by making connections with the frame. The alleged flexibility that a megastructure conferred tended to ally megastructuralism to 1960s thinking about modularity, where the component units could apparently be connected and disconnected from the frame at will. In some versions, the frame was seen as having a longer life-expectancy than the attached units, which in turn allowed for obsolescence and continuing modernisation. There was a powerful, if often implicit, utopian interest in megastructures as a vehicle for social transformation. As one enthusiast noted, megastructures might provide the catalyst to invigorate social and communal life, since they had

> the potential of making greater change and variety possible in life, the
> liberation and ecological recreation of more open land, and even the

more immediate response of the community to citizen and vice versa on a newly revealed interface of the individual with his social, political, and cultural, as well as his physical, environment.[46]

Such statements, however, conflated two different positions that sometimes sat uneasily together, namely, environmental responsibility and individual choice. The first, which became more apparent as the 1960s wore on, sought to rekindle the social commitment of modernism by aligning the development of new architecture with the turn towards environmentalism. This trend emphasised the need for greater responsibility in use of land and resources, which might *constrain* choice in the interests of the wider good. To Paolo Soleri, for example, this led to the principles of arcology – a combination of architecture plus ecology. Soleri devised a series of conceptual projects, including a model community (Arcosanti) that he developed near Phoenix, Arizona. The earliest, completed as an entry for the Luxembourg Bridge competition in 1958, proposed an inhabited bridge, using the interstices for housing. By 1964, Soleri had switched to city-sized megastructures ranging in size from Arcosanti (5000 people) to Babelnoah (6 million: see Figure 11.8). Deeply incensed at the spread of the urban realm, explicitly as manifested by Doxiadis' ecumenopolis, Soleri looked to miniaturise technology and concentrate population, so as to avoid the endless sprawl of developments at ground level. Outside would be the 'unblighted world of nature'.[47]

The second and rather more pervasive trend revolved around spelling out brand new forms that capitalised on the changing social and technological circumstances of the day to maximise choice. In 1961, the Dutch architect N. John Habraken offered a theory that suggested dividing mass housing projects into supports and infill: *supports* acting as the collective frame, and *infill* supplying the arena in which to exercise individual choice.[48] Arthur Quarmby, later noted for his innovations in earth-sheltered housing, had developed in 1962 the idea of corn-on-the-cob developments, hooking habitable cells on to a hollow tower or mast. The

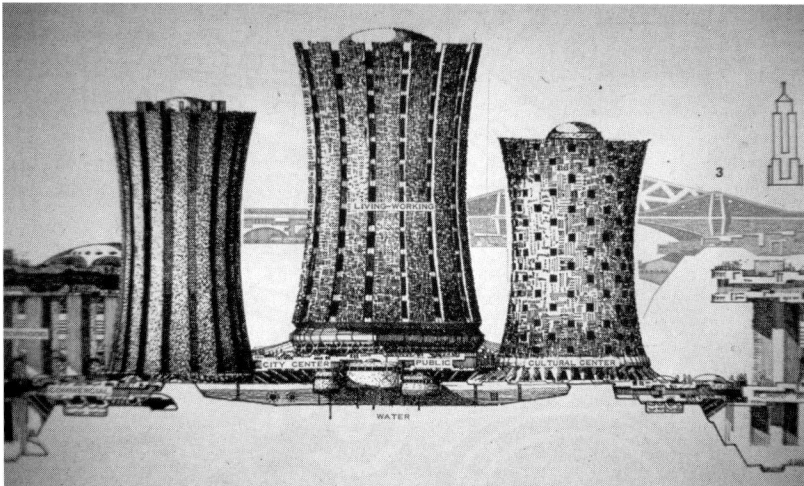

11.8
Paolo Soleri, Babelnoah (1969). Designed for a flat coastal region, Babelnoah was conceived as a settlement for 6 million people, with a density of 333 per acre (822 per hectare)

same idea would recur in Archigram's Plug-In City and in the work of Paul Rudolph in the USA,[49] with dwellings reduced to 'pods' in a manner reminiscent of the space industry.

Enormous multilevel creations developed this style of thought further. Yona Friedman's Groupe d'Etude d'Architecture Mobile, founded in 1958, married ideas of *urbanisme mobile*, in which citizens could freely change the plan and location of their homes, with giant 'space-frame' constructions filled with light-weight and adjustable units. Through this means, changes in constructional technology could introduce sufficient flexibility to allow the built environment to become self-regulating.[50] The photomontages and other illustrations displayed multilevel spatial constructions spanning areas of Paris such as Les Halles and the Beaubourg, assuring the reader that life 'underneath continues virtually undis-turbed'.[51] Friedman's group, however, was less forthcoming about how these colossal decks would be supported, how they would interact with ground level activities, or how life underneath *could* continue virtually undisturbed.

Even this scale of ambition would soon pale into insignificance compared with those megastructuralists who, similar to the hyper-linearists like Doxiadis, pushed the limits of their imaginative constructs to global extent. The Dutch artist Constant Anton Nieuwenhuys's New Babylon (1956–74), for instance, provided a project similar in some respects to Friedman's *urbanisme mobile*, but different in extent and underlying politics. Like Friedman, Constant had a city on stilts, with the traffic remaining at ground level. New Babylon, however, was a city of global extent and one in which social life formed in conditions where the city itself was completely automated. Given that the internal environments could be altered at will, life revolved around leisure and desire: a recipe originally celebrated as beneficial but later seen as increasingly dystopian.[52]

Perhaps the best known of 1960s work on megastructures were the projects produced by Archigram.[53] These combined a serious and omnivorous approach to technology with a characteristic 1960s prankster mentality. The group comprised six individuals, with other occasional contributors. Although, in the indulgent language of the time, they 'coalesced from a series of chance encounters and purposeful introductions',[54] more prosaically they shared a loosely based collaborative project born out of fascination with the new and boredom with the old. Its members worked in the London area, although they came from a variety of regional backgrounds. Peter Cook had studied architecture at the Bournemouth College of Art (1953–8) before taking the Architectural Association diploma (1958–60). Ron Herron attended evening classes at the Brixton School of Building (1950–4) before completing his professional education at the Regent Street Polytechnic in 1956. Both Warren Chalk and Dennis Crompton had studied in Manchester, respectively at the School of Art and the university's School of Architecture. David Greene was a Nottingham graduate; Michael Webb from Regent Street Polytechnic. The name 'Archigram' came from the group's magazine, a fusion of 'ARCHItecture' and 'teleGRAM' (or sometimes 'aeroGRAMme'),[55] to indicate something that was more analogous to the immediacy of a telegram – important, quickly read and, once understood, soon discarded.

The magazine ran to nine issues between May 1961 and 1970. The first issue was produced by a smaller group (Cook, Webb and Greene), with Herron, Chalk and Crompton (who had worked together at the LCC designing the South Bank Arts Centre) joining by *Archigram* III. The group reacted impatiently to the visual tedium of curtain walled office buildings and rectilinear slabs of housing then starting to engulf Britain's cities. Like Team X, with whom they shared a lukewarm relationship, they were modernist in their anticipations of socially beneficial technology-led change. Their programmatic project was fun, optimistic and playfully ironic, but also at times serious-minded and instrumental. In so far as they were serious, their projects responded to the established traditions of modernism.

Their work, rendered in colourful pop art-influenced designs and immersed in the rhetorical imageries of the 'space age', resists easy categorisation. Their starting point, if one can be detected, was the contemporary context of a nation wanting to exploit growing affluence after emerging from the hardships of war and the greyness of Austerity, only to find itself faced by 'dreary postwar modernism'.[56] Archigram argued that the 1960s would be shaped by consumerism and that view was reflected in their projects 'and everything that went with it, especially the ads. . . . A lot of their drawings had cut-outs from American magazines'.[57] To Reyner Banham, their work could offer 'an image-starved world a new vision of the city of the future, a city of components on racks, components in stacks, components plugged into networks and grids, a city of components being swung into place by cranes'.[58] The problem for architectural critics was to decide whether or not a particular project was utopian speculation, especially that which invited people to rethink 'architectural space and architectural technology',[59] or just merely flippant.

Ron Herron's 'Walking City' (1963) posed the problem. Easily the most recognisable alternative urban image of the 1960s, 'Walking City' drew in equal measure on science fiction, space technology and architectural megastructuralism (Figure 11.9). The drawings translated ideas about impermanence of settlement and mobility into visual form by means of comic book imagery, looking somewhat reminiscent of the alien war machines from H.G. Wells' *The War of the Worlds*.[60] Cities were depicted at rest as gigantic modules standing on retractable legs. They could hook up to the service infrastructure of existing cities, but when necessary, they could move away and take root elsewhere. This would not be by walking on the legs on which the module stands, given the immense damage that would cause, but by moving on cushions of air like giant hovercraft. The imagery suggests that this was an eye-catching scheme designed to see what response it might evoke, although some undoubtedly regarded it as a scheme that required firm rebuke:

> [Herron's] proposal is devoid of consideration of its implications for the quality of man's life and even how people might use such large, impermanent structures. Conditions in the city do shift incessantly. But the city would be totally chaotic without some guarantee of a reasonable amount of permanence, which permits necessary capital and human investment in city services, utilities and social organisation.[61]

11.9
**Ron Herron,
'Walking City'
(1963)**

11.9
**Ron Herron,
'Walking City'
(1963)**

Peter Cook's 'Plug-In City', however, was probably a fairer target for such analysis. Incorporating elements of linearity (see p. 253), the design allied ideas drawn from advanced science and technology with disposability and consumerism. Plug-In City envisaged the attachment of prefabricated units to an infrastructural framework of tubes that would contain the city's electricity, water and sewage services, as well as passenger lifts and goods distribution systems. The megastructural framework itself would have a projected lifespan of only 40 years. All other aspects of the city – dwellings, offices, shops, theatres, car parks and the rest – were factory-produced modular units (Figure 11.10) They would come in various colours, styles and shapes, and would have built-in obsolescence. The modular units would be brought to the site and simply clipped on to the framework in whatever manner was required, meaning that the city could be almost any shape, density or size required. Plug-In City, so the argument ran, would allow individuals maximum freedom to indulge their new-found affluence and supposed desires for novelty, change and leisure. People were rarely depicted in the drawings but, when shown, the strategy was often to use cuttings from the free colour supplements of Sunday newspapers. The new world became populated by the 'beautiful people' and not by the inhabitants of social housing. This, along with the absence of geometric harmony and Brutalist concrete, moved modernist-inspired city design as far from the prevailing imagery as it was possible to go.

The breeziness of the approach, however, did not go unchallenged, even in the 1960s. Critical opposition to optimistic technocentric visions designed for conventional consumer society mounted as the 1960s went on. Hans Hollein's collage 'Urban Construction above Vienna' (1963) satirically depicted megastructures on supports, in the shape of pieces of human excrement, dominating the city

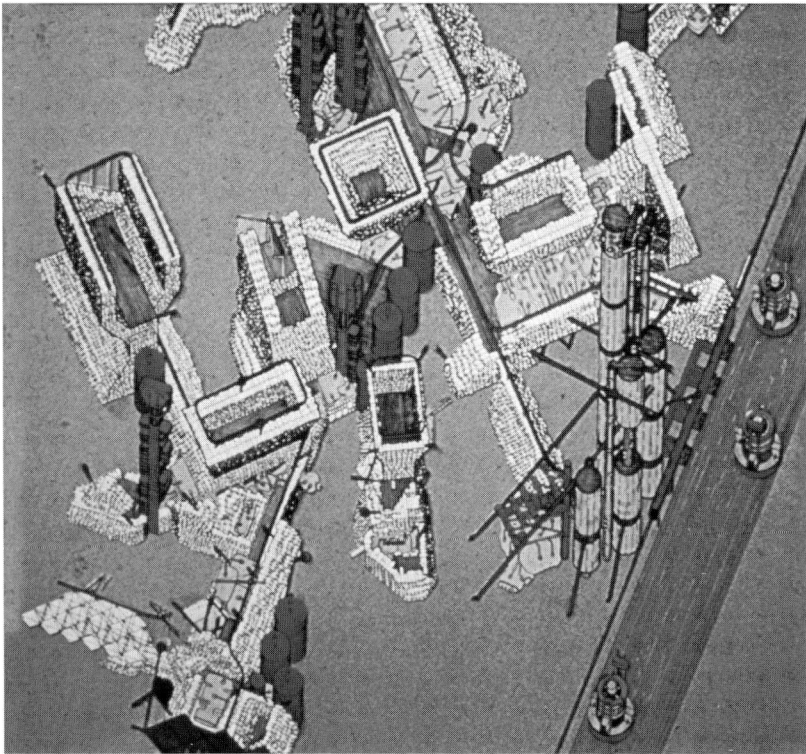

skyline.[62] The Italian Archizoom and Superstudio groups, founded in Florence in 1966, were eventually equally scathing. Although intellectually indebted to Archigram in their early days, both discarded initial utopianism in favour of a view of megastructures that detected the potential dystopia that lurked just ahead. In 1969, Superstudio unveiled their 'Continuous Monument' project. This satirised naive megastructural thought by means of collages of apparently endless, lifeless and identical three-dimensional grids imposed over existing cities or invading previously undeveloped areas, such as the Arizona desert, without any regard for the areas to be developed. The following year, their colleagues in Archizoom offered their 'No-Stop' City scheme, an underground, artificially lit and multilayered city where the incarcerated inhabitants only gain access to the surface – now a nature reserve – by lifts.[63] Patrick Hodgkinson, the designer of the megastructural Brunswick Centre in Bloomsbury (London) was particularly caustic about Plug-In City. He noted:

> Switch off the glitter and the Archigram blow-up house for instance . . .
> is seen to be a plastic inflatable semi-detached from Bournemouth
> pushed into 2001, without the Hollywood big screen G-plan furniture
> effects – a 'styling only' solution.[64]

Criticism at the direction embodied by Archigram, then, was already apparent at the time but, in keeping with the spirit of the 1960s, it was cheerfully disregarded. Archigram's approach was clearly different from that of the New Brutalists or others who tried to move modern architecture on to accommodate the ideas of a perceived new age and reach positions of influence in the Establishment:

> While Brutalists sought establishment credibility, Archigram made the avant-garde wild again and gave architecture a walk-on part in the British pop culture insurgency of the sixties. Archigram discovered the casual, expendable style of a leisured consumer society in which close-knit social structures and the buildings that accompanied them were largely irrelevant.[65]

Yet looked at another way, Archigram's projects were rooted in the old endeavour. The clarion call in *Archigram* I was: 'A new generation of architecture must arise with forms and spaces which seems to reject the precepts of "Modern" yet in fact retains those precepts'.[66] That connectivity with the past manifested itself in a commitment to revivify modernism and not to abandon it. Only superficially could Archigram's work be said to have consciously anticipated either the deeper anxieties of the 1970s or the wish to overthrow the strictures of modernism intrinsic to the turn to postmodernism.

## Mapping modernism

The changes in architectural thinking during the 1950s and 1960s led to renewed attempts to define and redefine what architectural modernism currently meant. John Summerson, for example, addressed that task in one of his last contributions before claiming that he had so much on his hands with other projects that he 'didn't really look at modern architecture at all'.[67] Summerson rejected the idea of building up a theory of modern architecture on the basis of the *existence* of modern buildings.[68] Rather, his answer to the question of what gave unity to modern architecture rested on the notion of the 'programme'.[69] He traced a process of development from the world of antiquity, where the architect focused on 'a world of form', through periods that emphasised the social factors surrounding architecture, to the modern age and 'the conception of the architect's programme as the source of unity – the source not precisely of forms but of adumbrations of forms of undeniable validity'.[70] He defined a programme as 'a local fragment of social pattern' and as 'a description of the spatial dimensions, spatial relationships, and other physical conditions required for the convenient performance of specific functions'. Programmes involve a process in time and imply 'some rhythmically repetitive pattern – whether it is a manufacturing process, the curriculum of a school, the domestic routine of a house, or the sense of repeated movement in a circulation system'.[71]

Summerson's attempt to reconceptualise modernist functionalism in this way, however, gained little support. The idea that this potential source of unity could replace the lost authority of the antique, for example, was necessarily limited to whatever programmes contemporary society can offer.[72] Moreover, the existence of programmes also necessarily implied a continuous process, whereby the development of constructible forms leads to a changing language of expression.[73] By contrast, Reyner Banham received much greater support for an analysis offered in his book *Theory and Design in the First Machine Age*,[74] which appeared in 1960. Based on his part-time doctorate from the Courtauld Institute and, before that, talks to the Independent Group, *Theory and Design* attacked the foundation myths established by the earlier historians of modernism and countered their selectivity, for example, resituating the Futurists in a central position in the origins and development of modernism. The analysis did not attempt 'to free architecture from observance of function, but rather to cast functionalism in a vastly expanded field that included . . . topology, perception, genetics, information theory, and technology of all kinds'.[75] Banham identified that the first Industrial Age, powered by the characteristic technology of the Industrial Revolution, had given way to a second that revolved around automated production systems. These were paralleled by two 'Machine Ages', which could be recognised in terms of buildings, transport media and the like. Although no exact dates are offered, the First Machine Age extended from the nineteenth century through to the 1930s and the Second from then up to and including the time when he was writing. Banham's concern in *Theory and Design* was the history of architecture and technology in the First Machine Age, but the book stressed the need for a body of theory 'proper to our own age – the Second Machine Age' and to understand the implications of that theory 'for an architecture integrally related to technology'.[76]

In making this argument, Banham focused attention on the new technology, about which he was enthusiastic and optimistic. It was a focus that led him, and others, to give serious attention to whatever looked new and promising in the technological field. This would include consumption as well as production, with the exhortation that: 'The architect who proposes to run with technology knows that he is in fast company and that in order to keep up, he may have to emulate the Futurists and discard his whole cultural load'.[77] A decade later, given the problems experienced in urban renewal as well as the advanced new thinking about architecture and technology, things had moved on. In addition to working out where modernism, and architecture in general, stood in relation to those problems, there was also the need for critical reflection on the nature and identity of the Modern Movement.

The most intriguing and influential rethinking came from the work of Charles Jencks.[78] Rapidly emerging as one of the leading architectural commentators of his generation, Jencks provided a series of incisive, but steadily evolving views of modernism at the turn of the 1970s. He was still, however, some way from being the critic whose writings helped to codify postmodernism's 'plural set of resistances to the hegemony of modernism'.[79] His book *Architecture 2000*,[80] published in 1971 but written in 1969, had conveyed a view of architecture moving optimistically forward into a period of rapid technological change and social fluidity without a hint of the problems that would arise in the 1970s. Jencks' analysis was both historical and futurological. A structural analysis located six traditions within modern architecture: Logical, Idealist, Self Conscious, Intuitive, Activist and Unselfconscious. These were semi-autonomous, but tended to stabilise around a common core. They were rendered pictorially as an evolutionary tree, which charted the individual traditions horizontally as flows over time. The chart indicated the relationships between the traditions in the period between 1920 and 1969 and then projected what new syntheses might spring from them in the period from 1970 to 2000. Reservations were immediately expressed about possible oversimplifications, but these carried the force only of polite caveats. Whatever emphasis was placed on the semi-autonomy of these traditions, they remained framed in the overarching envelope of modern architecture.[81] The impression was one of continuity – the unbroken trajectory into the twenty-first century of a movement starting around 1920.

Nevertheless, there remained palpable tensions in the writing. An essay dealing with London's South Bank Arts complex, for instance, saw Jencks identifying a design method that he termed 'adhocism', in which individuals designed their portion of the complex with little regard for the whole. This resulted in an architecture considered 'particularly suited to a pluralist age when no explicit, whole philosophy is shared by all'.[82] There were virtues in producing an architecture that was 'lively, pluralist and instantly expedient', but it had a fault that left Jencks hankering after something more profound:

> it is not expedient in the long term; it is not radically inventive and searching for ultimate truth. It remains content tinkering with its own conventions, its own tool box, from which the ideal scientist is always trying to extricate himself with a new theory.[83]

That unease, coupled with questions about the nature and outcomes of historical analysis, would soon lead to fundamental changes in the basic terms of the exercise, best expressed in his book *Modern Movements in Architecture*.[84] A revised version of a doctoral thesis written under the supervision of Reyner Banham at the Bartlett School, it brought together a compilation of Jencks' previous essays from the 1960s, with the addition of a revised theory of value. Its introduction uncompromisingly stated the case for the new approach:

> There is a conventional view among historians and the general public that some unified theory and practice called 'Modern Architecture' really exists. Perhaps, from time to time, this capital lettered concept has enjoyed a wide understanding and informed consensus, so that it does make sense to call this area of agreement Modern Architecture. But more often than not its use is generally informed by ignorance. Those who use it are either unaware of live architectural traditions, or else they hope to coalesce this plurality into some integrated movement.[85]

Historical analysis, exemplified by Pevsner and others, was elitist and prophetic, as well as conservatively reinforcing one ideology and one tradition of development, at the expense of a live plurality. After reprising familiar objections to the Zeitgeist and single strand theories, the development of modernism was reconceptualised as comprising six, now discontinuous, traditions. The histories of each of these traditions, and the movements to which they gave rise, were told through 'a series of discontinuous narratives and extended probes',[86] a non-linear writing style that had echoes of Marshall McLuhan and other contemporary writers.[87]

Jencks ameliorated the fragmentation inherent in this style of writing by two strategies. First, he offered a reworked version of the evolutionary tree as a cognitive map by which readers might orient themselves (Figure 11.11). The six traditions still existed, but the accompanying explanation subtly changed the terms of the exercise. The earlier version had stressed that there was 'a natural tendency for certain concepts and types of architecture to cluster together into a coherent whole'.[88] The text now emphasised autonomy rather than semi-autonomy (with its natural corollary of semi-attachment), stating that: 'The cumulative disciplines and the psychological coherence of values tend to keep each tradition distinct from and ideologically opposed to the others.'[89] The second strategy was to offer a theory of value that underpinned the selection of buildings or other edifices discussed in the book. The interpretive position that underpinned this history came by way of Samuel Taylor Coleridge and I.A. Richards.[90] The general idea was that some buildings had within their structure enough different but interrelated meanings continually to invite new and often opposing interpretations. They were therefore multivalued, a condition for which Jencks used the term 'multivalence'. Others,

11.11
**Charles Jencks, 'Evolutionary Tree, 1920–70' (1973)**

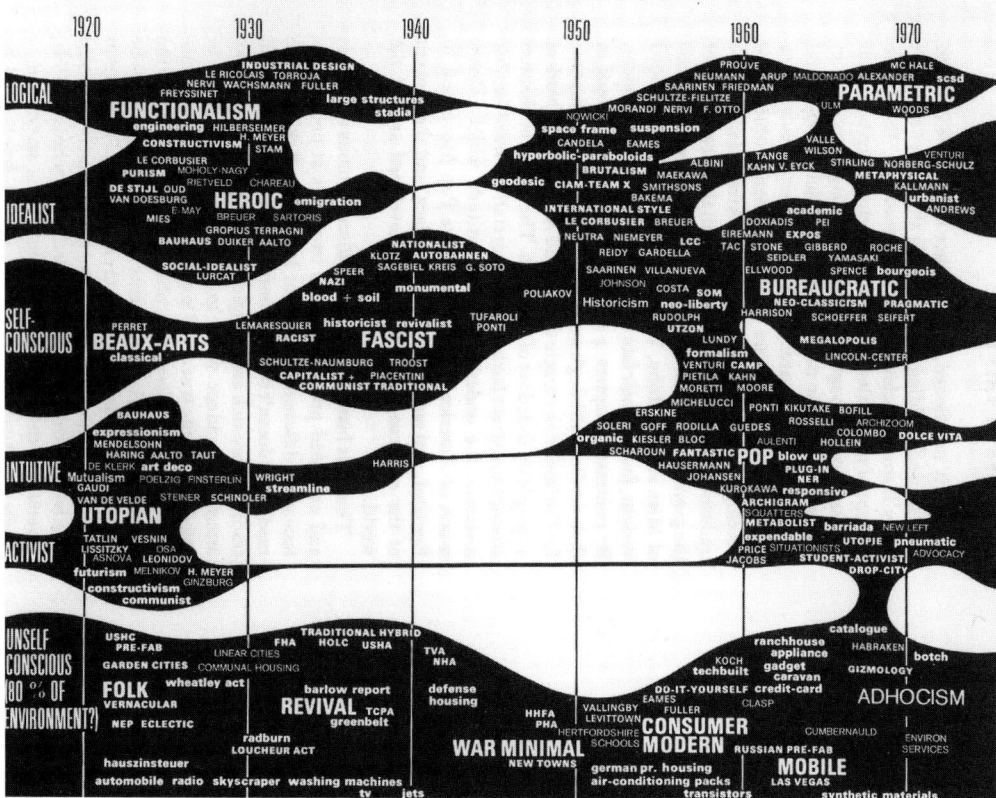

which lacked that quality and failed to communicate more than their manifest content, were termed 'univalent'.

By way of initial example, Jencks applied this theory to Le Corbusier's *unité d'habitation* in Marseilles and Frederick Gibberd's Liverpool Metropolitan Cathedral of Christ the King. The former was considered multivalent because its rich layers of manifest and latent meaning engaged the perceiver's powers of imaginative creation. Its multivalent form allowed opposite interpretations and thus diffused univalent criticism. Liverpool Cathedral was judged univalent because it excluded such possibilities. Its architecture comprised elements that can be read only in one way, with the finished building the result of dispassionate aggregation. There was much less to engage the perceiver's imagination. Rather later it would be realised that the theory of value carried the seeds of more radical interpretations, because the univalence of many modernist buildings could be equated to visual and spiritual impoverishment and that buildings that embraced multivalence could be presented as harbingers of the new architecture that might succeed modernism.

The hour of postmodernism, however, was not at hand. Jencks had not yet discerned the moment during 1972 when he later pronounced that the Modern Movement had died and Nathan Silver, his collaborator on a monograph about 'adhocism',[91] was some years short of his radio blast 'Why is British architecture lousy?' (upgraded to 'so lousy' in the book version).[92] *Modern Movements in Architecture* therefore closed on a strident note, but one cast within the prevailing intellectual climate. Jencks expressed distaste 'for the consumer societies for which architecture is built and the undeniable banality of their building tasks and commissions'.[93] Two things were necessary 'if architecture was to regain its credibility among both architects and the public'. First, architects needed to face up to 'giving certain tasks monumental and symbolic expression', and second, society needed to offer commissions that provided greater challenge for architects.[94] The current state of architecture reflected the state of the public realm. Jencks argued that a viable architecture needed to be able to express 'counter-themes, alternatives, ironic tensions, contradictions to the prevailing ideology'.[95] Half-a-century earlier, Le Corbusier had ended *Vers une architecture* with the words: 'Architecture or Revolution. Revolution can be avoided.'[96] Jencks believed that both were necessary: 'today if we are to have a credible architecture, it must be supported by a popular revolution that *ends* in a credible public realm, the council system. Architecture *and* revolution.'[97]

These were stirring words, suggesting greater boldness was needed by both architects and society if architecture was to recapture its edge and perform its role properly. The sentiments expressed were also based on an underlying premise that allotted architects a central cultural role: 'Architecture crystallises specific cultural values, and not others, and the architect, as opposed to, say, the sociologist or engineer, has been delegated to this role by society.'[98] The events and developments discussed in Chapter 12 would certainly initiate a radical reappraisal of that position. Unfortunately for architects that remained adherents to modernism, it would be in a manner that re-examined, highly critically, the record of architecture in practice and the nature of the architect's role in society.

# Chapter 12

# Storm clouds

**Futures not achieved are only branches of the past: dead branches.**
**Italo Calvino[1]**

Watersheds in the history of architecture can rarely be pinpointed to specific dates and are normally much easier to spot with hindsight than at the time. The experience of Great Britain during the 1960s was no exception. During the latter part of that decade, various events occurred that could be taken as *the* point at which the tide turned against architectural modernism. In terms of professional debate, one candidate would be the *Architectural Review*'s 'Housing and the Environment' issue of November 1967.[2] Coming from a journal and a publishing house that occupied a central place in the propagation of modernism, this issue's trenchant criticisms about the bleak conditions of public housing estates shocked and outraged in equal measures, but they were merely the harbinger of what was to come. Another candidate would be the Ronan Point disaster of May 1968. The progressive collapse of one corner of this 23-storey point block in Canning Town (London), when the basic design could not cope with a simple kitchen accident, created a deep sense of public outrage and brought a lasting media spotlight to bear on strategies of modern urban renewal.

At first glance, it is legitimate to ask why these two events should have inflicted this damage. Taking a critical line, of course, was not new to the *Architectural Review*. Its pages had always given space to dissenting voices wishing to direct friendly fire against directions taken by modern architecture in practice. Its 'Townscape' approach, first introduced in 1947, campaigned for realigning modernism with the Picturesque to reawaken interest in townscape and to counter the emotional boredom induced by the uniformity and straight-line geometry associated with modern architecture. The journal's editorials and features had also taken a fiercely hostile attitude towards poor office design and mediocre town centre renewal. There was no inherent reason why one such feature section from that journal, however disapproving, should have assumed the lasting importance that it did. Equally, although attracting international attention in the short term, the interest taken in Ronan Point might have soon dwindled despite the four fatalities that the disaster caused. Given that the cause was quickly diagnosed as a gas leak, a relatively commonplace problem, it would have seemed that the ensuing furore might have died down once the business of attributing blame and taking preventative measures (such as removal of gas appliances from such buildings) was complete. Moreover, deployment of tall flats was already past its peak in 1968. The number of local authority approvals was running at only 69 per cent of the figure for the peak year (1966) and was already destined to plummet further regardless of Ronan Point (see Chapter 8).

These, however, were not normal times. Both events had placed the spotlight on problems with flatted council estates, the area of urban renewal that had started to give most cause for concern. There was not, as yet, any reason to suggest that the problems were systemic, but they did lead to increasing critical scrutiny of the changes that had taken place within the previous 15 years. Earlier criticisms, which had perhaps been disregarded or downplayed, were revalorised now that they could be seen as part of a wider picture. Residents of council housing who might previously have felt that they, as individuals, had little chance of denting the prevailing wisdom now felt that they had a voice that would receive a hearing. Once the process of scrutiny began, it soon switched beyond housing to include the wider issue of approaching urban renewal through comprehensive redevelopment – increasingly seen as flawed – and to scrutinise the validity of alternative strategies. To substantiate these points, however, it is important to explore the anatomy of criticism as it unfolded in the 1950s and 1960s.

## Early stirrings

The writings of Jane Jacobs provide an apposite place to start. In an essay in *Fortune* magazine in 1957, for example, Jacobs offered an ironic view of what the new urban landscapes might be like in practice:

> What will the projects look like? They will be spacious, parklike, and uncrowded. They will feature long green vistas. They will be stable and symmetrical and orderly. They will be clean, impressive, and monumental. They will have all the attributes of a well-kept, dignified cemetery.[3]

Her point was to invite the reader to look critically at the reconstructed urban environments on offer from the major architectural and planning movements, which, despite their gleaming allure, might well be recipes for urban sterility. She later consolidated this point in her book *The Death and Life of Great American Cities*.[4] Like the Smithsons, Jacobs was a profound believer in the value and importance of street and neighbourhood life, but she believed they were things to be cherished *in their own right* rather than discarded and recreated by sensitive city design strategies. All too often, she felt, planning and architecture's preference for pristine reconstructed environments led them to brush aside lightly the unsung attractions of the existing neighbourhoods, seeing them as obsolete rather than as assets to be valued. Jacobs partly based her observations on Manhattan and particularly Hudson Street in West Greenwich Village where she lived (Figure 12.1). Hudson Street comprised three- and four-storey houses, with stores on the ground floor when the houses had not been converted to single-family use. Jacobs extolled the animated nature of the streets, the civility that people showed and the idea that they looked out for one another. In a city increasingly concerned about violence, she concluded: 'We are the lucky possessors of a city order that makes it relatively simple to keep the peace because there are plenty of eyes on the street'.[5]

Jacobs' paean of praise to apparent disorder complemented other studies. In their analysis of the social impact of migration in 1950s London, for example, Michael Young and Peter Willmott showed how rehousing people from Bethnal Green to an LCC housing estate at Debden ('Greenleigh') seriously dislocated existing social networks (see also Chapter 9).[6] The dislocation, however, turned out to be temporary, having largely disappeared after two years. In Boston, Walter Firey had recognised in the 1940s that the residents of the upper middle class Beacon Hill district shared deep attachments to where they lived;[7] attachments that were seemingly strong enough to have allowed the area to withstand pressures for redevelopment. Later research in Boston's West End by Mark Fried showed that residents exhibited genuine sadness when forced to relocate through comprehensive redevelopment of their neighbourhoods.[8] Fried reported that residents experienced a collective feeling of grief when their neighbourhood was destroyed by the clearance machine, which he compared to that which individuals suffer at the loss of a loved one.

Related themes emerged in Canon Norman Power's insider's account of urban renewal in the Ladywood area of Birmingham.[9] Power described a process of redevelopment, planning blight and community destruction that was a paradigm

12.1
**Hudson Street, West Greenwich Village (photograph March 2006)**

of the ill-conceived and poorly coordinated clearance process in many cities. The area, for example, possessed extremely poor housing, but Power observed that the better housing was cleared first, primarily because space was needed for the Inner Ring Road. Large areas of bulldozed land remained vacant for around seven years, but not cleared: a 'wilderness of brick-ends, tin cans, broken bottles and even half-demolished buildings'.[10] The council resisted its use for other purposes in the period awaiting redevelopment, leaving it to become vandalised and placing further pressure on the remaining community. Power described life in the new flats in equally bleak terms. The improved quality of the interior remained unquestioned, but the flat often became a refuge in a hostile environment, with 'little social life, and less cultural or spiritual life' particularly for elderly people.[11] Even things that officials in the Town Hall might regard as unequivocally beneficial could prove otherwise when seen in their true social context. Provision of a 'clean, splendid and modern clinic' replacing the 'doctor's house', for example, would sound like a major improvement, but destruction of the area's original physical fabric meant that the doctor was no longer part of the local community. Doctors, teachers and councillors now lived far away. There were no role models: the young 'see nobody whose opinion and respect they value'.[12] Power believed that the damage inflicted by this experience could take a generation to repair: these were the 'forgotten people'.

## Housing

The emphasis on the social context of housing was fully recognised by sections of the architectural community, notably those architects whose work was discussed in Chapter 9, but also by other perceptive critics. Reviewing a contemporary book on housing, for example, Elizabeth Denby castigated the way that the author had accepted from 'modern planners, architects and administrators much of their attitude to urban renewal. . . . Like them, he keeps his sights firmly fixed on bricks and mortar, on money bags and by-laws'.[13] Denby's opinion was well respected. As the 'housing manager' associated with such schemes as Kensal House, as a member of the MARS Group and as the author of several important texts,[14] she held an important place in the development of thinking about housing matters. Yet despite the tide in favour of clearance running powerfully through local authorities in the early 1960s, she recognised not only the extent to which perfectly serviceable homes were being demolished simply because of their age and location, but also that their demolition might run counter to 'human needs, human wishes and ultimate human satisfaction'.[15]

Having said this, it could scarcely be implied that architects and planners were arrogantly ignoring an incontrovertible weight of evidence running against the grain of their policies. Information about the public's wishes with regard to rehousing, especially in flats, was thin and ambiguous – largely because the users were rarely asked. Joan Demers' survey of residential satisfactions among the early residents of Park Hill (Chapter 9) merited comment because of its rarity. Architects themselves might express their dissatisfaction with what they saw, but they spoke as individuals (see Chapter 8). The Modern Movement, still in awe of the architecture's historic triumph, had always lacked sustained self-criticism, which it was certainly not receiving from an avant-garde that had decided that the path towards the future lay in ever-more abstruse technological fantasies. Little, therefore, prepared readers for the vehemence and breath of criticism directed at modern public-sector housing contained in the 'Housing and the Environment' issue of the *Architectural Review* in November 1967.[16]

The 'Housing Issue' did not start life as a pre-emptive strike on public-sector housing and seemed to take its senior editors as much by surprise as its readers. Nicholas Taylor, one of the assistant editors, had received instructions from the editor J.M. Richards to prepare a special issue on the 'best of current housing design', together with a text explaining 'what we think should be done'. When suggesting that some sociological evidence should be sought as to what people actually wanted, the proprietor Hubert de Cronin Hastings had replied: 'But we *know* what should be done'.[17] The elements of the issue contributed by Richards and the central editorial team gave that impression – a 'typical AR tract on the great god Urbanity, and his cosmetic soul-sister Townscape'. The editorial gave little sense of an attack on modern architectural practices. It appeared opposite two juxtaposed aerial photographs: the compact and human scale of Tewkesbury compared with the 'prairie planned' landscapes of the first generation New Town at East Kilbride. The use of aerial photography, conveniently reducing the three-dimensional to the two-dimensional, drew attention more to the deficiencies of planning rather than architecture. The editorial followed the same strategy. After criticising central government for its obsession with numbers rather than quality, the writer directed his attack towards the strategy of building housing ghettoes on the edges of cities, the failure to lock them into the existing pattern of communication, and for general inattention to urban structure. In typical fashion, the editorial's emphasis accented the positive. Citing a range of more encouraging examples, it concluded:

> The Editors are convinced that, taken as a whole, this issue will show that as a nation we are capable of thinking at the level called for. The task ahead is to lay aside arrogance and preconception, and equip ourselves by realistic study of needs and means to build a total environment – not a politically acceptable number of dwellings – suited to the changing needs of this century.[18]

In contrast to Hastings' dismissive self-confidence, Taylor concluded that 'we did not know [what people wanted] and that almost all the most renowned high-density housing schemes were dangerous rubbish, precisely because they were conceived of merely as "housing" and not part of a fabric of a total living community.'[19] Moreover, Taylor recognised the tendency to impose a 'bureaucratic anonymity which violates the individuality of family life – no pets, no washing lines, no trellises, no colour wash, and all the doors painted uniformly olive-green'.[20] This represented a major intrusion into individual freedoms in the name of estate management and aesthetics. Taylor's accompanying essay on the 'failure of housing' – interestingly, rendered in quotation marks – argued bleakly that: 'More slums are likely to be built in the next five years than in the past twenty. Slums, that is, by the "subjective" standards of a free society.'[21] By that criterion, slums were measured not only by availability of taps and cupboards, but also by whether they actively 'encourage the satisfaction and self-expression of those who call it "home"'.[22] Controversially, Taylor linked the tenant-assisted aspects of physical decay encountered even on showpiece estates with residents wanting to get their own back on those that had inflicted such architecture on them. With regard to the Greater London Council's Canada Estate in Bermondsey (Lucas and Bottomley, 1962–4), he argued:

> it is easier after three years to count the few unbroken panes of armoured glass than the multitude which are cracked and splintered; Brutalism is being given the rough justice of brutalism. Economy on materials and the inadequacy of detailing . . . can be assessed as 'objective' weaknesses; but what is more important, if less easy to pinpoint, is the 'subjective' hatred of the tenants for the rough-shuttered concrete that is thrust on them.[23]

The ensuing photographs themselves continued the long tradition of the selective art of black-and-white architectural photography, as value-laden in their way as were those taken by Dell and Wainwright in the 1930s. The main difference was that these were statements of censure rather than praise. The venom of the accompanying captioning was primarily directed at those schemes offering an overwhelming civic monumentality. Glasgow's Red Road development rose 'proudly in an exurban waste of spoilheaps (ironically enough on the main road to Cumbernauld)'. They possessed a 'nightmare sublimity of scale', have a 'total lack of individuality' and lack 'even the most perfunctory treatment of the crucial points where overcrowded liftshaft disgorges on to overmotorised access road'.[24] The 'prestige image' buildings of the same city's Hutchesontown-Gorbals redevelopment are seen as 'the monumental tenement run mad'. 'Women return from the shops to be blown about amid the appalling dinginess of rough-shuttered concrete; children of all ages run wild in the undefined wastes known to the faithful as pilotis.'[25] This was relatively mild compared with Birmingham's Cregoe Road (Lee Bank) condemned as 'architectural arrogance' in terms of its design, the obsession of management with suppressing displays of individuality 'in the interests of visually portraying communal cleanliness', the wilful destruction of communities 'and the failure to join them together again in tower blocks'.[26]

The breadth of the targeting gave the impression of widespread misplacement of trust, but the 'Housing Issue' was not simply a case of castigating public-sector housing architecture. Schemes where efforts had been made to design with social intent earned recognition, which included World's End, Park Hill, Lillington Gardens and Southwark's Bonamy Street estate.[27] Significantly too, Taylor provided brief mention of the Deeplish area in Rochdale, where the Ministry of Housing and Local Government had carried out a pilot study to explore the prospects for rehabilitation of housing.[28] Deeplish was an important proving ground for ideas embodied in the Housing Act 1969, with its provisions of statutory instruments for comprehensive improvement as another option besides comprehensive redevelopment.[29] This, combined with the Civic Amenities Act 1967 which permitted the formation of Conservation Areas, marked the start of important new thinking that prompted architects and others to reconsider what the traditional urban environment had to offer.[30] Change, therefore, was already occurring, with high-rise flats already past their peak and the prospect of urban rehabilitation threatening to shift the focus towards conservation. In military terms, perhaps, the attack was not decisive, but the *Architectural Review*'s 'salvo' was instrumental in launching the 'critical onslaught on modernist housing'; its strictures about the 'failure of housing' being taken-for-granted in the late 1970s by a 'new generation of forceful architect-journalists and housing pressure groups'.[31]

Some idea of the growing force of that criticism was supplied by Adams and Conway.[32] Surveying available research about living in high-rise flats for a professional audience, they noted the evidence from local and national surveys which said that the great majority of tenants would prefer houses to flats. The report pointed to the problems for families with younger children, with poorer opportunities for play outside, fewer chances for socialisation,[33] and the possibility of suffering significantly higher incidence of respiratory diseases than other children of the same age who did not live in high-rise flats.[34] Until the late 1960s, the majority of reports from places where comprehensive redevelopment had led to rehousing in flats had pointed to general satisfaction with the new living environments.[35] That conclusion readily invited the interpretation that while people might not find the new estates intrinsically attractive in advance, they were content enough once they had moved in. By the early 1970s, the mood had changed, perhaps in line with changing national attitudes or because council housing tenants now felt that speaking out against the prevailing wisdom had some purpose. The balance sheet identified by Adams and Conway saw high flats having the advantages of being bright and easy to manage, enjoying access to fresh air, and offering lack of noise, privacy and good views. The somewhat longer list of drawbacks included problems with lifts, poorly maintained access areas, lack of gardens, the noise caused by children cooped up in flats, blocked and unhygienic rubbish chutes, loneliness, inability to exert control or fulfil self-expression, and vandalism and crime. The authors' conclusion was tactfully damning: 'What is needed for the future is to sensitize those who provide and manage the residential environment to the preferences and needs of those who will live there.'[36]

## Ronan Point

The Ronan Point disaster provided another powerful reason for the shift in attitudes among the British public. Ronan Point was one of a batch of four blocks constructed as part of a clearance scheme at Custom House in Canning Town (London Borough of Newham). Designed by the Borough Architect Thomas North, they were built by Taylor Woodrow Anglian using the Larsen and Nielsen large panel system (see Chapter 8). Ronan Point itself contained 44 two-bedroom and 61 one-bedroom flats, grouped symmetrically five to a floor. It was newly completed, with the contractors handing over the block to Newham Council only on 11 March 1968. At

5.45 on the morning of Tuesday, 16 May 1968, Ivy Hodge, professional cake decorator and the tenant of flat 90 on the eighteenth floor, went into her kitchen to make tea. When striking a match to light the burner on her gas cooker, she inadvertently ignited gas that had accumulated from a leakage. This caused an explosion that blew out the non-load-bearing walls of the kitchen and the living room and, crucially, the external load-bearing wall of the living room. Given that there was no structural frame, the effect of the upper floor slab falling on to the floor below initiated a process of domino-like collapse, with the progressive collapse of wall and floor sections in the south-east corner down to ground level (Figure 12.2).

12.2
Ronan Point,
London, after
building collapse
1968)

The process, in the words of an eye witness, resembled the collapse of a 'pack of cards'. It was a readily understood metaphor invoking a sense of derisory flimsiness that subsequently haunted those who tried to explain the accident away as a wholly unforeseeable accident akin to an 'Act of God'. Reacting to it in an editorial published immediately after the disaster, the *Architects' Journal*'s leader writer admitted the accuracy of the description, while opening the inevitable campaign to limit longer-term damage:

> Architects knowing the principle of the Larsen-Nielsen system of construction of loadbearing precast slabs will appreciate this [pack of cards] metaphor is in this instance probably particularly significant. Inevitably this catastrophe will arouse opposition to high building and to system building, but we suspect this is unreasonable. The modern world is forcing the abandonment of traditional techniques in building and in the transitional period there are bound to be a few difficulties which emerge as technical setbacks to the innovators and stark tragedy to the users.[37]

The writer took reassurance from the way that the emergency services and evacuation procedures had worked. There was also relief in many quarters that casualties among those 'users' were remarkably light given that this was a 23-storey residential building. There were only 4 fatalities out of the 260 residents of the building, with 17 others injured (including Ivy Hodge, who escaped with burns). This was largely because the early hour meant that most occupants were still in bed. The blast caused the collapse of the living room portion of the flats, but left the bedrooms intact apart from the seventeenth to the twenty-second floors (where the fatalities occurred).

The government established a tribunal headed by Hugh Griffiths QC to hold an official inquiry, but two processes were in train long before it reported. First, the local authority and the major professional bodies rallied around to reassure the public that high-rise public housing, including system-built blocks, was perfectly safe. This was particularly important for Newham, because the blocks were a key element in tackling its housing problems. The second element comprised the involvement of the national press. The professional press had always covered the issue of high-rise in a largely matter-of-fact manner. They presented 'housing reviews', which offered selections of similar-looking blocks, along with technical specifications and brief descriptions of their mode of construction and fitments. Accompanying advertisements reinforced the benign character of the coverage. The national press, by contrast, had little overt interest in architectural matters, indeed largely ignoring urban renewal altogether unless important landmarks were involved.

Ronan Point transformed matters.[38] The reputation of multi-storey housing, especially those blocks associated with system building, was on the line. An almost-new building had partially collapsed due to a form of accident, which occurs from time to time in any city where there are gas supplies. Given that there were many other similar buildings like Ronan Point, there were palpable concerns that fundamental design flaws might cause the same problems elsewhere. The media latched on to the issues and helped to transform public debate. When Ministry of Housing and Local Government sent letters in August to the 73 authorities with system-built flats asking them to appraise their condition,[39] *The Times* ran an associated editorial. Reacting to the tribunal's initial findings and an admission by the minister that a collapse could arise from causes other than gas explosions, the leader writer commented:

> in spite of all the building regulations, flats have been built which are exposed to an unacceptable degree of danger from a variety of causes. How did it come about that such designs were passed as safe?[40]

Thereafter, the Ronan Point disaster affected architectural practice in two main ways. The first directly stemmed from the tribunal's report,[41] delivered in early November 1968, which made criticisms and recommendations. As expected, the report was sharply critical, although the evidence suggests that the analysis and recommendations were not as swingeing as they might have been for fear of causing public alarm.[42] Its most alarmist published element was to observe that over a lifetime of sixty years, itself a low figure compared with the normal lifespan of housing, one block in fifty might experience the same problems. In attributing blame for Ronan Point, it noted that its construction had suffered from poor design, inadequate workmanship and deficient project management. The tribunal exonerated the person who fitted the gas stove and distributed blame locally on the local authority for flouting by-laws, on the consulting engineers and on the specific design (although in recognisably measured terms). More widely, it spread blame through the system, indicting bodies intended to maintain construction standards, the professions, and the Ministry of Housing and Local Government. Bodies such as the Building Research Station and the National Building Agency were blamed for their failure even to consider the possibility of collapse. With regard to the design professions:

> In the broadest sense it could be argued that the two major professions – architects and structural engineers – had been found wanting, the latter for failure to call adequately upon the latter, and the latter for failing to take much interest in system-building.[43]

Lack of engineering skills was regarded as particularly significant, which also called into question the government's judgement:

> It was unfortunate that engineers were largely lukewarm or uninformed about system-building and it was in those unpropitious professional circumstances that the Ministry of Housing, without qualified engineering staff, launched the industrialised housing drive.[44]

The tribunal's recommendations did lead immediately to a highly expensive programme of building reinforcement that remedied the specific problem, but that further undermined the economics of constructing tall flats in the public sector.

The second long-term consequence of Ronan Point was to symbolise the beginning of the end for the special postwar relationship between architects and the public.[45] The standing of the 'expert' was already tarnished by the Aberfan disaster in October 1966, when 144 people, including 116 children, died from a landslip in circumstances described by the ensuing tribunal of inquiry as a 'terrifying tale of bungling ineptitude'.[46] Once again, at Ronan Point, experts had made basic mistakes with disastrous consequences. The public had accepted the extended use of flats for public housing, and tall flats in particular, on a manifesto that promised to deliver comfortable and well-designed housing speedily for all. System-building was accepted because it represented advanced technology that was supposedly vital for speed and cheapness.[47] Its aura faded when it was recognised that elementary mistakes had been made in design, standards of construction were poor and building regulations had been flouted. In this respect, it is pertinent to note that the architects suffered far more in terms of public opprobrium than the engineers, who were allotted a greater degree of responsibility in the tribunal's report. Ironically, the tribunal implicitly subscribed to an analysis of the engineer–architect relationship that the architects themselves favoured (see Chapter 4). The engineers were broadly seen as problem solvers who brought their scientific expertise to bear on problems that the architects identified. In this construction, the engineers' technical contribution was wrapped in dispassionate value-neutrality of science; it was the architects' failure to identify the appropriate problems that led to the deployment of that technology in inappropriate ways. A useful parallel here is with the protests of July–August 1970 against Westway, the 2.5 miles (4.1 kilometres) of elevated roadway that carried the extension of Western Avenue (A40(M)) road from the White City to Paddington Green in West London. With a history sketched as a path from *engineering* triumph to *planning* disaster,[48] the major culpability was attributed to the 'planners' rather than the highway engineers who helped initiate the scheme.[49]

## More bad news

Matters would not be helped by a constant diet of new problems arising from what one senior architect termed the 'daily drip of criticism, kept going by the mass media',[50] which contributed to the lasting climate of suspicion and hostility that suffused public and professional debate about modernist-inspired urban renewal. In April 1971, for example, *The Times* ran a full-page feature article on 'The revolt in the cities', linking together road, housing and conservationist protests as part of a general movement against a pipeline 'full of megalomaniac projects on an unexampled scale, which may yet savage everything that remains of the scarred countenance of our cities'.[51] While not quite at the levels of vitriol shown just a few years later with accusations about the 'sack of Bath' or more general 'rape of Britain',[52] the growing opprobrium steadily eroded the remaining vestiges of trust.

New developments added to the design professions' discomfort, with the next major problem concerning corruption. In the naively idealistic years after the war, local authorities were *entrusted* to handle the housing drive and, later, town centre renewal. It was doubly unfortunate for the architectural profession that, just as the spotlight revealed the constructional problems and maladministration of building systems, new scandals broke out from inquiries into corruption. The catalyst was the bankruptcy of the Pontefract-based architect, John Poulson, in November 1971 for arrears on income tax payments. While the details of this case lie outside the time-span of this book,[53] the Metropolitan Police began a fraud inquiry in July 1972 that would reveal corruption at all levels. The resulting prosecutions convicted T. Dan Smith, the former leader of Newcastle City Council, George Pottinger, a senior civil servant at the Scottish Office, and Andrew Cunningham, Leader of Durham County Council along with Poulson. Three Members of Parliament, including the Home Secretary Reginald Maudling, escaped prosecution on a legal technicality.

This came as no surprise to many architects familiar with dealing with medium-sized towns and boroughs. One respondent noted that 'trips, meals and sweeteners' were normal procedure in negotiating housing contracts in some cities.[54] Another gave his assessment of the role of the leader of the dominant party on a local council in relation to housing contracts:

> he was in the pay of [name withheld]. They got contract after contract, yet I know that they were never *that* competitive. Now, how do you think that came about?

Yet another recounted his experience when invited to see another political grandee:

> I've sat round a table with X and told him to go to hell. I wouldn't work for him; I wouldn't do what he wanted us to do. He was a crook. Everyone knew that Poulson was up to his eyeballs in it and he was taking bribes. It took his bankruptcy to bring [corruption] out into the open, although everyone knew about it – except that we did not have a gutter press then, otherwise it would have come out earlier I am sure. . . . My boss was furious because we could have had quite a nice job out of X. We were talking about fees and he wanted a percentage of our fees back. I told him, no, as a professional architect I was not prepared to discuss that . . . but it was openly discussed round the table. . . . I was a young architect trying to be professional; you can't do business like that.

The normality of the situation, however, almost appeared as a defence in 1976 when Birmingham's City Architect Alan Maudsley was successfully prosecuted for corrupt dealings with building contractors.

The specific topic of modern flats, both high and low rise, would receive continuing coverage as further difficulties emerged. During the 1970s, it became apparent that there was a variety of structural deficiencies, ranging from general though minor problems such as damp and condensation through to the major problems faced by some estates in terms of cladding, asbestos, joints and beams. It became clear that under-provision of lifts, their consequent overuse and poor maintenance created problems for people living on higher floors, especially elderly people. A number of the new estates also acquired unenviable reputations for crime and vandalism, suddenly given an added alarm quotient by the arrival of the 'defensible space' hypothesis from the USA. This seemed to threaten the very core of belief about the new architecture. 'Defensible space', a spatial concept spun off from the 1960s fascination with territoriality and other atavistic concepts, asserted that human beings have deep-seated needs to maintain certain types of bounded spaces in their domestic environments in order to preserve communal harmony. The design of new estates, particularly those involving high-rise blocks of flats, apparently denied these needs and led to all manners of social pathologies. The leading exponent of this idea was the Canadian-born architect Oscar Newman, the absent rapporteur of the CIAM '59 meeting at Otterlo (see Chapter 10). His theories appeared first in a text published in 1969 but achieved international prominence when expressed in his 1972 book *Defensible Space*.[55]

Newman had become a firm critic of modernist housing through work on public housing estates in New York and in St Louis (the ill-fated Pruitt-Igoe scheme). Funded in part by grants from US law enforcement agencies, Newman's research posited an areal correlation between high crime rates and high-rise public housing. In particular, using data drawn from the New York City Housing Authority, Newman claimed there was an association between abnormally high crime rates and the physical design of residential buildings. His key idea was that their layout denied people the possibility of establishing claims over the space around their dwellings, a characteristic that had traditionally been present in housing design:

> By its very nature, the single-family house is its own statement of territorial claim. It has defined ownership by the very act of its positioning on an integral piece of land buffered from neighbours and public street by intervening grounds. At times the buffer is reinforced by symbolic shrubs or fences, and in other cultures by high walls and gates. The positioning of lights and windows which look out on to the buffering ground also act to reinforce this claim.[56]

By contrast, those families living in high-rise blocks, mostly 'experience the space outside their apartment unit doors as distinctly public; in effect they relegate responsibility for all activity outside the immediate confines of their apartments to public authority'.[57] Thus, large areas of space within and immediately surrounding these buildings were open to everyone but subject to the control of no specific resident, primarily because these spaces were not overlooked from the dwelling units. These semi-public spaces – stairs, elevators (lifts), lobbies, roof spaces, halls, and social areas – became places where crime was rife. Table 12.1, which deals with statistics of felonies, would seem to reveal that as building height increased, so did the proportion of crime committed in the interior spaces of the buildings.

Newman's suggestions for alleviating crime reflected his analysis of the cause. He recommended changes to building design and layout to provide residents with opportunities to have 'defensible space', the name given to a residential environment in which latent territoriality and sense of community can be translated

**Table 12.1** Defensible space: the place of occurrence of felonies in buildings of different heights

|  | 3-storey buildings (%) | 6–7 storey buildings (%) | 13+ storey buildings (%) |
|---|---|---|---|
| Apartment interiors | 40.4 | 35.8 | 21.3 |
| Halls | 3.3 | 8.9 | 10.8 |
| Elevators | 1.3 | 9.8 | 22.6 |
| Lobbies | 7.2 | 11.1 | 8.1 |
| Stairs | 1.3 | 3.3 | 5.9 |
| Roofs | 1.3 | 3.9 | 4.0 |
| Social | 2.8 | 3.2 | 3.4 |
| Project grounds | 42.4 | 24.5 | 23.8 |
| Total | 100.0 | 100.0 | 100.0 |
| Proportion of crime in interior public spaces | 17.2 | 40.2 | 54.2 |
| Mean felony rate (per 1000 population) | 9 | 12 | 20 |

Source: data from New York City Housing Authority Police Report (1969), adapted from O. Newman, *Defensible Space*, New York: Macmillan, 1972, p. 33.

into responsibility for ensuring a safe, productive and well-maintained living space. Potential criminals would perceive such spaces as under the control of their residents, in which they would be readily visible as intruders. Newman made four sets of recommendations for design improvements specifically for high-rise blocks and estates, which included creating perceived territorial barriers, improving opportunities for surveillance, reducing the elements of design that stigmatise such blocks as social housing, and placing estates in more sympathetic locations.

Newman's work aroused great interest and controversy but, understandably, refutations based on proper consideration of evidence took some years to appear.[58] In the mean time, the mythology gathered pace. Regardless of the problems of the examples deployed by Newman, opponents of modernism in general and high-rise estates in particular gained a powerful deterministic theory to add to their armoury. They could claim that physical design in itself bred social pathology and could cite chapter and verse in support of a view that saw examples of crime-ridden estates as expected norm rather than the exception. The design improvements that Newman suggested also added to the plausibility of the analysis. The abandonment of the 'park' element of the 'city in the park' in all but rhetoric, the economies that made estates look and feel cheap, and the removal or non-employment of the concierge – a prime source of surveillance – went to the heart of many of the problems of such estates. Without doubt, *Defensible Space* contributed to a trend that would lead to radical reappraisal of many relatively new blocks of flats in the 1980s and 1990s, along with the loss of the enormous investment expended on their construction.

## Conflicting messages

This book began in 1954 with modern architects failing to realise that the architecture for which they had campaigned was on the threshold of becoming *the* dominant architecture of urban reconstruction and renewal. At the end of 1972, those adhering to modernism – still the majority in the profession – were again unaware that their favoured architecture stood on the threshold of considerable change. The New Year of 1973 would herald the end of the years of postwar affluence and all the assumptions that went with it. Ahead lay energy crises, mass unemployment, hyperinflation, disenchantment with the supposed linkage of progress and technology, and the rise of a postmodern architecture that partly replaced and partly extended modern architecture. That much, of course, was unforeseen. All that was apparent in 1972 was that sections of the profession, at least, were deeply uncertain about what lay ahead.

That impression certainly re-emerges when rereading the press from the early 1970s, with its powerful impression of deep division between optimism and pessimism. Notwithstanding Ronan Point, some quarters of the popular press could still manage enthusiasm about the prospects for comprehensive redevelopment. In early 1973, for example, one could find a journalist for *The Times* reviewing the progress made in rebuilding Glasgow with the headline: 'Bulldozers blitz a way to build place of beauty'. Noting the 'compelling excitement' of demolition and rebuilding on this scale, he reported foreign dignitaries as admiring the vision and 'the guts to go ahead'. He concluded that: 'the vast redevelopment programme is taking shape, and what is emerging is not only a modern city but one which, with essays in landscaping and use of greenery, will have a fair claim to being a place of beauty'.[59] By contrast, Sir Hugh Casson gave the same newspaper's readership a quite different impression of the state-of-the-art when commenting on the 'architect's responsibility for conserving and enhancing the new Britain'.[60] Casson addressed the gross disenchantment then confronting architecture:

> Among the more informed this disenchantment with architecture amounts today almost to paranoia. They claim to hate equally (though they continue to demand and gladly use) office blocks and car parks, motorways and airports, supermarkets, comprehensive schools, shopping centres and holiday hotels – the whole glum vulgar, intrusive, depersonalised set-up.
>
> Why is this? It used not to be so. . . . Is it just, as some would suggest, a sudden reflowering of traditional British philistinism, or a real decline in professional competence? Is it, perhaps, a failure of confidence or in communication, a resistance to novelty? Or is it no more than symptom of the general cultural unease of industrialised societies?
>
> Whatever the reasons, a situation has been created which is dispiriting and should be disturbing – and not only to architects – for it is leading to a paralysis of the nation's cultural nerve.[61]

While regretting the enervating effects of the media attention, he accepted a measure of the architect's responsibility for the current situation. The problem, in his opinion, was that the architect had suffered from a sense of inadequacy having failed to compete in technical expertise with the engineer and having lost traditional sources of patronage. Architects dreamed of monuments 'at a time when architectural rhetoric seems impertinent'. They were 'beguiled by images – the glass tower, the leafy suburb, the casbah – and torn apart by [their] wish to reconcile making a living with . . . obligations to society.' Nevertheless, Casson argued that the response should not be despair. Architecture, he argued, 'is democracy's true art'. While the architect should address people's real needs, there was also a need for recognising the importance of inculcating a better public understanding of architecture. He finished on a rousing note:

> To cultivate an eye for architecture, which means not just for buildings but for spaces and places, landscape and weather, is to cultivate an eye and a concern for human life. To ignore it, even to take refuge from it in Toytown, is to ensure that our environment will never be more than something to be endured.[62]

Casson's response, therefore, recognised crisis, but was prepared to offer hope for the future. Other architects, as indicated by the professional press, varied markedly in their assessments. The *Architectural Design*, which had long since superseded the *Architectural Review* as the chosen outlet for the radical wing of modernism, led the case for continued optimism about architecture, technology and progress. Issues for 1972 had already featured the works of Archizoom, Cedric Price, the Smithsons, Piano and Rogers, Frei Otto, Foster Associates and Peter Cook. Its subject matter, offered in a format that strove hard to preserve the links between progressive architecture and modern art, kept uncomfortable sociological evidence at bay. The avant-garde, once again, were turning their backs on the world's more unpleasant realities. Coverage centred instead on solar power stations, submarine oil tankers, extendible housing and domes, grids, systems and networks of all descriptions, the radical replanning of existing cities (London and Florence), and affectionate essays on heroes of the Modern Movement. True to form, the December 1972 issue ran a retrospective on the work of Richard Buckminster Fuller,[63] combined with an appreciative review of military con-structional techniques and advances, which demonstrated the art of the possible, and enthusiastic portraits of space cities, floating cities and all manner of other urban-scale megastructural projects. Few constraints, apart from desire, were accepted. For example, while reluctantly admitting that the construction of floating spheroid cloud cities of more than a half-mile diameter might be 'several decades hence', nevertheless:

> we may foresee that along with the floating tetrahedronal cities, air-deliverable skyscrapers, submarine islands, sub-dry surface dwellings, domed-over cities, flyable dwellings . . . that man may be able to converge and deploy around earth without its depletion.[64]

The view from the establishment was similarly supportive. The *Royal Institute of British Architects' Journal* presented its customary diet of technical notes, miscellaneous details of members' activities, reports on current legislation, book reviews and gentle positional articles. Its December 1972 edition saw discussion about consultative documents on the National Health Service, reports on a conference of 'salaried architects' (keen to play down hints of divisions in the profession) and a listing of the Department of Environment's 1972 awards for good housing design. A commentary on architects' work stressed the vocational elements of the architect's trade: 'I try not to measure success in terms of cash or material possessions. I cannot remember the last good architect who died a millionaire'.[65] Science was very much in the air, with analyses of the uses of sealants and mastics, David Medd responding to new guidelines on environmental design in schools,[66] and Bill Hillier and Adrian Leaman discussing the need for a new scientific approach to architectural research.[67]

Science, coupled with proto-environmentalism, was picked up elsewhere. The quarterly *Architectural Science Review* devoted its December 1972 issue to 'ecology', with its authors supporting the profession's lingering ideological claims to a greater stake in the design of the human environment. Wilson and Scott argued,[68] for example, for recognising the architect as 'the designer and organiser of a section of the man-made part of what is now known as the environmental continuum or supporting medium for human life.'[69] An unsigned associated article ran an appreciative eye over the prospects for cities offered by 'people movers' – small, electrically powered vehicles running on rubber wheels on their own 'guideways'. Urging readers to think of them as 'horizontal escalators', the writer hailed such systems as an economic and pollution-free system that, if tests proved favourable, would be 'likely to spring up all over the world'.[70]

Other journals were less prone to provide uncritical support for new technology as the solution for pervasive problems, and much less to entertain claims for extension to the architect's realm. The Architectural Press's periodicals, the *Architects' Journal* and *Architectural Review*, occupied a significant middle ground. Both retained their eye for the historic mission of the Modern Movement, with obituaries or retrospective exhibitions offering an opportunity to place the present in context.[71] For instance, an obituary on Hans Scharoun, a founder member of the Ring and CIAM, reflected on the deep divisions that ran through modern architecture then, as now, but added that 'he often succeeded in reconciling them'.[72] Equally a review on the work of Eileen Gray provided another opportunity to revisit nostalgically the ethos of a past age in which modern architects struggled valiantly against overwhelming odds to get their viewpoint across. These were balanced against the less satisfactory picture emerging from certain aspects of contemporary practice. Hence while the editorials of the *Architectural Review* would happily point to Patrick Hodgkinson's Brunswick Centre as 'a good bit of city',[73] and Jim Stirling's unsuccessful entry for Derby's Civic Centre competition as a work by 'probably Britain's most original architect',[74] there was biting criticism of the design of hotels, 'bad dreams coming true',[75] and the increasingly monolithic townscape brought by developers. The writer commented: 'The ultimate sterility towards which monumental redevelopment is heading is of no concern to the developers. They are gamblers on the giant scale, whose only interest is in the next fall of the dice.'[76]

The pessimistic end of the scale was found in the trenchant attacks that appeared in *The Architect*, the renamed successor to the venerable magazine *The Architect and Building News*. A signed editorial by Kate Wharton in December 1972 reflected on the decision to hold a European Architectural Heritage Year in 1975.[77] She stressed that not all 'the new buildings will be bad, some indeed will be good, even very good.' Nevertheless:

> At the risk of being called cynical I fail to see what European Architectural Heritage Year will show up other than an increasing deterioration in all things architectural, all things environmental. The housing estates will be more massive and monolithic, the office blocks cheaper and cheaper and taller and taller, the centre of cities deserted places save for people scuttling back to 'landscaped' suburbs and bleak shopping centres.

It was no more than a continuation of the journal's campaign against what its editorial team saw as poor standards in all aspects of the built environment. An editorial at the start of 1972 had reflected on the value of ivy in covering up poor architecture and about buildings so bad that not even the guiles of architectural photography could improve matters. After compiling a damning list of comments, the author referred to the same Housing Awards that the *Royal Institute of British Architects' Journal* had covered in anodyne terms, adding:

> A good example of all this were the recent D of E Housing Awards which in our opinion reached a new low. How they got past let alone – barring a few honourable exceptions – won medals beats us. 'As crummy a lot of designs as you'll find anywhere' was the unkind verdict of an American visitor looking at the photographs of them and not even a passionate chauvinism could do anything but hang its head in shame and more or less agree.[78]

The attacks went on relentlessly. Judith Chisholm's otherwise appreciative analysis of Acland Burghley school by Howell, Killick, Partridge and Amis was prefaced by an editorial introductory sentence: 'People can exist without architecture but architects cannot exist without people.'[79] Walter Segal reflected on the ill-devised patterns of legal responsibility in the profession, especially 'the entirely inadequate definition of the duties, obligations, rights and remedies of the practising architect'.[80] Colm Brogan lamented the impact of redevelopment policies on his home city of Glasgow – the dreary housing estates, the destruction of old patterns of life and the impact of unsympathetic high buildings on the city centre.[81] When reviewing an architectural competition for the new Parliamentary building in London, yet another editorial took the architects to task for their response to criticism:

> In reply to critics who have called the scheme 'calamitous', 'offensive', 'a monstrosity', 'adding to the ever-increasing list of architectural blunders', Robin Webster for the architects has hit back by claiming that

their design 'is intended to reflect the *culture of the 20th century*'. Brave words indeed. But what exactly does he mean by culture?[82]

Then after listing some of the possible works of such culture, which the writer felt could as easily be termed anti-culture, she concluded:

> One of the signs of the world's promised apocalypse is the collapse of true culture. And never has it been so apparent as today. Obviously architects should be allowed to reply to their critics but let them do so more intelligently than this. Such sweeping nonsense as Mr Webster's remark indicates merely makes the whole architectural profession seem sillier or more conceited than ever.

Poignantly, in view of the concern expressed in 1954 about lack of children's play space in modern housing estates (see Chapter 1), Paul Davies indicated that things had not progressed that much by 1972.[83] His favourable reviews of some recent developments on Greater London Council estates that 'at last' were making provision for children's real needs served only to show that in many 'large blocks live families with their children looking down from high windows on to pools of emptiness'.[84]

## Outlook uncertain

We now know that the pessimists proved to have a firmer grasp of the situation. Many cherished ideas were being challenged, calling into question the bases of the self-legitimising constellation of design and social imagery on which modernist intervention in the built environment rested. The process of reappraisal established in the late 1960s and early 1970s would prove pervasive, much as many architects would have preferred to re-establish business as usual. So too would the mood of public disenchantment. Understandably, however, the process of reappraisal and reformulation took longer to establish itself in architectural circles than more generally in society. That which now clearly seems to constitute a seismic movement in opinion did not necessarily seem an irretrievable position to architects at the time. Such faith had been invested in modernism as the architectural language of the day that it was understandable that architects would not light-heartedly abandon the whole impedimenta of belief and practice overnight – regardless of whether hindsight might suggest that course of action was inevitable. As Sir Andrew Derbyshire noted with regard to responses of older modernists to the shifting design currents of the early 1970s:

> One had to be conscious, however, of how deep these issues ran when viewed in light of the struggle to establish modernism. It was a big fight and a victory that was hard to deny – they had worked so hard to achieve it.[85]

Against that background, it was even harder for architects to foresee the willing, almost gleeful, destruction that was soon wrought on what society quickly regarded as yesterday's failed symbols of progress (Figure 12.3).

At the point at which this book closes, all that was incontrovertible was that modern architecture faced an awkward future, necessarily confronting a series of fundamental questions that recent events had brought into stark focus. Many went to the very heart of modern architecture's interventions in the built environment, dealing with the structures built, their arrangement in space and the architect's role as designer. For instance, given active efforts to reconceptualise the Modern Movement, perhaps as Modern *Movements*, where was the underlying unity of modernism to be found? Did functional principles still have any part to play in shaping the future city? What lessons, practical and moral, needed to be learned from the structural and material problems facing modern buildings, especially as a result of the poor use of concrete and industrialised building methods? How should modern architects respond to the growing trend towards urban rehabilitation and away from clearance and redevelopment? Did the future of modernism lie with the efforts of an adventurous avant-garde restoring the Modern Movement's cutting edge or perhaps with a return to first principles? Finally, could architects reinvigorate the social intent of modernism by devising new and socially responsive forms to replace the previous generation's now discredited visions of the future city? It was from the resolution of these and similar questions that the legacy of modernism would emerge.

12.3
**Partial demolition
of Central Area,
Cumbernauld
(2004)**

# Notes and references

All interview transcript references are listed in full on the first occasion that they are mentioned, thereafter with identifying name followed by interview number and the relevant page of transcript in square brackets.

## 1 On the threshold

1   D. Eccles, 'Message to the *Architects' Journal*', *Architects' Journal*, 1954, vol. 119, p. 67.
2   P. Addison, *Now the War is Over: a social history of Britain, 1945–51*, revised edition, London: Pimlico, 1995, p. 210. The Royal Festival Hall, always seen as the replacement for the Queen's Hall (destroyed by bombing in 1941), was excluded from the clearance.
3   Anon, 'Portrait of a year', *The Times*, 1 January 1954, p. 5; D. Porter, '"Never-never land"': Britain under the Conservatives, 1951–1964', in N. Tiratsoo (ed.) *From Blitz to Blair: a new history of Britain since 1939*, London: Weidenfeld & Nicolson, 1997, p. 109.
4   Our Special Correspondent, 'Burden of public spending – III: nation straining at the limit', *The Times*, 18 July 1953, p. 7.
5   Interview between Sir Philip Powell and Louise Brodie, 27 May 1997. National Sound Archive (NSA), tape F5515, side A.
6   Our Special Correspondent, 'Burden of public spending – III: nation straining at the limit', *The Times*, 18 July 1953, p. 7.
7   L. Mumford, 'East End urbanity', reprinted in L. Mumford, *The Highway and the City*, London: Secker & Warburg, 1964, p. 26. The original essay was written in 1953.
8   With regard to industrial regeneration, see the contrasting views of Corelli Barnett and Nick Tiratsoo: C. Barnett, *The Audit of War: the illusion and reality of Britain as a great nation*, London: Macmillan, 1986; N. Tiratsoo, *Reconstruction, Affluence and Labour Politics, 1945–60*, London: Routledge, 1990.
9   P. Dunleavy, *The Politics of Mass Housing in Britain, 1945–1975: a study of corporate power and professional influence in the Welfare State*, Oxford: Clarendon Press, 1981, pp. 39–41.
10  P. Balchin, 'Housing', in J.B. Cullingworth (ed.) *British Planning: 50 years of urban and regional policy*, London: Athlone, 1999, p. 17. This contrasts with around 65,000 completions in the private sector.
11  Interview between A.G. Sheppard Fidler and Miles Glendinning, 28 October 1987.
12  Interview between Dame Jane Drew and Margaret Garlake, 20 May 1995. NSA, tape 4826, side B.
13  G.E. Cherry, *Town Planning in Britain since 1900: the rise and fall of the planning ideal*, Oxford: Blackwell, 1996, p. 123.
14  Interview between Dame Jane Drew and Margaret Garlake, 20 May 1995. NSA, tape 4826, side B.
15  Interview with Pat Crooke, 21 February 2005 [T47/5].
16  See e.g. J.M. Richards, 'Failure of the New Towns', *Architectural Review*, 1953, vol. 114, pp. 29–32; G. Cullen, 'Prairie planning in the New Towns', *Architectural Review*, 1953, vol. 114, pp. 33–6.
17  The first notable results did not appear until the 1960s. See P. Hall, *Cities of Tomorrow: an intellectual history of urban planning and design in the twentieth century*, Oxford: Basil Blackwell, 1988, p. 172.

18    S.V. Ward, *Planning and Urban Change*, London: Paul Chapman, 1994, p. 179.

19    L. Rodwin, *The British New Towns*, Cambridge, MA: Harvard University Press, 1956, p. 141.

20    Interview with Pat Crooke, 21 February 2005 [T47/4].

21    These plans were perhaps the most tangible embodiment of Lord Reith's oft-repeated advice to 'plan boldly and comprehensively'. This remark, which dates from 1941, was made when Reith was Minister of Works and Buildings. It is quoted in P.J. Larkham, *Agents of Change in the Post-war Reconstruction: the interaction of architects, planners, politicians and the public*, Working Paper Series 91, Birmingham: University of Central England, 2004, p. 2. For more on the advisory plans, see P.J. Larkham and K.D. Lilley, *Planning the 'City of Tomorrow': British reconstruction planning, 1939–52 – an annotated bibliography*, Pickering, North Yorkshire: Inch's Books, 2001.

22    J. Drew, 'Memoirs'. British Architectural Library, file DrJ/1/1. These unpublished memoirs date from approximately 1983.

23    This point is based on N. Tiratsoo, J. Hasegawa, T. Mason and T. Matsumura, *Urban Reconstruction in Britain and Japan, 1945–1955: dreams, plans and realities*, Luton: University of Luton Press, 2002, p. 11.

24    A. Sinclair, *The War Decade: an anthology of the 1940s*, London: Hamish Hamilton, 1989, p. 323.

25    L. Keeble, *Principles and Practice of Town and Country Planning*, London: Estates Gazette, 1952, p. 215.

26    Anon, 'Sober confidence', *Official Architecture and Planning*, 1954, vol. 17, p. 19.

27    H. Robertson, *Modern Architectural Design*, revised edition, London: Architectural Press, 1952, p. 22.

28    A. Korn, *History Builds the Town*, London: Lund Humphries, 1953.

29    Ibid., p. 11.

30    F.E. Gibberd, *Town Design*, London: Architectural Press, 1953. This book would go through various editions during the period under consideration here, reaching its sixth edition in 1970.

31    C. Tunnard, *The City of Man*, London: Architectural Press, 1953.

32    Ibid., p. 234.

33    Ibid.

34    Anon, 'Tropical architecture 2', *Architectural Design*, 1954, vol. 24, pp. 1–20. Among the practices represented were James Cubitt and Partners, Fry, Drew and Partners, Norman and Dawbarn, and Richard Nickson and Partners.

35    E. Goldfinger, 'Focus on France', *Architectural Design*, 1954, vol. 24, pp. 193–223.

36    Interview with Trevor Dannatt, 26 February 1996 [T17/7].

37    T. Dannatt (ed.) *Architects' Year Book 5*, London: Elek, 1953.

38    J.B. Drew, 'Chandigarh, capital city', in Dannatt (ed.) *Architects' Year Book 5*, pp. 48–55.

39    A. Smithson and P. Smithson, 'An urban project', in Dannatt (ed.) *Architects' Year Book 5*, p. 54.

40    T. Dannatt, 'Foreword', in Dannatt (ed.) *Architects' Year Book 5*, p. 7. This reference to the 'New Elizabethan' age recalls the popular mood following the coronation of Elizabeth II on 2 June 1953. The coupling of the new reign with hopes for a better future infused much contemporary writing about the built environment. See also e.g. A. Hunt, 'Royal tour: modern houses in countries the Queen is visiting', *House and Garden*, 1954, vol. 9, pp. 16–23.

41    Anon, 'The Building Exhibition and "Operation Rescue"', *Architectural Design*, 1953, vol. 23, p. 330. For more on the exhibition itself, see D. Dean, *The Architect as Stand Designer: building exhibitions, 1895–1983*, London: Scolar Press for the Building Trades Exhibition, 1985, pp. 90–5.

42    Editor, 'The Building Exhibition and "Operation Rescue"', *Architectural Design*, 1953, vol. 23, p. 330.

43    Ibid.

44    Ibid., p. 331.

45    See Anon, 'Men of the year', *Architects' Journal*, 1954, vol. 119, pp. 68–75.

46    Ibid., p. 68.

47    A. Smithson and P. Smithson, 'What the Smithsons think', *Architects' Journal*, 1954, vol. 119, pp. 72–3 (original emphasis).

48    G. Stephenson, 'Those were (and these can be) the days', *Architects' Journal*, 1954, vol. 119, p. 69. In fairness to Stephenson, it must be pointed out that he could elsewhere be found indicating enthusiastic approval at plans for the imminent redevelopment of London's South Bank. See G. Stephenson, 'The permanent development of the South Bank', *Royal Institute of British Architects' Journal*, third series, 1954, vol. 56, pp. 95–101.

49  Astragal, 'AR Preview', *Architects' Journal*, 1954, vol. 119, p. 31.

50  Anon, 'Foreword', *Architectural Review*, 1954, vol. 115, pp. 5–6.

51  Although Denys Lasdun disputed this attribution for the flats. Information from an interview between Sir Denys Lasdun and Jill Lever, 12 November 1996. NSA, tape F5347, side B. See also Chapter 9.

52  At the risk of labouring the point about the content of surveys, it is worth noting that the *Architect and Building News* independently covered much the same territory in its annual review: see Anon, 'Review of 1953', *The Architect and Building News*, 1954, vol. 205, pp. 62–99. Indeed, its editor's choice of the three 'planning schemes . . . most likely to succeed' (p. 63) were Chamberlin, Powell and Bon's Golden Lane scheme, the London County Council's South Bank scheme, and a courtyard planning scheme for Sidgwick Avenue by Sir Hugh Casson and his partner Neville Conder.

53  J.M. Richards, 'Preview', *Architectural Review*, 1954, vol. 115, pp. 7–13.

54  Ibid., p. 12.

55  Anon, 'Coventry preview', *Architectural Review*, 1955, vol. 117, p. 5.

56  Anon, 'Foreword', *Architectural Review*, 1954, vol. 115, p. 6.

57  A. Ling, 'The London skyline', *Official Architecture and Planning*, 1954, vol. 17, pp. 166–71.

58  A.G. Jury, 'Multi-storey housing', *Official Architecture and Planning*, 1954, vol. 17, pp. 225–7.

59  Anon, 'Lack of playgrounds of modern estates: Lady Allen of Hurtwood's strictures', *The Builder*, 1954, vol. 186, p. 28.

60  J. Betjeman, '"Honour your forebears": Mr John Betjeman's address at the RIBA', *The Builder*, 1954, vol. 186, p. 48.

61  C. Tunnard, *Gardens in the Modern Landscape*, London: Architerctural Press, 1938.

62  Even if, by then, Gibberd himself did not necessarily still want to be associated with that style of building: interview with George Dunton, 12 May 2005 [T50/1].

63  Comment by Sir Hugh Casson. Interview with Cathy Courtney, 13 February 1990. NSA, tape F1087, side B.

64  Interview with Arthur Ling, 30 January 1987 [T8/16–17]. Transcript revised by personal communication, 27 February 1987.

65  Ibid.

66  P.R. Banham, 'Only an academic flywheel', *Royal Institute of British Architects' Journal*, 1972, vol. 79, p. 339.

67  R. Witemeyer, 'Introduction: modernism resartus', in R. Witemeyer (ed.) *The Future of Modernism*, Ann Arbor, MI: University of Michigan Press, 1997, p. 2.

68  P. Nuttgens, *The Flight from Utopia*, Part 1, *The Age of Euphoria*, BBC1 television, 18 September 1984.

69  J.R. Gold, *The Experience of Modernism: modern architects and the future city, 1928–1953*, London: E. & F.N. Spon, 1997.

70  A large literature on narratives and storytelling has appeared since the review of material on the operation of Grand Narratives that I offered in the previous volume; see ibid., pp. 1–13. For some more recent thoughts on narrative, see J.R. Gold, 'The power of narrative: the early writings of Charles Jencks and the historiography of architectural modernism', in L. Campbell (ed.) *Twentieth-Century Architecture and its Histories*, Otley: Society of Architectural Historians of Great Britain, 2000, pp. 206–21. For other sources, see B. Eckstein and J.A. Throgmorton (eds) *Story and Sustainability: planning, practice and possibility for American cities*, Cambridge, MA: MIT Press, 2003; L. Sandercock, 'Out of the closet: the importance of stories and storytelling in planning practice', in B. Stiftel and V. Watson (eds) *Dialogues in Urban and Regional Planning 1*, London: Routledge, 2005, pp. 299–321. I only belatedly became aware of William Mitchell's invaluable collection of essays about narrative and Avital Ronell's philosophically (and typographically) challenging approach to plural narratives. See W.J.T. Mitchell (ed.) *On Narrative*, Chicago, IL: University of Chicago Press, 1981; and A. Ronell, *The Telephone Book: technology, schizophrenia, electric speech*, Lincoln, NE: University of Nebraska Press, 1989.

71  Formal discussion of the perennial philosophical debate over free will versus determinism, and its recent recasting, first, in the debate over structuration and, latterly, actor-network theory lies outside the scope of this text. For more information, see J. Law and J. Hassard (eds) *Actor Network Theory and after*, Oxford: Blackwell, 1999; B. Latour, *Reassembling the Social: an introduction to actor-network-theory*, Oxford: Oxford University Press, 2005.

72   The page numbers marked in these notes always relate to this version.

73   S. Lubar, 'Exhibiting memories', in A. Henderson and A.L. Kaeppler (eds) *Exhibiting Dilemmas: issues of representation at the Smithsonian*, Washington, DC: Smithsonian Institution Press, 1997, p. 24.

74   The Preface lists the principal archives that I have used in writing this book.

## 2  Practising modernism

1   D. Sharp, 'The new architecture in Britain: the framework of the Welfare State', in H.J. Henket and H. Heynen (eds) *Back from Utopia: the challenge of the Modern Movement*, Rotterdam: 010 Publishers, 2002, p. 125.

2   Partly based on R. Gutman, *Architectural Practice: a critical view*, Princeton, NJ: Princeton University Press, 1988, p. 123; and R. Verges-Escuin, *The Economic Future of the Architect*, Paris: UNESCO, 1980, p. 99. These figures, however, were from the US Bureau of the Census and relied on self-description of job title rather than on licensed or registered status. For quite different figures for 1950, see M.B. Boyle, 'Architectural practice in America, 1986–1965: ideal and reality', in S. Kostof (ed.) *The Architect: chapters in the history of the profession*, New York: Oxford University Press, 1977, p. 332.

3   D. Langdon and Everest Consultancy Group, *Architectural Practice in Europe: Italy*, London: Royal Institute of British Architects, 1991, p. 86.

4   Partly based on D. Langdon and Everest Consultancy Group, *Architectural Practice in Europe: France*, London: Royal Institute of British Architects, 1990, p. 86.

5   F. Duffy and F. Hutton, *Architectural Knowledge: the idea of a profession*, London: E. & F.N. Spon, 1998, pp. xiii–xv.

6   Gutman, *Architectural Practice*, p. 33.

7   J.M. Freeland, *The Making of a Profession: a history of the growth and work of the Architectural Institutes in Australia*, Sydney: Angus and Robertson, 1971, p. 180.

8   J.M. Austin-Smith, A. Derbyshire, D. Howard, J.H. Madge and J.M.N. Milne, *The Architect and his Office*, London: Royal Institute of British Architects, 1962, p. 29.

9   M. Symes, J. Eley and A.D. Seidel, *Architects and the Practices: a changing profession*, Oxford: Butterworth Professional, 1995, p. 16.

10   Austin-Smith et al., *The Architect and his Office*, p. 29.

11   A point to which we return in Chapter 4, when considering professional rivalries in relation to town planning.

12   These figures are from N. Bullock, *Building the Post-War World: modern architecture and reconstruction in Britain*, London: Routledge, 2002, p. 220. Bullock also claims that 71 per cent of architects working in the public sector, or 35 per cent of the architectural profession as a whole, worked for a borough or council engineer.

13   Ibid., p. 33.

14   S. Stevens, *The Favoured Circle: the social foundations of architectural distinction*, Cambridge, MA: MIT Press, 1998, p. 103.

15   A letter from Max Fry to Jane Drew from Simla, dated 5 August 1951, describes the atmosphere of misunderstanding with Jeanneret caused by different temperaments and describes Le Corbusier as being 'distrusted by both Jeanneret and myself as a colleague'. British Architectural Library, file DrJ/1/5.

16   Initially the practice also included Michael Powell before he left to join the LCC.

17   For biographical details and background of other first generation modernists who practised before the Second World War, see J.R. Gold, *The Experience of Modernism: modern architects and the future city, 1928–1953*, London: E. & F.N. Spon, 1997, pp. 88–93.

18   Staff Architect, 'Is an architect an administrator?', *Official Architecture*, 1937, vol. 1, p. 3.

19   Interview between Sir Hubert Bennett and Louise Brodie, 18 February 1999. National Sound Archive (NSA), tape F6936, side A.

20   Interview with Oliver Cox, 2 November 2004 [T29/2].

21   Interview with Lionel Brett (Lord Esher), 15 April 1987 [T2/1–8].

22   National Service was not finally abolished until 1959: see L.V. Scott, *Conscription and the Attlee Governments: the politics and policy of National Service, 1945–1951*, Oxford: Oxford University Press, 1993, p. 1.

**Notes and references**

23    Interview between Kenneth Campbell and Miles Glendinning, 28 October 1987.

24    Interview with John Summerson, 4 December 1986 [T12/2].

25    Kenneth Campbell, for instance, was perfectly open with his affiliations: 'The horrors of the Spanish Civil War turned us all into Communists.' Interview with Miles Glendinning, 28 October 1987.

26    Quotes from a variety of sources, two of whom requested non-attribution.

27    Interview between Sir Anthony Cox and Andrew Saint, 12 July 1984. NSA, CD-ROM C447/07/01, Disk 1.

28    C. St.J. Wilson, 'Working at the LCC', unpublished paper, n.d., p. 2.

29    Ibid., p. 4.

30    Interview with Colin Boyne, 11 January 2005 [T45/5].

31    M. Crimson and J. Lubbock, *Architecture – Art or Profession? Three hundred years of architectural education in Britain*, Manchester: Manchester University Press, 1994, p. 108.

32    Interview with Peter Winchester, 23 November 2004 [T33/3].

33    G. Smith, 'Schools of architecture', *Architecture and Building*, 1958, vol. 33, p. 50.

34    Interview with Peter Carter, 7 April 2005 [T48/3]. The original was B.F. Fletcher, *A History of Architecture for the Student, Craftsman, and Amateur: Being a comparative view of the historical styles from the earliest period*, London: Batsford, 1896. The Architectural Press published its twentieth (centenary) edition in 1996 under the editorship of Dan Cruickshank.

35    Interview with Martyn Smith, 19 November 2004 [T32/2].

36    P.R. Banham, 'Historical studies and architectural criticism', *Transactions of the Bartlett Society*, 1962–3, vol. 1, p. 37

37    Interview with Sir Andrew Derbyshire, 16 December 2004 [T40/3].

38    Interview with Geoffrey Darke, 23 May 2006 [T52/1].

39    Ibid.

40    Peter Winchester noted, for example, after a student visit to Le Corbusier's *unité* at Nantes: 'I had . . . decided that this was not for me: I don't like these damned corridors'. Interview with Peter Winchester, 23 November 2004 [T33/12].

41    Interview with John Graham, 9 December 2004 [T38/4].

42    Ibid.

43    Interview with Sir Andrew Derbyshire, 16 December 2004 [T40/16].

44    Interview between Sir Neville Conder and Alan Powers, 8 August 1999. NSA, tape F7517, side B.

45    Interview with Frank Woods, 18 November 2004 [T31/9].

46    Interview with Oliver Cox, 2 November 2004 [T29/2–3].

47    Interview between Sir George Grenfell-Baines and Louise Brodie, 5 January 2000. NSA, tape F7840, side B.

48    Ibid.

49    Interview with John Graham, 9 December 2004 [T38/2].

50    See J. Gowan (ed.) *Projects: Architectural Association 1946–71*, London: Architectural Association, 1975, pp. 26–7.

51    Interview with Peter Winchester, 23 November 2004 [T33/3].

52    Interview with John Hummerston, 29 October 2004 [T28/5].

53    Interview with Jack Bonnington, 20 December 2004 [T42/8].

54    Quoted in interview with Charles Willis, 22 October 2004 [T27/4–5].

55    A list compiled from the responses of a number of interviewees.

56    Interview with Peter Carter, 7 April 2005 [T48/7].

57    Interview with Peter Carter, 7 April 2005 [T48/4].

58    Interview with Jack Bonnington, 20 December 2004 [T42/2].

59    Interview with Peter Hall, 30 November 2004 [T34/6].

60    See Gold, *The Experience of Modernism*, pp. 107–15.

61    L.M. Wood, *A Union to Build: the story of UCATT*, London: Union of Construction, Allied Trades and Technicians, 1979.

62    G. Stamp, 'Anti-ugly: campaigning against ugly buildings may seem admirable – but a recent call for demolitions is based on philistinism', *Apollo*, 2005, vol. 161 (January).

63    Interview with Trevor Dannatt, 26 February 1996 [T17/6]. See also Chapter 10.

64    Gold, *The Experience of Modernism*, p. 224. See also A. Massey, *The Independent Group: Modernism and mass culture in Britain, 1945–59*, Manchester: Manchester University Press, 1995.

65    From Lawrence Alloway's 'Introduction' to *This is Tomorrow*, London: Whitechapel Gallery, n.p., quoted in Sharp, 'The new architecture in Britain', p. 123.

66    Interview with Mary Banham, 16 January 2006 [T51/14].

67    K. Frampton, 'Obituary: Peter Smithson', *The Independent*, 20 March 2003.

68    For the former, see B. Highmore, 'Rough poetry: *Patio and Pavilion* revisited', *Oxford Art Journal*, 2006, vol. 29, pp. 269–90; the latter is a quotation from S. Sadler, 'British architecture in the Sixties', in C. Stephens and K. Stout (eds) *Art and the 60s: This was Tomorrow*, London: Tate Publishing, 2004, p. 124.

69    Interview between Peter Smithson and Louise Brodie, 17 September 1997. NSA, tape F5952, side B.

70    Interview with Peter Carter, 7 April 2005 [T48/3].

71    R.F. Jordan, 'LCC: new standards in official architecture', *Architectural Review*, 1956, vol. 119, p. 304.

72    A. Goss, 'Young architects and the public authority', *Official Architecture and Planning*, 1963, vol. 26, p. 35.

73    Anon, 'Architects' offices in local government', *Royal Institute of British Architects' Journal*, 1967, vol. 74(August).

74    Interview with Jack Bonnington, 20 December 2004 [T42/2].

75    Taken from an obituary of Bill Howell and referring to HKPA: see A. Gordon, 'Obituary: Bill Howell', *Royal Institute of British Architects' Journal*, 1975, vol. 82, p. 14.

76    Interview with Frank Woods, 18 November 2004 [T31/1].

77    Interview with Anthony Blee, 10 December 2004 [T39/6].

78    Interview between Sir Hubert Bennett and Louise Brodie, 18 February 1999. NSA, tape F6936, side B.

79    Interview with Sir Andrew Derbyshire, 16 December 2004 [T40/3, 6].

80    Interview with Colin St. John Wilson, 5 January 2005 [T44/3].

81    Robbins Report (1963) *Higher Education: Government statement on the report of the committee under the chairmanship of Lord Robbins, 1961–63*, Cmnd 2168, London: HMSO.

82    Interview with Pat Crooke, 21 February 2005 [T47/3].

83    Interview between John F.C. Turner and Roberto Chavez, 11 September 2000, transcript p. 1, http://www.worldbank.org/urban/forum2002/docs/turner-tacit.pdf.

84    P. Geddes, *Cities in Evolution*, London: Williams & Norgate, 1915.

85    See e.g. J.F.C. Turner and R. Fichter (eds) *Freedom to Build: dweller control of the housing process*, New York: Macmillan, 1972.

86    The quotation relates to Robert Frost's poem 'The Road Not Taken' (1915). See R.L. Frost, *The Road Not Taken: A selection of Robert Frost's poems*, New York: Henry Holt, 1951.

## 3  Public and private

1    D. Cuff, 'The political paradoxes of practice: political economy of local and global architecture', *ARQ* (*Architectural Research Quarterly*), 1999, vol. 3, pp. 79–80.

2    Crichel Down was a case of official malpractice in land transfer that led to the resignation of Sir Thomas Dugdale, the Minister of Agriculture. See R.D. Brown, *The Battle of Crichel Down*, London: J. Lane, 1955.

3    R.F. Jordan, 'LCC: new standards in official architecture', *Architectural Review*, 1956, vol. 119, pp. 303–24.

4    E. Layton, *Building by Local Authorities: the report of an inquiry by the Royal Institute of Public Administration into the organization of building and maintenance by local authorities in England and Wales*, London: George Allen and Unwin, 1961, pp. 15–16.

5    Ibid., p. 137; P. Dunleavy, *The Politics of Mass Housing in Britain, 1945–1975: a study of corporate power and professional influence in the Welfare State*, Oxford: Oxford University Press, 1981, p. 12.

6    Interview between George Bowie and Miles Glendinning, 3 November 1987.

7    J.M. Austin-Smith, A. Derbyshire, D. Howard, J.H. Madge and J.M.N. Milne, *The Architect and his Office*, London: Royal Institute of British Architects, 1962, p. 29.

8    The information about organisational structures comes from Layton, *Building by Local Authorities*, pp. 118–22.

9   Interview with Rodney Gordon, 11 November 2004 [T30/9].

10  R.F. Jordan, 'LCC: new standards in official architecture', *Architectural Review*, 1956, vol. 119, pp. 321, 325.

11  Interview with Sir John Summerson, 4 December 1986 [T12/9–10].

12  Interview with Professor Sir Colin St. John Wilson [T46/2].

13  Interview between John Partridge and Jill Lever, 3 September 2002. National Sound Archive (NSA), tape F12318, side A.

14  Interview between George Bowie and Miles Glendinning, 3 November 1987.

15  Interview between John Partridge and Jill Lever, 19 September 2002. NSA, tape F12322, side A.

16  Interview with Professor Sir Colin St. John Wilson, 17 February 2005 [T46/2].

17  Interview between George Bowie and Miles Glendinning, 3 November 1987.

18  Interview between Sir Hubert Bennett and Louise Brodie, 18 February 1999. NSA, tape F6936, side A.

19  B. Finnimore, *Houses from the Factory: system building and the Welfare State*, London: Rivers Oram Press, 1989, p. 73.

20  Interview between Walter Bor and Louise Brodie, 6 April 1997. NSA, tape F5630, side B.

21  M. Hebbert and W. Sonne, '*History Builds the Town*: on the uses of history in twentieth century city planning', in J. Monclus and M. Guardia (eds) *Culture, Urbanism and Planning*, Aldershot: Ashgate, 2006, p. 12.

22  F.R. Hiorns, *Town-Building in History: an outline review of conditions, influences, ideas, and methods affecting 'planned' towns through five thousand years*, London: Harrap, 1956, p. 412.

23  Interview between Kenneth Campbell and Miles Glendinning, 28 October 1987.

24  Interview with John Hummerston, 29 October 2004 [T28/6].

25  Interview with Martyn Smith, 19 November 2004 [T32/4] (original emphasis).

26  Ibid.

27  Interview with Charles Willis, 22 October 2004 [T27/3].

28  Interview with Rodney Gordon, 11 November 2004 [T30/4].

29  Principally by restrictions imposed by the London Building Acts of 1888 and 1894, which restricted building heights to the width of the street or to the height of a fireman's ladder (80 feet) plus a two-storey roof with some concession for 'architectural features'. Information from English Heritage (2005) 'Memorandum' (TAB 18), http://www.parliament.the-stationery-office.co.uk/pa/cm200102/cmselect/cmtlgr/482/48232.htm

30  L. Esher, *A Broken Wave: the rebuilding of England, 1940–1980*, London: Allen Lane, 1981, p. 112.

31  Interview between Walter Bor and Louise Brodie, 6 April 1997. NSA, tape F5628, side B.

32  N. Bullock, *Building the Post-War World: modern architecture and reconstruction in Britain*, London: Routledge, 2002, p. 249.

33  Interview with Maxwell Fry, 24 November 1986 [T/2].

34  This curt dismissal of the later work of Maxwell Fry, F.R.S. Yorke and Frederick Gibberd in these terms is found in A. Jackson, *The Politics of Architecture: a history of modern architecture in Britain*, London: Architectural Press, 1970, p. 179 (emphasis added). Sir Anthony Cox made similar comments: interview between Anthony Cox and Andrew Saint, 12 July 1984. NSA, CD-ROM C447/07/01 Disc 1.

35  A. Powers, *In the Line of Development: F.R.S. Yorke, E. Rosenberg and C.S. Mardall to YRM*, London: RIBA Heinz Gallery, 1992, p. 42.

36  D. Allford, 'FRS Yorke – a memoir, 1952–64: "If you don't like what you are doing, don't do it"', in J. Melvin (ed.) *F.R.S. Yorke and the Evolution of English Modernism*, Chichester: Wiley-Academy, 2003, p. 117.

37  See Chapter 1. His immunity to criticism may have been because he was classified as a 'Friend of Jim' (i.e. J.M. Richards); one of a group of former MARS members and other members of the interwar Modern Movement whose work could not be criticised in the publications of the Architectural Press.

38  Interview with George Dunton, 12 April 2005 [T50/1].

39  O. Luder, 'A long way to go', *Building* (30 November 1979), pp. 50–1.

40  A.J. Willis and W.N.B. George, *The Architect in Practice*, London: Crosby Lockwood, 1952, p. 11.

41  Interview with Geoffrey Darke, 23 May 2006 [T52/3].

42    C. Ward, 'Anarchy and architecture', in J. Hughes and S. Sadler (eds) *Non-Plan: essays on freedom participation and change in modern architecture and urbanism*, Oxford: Architectural Press, 2000, p. 45.

43    Interview with Frank Woods, 18 November 2004 [T31/7].

44    Interview with Geoffrey Darke, 23 May 2006 [T52/4].

45    Interview with Harry Teggin, 11 October 2004 [T26/6].

46    Interview between Lord Esher and Louise Brodie, July 1997. NSA, tape FS643, side A. It should be noted in passing that his withdrawal from the firm was not immediate. He agreed, however, to remain as consultant to the Portsmouth Guildhall Redevelopment, the firm's major project, after his departure for the Royal College of Art: see Minutes of Special Meeting, held at Portsmouth Guildhall, 10 February 1971. BAL, BrL/39/3.

47    Interview with Frank Woods, 18 November 2004 [T31/6].

48    Ibid., [T31/2].

49    Ibid., [T31/7].

50    Interview between John Partridge and Jill Lever, 19 September 2002. NSA, tape F12322, side A.

51    For more on Goldfinger's approach to his work and staff, see N. Warburton, *Ernö Goldfinger: the life of an architect*, London: Routledge, 2004, pp. 131–6.

52    Interview between Denys Lasdun and Jill Lever, 12 November 1996. NSA, tape F5348, side A.

53    To some extent, this impression of size is misleading. The Harlow work could easily have been done from the larger Percy Street office. The rationale of retaining a Harlow office lay partly in wanting to give the New Town an architectural practice and partly in allowing Gibberd a base from which to indulge his personal interests in creating a landscape garden, which became the seven-acre Gibberd Garden at Marsh Lane. He structured his week to spend Monday and Friday at the Development Corporation, leaving the weekend to make his garden.

54    Interview with John Graham, 9 December 2004 [T38/8].

55    Interview with Lady Patricia Gibberd, 8 December 2004 [T37/2].

56    Interview with Jack Bonnington, 20 December 2004 [T42/2].

57    Discussion of this point lies outside the scope of this account, but the consensus among former employees was that fragmentation of the office, and division of commissions, in the 1960s resulted from irreconcilable differences between Spence and Andrew Renton.

58    Interview with Peter Winchester, 23 November 2004 [T33/5].

59    Interview with Anthony Blee, 10 December 2004 [T39/12–13].

60    Austin-Smith et al., *The Architect and his Office*, p. 35.

61    Interview with Rodney Gordon, 11 November 2004 [T30/10].

62    Interview with Jack Bonnington, 20 December 2004 [T42/8].

63    Interview between Cecil Elsom and Louise Brodie on 2 April 1996. NSA, tape 5447, side A.

64    O. Marriott, *The Property Boom*, London: Hamish Hamilton, 1967, p. 32.

65    Ibid. See also the comments in Chapter 2 about the recognised lists of firms habitually interviewed for major projects.

66    Interview with John Hummerston, 29 October 2004 [T28/2]. He was talking about his experience of working on Arndale Centres for Shindler and Risdon.

67    Marriott, *The Property Boom*, p. 271.

68    Interview between Richard Seifert and Louise Brodie, 2 April 1996. NSA, tape F5075, side B. It must be said, however, that Seifert's approach was to get subcontractors to take care of the detailing. Interview with Rodney Gordon, 11 November 2004 [T30/10].

69    Ibid., [T30/13].

70    Interview with Professor Sir Colin St. John Wilson, 17 February 2005 [T46/3].

71    F. Pooley, 'Architects in local government', *Architecture and Building*, 1958, vol. 33, p. 321.

72    The fullest account of the workings of this cabal is in A. Saint, *Towards a Social Architecture: the role of school building in post war England*, New Haven, CT: Yale University Press, 1987, p. 245.

73    Letter from Percy Johnson-Marshall to Lionel Brett (Lord Esher), 3 January 1959. BAL, BrL Box 4 file 1.

74    Interview with Sir Andrew Derbyshire, 4 January 2005 [T43/3].

75    Austin-Smith et al., *The Architect and his Office*, p. 15.

76    A. Saint, *The Image of the Architect*, New Haven, CT: Yale University Press, 1983, p. 143.

77    Austin-Smith et al., *The Architect and his Office*, p. 14.

78   A few examples from a voluminous literature include: J.H.G. Archer, *Art and Architecture in Victorian Manchester: ten illustrations of patronage and practice*, Manchester: Manchester University Press, 1985; M. Hays, 'Patronage', *Harvard Architecture Review*, 1987, vol. 6, pp. 4–174; P. Bess, 'The architectural community and the polis: thinking about ends, premises, and architectural education', *Humanist Art Review*, July 2001, http://www.humanistart.net/features/bess/bess.htm, accessed 15 January 2006.

79   Interview with Sir Andrew Derbyshire, 16 December 2005 [T40/7].

80   Interview with Sir Andrew Derbyshire, 4 January 2005 [T43/7]. Derbyshire alluded to the fact that when the Central Lancashire New Town was in the offing, James Jones, the permanent secretary at the Ministry of Town and Country Planning, approached RMJM because he admired the practice's work on York University:

> So we brought together people in the office and he and Jimmy James spent a day with us having a seminar about New Town planning. As a result of that, he decided to appoint us. In those days, you did not have to go through a competition or anything like that.

81   See, respectively, interview between Sir Denys Lasdun and Jill Lever, 12 November 1996. NSA, tape F5348, side B; and S. Menin and S. Kite, *An Architecture of Invitation: Colin St John Wilson*, Aldershot: Ashgate, 2005, p. 64.

82   The allocation of work and contracts was affected by the strength of the building workers' union. See J.R. Short, *Housing in Britain: the postwar experience*, London: Methuen, 1982, p. 111.

83   Interview with Harry Teggin, 21 May 2003 [T23/5].

84   Interview between Sir Hubert Bennett and Louise Brodie, 18 February 1999. NSA, tape F6937, side A.

85   Interview between Peter Smithson and Louise Brodie, 17 September 1997. NSA, tape F5954, side A.

86   Interview with James Dunnett, 17 December 2004 [T41/1].

87   Interview with Jacob Blacker, 10 May 2005 [T49/5–6].

88   Interview with James Dunnett, 17 December 2004 [T41/6].

89   Ibid., [T41/7].

90   Interview with Anthony Blee, 10 December 2004 [T39/9].

91   Interview with Frank Woods, 18 November 2004 [T31/7].

92   Association of Consultant Architects, *Patronage*, London: Association of Consultant Architects, n.d.

## 4  Professions

1   R. Norman Shaw, 'The fallacy that the architect who makes design his first consideration, must be impractical', in R. Norman Shaw and T.G. Jackson (eds) *Architecture: A Profession or an Art? Thirteen short essays on the qualifications and training of architects*, London: John Murray, 1892, p. 13.

2   S. Alderson, *Britain in the Sixties: housing*, Harmondsworth: Penguin, 1962, p. 27.

3   See O. Arup, 'Architects, engineers and builders', *Royal Society of Arts Journal*, June 1970, pp. 390–401; K. Harries, *The Ethical Function of Architecture*, Cambridge, MA: MIT Press, 1997.

4   N. Pevsner, *An Outline of European Architecture*, third edition, Harmondsworth: Penguin, 1949, p. 19.

5   C. Norberg-Schulz, *Intentions in Architecture*, London: George Allen and Unwin, 1961, p. 17.

6   See e.g. A.J. Willis and W.N.B. George, *The Architect in Practice*, London: Crosby Lockwood, 1952, p. 1.

7   Ibid., p. 234.

8   A. Powers, 'John Summerson and modernism', in L. Campbell (ed.) *Twentieth-Century Architecture and its Histories*, Otley: Society of Architectural Historians of Great Britain, 2000, p. 170. See also P. Hodgkinson, 'Informing forms: continuity and innovation', in P. Carolin and T. Dannatt (eds) *Architecture, Education and Research: the work of Leslie Martin, papers and selected articles*, London: Academy Editions, 1996, p. 53.

9   Quoted in Anon, 'A steady process of change', *Interbuild*, 1963, vol. 1, p. 2.

10   B. Finnimore, *Houses from the Factory: system building and the Welfare State*, London: Rivers Oram Press, 1989, p. 4.

11    R. Bender, *A Crack in the Rear-View Mirror: a view of industrialised building*, New York: Van Nostrand Reinhold, 1973, p. 63.

12    K. Wachsmann, 'On building in our time', in J. Ockman (ed.) *Architecture Culture 1943–1968*, New York: Rizzoli, 1993, p. 267.

13    Interview with Professor Colin St. John Wilson, 17 February 2005 [T46/7].

14    Interview with Sir Andrew Derbyshire, 16 December 2004 [T40/3, 8].

15    A. McNab, 'Industrialisation in building: an introduction to a series', *Official Architecture and Planning*, 1964, vol. 27, p. 73.

16    Interview with Sir Andrew Derbyshire, 16 December 2004 [T40/3, 8].

17    Ibid.

18    M. Glendinning and S. Muthesius, *Tower Block: modern public housing in England, Scotland, Wales and Northern Ireland*, New Haven, CT: Yale University Press, 1994, p. 184.

19    A. Derbyshire, 'Review: the postwar university, Utopianist campus and college', *Architectural Review*, 2001, vol. 220, pp. 94–5.

20    See e.g. Ministry of Health, *Standardisation and New Methods of Construction Committee: report on the first year's work of the Committee*, London: HMSO, 1920; J.H. Bateman, *Introduction to Highway Engineering: a textbook for students of Civil Engineering*, fourth edition, New York: Wiley, 1942; British Road Federation, *Urban Motorways*, London: British Road Federation, 1957; F.M. Lea, *Science and Building: a history of the Building Research Station*, London: Building Research Station, 1971.

21    Institution of Municipal Engineers, 'A National Building Agency: observations on the White Paper presented to Parliament in December 1963', The National Archives (TNA), WORK 45/340.

22    For a commentary stressing the supposedly comfortable alliance of architecture and engineering for the good of society, see W.H.G. Armytage, *A Social History of Engineering*, London: Faber & Faber, 1961.

23    B.H. Fisher, 'Design for production', in *Industrialised Building and the Structural Engineer: a symposium organised by the Institution of Structural Engineers and held in London on 17–19 May 1966*, London: Institution of Structural Engineers, 1967, p. 21.

24    Interview between George Bowie and Miles Glendinning, 3 November 1987.

25    See P. Dunleavy, *The Politics of Mass Housing in Britain, 1945–1975: a study of corporate power and professional influence in the Welfare State*, Oxford: Clarendon Press, 1981, p. 136.

26    Royal Institute of British Architects, *The Industrialisation of Building*, London: RIBA, 1965, p. 32.

27    Ibid., p. 31.

28    Glendinning and Muthesius, *Tower Block*, p. 184.

29    J.G. Watson, *The Civils: the story of the Institution of Civil Engineers*, London: Thomas Telford, 1988, p. 86.

30    J.B.F. Earle, *Black Top: the history of the British flexible road industry*, London: Basil Blackwell, 1974, p. 23.

31    C.D. Buchanan, 'Comprehensive redevelopment: the opportunity for traffic', in T.E.H. Williams (ed.) *Urban Survival and Traffic*, London: E. & F.N. Spon, 1962, p. 2.

32    Ibid.

33    M. Laffin, *Professionalism and Policy: the role of the professions in the central–local government relationship*, Aldershot: Gower, 1986, p. 62.

34    S.V. Ward, *Planning and Urban Change*, second edition, London: Sage, 2004, p. 30.

35    Anon, 'Suggestions to promoters of town planning schemes', *Royal Institute of British Architects' Journal*, third series, 1911, vol. 18, p. 668.

36    G.E. Cherry, *The Evolution of British Town Planning*, London: Leonard Hill, 1974, p. 45.

37    See e.g. A.D. Greatorex, 'Address by the President', in T. Cole (ed.) *Housing and Town Planning Conference*, London: E & F.N. Spon, 1911, p. 3.

38    N. Taylor, 'Anglo-American town planning theory since 1945: three significant developments but no paradigm shifts', *Planning Perspectives*, 1999, vol. 14, p. 330.

39    Royal Institute of British Architects, *Report of the Special Committee on Architectural Education*, London: RIBA, 1946, p. 9.

40    Interview with Peter Moro, 15 December 1986 [T10/3].

41    Editor, 'Interview of the month: Sir William Holford', *Official Architecture and Planning*, 1962, vol. 25, p. 27.

42   S.V. Ward, *Planning and Urban Change*, London: Paul Chapman, 1994, p. 111.

43   The Town Planning Institute defined associate members as 'members of professions who had achieved an approved standard of proficiency in town planning'. Information from Cherry, *The Evolution of British Town Planning*, pp. 59 and 210; see also Taylor, 'Anglo-American town planning theory since 1945', p. 331.

44   Interview with Jack Bonnington, 20 December 2004 [T42/2].

45   Interview with H.T. Cadbury-Brown, 15 December 1987 [T2/5–6].

46   M. Crinson and J. Lubbock, *Architecture – Art or Profession? Three hundred years of architectural education in Britain*, Manchester: Manchester University Press, 1994, p. 4.

47   Dunleavy, *The Politics of Mass Housing in Britain*, p. 12.

48   These figures actually overestimate the number of architects, since a number of chief officers with architectural qualifications also had qualifications in engineering and primarily practised as the latter. Statistics from A. Goss, *The Architect and Town Planning*, London: Royal Institute of British Architects, 1965, p. 26.

49   Ibid. The raw figures of 33 out of 181 reflect double counting of chief officers with multiple qualifications (there were only 109 authorities listed as 'towns').

50   Ibid., p. 23.

51   Astragal, 'Oh Henry!', *Architects' Journal*, 1960, vol. 131, p. 566 (original emphasis).

52   L. Esher, 'Foreword', in Goss, *The Architect and Town Planning*, p. 5.

53   Goss, *The Architect and Town Planning*, p. 64.

54   Ibid.

55   Interview with Percy Johnson-Marshall, 18 December 1986 [T7/17].

56   Ibid.

57   Interview with Professor Arthur Ling, 30 January 1987 [T8/11].

58   P.N. Malpass, 'Professionalism and the role of architects in local authority housing', *Royal Institute of British Architects' Journal*, 1975, vol. 82, pp. 6–29.

59   Anon, 'Newcastle: City Planning Officer', *Architects' Journal*, 1960, vol. 131, p. 4.

60   J. Gower Davies, *The Evangelistic Bureaucrat: a study of a planning exercise in Newcastle upon Tyne*, London: Tavistock, 1972, p. 1.

61   Astragal, 'Notes and topics', *Architects' Journal*, 1960, vol. 131, p. 4.

62   This began with the 1961 *Plan for the Centre of Newcastle*: Planning Department, City of Newcastle upon Tyne, *Plan for the Centre of Newcastle*, Newcastle: City of Newcastle upon Tyne, 1961.

63   For more on this subject, see W. Burns, *New Towns for Old*, London: Leonard Hill, 1963; D. Byrne, 'The reconstruction of Newcastle: planning since 1945', in R. Colls and B. Lancaster (eds) *Newcastle upon Tyne: a modern history*, Chichester: Phillimore, 2001, pp. 341–60; T. Faulkner, 'Architecture in Newcastle', in R. Colls and B. Lancaster (eds) *Newcastle upon Tyne: a modern history*, Chichester: Phillimore, 2001, pp. 213–44.

64   Malpass, 'Professionalism and the role of architects in local authority housing', p. 16.

65   Ibid., p. 18.

66   P. Jones, 'Historical continuity and post-1945 urban redevelopment: the example of Lee Bank, Birmingham, UK', *Planning Perspectives*, 2004, vol. 19, p. 370.

67   J.L. Macmorran, *Municipal Public Works and Planning in Birmingham 1852–1972: a record of the administration and achievements of the Public Works Committee and Department of the Borough and City of Birmingham*, Birmingham: Public Works Committee, 1973, p. 156.

68   Interview between A.G. Sheppard Fidler and Miles Glendinning, 28 October 1987.

69   This is contrary to Elizabeth Layton's view that the 'City Architect is responsible for all architectural design' and that there was 'a small but growing Works department mainly for new housing under its own chief officer'. See E. Layton, *Building by Local Authorities: the report of an inquiry by the Royal Institute of Public Administration into the organization of building and maintenance by local authorities in England and Wales*, London: George Allen and Unwin, 1961, p. 119.

70   Interview with Charles Willis, 22 October 2004 [T27/4].

71   Glendinning and Muthesius, *Tower Block*, pp. 166–8.

72   Dunleavy, *The Politics of Mass Housing in Britain*, p. 264.

73   Letter from A.G. Sheppard Fidler to Miles Glendinning, 30 July 1988.

74   Dunleavy, *The Politics of Mass Housing in Britain*, pp. 274–5.

75  This episode is told in detail in A. Sutcliffe and R. Smith, *A History of Birmingham*, vol. 3, *Birmingham, 1939–1970*, Oxford: Oxford University Press, 1974, pp. 437–8. Dunleavy maintains that the reason for Sheppard Fidler's departure was disillusionment at the way in which the corporation marginalised the architects over industrialised building practices: Dunleavy, *The Politics of Mass Housing in Britain*, p. 286.

76  Interview with Sir Andrew Derbyshire, 16 December 2004 [T40/9].

77  H.A. Tripp, *Road Traffic and its Control*, London: Edward Arnold, 1938; H.A. Tripp, *Town Planning and Road Traffic*, London: Edward Arnold, 1942.

78  See J. Lynn, 'Sheffield', in D. Lewis (ed.) 'The Pedestrian in the City', *Architects' Year Book*, 11, London: Elek, 1965, pp. 73–5.

79  Ibid., [T40/12].

80  Interview with Sir Andrew Derbyshire, 16 December 2004 [T40/12].

81  Context and examples can be found in P. Crooke (ed.) 'Sheffield', *Architectural Design*, 1961, vol. 31, pp. 380–415.

82  Derbyshire left in 1960, Womersley in 1964.

83  Interview with Sir Andrew Derbyshire, 16 December 2004 [T40/13].

## 5  Towards renewal

1  D. Williams, 'The Scotland Guide', http://www.scotland-guide.co.uk, accessed 21 October 2005.

2  L.H. Reay, 'Conversation at CIAM 8', in J. Tyrwhitt, J.L. Sert and E.N. Rogers (eds) *The Heart of the City: towards the humanisation of urban life*, London: Lund Humphries, 1952, p. 39.

3  Interview with Peter Carter, 7 April 2005 [T48/9].

4  B.L.C. Johnson and M.J. Wise, 'The Black Country, 1800–1950', in R.H. Kinvig, J.G. Smith and M.J. Wise (eds) *Birmingham and its Regional Setting: a scientific survey*, Birmingham: Local Executive Committee, British Association for the Advancement of Science, 1950, pp. 229–48.

5  W.G. Hoskins, 'Chilterns to Black Country: a portrait', in G. Grigson (ed.) *About Britain*, vol. 5, *Chilterns to Black Country*, London: Collins for the Festival of Britain Office, 1951, p. 27.

6  Anon, 'Pits, pots, progress', *Britain's Shifting Centre: the West Midlands*, *Economist* survey supplement, 2 April 1966, London: The Economist, p. xxi.

7  The number of registered motorcars rose by 450 per cent between 1948 and 1965: figures quoted by J. Armstrong, 'Transport and the urban environment', in M. Daunton (ed.) *The Cambridge Urban History of Britain*, vol. 3, *1840–1950*, Cambridge: Cambridge University Press, 2000, p. 255.

8  C. Pooley and J. Turnbull, 'Commuting, transport and urban form: Manchester and Glasgow in the mid-twentieth century', *Urban History*, 2000, vol. 27, p. 376.

9  Interview between Kenneth Campbell and Miles Glendinning, 28 October 1987.

10  Ibid.

11  J. Sheail, *An Environmental History of Twentieth-Century Britain*, Basingstoke: Palgrave, 2002, pp. 248–50.

12  E. Ashby and M. Anderson, *The Politics of Clean Air*, Oxford: Clarendon Press, 1981, pp. 105–6. See also B. Luckin, 'Pollution in the city', in M. Daunton (ed.) *The Cambridge Urban History of Britain*, vol. 3, *1840–1950*, Cambridge: Cambridge University Press, 2000, pp. 225–6.

13  W.G. Holford, 'Rebuilding at the centre', *Town Planning Review*, 1961, vol. 32, p. 237.

14  This is from the memorandum of an informal meeting on the 1959 Symposium on Urban Renewal, written by George Grenfell-Baines and attended by G. Grenfell-Baines, P. Johnson-Marshall and Lionel Brett. RIBA Paper D.1799/58, SR 11, Crate 333, Percy Johnson-Marshall Collection, University of Edinburgh Library.

15  Interview with Charles Willis, 22 October 2004 [T27/2], who was alluding to the ideas of Patrick Geddes.

16  Ministry of Town and Country Planning, *The Reconstruction of Central Areas*, London: HMSO, 1947. Gordon Stephenson, however, argues that this interpretation is misleading because 'the proposed methodology had to be reduced to simple terms to meet immediate post-war needs when practical, creative planners would be few and far between': G. Stephenson, *On a Human Scale: a life in city design*, South Fremantle, WA: Fremantle Arts Centre Press, 1992, p. 66.

17  N. Tiratsoo, J. Hasegawa, T. Mason and T. Matsumura, *Urban Reconstruction in Britain and Japan, 1945–1955: dreams, plans and realities*, Luton: University of Luton Press, 2002, p. 25.

18  *Rebirth of a City*, 'Look at Life' series, Rank Film Productions, 1956.
19  Quoted in A. Goss, 'Young architects and the public authority', *Official Architecture and Planning*, 1963, vol. 26, p. 36.
20  Ibid.
21  For further information on this matter, see S.V. Ward, *Planning and Urban Change*, second edition, London: Sage, 2004, pp. 130–9.
22  O. Marriott, *The Property Boom*, London: Hamish Hamilton, 1967, pp. 57–65.
23  Anon, 'Swansea: another missed opportunity', *Architects' Journal*, 1959, vol. 129, p. 892.
24  Ibid. With regard to Blomfield, see R.T. Blomfield, *Modernismus*, London: Macmillan, 1934.
25  T.A. Markus, 'Comprehensive development and housing, 1945–75', in P. Reed (ed.) *Glasgow: the forming of the city*, Edinburgh: Edinburgh University Press, 1959, p. 152.
26  R. Bruce, *First Planning Report to the Highways and Planning Committee of the Corporation of Glasgow*, 2 vols, Glasgow: Glasgow Corporation, 1945.
27  P. Abercrombie and R.H. Matthew, *The Clyde Valley Regional Plan, 1946*, Edinburgh: HMSO, 1949. The plan itself was prepared from 1943 onwards and implemented from 1946, but not finally published until 1949. It was one of three regional plans prepared at this time in Scotland.
28  Pooley and Turnbull, 'Commuting, transport and urban form', p. 372; A. Gibb, 'Policy and politics in Scottish housing since 1945', in R. Rodger (ed.) *Scottish Housing in the Twentieth Century*, Leicester: Leicester University Press, 1989, p. 161.
29  Ibid.
30  Both sides presented their arguments in reports published in 1946: the city in the Bruce Report and the Scottish Office in the Clyde Valley Plan. This was also an important factor in the decision-making involved in the designation of Cumbernauld (see Chapter 7).
31  J.B. Singer, 'The Glasgow bourgeoisie', in S. Berry and H. Whyte (eds) *Glasgow Observed*, Edinburgh: John Donald, 1987, p. 236.
32  G.E. Cherry, *Birmingham: a study in geography, history and planning*, Chichester: Wiley, 1994, p. 211.
33  A. Sutcliffe, 'Case studies in modern British planning history: the Birmingham Inner Ring Road', paper presented to the Planning History Group meeting, Birmingham, 18 October 1975.
34  Cherry, *Birmingham*, p. 212.
35  E. Harwood, 'White light/white heat: rebuilding England's provincial towns and cities in the Sixties', *Twentieth Century Architecture*, 2002, vol. 6, p. 62.
36  N. Pevsner and A. Wedgwood, *The Buildings of England: Warwickshire*, Harmondsworth: Penguin, 1966, p. 106.
37  H.J. Manzoni, 'The Inner Ring Road', *Proceedings of the Institution of Civil Engineers*, 1961, vol. 18, p. 267.
38  Marriott, *The Property Boom*, p. 223.
39  See P.E.A. Johnson-Marshall, *Rebuilding Cities*, Edinburgh: Edinburgh University Press, 1966, pp. 177–98.
40  G.E. Cherry and L. Penny, *Holford: a study in architecture, planning and urban design*, London: Mansell, 1986, p. 175.
41  J.H. Forshaw and P. Abercrombie, *County of London Plan*, London: Macmillan, 1943.
42  Johnson-Marshall, *Rebuilding Cities*, p. 209.
43  S. Inwood, *A History of London*, London: Macmillan, 1998, p. 845.
44  Percy Johnson-Marshall Archive, University of Edinburgh, file GB 0237/PJM/LCC/E/5.
45  Interview with Jacob Blacker, 10 May 2005 [T49/5]. See also Chapter 3.
46  Quoted in Marriott, *The Property Boom*, p. 217.
47  H.R. Hitchcock, 'Notes of a traveller: England', *Zodiac*, 1960, vol. 5, p. 23.
48  Ward, *Planning and Urban Change*, second edition, p. 131.
49  Inwood, *A History of London*, p. 842.
50  Interview between Richard Seifert and Louise Brodie, 2 April 1996. NSA, tape F5076, side A.
51  Based on annual figures for permissions presented by Marriott, *The Property Boom*, p. 272.
52  A. Ravetz, *Remaking Cities: contradictions of the recent urban environment*, London: Croom Helm, 1980, p. 54.
53  J.M. Richards, 'Rebuilding the City: the City of London on the brink of disaster', *Architectural Review*, 1954, vol. 115, p. 379.

54  Ibid., p. 380.
55  Not all developers, however, realised this immediately. Richard Seifert, for instance, admitted to having failed to recognise 'the potential of new materials' until tackling Centre Point (which received planning permission in August 1959). Information from interview between Richard Seifert and Louise Brodie, 2 April 1996. NSA, tape F5076, side A.
56  Inwood, *A History of London*, p. 846.
57  Cherry and Penny, *Holford*, p. 175.
58  W.G. Holford, 'Rebuilding at the centre', in Department of Civic Design, University of Liverpool (eds) *Land Use in an Urban Environment: a general view of town and country planning*, Liverpool: Liverpool University Press, 1961, p. 233.
59  For much fuller information about the underlying negotiations, see ibid., pp. 175–7.
60  Ministry of Housing and Local Government, *Piccadilly Circus: Report of the Working Party*, London: HMSO, 1965, p. 17.
61  Correspondent, 'City Centre Properties Ltd', *The Times*, 27 October 1959, p. 19.
62  Cherry and Penny, *Holford*, p. 177.
63  Marriott, *The Property Boom*, p. 143.
64  Minutes of a meeting of the Executive Committee, 7 April 1952. British Architectural Library (BAL), file ArO/1/5/77(i), item 3d.
65  Report of the Executive for the year ending December 1952. BAL, file ArO/1/5/84(i), item 4d.
66  Minutes of the Annual General Meeting, 11 May 1953. BAL, file ArO/1/4/11(i).
67  Minutes of a meeting of the MARS Executive, 17 June 1953. BAL, file ArO/1/5/84, item 3a.
68  J. Tyrwhitt, J.L. Sert and E.N. Rogers (eds) *The Heart of the City: towards the humanisation of urban life*, London: Lund Humphries, 1952. For more on the Hoddesdon Congress, see Gold, *The Experience of Modernism*, pp. 215–19.
69  The term was first used in S. Giedion, 'The need for a new monumentality', in P. Zucher (ed.) *New Architecture and City Planning*, New York: Philosophical Library, 1944, pp. 549–68. For discussion, see Various authors, 'Monumentality and the city', *Harvard Architecture Review*, 1984, vol. 4, special issue (Spring), pp. 6–208.
70  C. Norberg-Schulz, *Intentions in Architecture*, London: George Allen and Unwin, 1961, p. 17.
71  MARS Group, CIAM 10 Sub-Committee, Bulletin 3. BAL, file GolEr/315/2.
72  Interview with Maxwell Fry, 24 November 1986 [T5/12].
73  The full list comprised John Bicknell, Misha Black, H.T. Cadbury Brown, Bertram Carter, Theo Crosby, Trevor Dannatt, Leo de Syllas, Jane Drew, Maxwell Fry, Ernö Goldfinger, Michael Grice, Bill Howell, R.S. Jenkins, Arthur Korn, Denys Lasdun, Ian McCallum, Monica Pidgeon, J.M. Richards, Alison Smithson and Peter Smithson.
74  Astragal, 'Notes and topics', *Architects' Journal*, 1955, vol. 121, p. 871.
75  MARS Group, *Turn Again: an exhibition presented by the MARS Group, Royal Exchange, July 1955*, London: MARS Group, 1955.
76  Ibid.
77  Minutes of the Annual General Meeting, 15 October 1956. BAL, file ArO/1/4/13(ii).
78  D. Lasdun, 'The MARS Group 1953–1957', in T. Dannatt (ed.) *Architects' Year Book 8*, London: Elek, 1957, pp. 57–61.
79  Minutes of the Annual General Meeting, 15 October 1956. BAL, file ArO/1/4/13(ii).
80  Interview with Sir Peter Shepheard, 15 March 1996 [T18/14].
81  Anon, 'Turn Again', *Architectural Design*, 1955, vol. 26.
82  Interview with Trevor Dannatt, 26 February 1996 [T17/3].
83  Our Architectural Correspondent, 'Standard of city rebuilding: architects' protest', *The Times*, 12 July 1955.
84  The group included David Gregory Jones, Ted Hollamby, Dick Toms, Graeme Shankland and Percy Johnson-Marshall.
85  F. Jones and D. Gregory Jones, with R.W. Toms, 'Housing the city dweller', *Keystone*, 1956, vol. 30, n.p.
86  Anon, 'City development: draft statement for the Continuing Committee of the ABT Housing the City Dweller Conference', 57/81/24. Percy Johnson-Marshall Collection (PJMC), Crate 333 SR 12.
87  Anon, 'A Council or Committee for the Promotion of City Redevelopment', unpublished typescript. PJMC, Crate 333 SR 12.

88  See items of correspondence. PJMC, Crate 333 SR 12.

89  Letter from M.C. Solomon to P. Johnson-Marshall, 17 June 1957. PJMC, Crate 333 SR 12.

90  Minutes of the 123rd Meeting of the Housing Centre's General Committee, 12 December 1957. PJMC, Crate 333 SR 12. A fuller version of these discussions is found in J.R. Gold, 'A SPUR to renewal', unpublished typescript, 2006.

91  R. McKown (ed.) *Official Architecture and Planning Year Book 1956*, London: Chantry Publications, 1956, p. 173.

92  Letter from Margaret Solomon to Lionel Brett, 29 November 1957. BAL, file BrL/4/1.

93  This document, dating from before the formal invitation to Brett to convene the group, accompanied a letter from Brett to Judith Ledeboer, 27 November 1957. BAL, file BrL/4/1.

94  Ibid.

95  'Urban renewal: brief report of a meeting held at the Housing Centre on the 4th February, 1958', p. ii. The fourth aim was added at a subsequent meeting: Minutes of Meeting, 1 April 1958. PJMC, Crate 333 SR 12.

96  Ibid., p. i.

97  Letter from George Grenfell-Baines to Lionel Esher, 10 February 1958. BAL, file BrL/4/1.

98  Letter to George Grenfell-Baines, 13 February 1958. BAL, file BrL/4/1.

99  Letter from M.C. Solomon to Percy Johnson-Marshall, 24 February 1958. PJMC, Crate 333 SR 12. This contradicts Lord Esher's recollection that he thought of the name. Interview between Lord Esher and Louise Brodie, July 1997. NSA, FS642, side B.

100  As such, the policy quickly gained a reputation for 'Negro removal' due to its impact on clearing African Americans from integrated areas and relocating them to areas where a high proportion of residents were already black. P. Marcuse, 'Enclaves yes, ghettos no: segregation and the state', in D.P. Varady (ed.) *Desegregating the City: ghettos, enclaves and inequality*, Albany, NY: State University of New York Press, 2005, p. 25.

101  D.M. Muchnick, *Urban Renewal in Liverpool: a study of the politics of redevelopment*, Occasional Papers on Social Administration 33, London: George Bell, 1970, p. 13.

102  Ibid.

103  Minutes of RIBA Town and Country Planning and Housing Committee, 21 July 1958 (D.1745/58). PJMC, Crate 333 SR 11. Minutes, General Committee, SPUR, 17 July 1958. BAL, file BrL/4/1.

104  Minutes, Special Meeting of the General Committee of SPUR, 23 September 1958. Item 24 'Cooperation with the RIBA'. BAL, file BrL/4/1.

105  Letter from Grenfell-Baines to Brett, 7 October 1958. BAL, file BrL/4/1. The other member was Leonard Vincent.

106  Letter from Brett to Solomon, 23 October 1958. BAL, file BrL/4/1.

107  Untitled document, accompanying letter from Brett to Solomon, 23 October 1958. BAL, file BrL/4/1.

108  Untitled draft, sent with letter from Brett to Solomon, 26 September 1958. BAL, file BrL/4/1.

109  This category was a slightly later addition. See Minutes, Fourth Meeting, General Committee, SPUR at Housing Centre, 21 October 1958. BAL, file BrL/4/1.

110  Postcard from Walter Bor to Brett, 14 October 1958. BAL, file BrL/4/1.

111  P. Chamberlin, G. Powell, C, Bon, G. Shankland, D. Gregory Jones and F. Millett, 'The living suburb: a special issue', *Architecture and Building*, 1958, vol. 33, pp. 323–62.

112  Minutes, Third Meeting, General Committee, SPUR, 18 September 1958. PJMC, Crake 333 SR 12.

113  Interview with Frank Woods, 18 November 2004 [T31/5].

114  J.J. Guerin, 'Vällingby', *Architecture and Building*, 1958, vol. 33, p. 444.

115  Minutes, Fifth Meeting, General Committee, 18 November 1958. BAL, file BrL/4/1.

116  'Notes on the exhibition', accompaniment to the Agenda of General Meeting, SPUR, 17 February 1959. BAL, file BrL/4/1.

117  M. MacEwan, 'SPUR: exhibition at RIBA', *Architects' Journal*, 1959, vol. 129, p. 794.

118  'Notes on the exhibition', accompaniment to the Agenda of General Meeting, SPUR, 17 February 1959, p. 2. BAL, file BrL/4/1.

119  Minutes, SPUR General Committee Meeting, 13 January 1959. Item 42, point 1. BAL, file BrL/4/1.

120  Minutes, Ninth Meeting, SPUR General Committee, 18 March 1959. BAL, file BrL/4/1.

121  Letter from Noel Tweddell (Civic Trust), 20 October 1958. BAL, file BrL/4/1.

122 Minutes, Ninth Meeting, SPUR General Committee, 18 March 1959. BAL, file BrL/4/1. For its part, SPUR was happy to accept assistance only 'with drawing and erecting, if the designers felt this would be helpful'.
123 BAL, file BrL/4/1.
124 Letter from Solomon to Brett, 1 May 1959. BAL, file BrL/4/1.
125 MacEwan, 'SPUR: exhibition at RIBA', p. 795.
126 Royal Institute of British Architects, *The Living Town*, London: RIBA, 1959.
127 Letter from Tweddell to Brett, 23 May 1959. BAL, file BrL/4/1.
128 Letter from Brett to Solomon, 11 June 1959. BAL, file BrL/4/1.
129 See *Architects' Journal*, 129, pp. 794–6.
130 Draft letter (undated) to SPUR General Meeting, 7 July 1959. BAL, file BrL/4/1.
131 Reprinted in full as Appendix C in L. Esher, *A Broken Wave: the rebuilding of England, 1940–1980*, London: Allen Lane, 1981, pp. 305–12.
132 T. Knight, B. Falk, R. Harbour and R. Vigars, *Let our Cities Live*, London: Bow Group, 1961.
133 Esher, *A Broken Wave*, p. 305.
134 Ibid., p. 307.
135 Ibid.

## 6 Heart and soul

1 Ministry of Housing and Local Government and Ministry of Transport, *Town Centres: approach to renewal*, London: HMSO, 1962, p. 2.
2 Ibid., p. 3.
3 Ibid.
4 S.V. Ward, *Planning and Urban Change*, second edition, London: Sage, 2004, p. 133.
5 J. Hughes, '1961', in L. Campbell (ed.) *Twentieth-Century Architecture and its Histories*, Otley: Society of Architectural Historians of Great Britain, 2000, p. 75.
6 Quoted in B.C. Waterhouse, '"Through the operations of private enterprise": the Prudential Insurance Company's corporate renewal in Boston', graduate paper presented to seminar on 'Building Boston in the 19th and 20th Centuries', Rappaport Institute for Greater Boston, Kennedy School of Government, Harvard University, http://www.ksg.harvard.edu/rappaport/downloads/building_boston/waterhouse_prudential.pdf, accessed 17 January 2006.
7 See e.g. S.B. Warner, *Private City: Philadelphia in three periods of its growth*, Philadelphia, PA: University of Pennsylvania Press, 1968.
8 Anon, 'Building big: Bovis chairman tells architects', *Architects' Journal*, 1961, vol. 133, p. 687.
9 Ministry of Transport, *Traffic in Towns: a study of the long term problems of traffic in urban areas* (Buchanan Report), London: HMSO, 1963.
10 W.G. Bor and G.C.L. Shankland, 'Renaissance of a city: a study in the redevelopment of Liverpool', *Journal of the Town Planning Institute*, 1965, vol. 51, p. 27.
11 Interview with Sir Peter Hall, 30 November 2004 [T34/8].
12 D. Hamer, 'Planning and heritage: towards integration', in R. Freestone (ed.) *Urban Planning in a Changing World*, London: E. & F.N. Spon, 2000, p. 195.
13 C.D. Buchanan, 'Architects are town-rebuilders', *Architects' Journal*, 1961, vol. 133, pp. 80–2.
14 Browne, a skilled illustrator, had a well-established interest in multilevel circulation systems: see e.g. K. Browne, 'A question of detail', *Architects' Journal*, 1960, vol. 131, pp. 858–61.
15 J. Armstrong, 'Transport and the urban environment', in M. Daunton (ed.) *The Cambridge Urban History of Britain*, vol. 3, *1840–1950*, Cambridge: Cambridge University Press, 2000, p. 257.
16 Anon, 'The Leicester Traffic Plan', *Official Architecture and Planning*, 1965, vol. 28, p. 67.
17 R. Smith, 'Great Britain', in M. Wynn (ed.) *Housing in Europe*, London: Croom Helm, 1984, p. 95.
18 M.J. Miller, *The Representation of Place: urban planning and protest in France and Great Britain, 1950–1980*, Aldershot: Ashgate, 2003, p. 198.
19 Interview with Paul Barker, 5 January 2005 [T44/4].
20 N. Tiratsoo, J. Hasegawa, T. Mason and T. Matsumura, *Urban Reconstruction in Britain and Japan, 1945–1955: dreams, plans and realities*, Luton: University of Luton Press, 2002, pp. 39–47.
21 Ibid., p. 45.
22 Correspondent, '£5M new look for Portsmouth', *The Times*, 12 April 1961, p. 5.

23  Minutes, item 1, 'Redevelopment of Guildhall Square and surrounding area', Portsmouth City Council, 4 September 1963. British Architectural Library (BAL), file BrL/39/3.

24  Portsmouth City Council, 'The new city centre, Portsmouth: additional information', n.d. BAL, file BrL/40/2.

25  Interview between Lionel Esher and Louise Brodie, July 1997. NSA, tape FS643, side A.

26  Interview with Harry Teggin, 11 October 2004 [T26/1].

27  Correspondent, 'Continental touch for Portsmouth', *The Times*, 10 April 1964, p. 10.

28  Minutes, Guildhall Area Redevelopment, Portsmouth City Council, 14 May 1964. BAL, file BrL/39/3.

29  Minutes, Guildhall Area Redevelopment (Action Group), Portsmouth City Council, 25 October 1967. BAL, file BrL/39/3.

30  L. Esher, *City of Portsmouth: the new city centre*, Report 2, London: Brett and Pollen Architects, 1970, p. 14.

31  Ibid., p. 17.

32  Interview between Lionel Esher and Louise Brodie, July 1997. NSA, tape FS643, side A.

33  Portsmouth City Council, 'The new city centre, Portsmouth: additional information', n.d. BAL, file BrL/40/2.

34  M. Webb, *Architecture in Britain Today*, Feltham, Middlesex: Country Life Books, 1969, p. 148.

35  Information from Portsmouth Corporation, 'The Tricorn Centre: information sheet', http://www. portsmouth.gov.uk/media/Tricorn.pdf, accessed 8 November 2005.

36  Report from the *Sunday Times*, quoted by Owen Luder, 'The Tricorn – the architect's view', *The Portsmouth Society – News*, http://www.portsmouthsociety.org.uk/news2004/TricornFeb04b.htm, accessed 9 November 2005.

37  Interview with Rodney Gordon, 11 November 2004 [T30/16].

38  Ibid.

39  Webb, *Architecture in Britain Today*, p. 150.

40  W. Burns, *New Towns for Old: the technique of urban renewal*, London: Leonard Hill, 1963, p. xi.

41  Planning Department, City of Newcastle upon Tyne, *Plan for the Centre of Newcastle*, Newcastle: City of Newcastle upon Tyne, 1961.

42  Quoted in T.D. Smith, 'Newcastle's regional initiative', *Official Architecture and Planning*, 1965, vol. 28, p. 922.

43  Burns, *New Towns for Old*, p. 211.

44  D. Byrne, 'The reconstruction of Newcastle: planning since 1945', in R. Colls and B. Lancaster (eds) *Newcastle upon Tyne: a modern history*, Chichester: Phillimore, 2001, p. 345.

45  Ibid.

46  T. Faulkner, 'Architecture in Newcastle', in R. Colls and B. Lancaster (eds) *Newcastle upon Tyne: a modern history*, Chichester: Phillimore, 2001, pp. 233, 238.

47  Ibid., p. 242.

48  C. McKean and J.M. McKean, 'Motorway city', *Architects' Journal*, 1971, vol. 154, pp. 902–4.

49  B. Paterson, *Dancing at the Wrecker's Ball*, BBC Radio 4, 12 June 2006.

50  A. Gibb, *The Development of Public Sector Housing in Glasgow*, Discussion Paper 6, Centre for Urban and Regional Research, University of Glasgow, 1982, p. 22.

51  M. Pacione, *Glasgow: the socio-spatial development of the city*, Chichester: Wiley, 1995, p. 165.

52  Gibb, *The Development of Public Sector Housing in Glasgow*, p. 25.

53  A. Gibb, *Glasgow: the making of a city*, London: Croom Helm, 1983, p. 180.

54  G. Stell, J. Shaw and S. Storrier (eds) *Scottish Life and Society: a compendium of Scottish ethnology*, vol. 3, *Scotland's Buildings*, East Linton, East Lothian: Tuckwell Press, 2003, p. 670.

55  L. Esher, *Conservation in Glasgow: a preliminary report*, Glasgow: Glasgow Corporation, 1971, p. 3.

56  D.T. Martin, 'Conservation and restoration', in P. Reed (ed.) *Glasgow: the forming of the city*, Edinburgh: Edinburgh University Press, 1999, pp. 166–86.

57  Interview with Paul Barker, 5 January 2005 [T44/1].

58  G.E. Cherry, *Birmingham: a study in geography, history and planning*, Chichester: Wiley, 1994, p. 213.

59  Anon, 'Birmingham Bull Ring', *Architectural Design*, 1965, vol. 35, p. 424.

60  Anon, 'Birmingham's Bull Ring Centre', *Architects' Journal*, 1960, vol. 131, p. 187.

61  The editors of the *Architects' Journal* expressed their anger at a situation in which because negotiations with the original developers broke down, 'the Corporation has, in effect, had the

services of a planning and architectural consultant free of charge, and all the competitors were able to build on his work and to develop or plagiarise his ideas.' See Editors, 'The dangers of the secret competition', *Architects' Journal*, 1960, vol. 131, p. 189.

62 Anon, 'The Bull Ring Centre, Birmingham', *Official Architecture and Planning*, 1964, vol. 27, p. 811.

63 T.B., 'Bull Ring: Birmingham's new shopping centre', *Architects' Journal*, 1961, vol. 133, p. 725.

64 M.B. Stedman, 'Birmingham builds a model city', *Geographical Magazine*, 1968, vol. 40, p. 1383; quoted in D. Parker and P. Long, '"The mistakes of the past": visual narratives of urban decline and regeneration', *Visual Culture in Britain*, 2004, vol. 5, pp. 42–3.

65 Cherry, *Birmingham*, p. 215.

66 Parker and Long, '"The mistakes of the past"'.

67 A. Higgott, 'Birmingham: building the modern city', in T. Deckker (ed.) *The Modern City Revisited*, London: Routledge, 2000, p. 158.

68 Will Alsop, from an interview quoted by L. Kennedy, 'Introduction: the creative destruction of Birmingham', in L. Kennedy (ed.) *Remaking Birmingham: the visual culture of urban regeneration*, London: Routledge, 2004, p. 1.

69 F. Price, *The New Birmingham*, Birmingham: The Birmingham Mail and the Public Works Committee, Birmingham Corporation, n.d.; see also M.B. Stedman and P.A.Wood, 'Urban renewal in Birmingham: an interim report', *Geography*, 1965, vol. 50, pp. 1–17.

70 See e.g. G. Moorhouse, *Britain in the Sixties: the other England*, Harmondsworth: Penguin, 1964, p. 98; D. Winder, 'British city tackles rebuilding tasks', *Christian Science Monitor*, 12 April 1968.

71 K. Lynch, *Image of the City*, Cambridge, MA: MIT Press, 1960.

72 B. Goodey, A. Duffett, J.R. Gold and D. Spencer, *The City Scene: an exploration into the image of central Birmingham held by area residents*, Research Memorandum 10, Centre for Urban and Regional Studies, University of Birmingham, 1972.

73 E. Harwood, 'White light/white heat: rebuilding England's provincial towns and cities in the Sixties', *Twentieth Century Architecture*, 2002, vol. 6, p. 66.

74 Interview with Peter Winchester, 23 November 2004 [T33/11–12].

75 P. Winchester, 'Nottingham Centre', in J. Donat (ed.) *World Architecture*, vol. 2, London: Studio Vista, 1965, p. 65.

76 Ibid., pp. 65–6.

77 S. Kadleigh, assisted by P. Horsbrugh, *High Paddington: a town for 8000 people*, London: The Architect and Building News, 1952.

78 Interview with Peter Winchester, 23 November 2004 [T33/12].

79 Winchester, 'Nottingham Centre', p. 67.

80 Interview between Walter Bor and Louise Brodie, 6 April 1997. NSA, tape F5630, side B.

81 City of Liverpool, *Interim Planning Policy Statement*, Liverpool: City Planning Department, Liverpool, 1965.

82 Interview between F.J.C. Amos and Miles Glendinning, 29 October 1987.

83 In this instance, the City Architect and Director of Housing, Ronald Bradbury, held the role of Chief Planning Officer.

84 Interview between Walter Bor and Louise Brodie, 6 April 1997. NSA, tape F5629, side B.

85 Anon, 'Central redevelopment at Liverpool', *Official Architecture and Planning*, 1962, vol. 25, pp. 232–3.

86 City Centre Planning Group, *Liverpool City Centre Plan*, Liverpool: City and County Borough of Liverpool, 1965.

87 J. Tetlow and A. Goss, *Homes, Towns and Traffic*, London: Faber & Faber, 1965, p. 209.

88 R. Pollard and N. Pevsner, *Lancashire: Liverpool and the Southwest*, New Haven, CT: Yale University Press, 2006, p. 105.

89 Anon, 'Liverpool City Centre Plan', *Official Architecture and Planning*, 1966, vol. 29, p. 109.

90 Rebroadcast in *High Society*, BBC Radio 4 'Archive Hour', 29 April 2006.

91 Pollard and Pevsner, *Lancashire*, p. 105.

92 City Centre Planning Group, *Liverpool City Centre Plan*, 1965, p. 69.

93 Interview with Colin St. John Wilson, 5 January 2005 [T44/4]. Additional detail on the other practices involved in tendering comes from S. Menin and S. Kite, *An Architecture of Invitation: Colin St John Wilson*, Aldershot: Ashgate, 2005, p. 133.

**Notes and references**

94  City Centre Planning Group, *Liverpool City Centre Plan*, 1965, p. 128.

95  The plans appeared in the *Architectural Design*, for instance, in the same month as the main pavilions for Expo '67, Frederick Gibberd and Partners' Metropolitan Cathedral of Christ the King in Liverpool, a study for the British Library by Martin and Wilson, and university buildings for Liverpool and Leicester by Denys Lasdun.

96  Along with the work of John Portman in the USA, although neither Wilson nor Portman invented this form of building, which had echoes of the Crystal Palace and arcades from Victorian cities. This point is amplified by Menin and Kite, *An Architecture of Invitation*, p. 137.

97  Anon, 'Civic and Social Centre, Liverpool: Colin St. John Wilson', *Architectural Design*, 1967, vol. 37, pp. 265–9.

98  Interview with Colin St. John Wilson, 5 January 2005 [T44/16].

99  Ibid.

100 Menin and Kite, *An Architecture of Invitation*, p. 138.

101 B. Cherry and N. Pevsner, *The Buildings of England: London 2: South*, Harmondsworth: Penguin, 1983, p. 217.

102 Harwood, 'White light/white heat', p. 61.

103 Cherry and Pevsner, *London 2: South*, p. 217.

104 J.S. Cockburn and T.F.T. Baker, 'Hillingdon, including Uxbridge: introduction', in *A History of the County of Middlesex*, vol. 4, *Harmondsworth, Hayes, Norwood with Southall, Hillingdon with Uxbridge, Ickenham, Northolt, Perivale, Ruislip, Edgware, Harrow with Pinner*, London: Boydell & Brewster, 1971, pp. 55–69.

105 M. Hebbert, *London: more by fortune than design*, Chichester: Wiley, 1998, p. 80.

106 Cockburn and Baker, 'Hillingdon', pp. 55–69.

107 Anon, 'Civic Centre', *Architecture and Building*, 1958, vol. 33, pp. 165–71.

108 B. Cherry and N. Pevsner, *London 4: London*, New Haven, CT: Yale University Press, 2002, p. 594.

109 Anon, 'Nothing to fear from "New Town" plan', *Ilford Recorder*, 28 June 1962, p. 24.

110 Anon, 'Civic Centre agreed on – so far', *Ilford Recorder*, 1 March 1962, p. 48.

111 Anon, 'New centre at Ilford', *Architects' Journal*, 1962, vol. 135, p. 774.

112 R. Miller, 'The plan for new town centre', *Ilford Recorder*, 8 February 1962, pp. 1, 48.

113 G. Wood, 'Secret "marriage" will create a super-town', *Ilford Recorder*, 22 February 1962, p. 27; Anon, 'Towns' merger could alter civic centre plan', *Ilford Recorder*, 5 April 1962, p. 3.

114 Anon, '3-year Civic Centre pause', *Ilford Recorder*, 29 March 1962, p. 1.

115 R. Miller, 'Town plan for year 2062', *Ilford Recorder*, 28 June 1962, p. 1.

116 Anon, 'Nothing to fear from "New Town" plan, *Ilford Recorder*, 28 June 1962, p. 24.

117 Anon, 'Towns' merger could alter civic centre plan', *Ilford Recorder*, 5 April 1962, p. 3.

118 Anon, 'Banners and cheers in Civic Centre row', *Ilford Recorder*, 3 May 1962, p. 10.

119 C. Ward, 'Anarchy and architecture', in J. Hughes and S. Sadler (eds) *Non-Plan: essays on freedom participation and change in modern architecture and urbanism*, Oxford: Architectural Press, 2000, p. 48.

120 B. Franks, 'New right/new left: an alternative experiment in freedom', in J. Hughes and S. Sadler (eds) *Non-Plan: essays on freedom participation and change in modern architecture and urbanism*, Oxford: Architectural Press, 2000, p. 38.

121 J.H. Forshaw and P. Abercrombie, *County of London Plan*, London: Macmillan, 1943; London County Council, *Administrative County of London Development Plan*, London: LCC, 1951.

122 Interview with Anthony Blee, 10 December 2004 [T39/13].

123 Ibid.

124 L. Esher, *A Broken Wave: the rebuilding of England, 1940–1980*, London: Allen Lane, 1981, p. 119.

125 P.E.A. Johnson-Marshall, *Rebuilding Cities*, Edinburgh: Edinburgh University Press, 1966, p. 184.

126 Interview with Martyn Smith, 19 November 2004 [T32/3].

127 Ibid., p. 185.

128 The National Theatre languished for many years. The project was briefly abandoned in 1961 in favour of replacing Sadler's Wells by a National Opera House on the South Bank, but was reinstated in 1965 after recognition of the unrealistic nature of that plan. See Cherry and Pevsner, *London 2: South*, p. 352.

129 Webb, *Architecture in Britain Today*, pp. 195–205.

130 Ibid., p. 201.

131 P. Moro, 'Queen Elizabeth Hall and Purcell Room appraised', *Architects' Journal*, 1967, vol. 145, pp. 1002–3.

132 Anon, 'Proposed traffic segregation at Holborn-Kingsway Crossing', *Official Architecture and Planning*, 1963, vol. 26, p. 219.

133 L. Martin and C.D. Buchanan, *Whitehall: a plan for the National and Government Centre*, London: HMSO, 1965. For background, see also I. Rice, '"Ziggurats for Bureaucrats": Sir Leslie Martin's Whitehall Plan', *Architectural Research Quarterly*, 2004, vol. 8(3/4), pp. 313–23.

134 G.E. Cherry and L. Penny, *Holford: a study in architecture, planning and urban design*, London: Mansell, 1986, p. 177; Astragal, 'Ripe for a change', *Architects' Journal*, 1961, vol. 133, p. 40.

135 Anon, 'Architects and planners say "Reject the Application"', *Architects' Journal*, 1960, vol. 131 (14 January), p. 45.

136 H.F. Ellis, 'Eros in Wonderland', *Architects' Journal*, 1960, vol. 131, pp. 144–6.

137 Quoted in Ministry of Housing and Local Government, *Piccadilly Circus*, p. 17.

138 See Anon, 'Piccadilly Circus competition', *Architects' Journal*, 1961, vol. 133, p. 255.

139 W.G. Holford, 'Rebuilding at the centre', in Department of Civic Design, University of Liverpool (eds) *Land Use in an Urban Environment: a general view of town and country planning*, Liverpool: Liverpool University Press, 1961, p. 233.

140 Ibid.

141 Editors, 'Piccadilly Circus: the next step', *Architects' Journal*, 1961, vol. 133, p. 235.

142 Cherry and Penny, *Holford*, p. 177.

143 Editorial, 'Piccadilly forever!', *The Times*, 5 August 1966, p. 11.

144 Holford, 'Rebuilding at the centre', p. 233.

145 'Mansion House project, London, 1962–1975', box C39, Papers of William Graham, Baron Holford of Kemp Town, University of Liverpool.

146 Interview with Peter Carter, 7 April 2005 [T48/17].

147 Ibid.

148 Anon, 'History of the Palumbo tower scheme', *The Times*, 22 May 1985, p. 3.

149 P. Carter, *Mies van der Rohe at Work*, London: Phaidon, 1969, p. 150.

## 7 Second generation

1 G. Copcutt, 'Reflections on Cumbernauld Town Centre', in A. Burton and J. Hartley (eds) *New Towns Record* (NTR) CD-ROM 1, Glasgow: Planning Exchange, 1967.

2 Interview between Lord Esher and Louise Brodie, July 1997. National Sound Archive (NSA), tape FS642, side A.

3 For example, see the cross-cultural analyses found in G.H. Oglesby and L.I. Hughes, *Highway Engineering*, second edition, New York: Wiley, 1963; P. Ritter, *Planning for Man and Motor*, Oxford: Pergamon, 1968.

4 W. Houghton-Evans, *Planning Cities: legacy and portent*, London: Lawrence & Wishart, 1975, p. 106.

5 *Cumbernauld: Town for Tomorrow*, dir. R. Crichton, Edinburgh Films Production for Films of Scotland/Cumbernauld Development Corporation, 1970.

6 Originally from an article by P. Hall, 'The pattern of cities to come', *New Society*, 10 March; reprinted in P. Barker (ed.) *One for Sorrow, Two for Joy*, London: George Allen and Unwin, 1972, p. 187.

7 This section draws on J.R. Gold, 'The making of a megastructure: architectural modernism, town planning and Cumbernauld's central area, 1955–75', *Planning Perspectives*, 2006, vol. 21, pp. 109–31. I am grateful to the editor for allowing me to use it here.

8 P. Abercrombie and R.H. Matthew, *The Clyde Valley Regional Plan, 1946*, Edinburgh: HMSO (implemented in 1946, but not formally published until 1949).

9 Ibid., Chapter 4, quoted in NTR CD-ROM 1; J.B. Cullingworth, *Environmental Planning*, vol. 3, *New Towns Policy*, London: HMSO, 1979, pp. 33, 39.

10 Information from an unpublished aide-memoire written by Alec Kerr, December 2004.

11 Cullingworth, *New Towns Policy*, p. 89. McNeil's tenure as Secretary of State for Scotland, however, was only between February and October 1951.

12 Cullingworth, *New Towns Policy*, pp. 116–63.

13 Sir Robert Grieve (in conversation with Kirsteen Borland), 'The Clyde Valley Plan and its legacy'. Unpublished transcript of Royal Fine Arts Commission for Scotland (RFACS) seminar, Edinburgh, 1994.

**Notes and references**

14 Interview with Alec Kerr, 2 December 2004.

15 Interview with Dr Derek Lyddon, 3 December 2004.

16 R. Grieve, 'The region', in R. Grieve and D.J. Robertson, *The City and the Region*, Occasional Papers 2, University of Glasgow Social and Economic Studies, Edinburgh: Oliver & Boyd, 1964, p. 26.

17 M. Glendinning and D. Page, *Clone City: crisis and renewal in contemporary Scottish architecture*, Edinburgh: Polygon, 1999, p. 180.

18 H. Wilson, *Cumbernauld New Town: preliminary planning proposals*, Cumbernauld: CNTDC. See also Houghton-Evans, *Planning Cities*, 1958, p. 103.

19 CNTDC, *Cumbernauld Technical Brochure*, n.d.; cited in J. Johnson and K. Johnson, 'Cumbernauld revisited', *Architects' Journal*, 1977, vol. 166, p. 639.

20 Interview with Sir Robert (Bob) Grieve by Dr Derek Lyddon, December 1994, NTR CD-ROM 1.

21 F.J. Osborn and A. Whittick, *New Towns: their origins, achievements and progress*, third edition, London: Leonard Hill, 1977, p. 419.

22 Anon, 'Cumbernauld New Town: preliminary planning proposals', *Architects' Journal*, 1958, vol. 127, pp. 858–9.

23 The information is from an unpublished aide-memoire written by Alec Kerr, December 2004.

24 CNTDC, *Preliminary Planning Proposals*, Cumbernauld: CNTDC, 1958.

25 K. Young and P. Garside, *Metropolitan London: politics and urban change, 1837–1981*, London: Edward Arnold, 1982, pp. 289–91 (original emphasis).

26 Interview between Oliver Cox and Neil Bingham, 1 March 2000. NSA, tape F15579, side A.

27 Interview with Oliver Cox, 2 November 2004 [T29/6].

28 Interview between Oliver Cox and Neil Bingham, 1 March 2000. NSA, tape F15579, side A.

29 London County Council, *The Planning of a New Town: design based on a study for a New Town of 100,000 at Hook, Hampshire*, London: LCC, 1961.

30 Quoted in Anon, 'Hook New Town', *Architects' Journal*, 1961, vol. 133, p. 168.

31 E. Dennington, 'Introduction', in London County Council, *The Planning of a New Town: design based on a study for a New Town of 100,000 at Hook, Hampshire*, London: LCC, 1961, p. 10.

32 Ibid.

33 Ibid., p. 53.

34 Ibid.

35 Interview with Oliver Cox, 2 November 2004 [T29/6].

36 London County Council, *The Planning of a New Town*, p. 29.

37 Interview with Oliver Cox, 2 November 2004 [T29/6].

38 F. Schaffer, *The New Town Story*, London: MacGibbon & Kee, 1970, p. 64.

39 Osborn and Whittick, *New Towns*, p. 159.

40 Ibid., pp. 398–400, 411–12.

41 P. Hall. and C. Ward, *Sociable Cities: the legacy of Ebenezer Howard*, London: Wiley, 1988, p. 56.

42 Initially it simply comprised Copcutt, Alec Kerr and Ronald Simpson.

43 It may be speculated that Edinburgh, especially the Old Town, supplied exemplars of how to fit buildings to awkward topography. Interview with Alec Kerr, 2 December 2004.

44 Anon, 'Garage at Loughborough: Copcutt, Hancock and Hawkes', *Zodiac*, 1958, vol. 1, pp. 169–72. Maxwell Fry, in particular, commented how the work of Copcutt's practice and that of Chamberlin, Powell and Bon, with their Cooper Taber factory at Witham, gave a 'rather clear idea about some trends of contemporary architecture in Great Britain'. See E.M. Fry, 'Factory at Hemel Hempstead', *Zodiac*, 1958, vol. 1, p. 182.

45 Anon, 'Garage at Loughborough, Leicestershire', *Architectural Design*, 1957, vol. 27, pp. 247–8.

46 Copcutt seems to dispute this and stated that the reason that he received this portfolio rather than Derek Lyddon was by tossing a coin. See G. Copcutt, 'Reflections on Cumbernauld Town Centre', in A. Burton and J. Hartley, *NTR*, CD-ROM 1, 1997. Derek Lyddon, however, has no recollection of this and suggests it was highly unlikely: interview with Dr Derek Lyddon, 3 December 2004.

47 Ibid., p. 2.

48 Johnson and Johnson, 'Cumbernauld revisited', p. 639.

49 It is impossible to go into the detail of these reports here. Material relating to this subject here and in the ensuing paragraph come from the manuscript draft of Chapter 6 of R. Hardy (ed.) 'Building a New Town', an unpublished edited collection of essays compiled in 1963–4. The chapter bears the initials of Hugh Wilson.

50  Interview with Sir Andrew Derbyshire, 16 December 2004. A profile of the Castle Market development can be found in P. Crooke (ed.) 'Sheffield', *Architectural Design*, 1961, vol. 31, pp. 405–11.

51  Ibid., p. 4 (emphasis added).

52  CNTDC, *Cumbernauld Town Centre: preliminary report*, Cumbernauld: CNTDC, 1960, p. 3.

53  The information is from an unpublished handwritten note by Alec Kerr, December 2004.

54  Ibid.

55  An example is shown in G. Copcutt, 'Cumbernauld New Town Central Area', *Architectural Design*, 1963, vol. 33, p. 210. A description is found in Hardy, 'Building a New Town', Chapter 6, p. 7.

56  Hardy, 'Building a New Town', Chapter 6. This point also draws on CNTDC, *Planning Proposals – Second Revision: second addendum report to the preliminary planning proposals*, Cumbernauld: CNTDC, 1962.

57  Ministry of Transport, *Traffic in Towns: a study of the long term problems of traffic in urban areas* (Buchanan Report), London: HMSO, 1963, p. 166 (original emphases).

58  Interview with Alec Kerr, 2 December 2004. Each was ruled out on grounds of cost.

59  Peter Youngman, cited in Johnson and Johnson, 'Cumbernauld revisited', p. 640.

60  By Professor A. Hendry (Liverpool University).

61  Anon, 'Cumbernauld New Town Central Area', *Architectural Design*, 1963, vol. 33, p. 229.

62  D. Whitham, 'Coming of age: Scottish new towns in the 21st century', paper presented to the Sixth International DOCOMOMO Conference, Brasilia, Brazil, September 2000.

63  M. Glendinning, 'Cluster Citadel: the architecture and planning of Cumbernauld Town Centre', unpublished manuscript, 1991.

64  Copcutt, 'Cumbernauld New Town Central Area', p. 210.

65  Ibid; see also M. Glendinning, 'Megastructure and genius loci: the architecture of Cumbernauld New Town', in *Proceedings Fourth DOCOMOMO International Conference*, Bratislava: DOCOMOMO, 1996, p. 125.

66  Hardy, 'Building a New Town', p. 10.

67  Interview with Alec Kerr, 2 December 2004.

68  Interview with Dr Derek Lyddon, 3 December 2004 [T36/3].

69  Ibid.

70  CNTDC, *Annual Report, 1963*, *NTR*, CD-ROM 2.

71  Schaffer, *The New Town Story*, p. 124. For a flavour of the international reaction see Anon, 'Une importante experience anglaise: la nouvelle ville de Cumbernauld', *Architecture d'Aujourd'hui*, 1963 (January–February); H. Stumme, 'Das Zentrum der "Neuen Stadt" Cumbernauld in Schottland', *Bauwelt*, 1963, vol. 54, pp. 995ff.

72  Anon, 'Town Centre: Cumbernauld', *Architectural Review*, 1967, vol. 142, pp. 445–51.

73  Our Architectural Correspondent, 'Scope of New Town begins to show', *The Times*, 16 September 1966.

74  Schaffer, *The New Town Story*, pp. 124–5.

75  Osborn and Whittick, *New Towns*, p. 86.

76  Anon, 'Town centre: phase 1', *Architects' Journal*, 1968, vol. 147, p. 304.

77  Ibid., p. 307.

78  P. Nuttgens, 'Criticism: Cumbernauld Town Centre', *Architectural Review*, 1967, vol. 142, p. 444.

79  Glendinning, 'Cluster Citadel'.

80  Ibid.

81  P. Hall, 'Monumental follies', *New Society*, 1968, vol. 12 , pp. 602–3.

82  Information Centre, CNTDC, 'Cumbernauld New Town', Cumbernauld: CNTDC, 1968, p. 8.

83  F. Zweig, *The Cumbernauld Study*, London: Urban Research Bureau, 1970, p. 37.

84  N. Wates, 'Preface', in F. Zweig, *The Cumbernauld Study*, London: Urban Research Bureau, 1970, p. 6.

85  P.R. Banham, P. Barker, C. Price and P. Hall, 'Non-plan: an experiment in freedom', *New Society*, 1969, vol. 13, p. 436.

86  N. Taylor, *The Village in the City*, London: Maurice Temple Smith, 1973, p. 17.

87  Cowan, 'Individual thoughts on Cumbernauld Town Centre'.

88  Ibid.

89  Ibid.

90  Interview with Sir Andrew Derbyshire, 16 December 2004 [T40/3, 5–6].

91  Interview with Alec Kerr, 2 December 2004.

92  This comes from an anecdote told by Alec Kerr (ibid.). He recalled visiting Cumbernauld with Copcutt in the mid-1960s, after he had moved to the Scottish Office and Copcutt had moved to Dublin. Inspecting the scene when Phase 1 was being constructed, Copcutt noted wistfully that 'at least we got a tiny wee bit of it'.

93  A reference back to footnote 1: Copcutt, 'Reflections on Cumbernauld Town Centre'.

## 8  The pursuit of numbers

1   Comments made by Bruce Goff in 1956 and quoted in J. Peter, *The Oral History of Modern Architecture*, New York: Harry N. Abrams, 1994, p. 289.

2   See e.g. Anon, 'West Germany: International Building Exhibition, Berlin 1957', *Architectural Design*, 1957, vol. 27, p. 314.

3   G. Friehe and W. Leopold (eds) *Interbau Industrie Ausstellung Berlin 1957: Amtlicher Messekatalog*, Berlin: Berliner Ausstellungen, 1957.

4   Abner, 'Interbau', *Architect and Building News*, 1957, vol. 212, p. 371.

5   A. Colquhoun, 'On modern and postmodern space', in J. Ockman (ed.) *Architecture, Criticism, Ideology*, Princeton, NJ: Princeton University Press, 1985, p. 113.

6   L. Dawson, 'View: two Germanys, one architecture', *Architectural Review*, 2004, vol. 216, pp. 23–8.

7   Albeit at too low a density for some, who complained about walking excessive distances in order to visit the exhibits.

8   Our Own Correspondent, 'The New Berlin: striking exhibition of modern building', *The Times*, 2 July 1957, p. 8.

9   Interview with John Hummerston, 29 October 2004 [T28/12].

10  See e.g. http://www.galinsky.com/buildings/niemeyerinterbau/index.htm, accessed 13 May 2006.

11  Our Own Correspondent, 'The New Berlin: striking exhibition of modern building', *The Times*, 2 July 1957, p. 8.

12  R. Paine, 'Commentary', *Architect and Building News*, 1957, vol. 212, p. 375.

13  Our Own Correspondent, 'New Hansa Quarter rising from the ashes', *The Times*, 22 July 1957, p. 7.

14  Deutschen Bauzentrum, *Taschenbuch der Internationalen Bauliteratur*, Berlin: Berliner Verleger- und Buchhändlervereinigung, 1957, p. 9.

15  With particular relevance to this study, see P. Dunleavy, *The Politics of Mass Housing in Britain, 1945–1975*, Oxford: Oxford University Press, 1981; M. Glendinning and S. Muthesius, *Tower Block: modern public housing in England, Scotland, Wales and Northern Ireland*, New Haven, CT: Yale University Press, 1994; and A. Power, *Estates on the Edge: social consequences of mass housing in modern Europe*, London: Macmillan, 1997. For more general treatments, see J.B. Cullingworth, *English Housing Trends: a report to the Rowntree Trust Housing Study*, Occasional Papers on Social Administration 13, London: George Bell, 1965; J.R. Short, *Housing in Britain: the postwar experience*, London: Methuen, 1982; and J. Burnett, *A Social History of Housing, 1815–1985*, second edition, London: Methuen, 1986.

16  E. Layton, *Building by Local Authorities: the report of an inquiry by the Royal Institute of Public Administration into the organization of building and maintenance by local authorities in England and Wales*, London: George Allen and Unwin, 1961, p. 16.

17  R.H. Ducland-Williams, *The Politics of Housing in Britain and France*, London: Heinemann, 1978, p. 176.

18  A. Sills, G. Taylor and P. Golding, *Housing and the Inner City*, Leicester: Centre for Mass Communication Research, University of Leicester, 1982, p. 23.

19  Ducland-Williams, *The Politics of Housing in Britain and France*, p. 161.

20  Ibid., p. 176.

21  Central Housing Advisory Committee, *Homes for Today and Tomorrow* (Parker Morris Report), London: HMSO, 1961.

22  R. Crossman, *The Diaries of a Cabinet Minister*, vol. 1, *Minister of Housing 1964–66*, London: Hamish Hamilton and Jonathan Cape, 1975, p. 230.

23  Community Development Project, *Whatever Happened to Council Housing?*, London: CDP Information and Intelligence Unit, 1976, p. 25.

24  Dunleavy, *The Politics of Mass Housing in Britain*, p. 37.

25  Glendinning and Muthesius, *Tower Block*, p. 175.

26  Dunleavy, *The Politics of Mass Housing in Britain*, p. 37.

27  E. Sharpe, 'Speech by Dame Evelyn Sharpe, Deputy Secretary, the Ministry of Housing and Local Government', in Royal Institute of British Architects, *High Flats: report of a symposium held on 15 February 1955 by the Royal Institute of British Architects at 66 Portland Place, London W1*, London: RIBA, 1955, p. 5.

28  Ibid.

29  Ministry of Housing and Local Government, *Flats and Homes 1958: design and economy*, London: HMSO, 1958.

30  Ministry of Public Building and Works, *A National Building Agency*, Cmnd 2228, London: HMSO, 1963, pp. 1–2.

31  Glendinning and Muthesius, *Tower Block*, p. 157.

32  *Portsmouth Evening News*, 9 March 1959, p. 5; quoted in E.W. Cooney, 'High flats in local authority housing in England and Wales since 1945', in A. Sutcliffe (ed.) *Multi-Storey Living: the British working-class experience*, London: Croom Helm, 1974, p. 162.

33  Community Development Project, *Whatever Happened to Council Housing?*, p. 48.

34  Interview between Kenneth Campbell and Miles Glendinning, 28 October 1987.

35  Ibid.

36  From Our Correspondent, 'Brighter shopping: perambulator parks', *The Times*, 13 September 1955, p. 10.

37  Community Development Project, *Whatever Happened to Council Housing?*, p. 66.

38  Although cities such as Leeds had continued to sweep away individually unfit houses even at the height of the postwar housing shortage, other towns struggled to launch programmes that would make any real difference. In 1953, for example, the Council of the City of Birmingham had tried to gain special power through a Corporation Bill that would allow it to acquire areas of poorly laid-out and obsolete development, but the property owners' associations won majorities in the town's meeting and poll to prevent implementation of this clause. See O. Hartley, 'The Second World War and after, 1939–74', in D. Fraser (ed.) *A History of Modern Leeds*, Manchester: Manchester University Press, 1980, pp. 448–9; A. Sutcliffe and R. Smith, *A History of Birmingham*, vol. 3, *Birmingham, 1939–1970*, Oxford: Oxford University Press, 1974, p. 230.

39  Burnett, *A Social History of Housing*, p. 279.

40  Ducland-Williams, *The Politics of Housing in Britain and France*, pp. 285–8.

41  J.B. Cullingworth, *Housing Needs and Planning Policy*, London: Routledge & Kegan Paul, 1960; quoted in S. Alderson, *Britain in the Sixties: housing*, Harmondsworth: Penguin, 1962, p. 37.

42  Councillors such as David Gibson in Glasgow, Karl Cohen in Leeds or David Nickson in Liverpool exerted powerful and enduring influence over the shape of housing strategy. Not surprisingly, in cities where voting patterns seldom produced changes sufficient to oust the ruling political party, the housing domain could almost become a private fiefdom. When visiting Leeds in 1965 as Minister of Town and Country Planning, for example, Richard Crossman reflected on the role played by Councillor Cohen as Housing Committee Chairman (Crossman, *The Diaries of a Cabinet Minister*, p. 127):

> One thing which seemed to me wrong was the [Labour] group's decision that the chairmen of key committees can stay chairmen for a long time. Cohen has been chairman of housing for ten years and he runs it very much as his personal possession. If he's ever robbed of the chairmanship, he will feel that his personal property has been taken away.

43  Glendinning and Muthesius, *Tower Block*, p. 173.

44  Interview transcript, 5 October 2004 [T25/16].

45  N. Bullock, *Building the Post-War World: modern architecture and reconstruction in Britain*, London: Routledge, 2002, pp. 199–218.

46  J.H. Forshaw and P. Abercrombie, *County of London Plan*, London: Macmillan, 1943.

47  H.J. Whitfield Lewis, 'The principles of mixed development', in Royal Institute of British Architects, *High Flats: report of a symposium held on 15 February 1955 by the Royal Institute of British*

*Architects at 66 Portland Place, London W1*, London: RIBA, 1955, p. 6. For more recent commentary on the LCC's policy, see Bullock, *Building the Post-War World*, pp. 199–218.

48  M. Richardson, 'Housing: the architect's contribution', *Official Architecture and Planning*, 1965, vol. 28, p. 786.

49  A. Sutcliffe, 'A century of flats in Birmingham, 1875–1973', in Sutcliffe (ed.) *Multi-Storey Living*, p. 192.

50  A. Briggs, *History of Birmingham*, vol. 2, *Borough and City, 1865–1938*, London: Oxford University Press for Birmingham City Council, 1952, p. 304.

51  P. Jones, 'Bigger is better? Local authority housing and the strange attraction of high-rise, 1945–70', paper presented to a workshop on 'Entrepreneurship and new community development in twentieth century Britain', Centre for International Business History, University of Reading, 25 October 2002. See: http://www.gees.bham.ac.uk/research/umrg/membersfiles/phil/biggerbetter.pdf, accessed 7 June 2006.

52  Interview between A.G. Sheppard Fidler and Miles Glendinning, 28 October 1987.

53  M. Tomlinson, 'Secular architecture', in W.B. Stephens (ed.) A History of the County of Warwickshire, vol. 7, *The City of Birmingham*, London: Oxford University Press for the Institute of Historical Research, University of London, 1964, p. 57.

54  Dunleavy, *The Politics of Mass Housing*, p. 267.

55  Layton, *Building by Local Authorities*, p. 302.

56  B. Finnimore, *Houses from the Factory: system building and the Welfare State*, London: Rivers Oram Press, 1989, p. 78.

57  Glendinning and Muthesius, *Tower Block*, p. 252.

58  Finnimore, *Houses from the Factory*, p. 78.

59  Package deals were seen as a threat to local authority architects, although the City and Borough Architects' Society did attempt to place a positive view on matters by suggesting that members should see continuous programmes of work as a benefit and press for a small amount of the estimated savings to be redirected into research and development. See Anon, 'Borough architects' views on the package deal', *Official Planning and Architecture*, 1964, vol. 27, p. 597.

60  Jones, 'Bigger is better?'

61  N. Pevsner and A. Wedgwood, *The Buildings of England: Warwickshire*, Harmondsworth: Penguin, 1966, p. 163.

62  M. Mitchell, 'Landscaping of housing areas', *Official Architecture and Planning*, 1962, vol. 25, p. 194.

63  G.E. Cherry, *Birmingham: a study in geography, history and planning*, Chichester: Wiley, 1994, p. 179.

64  Glendinning and Muthesius, *Tower Block*, p. 252.

65  M. Pacione, *Glasgow: the socio-spatial development of the city*, Chichester: Wiley, 1995, p. 171.

66  J.B. Cullingworth, *A Profile of Glasgow Housing 1965*, Occasional Papers 8, Edinburgh: Oliver & Boyd, 1961, p. 14.

67  R. Smith, 'Multi-dwelling building in Scotland 1750–1970: a study based on housing in the Clyde valley', in Sutcliffe (ed.) *Multi-Storey Living*, p. 226.

68  Ibid., p. 227.

69  T. Brennan, 'Most publicised British slum', *The Times*, 6 March 1958, p. 11.

70  Pacione, *Glasgow*, p. 168.

71  Brennan, 'Most publicised British slum'.

72  From Our Special Correspondent, 'Rebuilding the Gorbals: hanging gardens on 20 storeys', *The Times*, 28 August 1958, p. 10.

73  Interview between Tom Smyth and Miles Glendinning, 5 July 1987.

74  M. Horsey, *Tenements and Towers: Glasgow working class housing, 1890–1990*, Edinburgh: Royal Commission on the Ancient and Historical Monuments of Scotland, 1990.

75  Glendinning and Muthesius, *Tower Block*, p. 228.

76  R. Smith, 'Great Britain', in M. Wynn (ed.) *Housing in Europe*, London: Croom Helm, 1984, p. 95.

77  Glendinning and Muthesius, *Tower Block*, p. 228.

78  Ibid., p. 318.

79  E. Williamson, A. Riches and M. Higgs, *The Buildings of Scotland: Glasgow*, London: Penguin, 1990, p. 433.

80  Anon, 'Outer housing zone development at Cranhill, Glasgow', *Official Architecture and Planning*, 1963, vol. 26, p. 116.

81  Interview between George Bowie and Miles Glendinning, 3 November 1987.

82  Ibid.

83  R. Bradbury, 'Some aspects of experience in the USA and their possible application in this country', in Royal Institute of British Architects, *High Flats: report of a symposium held on 15 February 1955 by the Royal Institute of British Architects at 66 Portland Place, London W1*, London: RIBA, 1955, p. 10.

84  Ibid., p. 14.

85  Ibid.

86  Dunleavy, *The Politics of Mass Housing*, p. 126.

87  Glendinning and Muthesius, *Tower Block*, p. 164.

88  R. Bradbury (ed.) *Liverpool Builds, 1945–65*, Liverpool: Public Relations Office, City of Liverpool, 1965, p. 42.

89  Port Cities Liverpool, 'Housing problems in Liverpool', http://www.mersey-gateway.org/, accessed 15 July 2006.

90  R. Bradbury, 'Planning a major industrialised housing scheme', *Industrialised Building: Systems and Components*, 1963, vol. 1(1), pp. 20–2; Anon, 'Camus factory: annual capacity of 1000 dwellings', *Industrialised Building: Systems and Components*, 1964, vol. 1(8), p. 48.

91  D.M. Muchnick, *Urban Renewal in Liverpool: a study of the politics of redevelopment*, Occasional Papers on Social Administration 33, London: George Bell and Sons, 1970, p. 39.

92  Letter from Charles Parnell to T.V. Prosser, 10 March 1966. TNA WORK 45/471, 'National Building Agency'.

93  National Building Agency, *Report for Liverpool City Council on the City's Housing Requirements*, London: NBA, 1965.

94  Ibid., pp. 2–7. For commentary, see Anon, 'Computer in campaign to end slums', *Guardian*, 9 December 1966.

95  Muchnick, *Urban Renewal in Liverpool*, p. 45.

96  Figures from Dunleavy, *The Politics of Mass Housing*, p. 259, although my interpretations are slightly different.

97  Ibid., p. 51.

98  Industrialised Building Study Teams, Royal Institute of British Architects, *The Industrialisation of Building*, London: RIBA, 1965, p. 9.

99  Dunleavy, *The Politics of Mass Housing*, p. 64.

100  Sills et al., *Housing and the Inner City*, p. 24.

101  Dunleavy, *The Politics of Mass Housing*, p. 44.

102  This acted on an interpretation of the 1944 *Housing Manual* which emphasised the provision of three-bedroom, two-storey housing and gave only one page of coverage to flats, seeing flats primarily regarded as dwellings for special circumstances as in locations where high densities were unavoidable. See Ministry of Health and Ministry of Works, *Housing Manual 1944*, London: HMSO, 1944; Papillon Graphics, 'Manchester in modern times: 20th century history of Manchester', *Virtual Encyclopaedia of Greater Manchester*, http://www.manchester2002-uk.com/history/modern/20thcent-2.html, accessed 18 January 2006.

103  Dunleavy, *The Politics of Mass Housing*, p. 55.

104  Glendinning and Muthesius, *Tower Block*, p. 203.

105  Interview between George Bowie and Miles Glendinning, 3 November 1987.

106  A. Saint, 'A.W. Cleeve Barr', *Guardian*, 8 June 2000.

107  Interview with Professor Colin St. John Wilson, 17 February 2005 [T46/10–11].

108  Interview with Peter Carter, 7 April 2005 [T48/5–6].

109  Finnimore, *Houses from the Factory*, p. 74.

110  Ibid., p. 75.

111  Anon, 'Myton', *The Times*, 19 April 1963, p. 20.

112  Anon, 'Taylor Woodrow Limited Twenty-Eighth Annual General Meeting', *The Times*, 10 May 1963; p. 24.

113  Much of the council's work in housing and town expansion schemes was largely unaffected by the creation per se of the Greater London Council in 1965: Greater London Council, *GLC Architecture 1965/70*, Publication 7168, London: Greater London Council, 1970, p. 6.

## Notes and references

114 Letter from Sir William Hart, Clerk of the LCC to Geoffery Rippon MP, Minister of Public Building and Works, 20 January 1964. National Archives, WORK 45/340.

115 This was designed by the Borough Architect, Thomas E. North, and was not to exactly the same design as those built by the LCC and its successor the GLC.

116 RIBA, *The Industrialisation of Building*, p. 9.

117 K. Campbell, 'Industrialised building: a brief survey of the present position', *Official Architecture and Planning*, 1963, vol. 26, p. 439.

118 B. Cherry and N. Pevsner, *The Buildings of England: London 2: South*, Harmondsworth: Penguin, 1983, p. 595.

119 Ibid., p. 596.

120 Advertisments, 'Laing System Building Speeds Construction', *Interbuild Supplement*, 'System Building', 1963, p. 40; 'Bison Wall Frame', *Interbuild Supplement*, 'System Building', 1963, p. 40.

121 Industrialised Building Study Teams, *The Industrialisation of Building*, p. 19.

122 An idea derived from K. Harries, *The Ethical Function of Architecture*, Cambridge, MA: MIT Press, 1997, p. 2; also A. Pérez-Gómez, *Architecture and the Crisis of Modern Science*, Cambridge, MA: MIT Press, 1983.

123 Interview with Rodney Gordon, 11 November 2004 [T30/5].

124 Cleeve Barr, 'Not a panacea', *Interbuild*, 1963, vol. 10(7), p. 27.

125 Ibid.

126 Ministry of Public Building and Works, *A National Building Agency*, p. 1.

127 Designed in association with Robert Matthew, Stirrat Johnson Marshall and Partners: see Anon, 'Computer building near Winchester', *Architects' Journal*, 1961, vol. 133, p. 2.

128 Memorandum, 'New responsibilities of the Ministry of Public Building and Works, 7 February 1963. NA PREM 11/4837, '1962–1964 Government'.

129 Interview with Sir Andrew Derbyshire, 16 December 2004 [T40/18].

130 From handwritten notes supplied by Oliver Cox, November 2004.

131 N. Taylor, *The Village in the City*, London: Maurice Temple Smith, 1973, p. 110.

132 Interview with Oliver Cox, 2 November 2004 [T29/9–10].

133 Both had previously served as parliamentary secretary to the Minister of Housing and Local Government.

134 Our Political Correspondent, 'The tasks of cabinet management', *The Times*, 27 January 1963, p. 7.

135 Anon, 'Minister looks for industrial revolution in building', *The Times*, 3 May 1963, p. 9.

136 Cited in Anon, 'Industrialised housing: preferred dimensions for standardised components', *Industrialised Building: Systems and Components*, 1963, vol. 1(1), p. 39.

137 Interview with John Delafons, 3 July 2003 [T24/2–3].

138 Crossman, *The Diaries of a Cabinet Minister*, p. 81. For more on the development of housing at St Mary's Oldham, see Anon, 'Oldham', *Official Architecture and Planning*, 1965, vol. 28, pp. 637–54.

139 R. Crossman, 'Message', in *Industrialised Building and the Structural Engineer: a symposium organised by the Institution of Structural Engineers and held in London on 17–19 May 1966*, London: Institution of Structural Engineers, 1967, p. 10.

140 Crossman, *The Diaries of a Cabinet Minister*, p. 127.

141 Ibid., p. 131.

142 H. Emmerson, *Survey of Problems before the Construction Industries: A Report prepared for the Minister of Works*, London: HMSO, 1962.

143 Extract from a speech by the Rt. Hon. Geoffrey Rippon MP, Caxton Hall, London, 8 October 1962. NA PREM 11/4837, '1962–1964 Government'.

144 Memorandum by the Minister of Public Building and Works, 'Central Building Agency', 23 January 1963, pp. 1–2. NA PREM 11/4837, '1962–1964 Government'.

145 Ibid., p. 2 (original emphasis).

146 Ibid.

147 Personal and Secret Memorandum by the Minister of Public Buildings and Works, 23 January 1963, p. 1. NA PREM 11/4837, '1962–1964 Government'.

148 Internal Memorandum, Prime Minister's Office, 16 May 1963. NA PREM 11/4837, '1962–1964 Government'.

149 Letter to Geoffrey Rippon from Enoch Powell, Minister of Health, 4 September 1963. NA PREM 11/4837, '1962–1964 Government'.

150 Draft Memorandum for the Minister of Public Building and Works, c. March 1963. NA WORK 45/339, 'Establishment of NBA White Paper'.

151 Respectively 'New Building Agency required?', speech by Geoffrey Rippon, p. 2; and minutes of meeting with secretaries of the local authorities' associations, Lambeth Palace House, 19 June 1963. NA PREM 11/4837, '1962–1964 Government'.

152 Letter from L. Petch to F.J. Root, Deputy Secretary, Ministry of Public Building and Works, 14 November 1963. NA WORK 45/339, 'Establishment of NBA White Paper'.

153 First suggested in memorandum from W.O. Ulrich, private secretary to minister, to F.J. Root, 11 November 1963. The suggestion by Sir Keith Joseph is contained in a letter from B.H. Chapman to W.O. Ulbrich, 28 November 1963. Both are found in NA WORK 45/339, 'Establishment of NBA White Paper'.

154 Minutes by W.O. Ulrich, meeting at Ministry of Public Building and Works, 6 December 1963. NA WORK 45/339, 'Establishment of NBA White Paper'.

155 Draft brief 'The National Building Agency', Ministry of Public Building and Works. NA WORK 45/339, 'Establishment of NBA White Paper'.

156 Anon, 'National Building Agencies', Irish Builder and Engineer, 1964, vol. 106(3), p. 73.

157 Memorandum by H.J. Whitfield Lewis, 'The future of the National Building Agency', Ministry of Public Building and Works. NA WORK 45/383, 'General Correspondence'.

158 Ibid.

159 Note 'Services available from the National Building Agency for housing authorities'. NA WORK 45/383, 'General Correspondence'.

160 Memorandum by G.W.M., 'Discussion with National Building Agency', 17 December 1964. NA WORK 45/383, 'General Correspondence'.

161 NBA, 'Note for the Minister of Housing and Local Government: system building and the housing programme'. NA WORK 45/383, 'General Correspondence'.

162 Memorandum by G.W.M., 'Discussion with National Building Agency', 17 December 1964. NA WORK 45/383, 'General Correspondence'.

163 T.V. Prosser and A.W.C. Barr, 'Note for the Minister of Housing and Local Government: system building and the housing programme', 7 January 1965. NA WORK 45/383, 'General Correspondence'.

164 Anon, 'Building agency chief resigns', The Times, 20 March 1963.

165 M.E. Petsche, 'Future of the NBA', MO 8284/69. TNA WORK 45/635, 'National Building Agency: future role and reorganisation'.

166 Ibid.

167 Ibid.

168 'National Building Agency: new statement on future activities'. TNA WORK 45/471, 'National Building Agency: future role and reorganisation'.

169 Finnimore, Houses from the Factory, p. 254.

170 Interview with Geoffrey Darke, 23 May 2006 [T52/6].

171 N. Taylor, 'The failure of housing', Architectural Review, 1967, vol. 149, p. 342.

172 Ibid.

173 Interview with Rodney Gordon, 11 November 2004 [T30/5].

174 M. Richardson, 'Housing: the architect's contribution', Official Architecture and Planning, 1965, vol. 28, pp. 784–5.

175 I. Smith, 'Architects' approach to architecture: Ivor Smith', Royal Institute of British Architects' Journal, 1967, vol. 74, p. 271.

## 9 With social intent

1 R. Jensen, High Density Living, London: Leonard Hill, 1966, p. 30.

2 H. Sanoff, 'Son of rationality', in B. Honikman (ed.) Responding to Social Change, Stroudsburg, PA: Dowden, Hutchinson and Ross, 1975, p. 227.

3 Le Corbusier, La Ville radieuse, Boulogne sur Seine: Vincent, Freal, 1933; translated as The Radiant City, London: Faber & Faber, 1966, p. 64.

4 From the opening panel of the 'Modernism, 1914–1939' exhibition, held at the Victoria and Albert Museum, 6 April–23 July 2006.

5  M. Glendinning and D. Page, *Clone City: crisis and revival in contemporary Scottish architecture*, Edinburgh: Polygon, 1999, p. 138.

6  See Chapter 12 for further discussion and relevant sources. With regard to the then-current British traditions of community studies, see H.E. Bracey, *Social Provision in Rural Wiltshire*, London: Methuen, 1952; and R. Frankenberg, *Communities in Britain: social life in town and country*, Harmondsworth: Penguin, 1966.

7  A. Saint, 'Park Hill: what next?', in A. Saint (ed.) *Park Hill: what next?*, AA Documents 1, London: Architectural Association, 1996, p. 25.

8  Ibid.

9  K. Lynch, 'The form of cities', *Scientific American*, 1954, vol. 190(4), pp. 54–63.

10  This summary draws on Anon, 'Cluster blocks at Usk Street, Bethnal Green, London', *Architectural Design*, 1958, vol. 28, p. 62.

11  Technically Lasdun was part of Fry, Drew, Drake and Lasdun, but Lasdun asserts that this was essentially an administrative arrangement while Fry and Drew were working in Chandigarh: 'there was never any, and there couldn't have been any design collaboration'. Interview between Denys Lasdun and Jill Lever, 12 November 1996. National Sound Archive (NSA), tape F5348, side A.

12  Interview between Denys Lasdun and Jill Lever, 12 November 1996. NSA, tape F5348, side A.

13  W. Curtis, 'A language and a theme: the architecture of Denys Lasdun and Partners', in D. Lasdun, *A Language and a Theme: the architecture of Denys Lasdun and Partners*, London: RIBA Publications, 1976, pp. 11, 21.

14  Anon, 'Flats: Bethnal Green', *Architectural Review*, 1954, vol. 115, p. 49.

15  Anon, 'Cluster blocks at Bethnal Green, London', *Architectural Design*, 1956, vol. 26, p. 125.

16  Anon, 'Cluster blocks at Usk Street, Bethnal Green, London', p. 62.

17  Interview between Denys Lasdun and Jill Lever, 12 November 1996. NSA, tape F5348, side A.

18  Anon, 'Housing: Bethnal Green, London', *Architectural Review*, 1960, vol. 127, p. 304.

19  Ibid.

20  Ibid.

21  D. Lasdun, 'Random thoughts', *Journal of the Royal Institute of British Architects*, 1977, vol. 84, p. 173.

22  Reproduced in J.W. Murray, *A Walk into History: Bethnal Green*, London: Polytechnic of Central London, 1991, p. 19.

23  These findings by Cooney are taken from N. Taylor, *The Village in the City*, London: Maurice Temple Smith, 1973, pp. 87–8.

24  One of the best available analyses is found in Saint, 'Park Hill: what next?', pp. 7–40.

25  M. Hebbert, 'The City of London walkway network', *Journal of the American Institute of Planners*, 1992, vol. 59, pp. 433–50.

26  The details of this were discussed previously in J.R. Gold, *The Experience of Modernism: modern architects and the future city, 1928–1953*, London: E. & F.N. Spon, 1997, pp. 224–6.

27  Interview between Trevor Dannatt and Alan Powers. NSA, tape F11648, side A.

28  T. Crosby (ed.) *Urban Structuring: studies of Alison and Peter Smithson*, London: Studio Vista, 1970, pp. 20–1.

29  A. Smithson and P. Smithson, 'An urban project', in T. Dannatt (ed.) *Architects' Year Book 5*, London: Elek, 1953, p. 49 (original emphases).

30  Ibid., p. 52.

31  J. Lynn, 'The development of the design', *Royal Institute of British Architects' Journal*, 1962, vol. 69, p. 448; the reference is to Smithson and Smithson, 'An urban project', p. 54.

32  N. Wiener, *The Human Use of Human Beings: cybernetics and society*, London: Eyre & Spottiswoode, 1950.

33  A. Colquhoun, *Modern Architecture*, Oxford: Oxford University Press, 2002, p. 220.

34  Crosby, *Urban Structuring*, pp. 20–1.

35  A. Smithson and P. Smithson, *Ordinariness and Light: urban theories 1952–1960 and their application in a building project 1963–1970*, London: Faber & Faber, 1970, p. 45.

36  Ibid., p. 52.

37  Smithson and Smithson, 'An urban project', p. 54.

38  Most fully stated in Smithson and Smithson, *Ordinariness and Light*, pp. 53–61, with an important early synthesis into CIAM traditions in A. Smithson, 'Team 10 Primer', *Architectural Design*, 1962, vol. 32, pp. 559–602.

39  Crosby, *Urban Structuring*, p. 33.
40  A. Smithson and P. Smithson, 'The New Brutalism', *Architectural Review*, 1957, vol. 115, p. 274.
41  Berlinische Galarie (1990) *Haupstadt Berlin: Internationaler Städtebaulicher Ideenwettbewerb 1957/8*, Berlin: Gerb. Mann Verlag.
42  A. Colquhoun, 'On modern and postmodern space', in J. Ockman (ed.) *Architecture, Criticism, Ideology*, Princeton, NJ: Princeton University Press, 1985, p. 112.
43  M. Vidotto, *Alison + Peter Smithson*, Barcelona: Editorial Gustavo Gil, 1997, pp. 64, 66.
44  Interview between Peter Smithson and Louise Brodie, 17 September 1997. NSA, tape F5954, side A.
45  Ibid.
46  H. Webster, 'Modernism without rhetoric: the work of Alison and Peter Smithson', in H. Webster (ed.) *Modernism without Rhetoric: essays on the work of Alison and Peter Smithson*, London: Academy Editions, 1997, p. 73.
47  D. van den Heuvel, 'Robin Hood Gardens housing estate, London 1966–72', in M. Risselada and D. van den Heuvel (eds) *Team 10, 1953–81: in search of a utopia*, Rotterdam: NAI, 2005, p. 174.
48  Lynn, 'The development of the design', p. 448.
49  J. Lynn, 'Sheffield', in D. Lewis (ed.) 'The Pedestrian in the City', *Architects' Year Book 11*, London: Elek, 1965, p. 59.
50  Interview with Lewis Wolmersley, *c.*1963; rebroadcast in *The Flight from Utopia*, Part 1, *The Age of Euphoria*, BBC1 television, 18 September 1984.
51  Housing Development Committee of the Corporation of Sheffield, *Ten Years of Housing in Sheffield*, Sheffield: City Architect's Department, 1962, p. 3.
52  Lynn, 'The development of the design', pp. 448–50.
53  P. Crooke, 'Sheffield', *Architectural Design*, 1961, vol. 31, p. 406.
54  Anon, 'Impressive planning for rehousing in Sheffield: imaginative use of topography', *The Times*, 15 September 1961, p. 19.
55  Anon, 'High density redevelopment, Park Hill, Sheffield', *The Builder*, 1955, vol. 188, p. 668.
56  Housing Development Committee, *Ten Years of Housing in Sheffield*, p. 43.
57  R. Landau, *New Directions in British Architecture*, New York: George Braziller, 1968, p. 31.
58  Anon, 'Impressive planning for rehousing in Sheffield: imaginative use of topography', *The Times*, 15 September 1961, p. 19.
59  M. Webb, *Architecture in Britain Today*, Feltham, Middlesex: Country Life Books, 1969, p. 88.
60  See Anon, 'Kelvin', *Official Architecture and Planning*, 1966, vol. 29, p. 232.
61  Anon, 'High density redevelopment, Park Hill, Sheffield', p. 668.
62  Anon, 'Park Hill', *Architects' Journal*, 1961, vol. 133, p. 276.
63  Housing Development Committee, *Ten Years of Housing in Sheffield*, p. 42.
64  Lynn, 'Sheffield', p. 58.
65  Ibid.
66  Ibid., pp. 65, 67.
67  Ibid., p. 69.
68  Ibid.
69  J. Demers, 'Park Hill survey', unpublished report, Sheffield City Architect's Department, 1962.
70  A.E.J. Morris, 'Park Hill 1966: a reappraisal', *Official Architecture and Planning*, 1966, vol. 29, pp. 225, 229.
71  Editor, 'Housing and the environment', *Architectural Review*, 1967, vol. 142, p. 350.
72  Ibid., p. 351.
73  Saint, 'Park Hill: what next?', p. 37.
74  Cited in W. Bor, 'A fresh approach to high density housing', *Official Architecture and Planning*, 1962, vol. 25, p. 173.
75  Bor, 'A fresh approach to high density housing', p. 175.
76  K. Joseph, 'Foreword', in Ministry of Housing and Local Government, *Residential Areas: higher densities*, Planning Bulletin 2, London: HMSO, 1962, p. 3.
77  S.L. Elkin, *Politics and Land Use Planning: the London experience*, London: Leonard Hill, 1974, p. 35.
78  P.E.C. Croot (ed.) *A History of the County of Middlesex*, vol. 12, *Chelsea*, London: Boydell Press for the Victoria County History of the Counties of England, 2004, pp. 91–101; quoted from

'Settlement and building: twentieth century: after the Second World War', http://www.british-history.ac.uk, accessed 20 July 2006.

79  Eric Lyons v London County Council (LCC), Blackheath Planning Appeal, 1961, FR 11, Crate 283, Percy Johnson-Marshall Collection, University of Edinburgh Library.

80  Quoted in Anon, 'Chelsea (World's End): Eric Lyons and Partners', *Architectural Review*, 1967, vol. 142, p. 379.

81  B. Cherry and N. Pevsner, *The Buildings of Britain: London 3: North West*, Harmondsworth: Penguin, 1991, p. 585.

82  Ibid.

83  Bor, 'A fresh approach to high density housing', p. 199.

84  Anon, 'Westminster housing competition', *Architects' Journal*, 1961, vol. 134, p. 156.

85  Ibid.

86  Anon, 'Preview: housing', *Architectural Review*, 1965, vol. 137, p. 39.

87  Interview with Geoffrey Darke, 23 May 2006 [T52/8].

88  Ibid [T52/18].

89  Ibid [T52/17].

90  Ibid.

91  Editor, 'Housing and the environment', p. 380.

92  Anon, 'Lillington 3', *Architects' Journal*, 1972, vol. 155, p. 57.

93  Interview with Geoffrey Darke, 23 May 2006 [T52/8].

94  Editor, 'Housing and the environment', p. 380.

95  Anon, 'Lillington 3', pp. 57–8.

96  See L. Esher, *A Broken Wave: the rebuilding of England, 1940–1980*, London: Allen Lane, 1981, p. 119.

97  Interview with Geoffrey Darke, 23 May 2006 [T52/6].

98  Anon, 'Housing: Marquess Road, Islington', *Architectural Review*, 1974, vol. 142, p. 144.

99  Darbourne and Darke, *The Architecture of Darbourne & Darke: a handbook to an exhibition at the Royal Institute of Architects Heinz Gallery, 17 May–29 July 1977*, London: RIBA Publications, 1977, p. 62.

100  Interview with Geoffrey Darke, 23 May 2006 [T52/9].

101  C. Amery, 'Housing, Marquess Road, Islington, London', *Architectural Review*, 1974, vol. 142, pp. 151–2.

102  Homes for Islington, 'New River Green Project', http://www.homesforislington.org.uk/homes forislington/repairs/NewRiverGreen/index.asp, accessed 30 July 2006.

103  Interview with Geoffrey Darke, 23 May 2006 [T52/3].

## 10  Succession

1   L. Brett, 'Note from the chairman', unpublished memorandum, 1962, SPUR. British Architectural Library (BAL), file BrL/5/2.

2   Letter from Ted Hollamby to Lionel Brett, 20 November 1962. BAL, file BrL/5/2.

3   Item 231a 'Architects' Action Group Exhibition', Minutes, Thirty-Second Meeting of the General Committee of SPUR on 24 July 1962. BAL, file BrL/5/2.

4   Letter from John Smith to Margaret Baker, 10 July 1962. BAL, file BrL/5/2.

5   'Note from the chairman', 8 November 1962. BAL, file BrL/5/2.

6   Letter to members of SPUR from Lionel Brett, 31 December 1962. BAL, file BrL/5/2.

7   Letter from Brett to Donald Insall, 8 January 1963. BAL, file BrL/5/2.

8   Letter from Brett to Jeremy Mackay-Lewis, 1 February 1963. BAL, file BrL/5/2.

9   Letter from Jeremy Mackay-Lewis to Brett, 15 February 1963. BAL, file BrL/5/2.

10  Letter from Mackay-Lewis to Lord Esher, 25 October 1963. BAL, file BrL/5/2.

11  BAL, ArO/1/1/5.

12  See e.g. the following files: BAL, ArO/2/2/1–12 and ArO/2/5/1.

13  D. Lasdun, 'MARS Group, 1953–1957', in T. Dannatt (ed.) *Architects' Year Book 8*, London: Elek, 1957, p. 57.

14  Interview with Cyril Sweett, 6 March 1987 [T13/3].

15  Interview with Maxwell Fry, 24 November 1986 [T5/16].

16 Interview with J.M. Richards, 3 December 1986 [T11/15].
17 Lasdun, 'MARS Group, 1953–1957', p. 59.
18 The eventual outcome was S. Cantacuzino, *Wells Coates: a monograph*, London: Gordon Fraser, 1978.
19 Interview between Trevor Dannatt and Alan Powers. National Sound Archive (NSA), tape F11648, side B.
20 Ibid.
21 J.R. Gold, 'Creating the Charter of Athens: CIAM and the functional city, 1933–43', *Town Planning Review*, 1998, vol. 69, pp. 221–43.
22 Pierre-André Emery, for example, writing to Sert to complain of 'la terrible obstination des jeunes turcs Peter et Alison'. Letter from P.A. Emery to J.L. Sert, 24 September 1955. Folder C15, CIAM Archive, Frances Loeb Library, Harvard University.
23 Interview with Sir Andrew Derbyshire, 4 January 2005 [T43/6].
24 Interview between Peter Smithson and Louise Brodie, 1997. NSA, tape F5952, side A.
25 Ibid.
26 J.R Gold, *The Experience of Modernism: modern architects and the future city, 1928–1953*, London: E. & F.N. Spon, 1997, pp. 226–9.
27 S. Giedion, 'The heart of the city: a summing up', in J. Trywhitt, J.L. Sert and E.N. Rogers (eds) *The Heart of the City: towards the humanisation of urban life*, London: Lund Humphries, 1952, p. 163.
28 CIAM Meeting 29–30–31 January 1954, Doorn 'Statement on Habitat'. BAL, ArO/2/11/6(i).
29 A. Smithson and P. Smithson, *The Charged Void: Urbanism*, New York: Monacelli Press, 2005, p. 24.
30 Although van Ginkel's name is omitted from some versions: e.g. CIAM Meeting 29–30–31 January 1954, Doorn 'Statement on Habitat'. BAL, ArO/2/11/6(i).
31 MARS Group, London CIAM X Committee, 22 March 1954. BAL, ArO/2/11/6(i).
32 The listing included Pat Crooke, Trevor Dannatt, Ernö Goldfinger, Gordon Graham, Bill Howell, Denys Lasdun, Alison Smithson, Peter Smithson and John Voelcker. MARS Group, CIAM 10 Sub-Committee, Bulletin 3. BAL, GolEr/315/2.
33 MARS Group, London CIAM X Committee, 22 March 1954. BAL, ArO/2/11/6(ii).
34 MARS Group, CIAM X Sub-Committee, Minutes, 23 April 1954. BAL, ArO/2/11/9.
35 Ibid.
36 Lasdun, 'MARS Group, 1953–1957', p. 58.
37 MARS Group, CIAM 10 Sub-Committee, Bulletin 2. BAL, GolEr/315/2.
38 CIAM, CIRPAC Meeting, Paris, 30 June 1954. BAL, GolEr/315/2.
39 The account is found in MARS Group, 'Draft Framework 5: CIAM X', December 1954. BAL, ArO/2/11/10.
40 M. Risselada and D. van den Heuvel (eds) *Team 10, 1953–81: in search of a utopia*, Rotterdam: NAI, 2005, p. 44.
41 C. Tuscano, 'How can you do without history? Interview with Giancarlo De Carlo', in Risselada and van den Heuvel (eds) *Team 10, 1953–81: in search of a utopia*, p. 340.
42 Interview between Dame Jane Drew and Margaret Garlake, 20 May 1995. NSA, tape 4826, side B.
43 Interview with Peter Carter, 7 April 2005 [T48/4].
44 A. Smithson (ed.) *The Emergence of Team 10 out of CIAM*, London: Architectural Association, 1982.
45 M. Risselada and D. van den Heuvel 'Introduction: looking into the mirror of Team 10', in Risselada and van den Heuvel (eds) *Team 10, 1953–81: in search of a utopia*, p. 11.
46 MARS Group, 'Draft Framework 5: CIAM X', December 1954. BAL, ArO/2/11/10.
47 Ibid.
48 Letter from Alison Smithson, Peter Smithson, Bill Howell and John Voelcker to Sigfried Giedion, 4 January 1955. Folder C15, CIAM Archive, Frances Loeb Library, Harvard University. Giedion, in forwarding a copy to Sert, was happier to observe that they (the English and Dutch groups) seemed not to agree with one another.
49 A. Colquhoun, *Modern Architecture*, Oxford: Oxford University Press, 2002, p. 218.
50 Circular Letter from P.A. Emery, 'CIAM International Congress for Modern Architecture, Congress 10', 15 June 1955. BAL, ArO/2/1/11(i).

51 CIAM Meeting of Delegates at La Sarraz, Minutes, 8–10 September 1955. Folder C15, CIAM Archive, Frances Loeb Library, Harvard University (original emphasis).

52 Ibid.

53 CIAM Meeting of Delegates at La Sarraz, Minutes, 8–10 September 1955, Appendix II 'Proposal of S. Giedion'. BAL, ArO/2/11/12/(i).

54 Ibid.

55 CIAM Team X, statement, November 1955. BAL, GoEr/315/2.

56 Ibid. (original emphasis).

57 CIAM, Preparation for CIAM X, Document 3, undated. BAL, ArO/2/11/14 (ii).

58 Letter from Giedion (30 May 1956) circulated in MARS Group, 'CIAM X', June 1956. BAL, ArO/2/11/16/(i).

59 Letter from Le Corbusier to J.L. Sert, 22 May 1956. BAL, ArO/2/11/17/(i).

60 Ibid.

61 A. Pedret, 'Scales of association', in Risselada and van den Heuvel (eds) *Team 10, 1953–81: in search of a utopia*, p. 53.

62 Interview with Peter Carter, 7 April 2005 [T48/7].

63 S. Menin and S. Kite, *An Architecture of Invitation: Colin St John Wilson*, Aldershot: Ashgate, 2005, pp. 55–6.

64 M. Girouard, *Big Jim: the life and work of James Stirling*, London: Pimlico, 2000, p. 84.

65 Ibid.

66 CIAM, 'The 10th Congress of CIAM, Dubrovnik, 3–13 August 1956'. BAL, ArO/2/11/18(i).

67 E. Mumford, *The CIAM Discourse on Urbanism, 1928–1960*, Cambridge, MA: MIT Press, 2000, p. 267.

68 CIAM, 'The 10th Congress of CIAM, Dubrovnik, 3–13 August 1956'. BAL, ArO/2/11/18(i).

69 Mumford, *The CIAM Discourse on Urbanism, 1928–1960*, p. 259.

70 O. Newman, *CIAM '59 in Otterlo: Group for the Research of Social and Visual Inter-Relationships*, Stuttgart: Karl Krämer, 1961, p. 7.

71 Quoted in Mumford, *The CIAM Discourse on Urbanism, 1928–1960*, p. 260.

72 See e.g. T. Crosby, 'Introduction', in T. Crosby (ed.) *Urban Structuring: studies of Alison and Peter Smithson*, London: Uppercase Books, 1960, p. 7.

73 P. Collymore, *The Architecture of Ralph Erskine*, London: Granada, 1994, p. 23.

74 Colquhoun, *Modern Architecture*, p. 223.

75 C. Levi, *Christ Stopped at Eboli: the story of a year*, New York: Farrar, Straus & Giroux, 1947.

76 Comments by Giancarlo De Carlo, see C. Tuscano, 'How can you do without history? Interview with Giancarlo De Carlo', p. 340.

77 Newman, *CIAM '59 in Otterlo*, p. 76.

78 Mumford, *The CIAM Discourse on Urbanism, 1928–1960*, pp. 260–1.

79 P.R. Banham, 'Premature monument', *Architectural Review*, 1962, vol. 131, p. 7.

80 Newman, *CIAM '59 in Otterlo*, p. 7.

81 A. Smithson, *Team 10 Meetings, 1953–1984*, Delft: Delft University of Technology, 1991, p. 26.

82 Reported in Newman, *CIAM '59 in Otterlo*, p. 221.

83 This is taken from the draft of a statement sent to the architectural press by J.L. Sert, Walter Gropius, Le Corbusier and Sigfried Giedion in 1961 in defence of their own record. Folder E7, CIAM Archive, Frances Loeb Library, Harvard University, p. 3. For published versions, see J.L. Sert, W. Gropius, Le Corbusier and S. Giedion, 'What became of CIAM?', *Architectural Review*, 1961, vol. 129, p. 154; J.L. Sert, W. Gropius, Le Corbusier and S. Giedion, 'The truth and CIAM: letter from four founders', *Architectural Design*, 1961, vol. 31, p. 5.

84 Ibid.

85 J. Bakema, 'The truth and CIAM: a reply from Bakema', *Architectural Design*, 1961, vol. 31, p. 55.

86 Letter from Jaap Bakema to J.L. Sert, 19 June 1961. Folder C17, CIAM Archive, Frances Loeb Library, Harvard University.

87 Ibid.

88 Letter from Jaap Bakema to Ernö Goldfinger (and others). BAL, GolEr/315/2.

89 M. Risselada, 'Between understatement and overdesign', in Risselada and van den Heuvel (eds) *Team 10, 1953–81: in search of a utopia*, p. 121.

90 S. Samassa, 'Team 10 in crisis: to move or to stay?', in Risselada and van den Heuvel (eds) *Team 10, 1953–81: in search of a utopia*, p. 142.

91    A. Smithson (ed.) 'Team 10 Primer 1953–1962', *Architectural Design*, 1962, vol. 32, pp. 559–600;
      A. Smithson (ed.) *Team 10 Primer*, Cambridge, MA: MIT Press, 1962.
92    Smithson, *Team 10 Primer*, pp. 99–119 and 163–79.
93    Comment by Giancarlo De Carlo, see C. Tuscano, 'How can you do without history? Interview with
      Giancarlo De Carlo', p. 341.

## 11   Late-flowering modernism

1     Paul Kantner, attributed www.brainyquote.com/quotes/authors/p/paul_kantner.html, accessed 31
      July 2006.
2     S. Sadler, 'British architecture in the Sixties', in C. Stephens and K. Stout (eds) *Art and the 60s: this
      was tomorrow*, London: Tate Publishing, 2004, p. 124.
3     C. Jencks, *Modern Movements in Architecture*, Harmondsworth: Penguin, 1973, p. 239.
4     P.A. Stone, 'Resources and the economic framework', in P. Cowan (ed.) *Developing Patterns of
      Urbanisation*, Edinburgh: Oliver & Boyd, 1970, p. 34.
5     P. Hall, 'The pattern of cities to come', *New Society*, 10 March 1966; reprinted in P. Barker (ed.)
      *One for Sorrow, Two for Joy*, London: George Allen and Unwin, 1972, p. 183.
6     U. Conrads and H.G. Sperlich, *Fantastic Architecture*, trans. C.C. Collins and G.R. Collins, London:
      Architectural Press, 1963, p. 6 (originally published in German in 1960).
7     P.R. Banham, P. Barker, C. Price and P. Hall, 'Non-Plan: an experiment in freedom', *New Society*,
      1969, vol. 13, pp. 435–43; P.R.R. Calder, *Hurtling towards 2000 AD*, Matlock: Derbyshire Education
      Committee, 1969; P. Cook, *Experimental Architecture*, London: Studio Vista, 1970; P. Cowan (ed.)
      *Developing Patterns of Urbanisation*, Edinburgh: Oliver & Boyd, 1970; H. Cox, *The Secular City*,
      Harmondsworth: Penguin, 1968; C. Doxiadis, *Ekistics*, London: Hutchinson, 1968; R. Eells and C.
      Walton (eds) *Man in the City of the Future*, London: Collier-Macmillan, 1968; D.F. Knight, *Cities of
      Wonder*, London: Dobson, 1968; D. Lewis, 'New urban structures', in K. Baier and N. Rescher (eds)
      *Values and the Future*, New York: Free Press, 1969, pp. 320–35; I.L. McHarg, *Design with Nature*,
      Garden City, NY: Doubleday, 1969; P. Soleri, *Arcology: the city in the image of man*, Cambridge,
      MA: MIT Press, 1969; W.H. Whyte, *The Last Landscape*, New York: Doubleday, 1968.
8     See e.g. D. Velez, 'Late nineteenth-century Spanish progressivism: Arturo Soria's linear city',
      *Journal of Urban History*, 1982, vol. 9, pp. 131–64; K. Frampton, 'The other Le Corbusier: primitive
      form and the linear city', in M. Raeburn and V. Wilson, (eds) *Le Corbusier: architect of the century*,
      London: Arts Council of Great Britain, 1986, pp. 29–34; J.R. Gold, 'The MARS plans for London,
      1933–1942: plurality and experimentation in the city plans of the early British Modern Movement',
      *Town Planning Review*, 1995, vol. 66, pp. 243–67.
9     See, in particular, the discussion of the Bull Ring Shopping Centre in Chapter 6 and the discussion
      of the Central Areas at Cumbernauld and in the plans for Hook (Chapter 7).
10    P.R. Banham, 'Megastructure: large multi-functional urban complexes containing transient smaller
      units adaptable to changing needs', *Architectural Design*, 1975, vol. 45, pp. 400–1.
11    Percival Goodman and Paul Goodman, *Communitas: means of livelihood and ways of life*, Chicago,
      IL: University of Chicago Press, 1947, p. 69.
12    Ibid., p. 71.
13    See e.g. J. Gottmann, *Megalopolis: the urbanized Northeastern Seaboard of the United States*,
      Cambridge, MA: MIT Press, 1961; B.J.L. Berry, 'The geography of the United States in the year
      2000', *Transactions of the Institute of British Geographers*, 1971, vol. 51, pp. 21–54.
14    P. Hall, *London 2000*, second edition, London: Faber & Faber, 1969 (originally published 1963).
15    M.M. Webber, 'Order in diversity: community without propinquity', in L. Wingo (ed.) *Cities in Space*,
      Baltimore, MD: Johns Hopkins University Press, 1963, pp. 23–56.
16    P. Hall, 'The urban culture and the suburban culture', in R. Eells and C. Walton (eds) *Man in the City
      of the Future*, London: Collier-Macmillan, 1969, p. 109.
17    R. Matthews and G. Cullen, *A Town Called Alcan*, London: Alcan Industries, 1964, p. 9.
18    Ibid., p. 17.
19    W. Houghton-Evans, *Planning Cities: legacy and portent*, London: Lawrence & Wishart, 1975, pp.
      126–39.
20    Robert Matthew, Johnson-Marshall and Partners, *Central Lancashire: study for a city*, 1964,
      London: RMJM; see also W.L. Waide, 'Central Lancashire new town: masterly Leyland-Chorley
      study', *Official Architecture and Planning*, 1967, vol. 30, pp. 1145–51.

21    Interview with Sir Andrew Derbyshire, 4 January 2005 [T43/7].

22    Ibid. [T43/10].

23    P. Cook, 'Plug-in City', in M. van Schaik and O. Máčel (eds) *Exit Utopia: architectural provocations, 1956–76*, Munich: Prestel, 2005, p. 83.

24    Doxiadis, *Ekistics*, p. 217.

25    E. Jones, *Metropolis*, Oxford: Oxford University Press, 1990, p. 137; N. Brown, 'Constantinos Doxiadis: Ekistics', http://www.csiss.org/classics/content/36, accessed 21 April 2006.

26    Banham et al., 'Non-Plan', pp. 435–43.

27    Interview with Paul Barker, 5 January 2005 [T44/8].

28    Banham et al., 'Non-Plan', p. 435 (original emphases).

29    Ibid., p. 437.

30    P. Barker, 'Non-Plan revisited: or the real way cities grow', *Journal of Design History*, 2003, vol. 12, pp. 95–110.

31    Interview with Peter Hall, 30 November 2004 [T34/6].

32    P.R. Banham, *Los Angeles: the architecture of the four ecologies*, London: Pelican, 1971, p. 21.

33    Banham, *Los Angeles*. Commentary from N. Whiteley, *Reyner Banham: historian of the immediate future*, Cambridge, MA: MIT Press, 2002, p. 225.

34    S. Mathews, 'The Fun Palace as virtual architecture: Cedric Price and the practices of indeterminacy', *Journal of Architectural Education*, 2006, vol. 59, p. 40. See also J. Littlewood, 'A laboratory of fun', *New Scientist*, 1964, vol. 38, pp. 432–3.

35    Banham et al., 'Non-Plan', pp. 437–41.

36    See e.g. E. Relph, *Place and Placelessness*, London: Pion, 1976.

37    J. Miller, 'Expo '67: a search for order', *Canadian Architect*, 1967, vol. 12(5), pp. 45–6.

38    Anon, 'How the Fair was planned', *Progressive Architecture*, June 1967, p. 123.

39    Interview with Gilles Gagnon, 5 October 1998 [T21/6].

40    M. Safdie and W. Kohn, *The City after the Automobile: an architect's vision*, Toronto: Stoddart, 1967, p. 81.

41    J.R. Gold, 'Exposition and imagination: revisiting the future city at Montreal's Expo '67 and New York's World's Fair', *Fennia*, 2000, vol. 178(1), pp. 113–24; J.R. Gold and M.M. Gold, *Cities of Culture: staging international festivals and the urban agenda, 1851–2000*, Aldershot: Ashgate, 2005.

42    A sample of the enormous range of schemes put forward can be found in V.M. Lampugnani, *Visionary Architecture of the 20th Century: master drawings from Frank Lloyd Wright to Aldo Rossi*, London: Thames & Hudson, 1982; M. Pawley, *Theory and Design in the Second Machine Age*, Oxford: Blackwell, 1990, pp. 102–11; C.W. Thomsen, *Visionary Architecture: from Babylon to virtual reality*, Munich: Prestel, 1994; S. Sadler, *The Situationist City*, Cambridge, MA: MIT Press, 1998; M. Wigley, *Constant's New Babylon: the hyper-architecture of desire*, Rotterdam: Witte de With, Centre for Contemporary Art, 1998; E. Burden, *Visionary Architecture: unbuilt works of the imagination*, New York: McGraw-Hill, 2000; R. Eaton, *Ideal Cities: utopianism and the (un)built environment*, London: Thames & Hudson, 2001, pp. 216–35; and D. Pinder, *Visions of the City: utopianism, power and politics in twentieth-century urbanism*, Edinburgh: Edinburgh University Press, 2005.

43    F. Maki, *Investigations in Collective Form*, St. Louis, MO: School of Architecture, Washington University, 1964. This point comes from P.R. Banham, *Megastructure: urban futures of the recent past*, London: Thames & Hudson, 1976, p. 12, with Banham himself acknowledging source to R. Wilcoxen, *Megastructures: a bibliography*, Monticello, IL: Council of Planning Librarians, 1968.

44    Editors, 'Omnibuilding: special section', *Progressive Architecture*, 1968, vol. 44 (June), pp. 89–158.

45    A. Colquhoun, *Modern Architecture*, Oxford: Oxford University Press, 2002, p. 229.

46    J.T Burns, Jr, 'Social and psychological implications of megastructures', in G. Kepes (ed.) *Arts of the Environment*, London: Aidan Ellis, 1972, p. 135.

47    Jones, *Metropolis*, p. 156. See also H. Skolimowski, 'Paolo Soleri: the philosophy of urban life', *Architectural Association Quarterly*, 1970, vol. 3, pp. 34–42. Additional information from J. Cook, 'Soleri, Paolo', in R.J. van Vynckt (ed.) *International Dictionary of Architects and Architecture 1*, London: St James Press, 1993, pp. 842–4.

48    N.J. Habraken, *Supports: an alternative to mass housing*, New York: Praeger, 1972.

49　Some indication of Quarmby's work is found in A. Quarmby, *The Plastics Architect*, London: Pall Mall Press, 1974. Quarmby's influence on megastructuralism was recognised by the exhibition, 'Future City: experiment and utopia in architecture, 1956–2006', Barbican Art Gallery, 2006.

50　Colquhoun, *Modern Architecture*, p. 223.

51　Y. Friedman, 'Paris Spatial: a suggestion', reprinted in van Schaik and Máčel (eds) *Exit Utopia*, p. 24.

52　Wigley, *Constant's New Babylon*.

53　For a 17-page bibliography on Archigram, see A. Smith, *Archigram: a selective bibliography*, London: Library, Architectural Association, 2006; available on http://www.aaschool.ac.uk/library/archigram.pdf.

54　P. Drew, *Third Generation: the changing meaning of architecture*, London: Pall Mall Press, 1972, p. 102.

55　P. Cook, 'Some notes on the Archigram syndrome', *Perspecta*, 11(supplement), 1967, p. 153.

56　M. van Schaik, 'Introduction', in van Schaik and Máčel (eds) *Exit Utopia*, p. 9.

57　Interview with Mary Banham, 16 January 2006 [T51/8].

58　P.R. Banham, 'A clip-on architecture', *Design Quarterly*, 1965, vol. 63, p. 30.

59　S. Sadler, *Archigram: architecture without architecture*, Cambridge, MA: MIT Press, 2005, p. 11.

60　H.G. Wells, *The War of the Worlds*, London: Heinemann, 1898; P.R. Banham, *The Visions of Ron Herron*, Architectural Monographs 38, London: Academy Editions, pp. 72–81.

61　P. Wolf, *The Future of the City: new directions in urban planning*, New York: Watson-Guptill Publications for the Whitney Library of Design, 1974, p. 101.

62　Eaton, *Ideal Cities*, p. 233.

63　Ibid.

64　P. Hodgkinson, 'Plug In City', *Architectural Design*, 1969, vol. 39, p. 586.

65　Sadler, 'British architecture in the Sixties', p. 131.

66　Reprinted in: Mito Art Tower, *Archigram: experimental architecture, 1961–1974*, Tokyo: Pie, 2005, n.p.

67　Interview with John Summerson, 4 December 1986 [T12/2].

68　A. Vidler, 'Toward a theory of the architectural program', *October*, 2003, vol. 106, p. 62.

69　J. Summerson, 'The case for a theory of modern architecture', *Royal Institute of British Architects' Journal*, 1957 (June), pp. 307–10. This essay has been reprinted in several places: the version used here is in J. Ockman (ed.) *Architecture Culture 1943–1968*, New York: Rizzoli, pp. 227–36.

70　Ibid.

71　Ibid., pp. 232–3.

72　A. Powers, 'John Summerson and modernism', in L. Campbell (ed.) *Twentieth-Century Architecture and its Histories*, Otley: Society of Architectural Historians of Great Britain, 2000, p. 170.

73　P. Hodgkinson, 'Informing forms: continuity and innovation', in P. Carolin and T. Dannatt (eds) *Architecture, Education and Research: the work of Leslie Martin, papers and selected articles*, London: Academy Editions, 1996, p. 53.

74　P.R. Banham, *Theory and Design in the First Machine Age*, London: Architectural Press, 1990.

75　Vidler, 'Toward a theory of the architectural program', p. 61.

76　Whiteley, *Reyner Banham*, p. 143.

77　Banham, *Theory and Design in the First Machine Age*, p. 239.

78　The material in this section draws on J.R. Gold, 'The power of narrative: the early writings of Charles Jencks and the historiography of architectural modernism', in L. Campbell (ed.) *Twentieth-Century Architecture and its Histories*, Otley: Society of Architectural Historians of Great Britain, 2000, pp. 206–21.

79　S. Connor, *Postmodernist Culture: an introduction to theories of the contemporary*, second edition, Oxford: Blackwell, 1997, p. 78.

80　C. Jencks, *Architecture 2000: predictions and methods*, London: Studio Vista, 1971.

81　Ibid., p. 48.

82　Jencks, 'Adhocism on the South Bank', *Architectural Review*, 1998, vol. 144, pp. 27–30.

83　Ibid., p. 30.

84　Jencks, *Modern Movements in Architecture*.

85　Ibid., p. 11.

86　Ibid., p. 27.

87　See P. Marchand, *Marshall McLuhan: the message and the messenger*, Cambridge, MA: MIT Press, 1990, p. 121.

88 Jencks, *Architecture 2000*, p. 36.
89 Jencks, *Modern Movements in Architecture*, p. 30.
90 Particularly I.A. Richards, *Principles of Literary Criticism*, London: Kegan Paul, 1924.
91 C. Jencks and N. Silver, *Adhocism: the case for improvisation*, New York: Doubleday, 1972.
92 N. Silver, 'Why is British architecture lousy?', in N. Silver and J. Boys (eds) *Why is British Architecture so Lousy?*, London: Newman Communications, 1979.
93 Jencks, *Modern Movements in Architecture*, p. 371.
94 Ibid., pp. 371–3.
95 Ibid., p. 380.
96 Le Corbusier, *Vers une architecture*, Paris: Editions Crès, 1923; trans. F. Etchells as *Towards a New Architecture*, London: John Rodker, 1927 (13th edition quoted here, London, Architectural Press, 1987).
97 Jencks, *Modern Movements in Architecture*, p. 380 (original emphases).
98 Ibid., p. 372.

## 12 Storm clouds

1 I. Calvino, *Invisible Cities*, London: Pan, 1979, p. 25.
2 N. Taylor (ed.) 'Housing and the environment', *Architectural Review*, 1967, vol. 142, pp. 325–408.
3 This quote is taken from the reprinted version of this essay: see J. Jacobs, 'Downtown is for people', in W.H. Whyte, Jr. (ed.) *The Exploding Metropolis*, Garden City, NY: Doubleday, 1958, p. 157.
4 J. Jacobs, *The Death and Life of Great American Cities*, New York: Random House.
5 Ibid., p. 54.
6 M.D. Young and P. Willmott, *Family and Kinship in East London*, London: Routledge & Kegan Paul, 1957. See also M. Kerr, *The People of Ship Street*, London: Routledge & Kegan Paul, 1958.
7 W. Firey, *Land Use in Central Boston*, Cambridge, MA: Harvard University Press, 1947.
8 M. Fried, 'Grieving for a lost home', in L.H. Duhl (ed.) *The Urban Condition*, New York: Basic Books, 1963, pp. 151–71; and M. Fried and P. Gleicher, 'Some sources of residential satisfaction in an urban slum', *Journal of the American Institute of Planners*, 1961, vol. 27, pp. 305–15.
9 N.S. Power, *The Forgotten People: a challenge to a caring community*, Evesham, Worcs.: Arthur James, 1965.
10 Ibid., pp. 37–8.
11 Ibid., p. 46.
12 Ibid., p. 48.
13 E. Denby, 'The waste of homes', *Architectural Review*, 1963, vol. 133, p. 6. She was reviewing S. Alderson, *Britain in the Sixties: housing*, Harmondsworth: Penguin, 1962.
14 E. Denby, *Europe Re-housed*, London: George Allen and Unwin, 1938.
15 Denby, 'The waste of homes', p. 6.
16 Taylor, 'Housing and the environment', pp. 325–408.
17 Reported in N. Taylor, *The Village in the City*, London: Maurice Temple Smith, 1973, p. 79 (original emphasis).
18 Taylor, 'Housing and the environment', p. 334.
19 Ibid.
20 Taylor, *The Village in the City*, p. 81.
21 N. Taylor, 'The failure of housing', *Architectural Review*, 1967, vol. 142, p. 341.
22 Ibid.
23 Ibid.
24 Taylor, 'Housing and the environment', p. 344.
25 Ibid., p. 348.
26 Ibid., p. 345.
27 See Chapter 9.
28 Ministry of Housing and Local Government, *The Deeplish Study: improvement possibilities in a district of Rochdale*, London: HMSO, 1966.
29 It was actually presented as a parallel rather than an alternative approach: see S.V. Ward, *Planning and Urban Change*, second edition, London: Sage, 2004, p. 147.

30 In this context, see J.R. Gold, 'York: a suitable case for conservation', *Twentieth Century Architecture*, 2004, vol. 7, pp. 87–99.

31 Respectively: S. Sadler, 'British architecture in the Sixties', in C. Stephens and K. Stout (eds) *Art and the 60s: this was tomorrow*, London: Tate Publishing, 2004, p. 122; M. Glendinning and S. Muthesius, *Tower Block: modern public housing in England, Scotland, Wales and Northern Ireland*, New Haven, CT: Yale University Press, 1994, p. 307.

32 B. Adams and J. Conway, *The Social Effects of Living off the Ground*, Information Paper 8, London: Department of the Environment, 1975.

33 J. Maizels, *Two to Five in High Flats*, London: Housing Centre, 1961.

34 D.M. Fanning, 'Families in flats', *British Medical Journal*, 1967, vol. 4, pp. 382–6.

35 P. Dunleavy, *The Politics of Mass Housing in Britain, 1945–1975: a study of corporate power and professional influence in the Welfare State*, Oxford: Clarendon Press, 1981, pp. 94–5.

36 Adams and Conway, *The Social Effects of Living off the Ground*, p. 9.

37 Anon, 'Point-block disaster', *Architects' Journal*, 1968, vol. 147, p. 91.

38 Dunleavy, *The Politics of Mass Housing*, pp. 143–6.

39 Anon, '73 authorities with system-built flats', *The Times*, 16 August 1968, p. 3.

40 Editorial, 'After Ronan Point', *The Times*, 16 August 1968, p. 7.

41 Ministry of Housing and Local Government, *Report of the Inquiry into the Collapse of Flats at Ronan Point, Canning Town; presented to the Minister of Housing and Local Government by Hugh Griffiths, Sir Alfred Pugsley, Sir Owen Saunders*, London: HMSO, 1968.

42 The National Archives, HLG 157/38.

43 F. Roberts, 'One in 50 chance of new tower block disaster', *The Times*, 7 November 1968, p. 10.

44 Ibid.

45 S. Lyall, *The State of British Architecture*, London: Architectural Press, 1980, p. 41.

46 H.E. Davies, *Report of the Tribunal Appointed to Inquire into the Disaster at Aberfan on October 21st, 1966* (Chairman: Sir Herbert Edmund Davies), London, 1967.

47 Lyall, *The State of British Architecture*, p. 41.

48 See e.g. A. Duncan, *Taking on the Motorway : North Kensington Amenity Trust 21 years*, London: Kensington and Chelsea Community History Group, 1992.

49 See e.g. Highways Committee: Clerk's Department, LCC. Western Avenue Extension (Westway) – London Metropolitan Archives, LCC/CL/HIG/2/144. More generally, see R. Goodman, *After the Planners*, Harmondsworth: Penguin, 1972.

50 H. Casson, 'One man's formula for overcoming a nation's disenchantment', *The Times*, 27 February 1973, p. 30.

51 D. Wiggins, 'The revolt in the cities', *The Times*, 3 April 1971, p. 19.

52 Respectively: A Ferguson, *The Sack of Bath: a record and an indictment*, Salisbury: Compton Russell, 1973; C. Amery and D. Cruickshank, *The Rape of Britain*, London: Elek.

53 See M. Gillard, *Nothing to Declare: The Political Corruptions of John Poulson*, London: John Calder, 1980. Poulson's blank denials of any wrong-doing are found in J. Poulson, *The Price*, London: Michael Joseph, 1981.

54 Names in this section are withheld.

55 Respectively, O. Newman, *Physical Parameters of Defensible Space: past experiences and hypotheses*, New York: Columbia University Press, 1969; O. Newman, *Defensible Space: people and design in the violent city*, New York: Macmillan, 1972.

56 Newman, *Defensible Space*, pp. 51–2.

57 Ibid., p. 52.

58 For discussion of the immediate response, see J.R. Gold, 'Territoriality and human spatial behaviour', *Progress in Human Geography*, 1982, vol. 6, pp. 44–67.

59 F.W., 'Bulldozers blitz a way to build place of beauty', *The Times*, 18 May 1973, p. iii.

60 S. Cantacuzino, 'The architect and the environment', *The Times*, 27 February 1973, p. 29.

61 Casson, 'One man's formula for overcoming a nation's disenchantment', p. 30.

62 Ibid.

63 'R. Buckminster Fuller retrospective', *Architectural Design*, 1972, vol. 42, pp. 728–91.

64 Anon, 'Floating spheres', *Architectural Design*, 1972, vol. 42(12), p. 764.

65 Anon, 'At work: 12', *Royal Institute of British Architects' Journal*, third series, 1972, vol. 79, p. 530.

66 D. Medd, 'Responding to change', *Royal Institute of British Architects' Journal*, third series, 1972, vol. 79, p. 522.

**Notes and references**

67  B. Hillier and A. Leaman, 'A new approach to architectural research', *Royal Institute of British Architects' Journal*, third series, 1972, vol. 79, pp. 517–21.

68  S. Wilson and G. Scott, 'Architecture and an ecology of man', *Architectural Science Review*, 1972, vol. 15(4), p. 69.

69  Ibid.

70  Anon, 'Preview on people movers', *Architectural Science Review*, 1972, vol. 15(4), p. vii.

71  W. Segal, 'Hans Scharoun, 1893–1972', *Architects' Journal*, 1972, vol. 156, pp. 1276–8.

72  Ibid., p. 1278.

73  Anon, 'A good bit of city', *Architectural Review*, 1972, vol. 152, p. 195.

74  Anon, 'Editorial', *Architectural Review*, 1972, vol. 152, p. 257.

75  Anon, 'Hotels', *Architectural Review*, 1972, vol. 152, p. 134.

76  Anon, 'Death of the heart', *Architectural Review*, 1972, vol. 152, p. 3.

77  K. Wharton, 'Architectural heritage – Ha! Ha!', *The Architect*, 1972, vol. 2, p. 35.

78  Anon, 'Bare bones of buildings', *The Architect*, 1972, vol. 2, p. 31.

79  J. Chisholm, 'People vs architects', *The Architect*, 1972, vol. 2(January), p. 44.

80  W. Segal, 'Things can't go on as they are', *The Architect*, 1972, vol. 2(February), p. 46.

81  C. Brogan, 'Goodbye to Glasgow', *The Architect*, 1972, vol. 2(July), pp. 42–4.

82  Anon, 'Competitions and controversy', *The Architect*, 1972, vol. 2(April), p. 35.

83  P. Davies, 'Somewhere to play', *The Architect*, 1972, vol. 2(June), pp. 23–7.

84  Ibid., p. 25. The quote was from a book by Jane Cass that Davies' article was reviewing at length: see J. Cass, *The Significance of Children's Play*, London: Batsford, 1972.

85  Interview with Sir Andrew Derbyshire, 4 January 2005 [T43/13].

# Index

# Index